BACK TO NATURE
IN
CANOES

BACK TO NATURE
IN
CANOES

A Guide to American Waters

•

RAINER ESSLEN
MAPS BY BIL CANFIELD

COLUMBIA PUBLISHING COMPANY, INC.
FRENCHTOWN, NEW JERSEY 08825

Manufactured in the United States of America

Typography by Pine Tree Composition, Lewiston, Maine

Interior book design by Laszlo Matulay

Columbia Publishing Company, Inc.
Frenchtown, New Jersey 08825

Distributed by Whirlwind Book Company

CONTENTS

TO THE LOVERS OF A
GRACEFUL PASTIME

Travelling on business or for pleasure to many parts of the country, I am tempted often to add a weekend or several days to my trips to get to know local canoeing waters and enjoy the scenery. I often find it difficult, or impossible, at least on short notice, to get information on canoeing opportunities from the stacks of local tourist literature or from information offices and public directories. Moreover, most of the literature on canoeing waters confines itself to whitewater. When it comes to observing nature, I prefer birds, plants, and scenery to rocks, chutes, eddies, and haystacks even though I am not entirely immune to the thrill of steering a canoe over a fast course. So, I compiled this guide primarily for lovers of flat water.

I am an amateur — a "lover" — of the pleasures canoeing has to offer, the graceful gliding of the boat through quiet or rippling water and the enjoyment of nature untouched by human hands and tools and out of earshot of automobiles and motor boats. When it comes to the fine details of equipment and paddling techniques, I defer to the people who have spent their lives developing them. Thus, this book only touches on these subjects. A reader wanting to know about the technical points is referred to some of the excellent books listed in the bibliography.

My purpose is to share in these pages some of the joys of canoeing with like-minded amateurs, to win new converts to this graceful pastime, to broaden the understanding of the spiritual needs of conserving whatever nature we have left, and to help readers find the best safe canoeing waters wherever they may live or travel in the United States.

Who Canoes?

Canoe manufacturers are cagey about their output. No industry statistics are available on the total number of canoes on American waters today. Cautious estimates put it at 2 million canoes in 1975, with some 100,000 new ones being added each year and far fewer dropping out.

Since most canoes have a crew of two, up to 4 million people could, in theory, be paddling at any given time. Fortunately, not all canoes are in use at the same time, even though it may seem so to anyone paddling down the Russian River in California or the Current River in Missouri on a weekend in the peak season. On the other hand, each rented canoe is used by scores of different people each year, so the total number of Americans who dip a canoe paddle in the water at least once a year must be many millions.

Canoeists vary greatly in their interests. When the canoe ceased to be a utility craft for transportation on the vast roadless areas of the north, it was kept alive as a pleasure craft by sports fishermen, hunters, bird watchers, and lovers of the outdoors living in urban areas who found the canoe to be the most practical and economical means of being in nature. Some of them banded together in informal groups to share their adventures and their common interest in preserving the waterways. These traditions are kept alive in many of the canoeing clubs active today.

Much more in the limelight than these traditional canoeists are the whitewater fans — a special breed which finds thrills in highly perfected skills, breath-taking speed, the spur of competition, and the sensation of danger successfully overcome.

On the other end of the range are the "what-shall-we-do-this-weekend?" adventurers. They hear about canoeing as a new "in" thing. They form a group to float downstream together with much shouting, screaming, splashing, and banging, often with a spill or two, and sometimes with graver mishaps. Fortunately, most of them soon lose interest.

Having once watched the regimented way in which a large group of Scouts was drilled in the techniques of various canoeing strokes, I am not surprised that relatively few of them seem to pursue their skills in adult life. However, canoeing techniques, unlike algebraic formulas, are not easily forgotten, and they are easily revived with the right incentive.

People who own property on quiet waterways are often sporadic users of canoes. You see their boats ashore, propped on supports upside down, ready at any time for a quick spin to fish, to swim, or for fun with the children. The number of hours such canoes are in use is small, but the canoe seems to be the most popular boat for this purpose because of its relatively low cost, durability, low maintenance, and easy portability.

A special breed is the canoe camper — the campers at heart for whom there is no greater joy than to pitch one or several tents in a remote wilderness area, engage in wood gathering, fishing, outdoor cooking, and other housekeeping chores in a spirit of camaraderie and self-sufficiency that revives the memory and mood of the pioneers and voyageurs. These campers know that there is no better means of transporting equipment into wilderness areas inaccessible to automobiles, motor boats, and airplanes than a canoe. It certainly beats backpacking and the only other choice — a horse — both of which are more limited in their carrying capacities.

Until about 1960, canoeing was a pastime confined to a happy few.

8

The real boost to canoeing seems to have come at about this time from what, for lack of a better term, I call the "back-to-nature" movement. Campers and sports fishermen have always been nature lovers in their own ways. These new nature lovers are different. They are the ones who have created the present urgency for saving the ecology and the quality of life.

The back-to-nature movement has been triggered, I believe, by an unhappiness with excessive mechanization and its cacophony, foul air, putrid waters, industrial debris, stereotyped suburbs, and the ribbon wastelands of highways. Noise, in particular, has become a new pollution problem. Many Americans seem to equate it with power, excitement, and self-assertion. Yet there is enough evidence to prove that continued high noise levels cause hearing loss and damage to the sensibilities of the nervous system of all living things. As reported in *The New York Times Magazine* (November 23, 1975), house plants exposed to acid rock "leaned away from the sound as if trying to escape ... At the end of three weeks they were dying."

Many have discovered that canoeing is a simple, quick, and inexpensive way to return to nature. Relatively unspoiled, quiet canoeing waterways still exist within short driving distances of large cities, often only several hundred yards from busy highways and residential and industrial developments.

A canoe can move on waterways that are completely inaccessible to motor boats. It is more versatile in this respect than any other craft. It can go up or down narrow, winding, and shallow rivers on which it would be difficult to maneuver any other boat. When the water level gets lower than two inches one can "walk" it over the shallows.

A canoe is relatively inexpensive to own or rent. It requires practically no maintenance unless damaged by careless use. It can easily be taken out of the water to be beached, stored, portaged, or transported to another launching point. Most importantly, a canoe harmonizes with nature. It works without motors or other mechanical contraptions. It teaches the canoeist to know the elements and become part of them. Canoeing is an esthetic and spiritual pleasure.

Thus, its new popularity. Many start clumsily on a river close to home. Once they learn to handle a canoe, they go further afield, exploring more distant waterways; becoming campers, wildlife photographers, bird watchers, botanists, or ardent fishermen; graduating to whitewater skills; or seeking the rough wilderness country of the north.

Who to Canoe With

Solo canoeing is a discipline in competitive racing. It also serves a purpose in fishing, bird watching, duck hunting, wildlife photography, and other pastimes which may bore a partner. But in most other cases, the great attraction of canoeing lies in the companionship it provides, and demands, if only for one reason — the shape of the boat makes it easier and safer for two to paddle than for one.

I started to canoe around 1930 in Hamburg, Germany, where the canoe was particularly popular among teenagers as the most practical and comfortable means for dating. The city is built around a three-mile-long lake, the Alster, which on a fine summer day would be crowded with sail boats, row boats, canoes, and small passenger steamers providing a scheduled service from downtown to the residential sections. On one side of the lake was a large restaurant with outdoor tables under linden trees and a band shell from which a brass-dominated orchestra would offer light musical fare, such as the Boston Pops plays today at Hatch Shell on the Charles River.

The Hamburg restaurant had built a small mole close to the bandstand for the benefit of canoeists. On a fine day, this enclosure would be jammed, gunwale to gunwale, with canoes, many of them occupied by young couples, reclining at the bottom of the boats made of wood and canvas, painted in different colors, with two thwarts, one halfway forward, one halfway aft; none in the middle. We would prop wood headboards on a slant against the thwarts, deck them generously with cushions, and cover the bottom of the boat with a mattress and blankets.

The absence of center thwarts also made the canoes an excellent overnight camping shelter for two, eliminating the need for bulky camping equipment. Overnight camping involved nothing more than securing the boat on a scenic bank, removing one of the headboards to provide room for stretched-out legs, covering oneself with blankets, and pulling a tarpaulin across the boat.

Judging by the traffic on many of our United States and Canadian waterways, the canoe is still a very popular means for young dating couples to enjoy one another's company away from the crowd. It offers a rare privacy in a setting conducive to private moods.

By the same token, it is a pleasure to paddle with your spouse if he or she shares your interest or is willing to learn. If not, you may be in the same boat as the author of a canoeing book with this dedication:

> To my wife . . . and to my son and daughter . . . who have understood the self-imposed exile from family life required to complete this book . . . To the companionable men, women, and to the youths who have shared with me in the paddling, camping, singing . . . as well as in the enjoyment of woods and waters, in sunshine and storm . . . I affectionately dedicate this book.

No matter whether of different or the same sex, two like-minded

10

canoeists often find that an outing in a single canoe gives them more privacy and independence and a greater enjoyment of the quieter parts of nature than they would find in larger crowds. But an outing for two has some drawbacks. It limits you to the safer, smoother waters. *Single-canoe outings should never be undertaken on difficult or cold water. Two canoes is a minimum, three are recommended.* (More on this later.)

On a one-way river trip, two in a single canoe have the problem of getting back to their car, unless they use the services of a canoe livery that provides transportation to the put-in and/or the take-out point. Many liveries will do this for a charge, even for privately-owned canoes, but on a busy day this often involves a good deal of waiting.

The transportation problem for privately-owned canoes is easily solved if four congenial people in two canoes and two cars get together.

The same procedure with more than two canoes involves an increasing amount of waiting and shuttling time for each additional canoe — one reason why some people shun the often well-organized outings of clubs. On the other hand, a canoe club outing under seasoned leadership is an excellent training ground for beginners. And these trips are good opportunities to meet like-minded people.

For family activities with children, there is very little, if anything, to match canoeing in interest, excitement, and pleasure of the whole family over extended periods of time.

Small children can be easily placed in the middle of the canoe wearing the essential head-supporting life jackets. The changing scenery, the spirit of exploration, a stop for a dip in the water, the exploration of the shore, and a picnic will usually keep children excited and interested for an entire day and fill their minds with impressions that may shape their outdoor tastes for a lifetime.

When children are old enough to paddle at the bow, the spirit of joint adventure intensifies, and this is more true when they can take over the responsibility of steering a canoe at the stern. Most children are good for joint family canoeing until dating interests take precedence (and, for all you know, they may take their dates on canoeing trips).

Even grandparents, or those who could theoretically be grandparents, can canoe all waterways that do not require the strength of an athlete. Canoeing, in fact, is a good cure for one of the most common ailments of tense and desk-bound Americans — the aching back. Like hiking, it is a gentle and graceful exercise that can be continued into great age. The two supplement each other excellently in keeping a body limber.

Parties of three or more canoes can offer special pleasures and practical advantages on extended trips down long and difficult rivers, and into remote areas such as the voyageurs trails of Maine, Minnesota, and Canada. The camaraderie and mood of such canoeing parties was summed up by Supreme Court Justice William O. Douglas in his farewell letter to his colleagues in November, 1975:

I am reminded of many canoe trips I have taken in my lifetime. Those who start down a water course may be strangers at the beginning but almost invariably are close friends at the end. There were strong headwinds to overcome and there were rainy as well as sun-drenched days to travel. The portages were long and many and some very strenuous. But there was always a pleasant camp in a stand of white birch and water concerts held at night to the music of the loons; and inevitably there came the last campfire, the last breakfast cooked over the last night's fire, and the parting was always sad. And yet, in fact, there was no parting because each happy memory of the choice parts of the journey — and the whole journey — was a harmonious, united effort filled with fulfilling and beautiful hours as well as dull and dreary ones.

Where to Canoe

Except for some of the drier states in the southwest, canoeing waters abound throughout the United States. It is impossible to do justice to them all. This book tries to concentrate on the more accessible ones, with stress on nature cruising rather than whitewater canoeing.

The information is gathered mostly from local and regional publications, many of which are listed at the end of each chapter. These publications usually give details of distances and difficulties of each river and sometimes describe scenic merits. However, a word of caution: broad descriptions of traveling time and difficulties in these publications would hinge, for accuracy, on an individual's canoeing skill and the water conditions in different seasons, and scenic merit can change quickly. A once beautiful river can be wrecked by dams, industrial or residential developments, pollution, or overuse. On the other hand, many formerly polluted rivers are being cleaned up thanks to the lobbying efforts of outdoor organizations and stricter state and Federal laws.

The judgment of the respective merits of canoeing waters is best left to the research efforts, exploring spirit, and personal preferences of the reader. Here are some general observations, tinged by my own personal preferences.

There is very little nature left in the United States still in the condition in which the white man found it on his arrival. Practically all woods and forests, except for some redwoods and sequoias in the west and other stands in national parks, are second growth. This is true even of the "wilderness" areas of the Allagash in Maine and the Boundary Waters of Minnesota. Much of the farmland in the east has reverted

12

*Vermont's Winooski River is typical of the streams and scenery
a canoeist would see in New England*
PHOTO COURTESY STOWE CANOE CO., STOWE, VT.

to brush or second growth. The difference between virgin and second growth is obvious to anyone who has ever seen both. In a virgin forest, only the large trees survive. The forest ground is relatively clean and open, often covered with moss or grass. The tree crowns are high above the ground, and the trunks generally without lower branches. This seems to suggest to some local poets the image of arches in a church, as evidenced by such names as Forest Cathedral or Cathedral Woods.

Second growth, especially in its early stages, is dense, full of underbrush, and often impenetrable. Much of it looks forbidding. However, as it grows, the larger trees prevail, and some of the tangle disappears. Often, government foresters or tree farmers give a helping hand by cleaning out the underbrush. Thus, a good deal of second growth has developed its own "natural" beauty.

Man has also eliminated many of the swamps — particularly vital parts of nature. Swamps retain moisture and provide a natural regulation of water supply and drainage. They are a key element in the chain of much animal life. And for a canoeist they provide some of the most scenic trips.* Finally, innumerable dams have changed the natural flow of the majority of rivers.

The largest tracts of virgin nature in the United States are found in the Rocky Mountains, including the Sierra Nevada chain in the west, and the swamps, bayous, and subtropical rivers of Georgia and Florida and the Gulf Coast, notably the Okefenokee Swamp and the Everglades.

The Rockies and the Sierra Nevada mountains offer primarily whitewater canoeing. Rough and inaccessible waters often offer nature in its purest form because they are so inaccessible and difficult to tame. It is worth knowing, however, that most of the whitewater streams in the mountains have stretches of quiet water. There is probably nothing more satisfying than gliding down a glistening crystal-clear stream in the snowmelting season, meandering through a meadow carpeted with myriads of gentians, buttercups, primroses, globeflowers, columbines, poppies, shooting stars, and other alpine flowers, surrounded by snow-capped peaks silhouetted against a pale-blue sky. To enjoy this great treat of nature, you must bring your own canoe or join a guided party, taking pot luck with the company and the amount of whitewater thrills included in the bargain. Most canoe liveries in whitewater areas have given up renting without guides. Too many customers who promised to stay on calmer waters could not resist the temptation to wreck their canoes, and often break their necks, on the nearest rapids.

---

* For a particularly good case history of the benefits derived from preserving bogs and swamps, see "A Lesson to be Learned from a Pennsylvania Bog" in Vincent Abraitys' book, The Backyard Wilderness: From the Canadian Maritimes to the Florida Keys, Columbia Publishing Company, Inc. (Frenchtown, N. J. 08825), 1975, pp. 75 et seq.

Bayous have their own mystery. A pirogue, cousin of the canoe, glides through a moss-draped cypress stand on Lake Mystic in Florida.

PHOTO COURTESY NEWS BUREAU, FLORIDA DEPARTMENT OF COMMERCE

On the other extreme of canoeing pleasure are the intimacy and mystery of the swamps, bayous, and winding rivers of the southeast. Except for the grasslands of the Everglades, the view here is confined by dense vegetation — cyprus, bay, gum, and swamp oaks hung with streamers of Spanish moss and entangled in vines and creepers.

It is ideal territory for watching birds — both the permanent population and the innumerable migratory visitors passing through or stopping for the winter. You are likely to see many turtles and occasionally an alligator, betraying his presence by two blobs, like floating black balls, on the water's surface. If the blobs are close together, the alligator is small; if far apart, it is a large one. As you get nearer, the blobs disappear under the water. Alligators are shy and quite harmless. They like to sun themselves ashore, and if you paddle quietly, you can sometimes see one sliding quickly into the water.

As confined as the views are, so are the waters extensive and confusing to paddle. Before setting out on swamps, bayous, and the Everglades — anything, in fact, except clearly defined river courses without confusing forks — be sure you know where you are going with the help of maps or advice from local experts.

The Gulf Coast and the coastal bays of the southeastern Atlantic states offer many tidewater and saltwater canoeing opportunities. A canoe is an ideal clam digging craft. It gets to spots that cannot be otherwise reached. It can go over shallow water and sandbanks that no other boat, except perhaps a kayak, can negotiate. But a canoe is a much better cargo vessel than a kayak should you be blessed with a record haul.

A canoe is also ideal for shell collecting in shallow saltwater lagoons. You can drag it behind you, wading ankle-deep over mud flats, to look for Kings Crowns, hardly known to beach shellers, and considered almost a pest by back bay dwellers who will not raise an eyebrow if you take a bucket full of live ones back to your vacation place, clean and cook them, and bring home a collection of all sizes of delicately formed and shaded cones, each ringed with spiral bands of spikes. It's another story with the pure white Angels Wing, a bivalve, hiding out a foot or two deep in the mud, sending its tongue-like body to the surface to feed. They have become very rare, and I have promised my friends in Florida not to reveal how to spot them and dig them up. Much easier to find on mud flats are perfect, and often quite large, specimens of live whelks, tulips, and horse conches. Occasionally, you may come across a much coveted Chinese alphabet cone.

Water bird watching is usually excellent on the bays, bayous, and swamps of the southeast — herons, egrets, ibises, cormorants, the ubiquitous pelicans, a rare sandhill crane, the noisy ducks splashing away as if walking on water, and the strange anhinga, or water turkey, really not made for the water, but nevertheless diving down deep for his food and then pathetically sitting on a branch spreading his wings to dry it.

16

I'll never forget the excitement of seeing, for the first time, a flock of frigate birds settling high on trees on a small island off the west coast of Florida — the males with their puffed-up crimson breasts protruding like balloons from their small black bodies and wings wide enough for birds four times their size. Paddling a canoe through mangrove-lined inlets and island clusters gives you a whiff of tropical nature as exotic as you will find in the United States.

Very few official canoe routes exist on lagoons and back bays — one of the few exceptions is the 100-mile Everglades Wilderness Waterway in Florida, and a new one is being created in the Assateague Island National Seashore in Maryland — but coastal waterways are among the best mapped waterways in the country, and local marinas and marine supply stores usually carry maps for their particular regions. While intended for larger craft, from sail and motor boat to ocean-going vessels, these maps are more than adequate for all canoeing purposes.

If I were asked to name the ideal river for the nature-loving family canoeist, I would probably specify most of the features found on the Little River in Virginia, which is typical of hundreds of other rivers throughout the country. It is narrow and winding, wide enough for one canoe to pass another, but rarely so wide that three canoes could paddle abreast. Most importantly, it is quite unsuitable for even the smallest power boat. It is swift, with enough riffles and miniature falls to add a few thrills and give a sense of accomplishment to the more skilled paddler, but not so wild as to pose a serious danger to the beginner. Its banks of varying heights are lined with a mixed stand of trees open enough to provide pleasant vistas and occasionally interspersed with dramatic rock formations. There are no dwellings along the canoeable course, and practically no farmland. Picnic spots abound. Although close to main highways (U.S. 1 near Richmond, Virginia), no mechanical noises are heard along most of its course. It provides a feeling of remote nature. If it has a drawback it is its relative shortness — barely long enough for a good day's paddling — and the fact that it may get too shallow in dry spells.

"Little Rivers," such as the one in Virginia, and many of greater length, can be found in great number in the flatter sections of the Atlantic Coastal states from New Jersey to Georgia, and in even greater number in the states of the Great American Plains — Ohio, Michigan, Indiana, Illinois, Wisconsin, and Missouri. Along the Appalachian chain from Georgia to Maine and in other mountain areas, rivers are usually less tame, yet rarely without smooth stretches.

Some people like the Huckleberry Finn romance of leisurely floating down the wide, open rivers, such as the Ohio, Mississippi, and Missouri, forgetting time and place and putting ashore wherever the spirit moves them. One of the problems, at least in the upper reaches of such rivers, are the many locks and dams requiring portages and often resulting in

17

a good deal of slack water. In the lower reaches one encounters much commercial traffic.

One of the loveliest big-river floats left, unencumbered by locks and dams, is the 160-mile stretch of the Missouri in Montana, starting at Fort Benton and ending at James Kipp State Park. Much of this trip looks as it must have to Lewis and Clark in 1804. Another wilderness big-river float is down the Green River in Utah, about 120 miles through canyon scenery, yet without whitewater. The most actively used big river is probably the Delaware from Hancock, New York, to Trenton, New Jersey, about 200 miles of swift and thrilling floating, with a few hazards along the way when the water is high.

Lake canoeing can be fine if the lake is relatively small or narrow, or has canoeable bays and feeder streams, and as long as it is closed to motor boats. Large lakes often have strong winds and high waves. Man-made lakes and reservoirs and large back-up river waters above dams make for dull canoeing. When the water level is low, many of these artificial lakes have ugly banks. Motor boats, of course, put them completely beyond the pale. Here is what a marina owner from upstate New York wrote to me about the subject:

> The lake would be very nice for canoeing but many big yachts and barges are going back and forth on summer vacation, and with every year they are getting rougher. About 70- to 90-foot yachts do not slow down for small craft. The lake is getting more and more dangerous every year. Nobody (or almost nobody) has time or cares.

Last but not least, there is the very special kind of canoeing you find in the wilderness or semi-wilderness of Maine, Minnesota, and Canada. It is a mixture of lake, channel, and river canoeing, interspersed with portages on trails that were first blazed by American Indians followed by the voyageurs — the fur traders — who traveled by canoe from Montreal to the distant Rockies and the Arctic waters of the Hudson Bay. A wilderness trip takes you to vaster areas of nature than you can find anywhere else on the North American continent, especially if you have enough time to put some distance between yourself and your fellow canoeists who are beginning to crowd some of the starting points and nearby waters. It often includes whitewater and other difficulties. Wilderness trips usually involve camping in a different spot every night with all the pleasures and chores that this entails. A skilled fisherman may be able to supply a good part of the calories needed to sustain the energies of the party. The best fishing is between May and July, when the flies and mosquitos have their heyday. People sensitive to, or nervous about, insects feel more comfortable in August and September. A camping trip rarely lasts less than a week, often several weeks, and some en-

18

thusiasts, lucky enough to have the time, spend an entire summer in the wilderness. Outfitters provide boats and all food and camping gear needed for any length of trip, as well as guides, if desired.

Those who don't like camping or portaging need not forego the scenic pleasures of wilderness waters. Many canoe outfitters have overnight accomodations under a roof, or there are motels nearby, often with housekeeping units. Non-camping canoeists can rent a canoe by the day without camping paraphernalia, have it towed on the water or have it transported on land to different waterways, take a picnic along, and come back at night to a comfortable bed. It is more costly, but worth the expense if you like to combine wilderness with comfort.

When I arrived for the first time at a remote wilderness outfitter's base on the Boundary Waters of Minnesota, and had hardly turned off the engine in my rented car, I was slightly taken aback when two eager boys, who served as handymen and guides, showed me a map on which they had marked in great detail the week-long canoe route they recommended as the most scenic of the area. It involved a different campground every night, and a minimum of three portages per day. They also pointed to three huge waterproof duffles with my name on them.

I was not aware of the progress made by the American tenting industry in the development of one-piece pup tents, easily propped up on a collapsible aluminum tree. I had visions of myself enveloped by a number of tarps flapping in the strong wind, getting entangled in ropes, and struggling with collapsing stakes. I also had more realistic visions of four round trips per portage, three with a 50-pound duffle on my back and one with an 80-pound canoe balanced on my shoulders — because my companion, a fairly good bow paddler, was not the portaging type.

I studied the map carefully, then pointed to the remotest spot that could apparently be reached without portage — at least 25 miles away, on the other side of the Canadian border — and asked the boys: "Isn't there a campsite around here?"

There was, in fact an ideal one, on a miniature peninsula, with a 270° field of vision, a small sandy beach, a flat, clean camping space trodden firm by thousands of users since the voyageurs' days, neatly arranged stones for a fire, and a heap of kindling wood left by the previous campers (a custom established by the voyageurs and still followed in good canoeing circles). Our guide, who had towed us to the spot with another canoe powered by a small outboard motor, set up the tent, caught half a dozen small bass in a jiffy, and then left us to ourselves. We stayed at this focal point during the entire week, feeding on fresh fish and freeze-dried pork chops with apple sauce, taking a side trip each day in a different direction, with rarely more than two portages of an empty canoe, and seeing, no doubt, as much different scenery as we would have camping at a different spot every night. Admittedly my companion never felt entirely comfortable after having discovered bear droppings behind our

19

campsite on the day of our arrival, seeing me hoist our food into a tree before retiring, and living through a thunderstorm the first night that sounded as though it was going to wash our tent away. Not to make matters worse, I didn't tell her until we were home that on the first morning, as I crawled out of the tent at dawn, I saw a moose towering over the tent, with his antlers at least three times as high. He seemed to give me a reproachful look, more in sorrow than in anger; then slowly retreated backwards, with his eyes fixed on me, until he disappeared behind bushes and a patch of fog. It was the first time I had seen a moose in nature. It was also the first time, on that trip, that I saw beavers at work. You have to wait patiently and still for a long time to make them feel safe. It was that stillness, above all, that I remember best — stillness occasionally broken by the plop of a fish catching an insect and by the hoot of a loon gliding by as the dusk settled.

Unfortunately, the more accessible of the Boundary Waters and of other wilderness areas have lost this stillness since my first visit some 10 years ago, and the same is true of many rivers that were once pristine and idyllically quiet. This trend is expressed in the distress of the biologist, a nature lover and author of an excellent regional canoeing guide, who wrote to me:

> [The rivers] are overcrowded now to the extent that some have been literally destroyed. If I had to do it again, I probably would never write the book I did, though it was written with the intent of emphasizing . . . conservation and good landowner relations, as well as being a guide book. If I were to tell you which of our rivers are most pristine, they would no longer remain so . . . .

I sympathize with his feelings and share them. They are probably akin to those of the American Indian when the first white man started to clear the forest to farm. Yet nothing the biologist or I do can arrest or change the major trends in human interests and endeavors. If the current back-to-nature trend proves genuine and durable, we tend to gain as much as we lose. We may gain converts to the art of quiet nature enjoyment. We may find more allies in our fight against further encroachment on nature by commerce and industry and the infernal combustion engine, as well as against the U.S. Army Corps of Engineers which seems to feel that the only good river is a dammed river.. We may increase the number of kindred people who set examples on how to keep nature clean and preserve it.

Finally, canoeing for the crowd is like going to shows. Many of them want to see only the hits, leaving innumerable intimate productions to the connoisseur.

You don't need 20 miles of river to get back to nature. Often an uncharted small creek, leading one mile up to a swamp, serves better.

How to Choose a Canoe

The canoe is undoubtedly one of the North American Indian's greatest contributions to civilization. When the white man arrived, the birch bark canoe was fully developed in essentially the same form found in canoes made of different materials today. Such ultimate perfection of design often results from a need for maximum utility combined with the complete harmony between craftsman and nature.

The birch bark canoe had a wooden frame covered by wooden sheathing over which the bark was tightly stretched. There is still at least one man left — Henri Vaillancourt, in Greenville, New Hampshire — who makes birch bark canoes, as reported by John McPhee in his book *The Survival of the Bark Canoe* (*see* bibliography). A good history of the birch bark canoe and its use by the American Indian and the fur-trading French-Canadian voyageurs is in John Malo's *Complete Guide to Canoeing and Canoe Camping* (*see* bibliography).

The birch bark was followed by the wood and canvas canoe, constructed along the same lines, except that painted canvas replaced the bark. Wood and canvas canoes are still used by purists who prefer "natural" materials to the synthetic man-made ones used for the vast majority of canoes built today. They can still be obtained from several makers, but they are more expensive and they require a good deal of maintenance and careful storage to prevent rot and the absorption of moisture by the wood.

The three most popular materials of which canoes are made today are aluminum, Fiberglass, and ABS (acrylonitrile butadiene styrene) plastic — the latter a newcomer with only a limited in-use history at the moment. Aluminum accounts for the greatest number of canoes in use. All three materials are eminently serviceable. Their respective merits are a matter of fine degree rather than major proportion, and are best left to others to discuss. As a generalization it can be said that aluminum has demonstrated great durability with practically no maintenance. Fiberglass and plastic are quieter in use and more flexible, an advantage for the less skilled when trying to get off a submerged rock.

When you rent a canoe you usually have little choice and take what the livery gives you, but frequent renting from different liveries exposes you to a good cross section of different types and sizes of canoes, helping you to develop your own preferences.

When you want to buy a canoe, you are confronted with a plethora of different sizes, shapes, weights, carrying capacities, and prices in each of the main canoe materials on the market today. Expert advice and sales talk may often add to the confusion. Most of the canoe books listed in the bibliography go into great detail about canoe design, construction, and selection. A reader who wants to be thorough about the subject is well advised to consult one or several of the recently published books. *Canoe Magazine* publishes a canoe and kayak buyer's guide every year.

Here is a general observation on the most important features in a canoe for anyone wanting to use the boat for back-to-nature purposes on all types of available waterways. The canoe should be light enough to be portaged and lifted on top of a car with relative ease. It should be large enough to carry, in addition to the two paddlers, two children under 10 or camping equipment and other gear up to 500 pounds. It should be equally suitable for river and lake canoeing; and it should be relatively stable. This all-purpose, non-racing compromise would give you a canoe 15'–17' long with a 36" beam, 12" deep, weighing 60–80 pounds, with a fairly flat bottom, no keel, a medium taper, and a fairly low peak at both ends. Sharp tapers may add some speed but they ship in water more easily in riffles and waves, and high peaks are a nuisance in winds.

If you want a canoe primarily for extensive camping and wilderness trips, you may be better off with an 18'–20' boat, but at that length canoes are heavy to lift or portage.

Boats smaller than 15' may be fine for taking short spins close to home or on solo outings for fishing, hunting, bird watching, etc., especially if carrying or portaging is involved, but they are not recommended for family or long-distance outings.

How to Choose a Paddle

When you rent a canoe these days, you have practically no other choice but a wide, square blade attached to a hollow shaft made of aluminum, Fiberglass, or plastic. This type of paddle was developed for racing, and is no doubt the most effective tool for propelling the boat forward at maximum speed.

Since canoeing is also an esthetic pleasure, some, including the author, still prefer the elegant shapes of wood paddles. I like a sturdy, flexible maple paddle with a medium-wide blade, rounded almost to a point at the end, and with a pear-shaped grip. The taper of the blade makes it possible (probably to the horror of any purist reading this) to use the paddle for poling in shallow water or execute some fast maneuvers in difficult waters. Poling, as not all canoeists seem to know, propels the canoe much faster than paddling ever can, and it is especially useful for going upstream. Consistent poling over some distance and with varying depths of water requires a pole at least 12′ long and some special skills for standing upright in a moving canoe. A reader seriously interested in poling is referred to Bill Riviere's *Pole Paddle & Portage* (*see* bibliography).

Paddles should reach at least to your chin, and some canoeists prefer them to be as tall as their own height. Wood paddles should not be left in the sun when wet, nor lying around where they can be stepped on. They may break. Always carry a spare paddle for paddles have been known to sneak away unobserved.

Most of the canoeing books given in the bibliography review the various paddle types and their best uses in great detail.

How to Paddle

When on a fine weekend you go out on one of the more popular waterways close to a city, you are surprised to see how many of the paddlers don't know how to keep a canoe on course without switching the paddle from one side of the canoe to the other every second stroke, and even then they usually steer an unsettled, zigzag course. No less authoritative a figure than the American Indian who appeared in a TV commercial to plead, with a tear in his eye, for keeping American waterways clean seemed to use his paddle on both sides to stay on course.

Struggling for a whole day with a boat that acts like a willful, skittish foal can take much of the pleasure away from the trip and discourage a repeat performance. Yet the few basic strokes needed by a beginner are relatively easy to learn. Many of the canoe liveries, when they are not too busy, offer instruction, or an experienced canoeist friend or a canoe club member may be willing to help.

Paddling, like swimming and dancing, cannot be learned from a book. You learn by doing it. But a little theory may help, and anyone interested in detailed theory is again referred to the bibliography. Here are some general observations:

With two people in a boat, only the stern paddler needs to know how to steer a boat on all but the most difficult waters. All the bow paddler has to do is to help propel the boat forward with a straight stroke, starting and stopping on command. Anyone can do that. So, ideally, a beginner should try to team up with a more experienced canoeist on the first outing, learning as they go along, and becoming a good canoeist himself after a few trips.

When both the bow paddler and the stern paddler paddle with about equal force on opposite sides of the boat, very little steering is necessary for a straight course. However, a canoe has the habit of veering when paddled only on one side or when paddled more forcefully on one side than the other. Moreover, on an average river a great many bends and other obstacles must be negotiated, and some steering knowledge is essential. Only a few strokes are needed to maneuver a canoe on any but the really tricky whitewaters. To keep the boat on a straight course, the stern paddler has two main strokes at his disposal. Either he turns the paddle outward and away from the boat as he finishes his stroke (the "J" stroke) counteracting the boat's tendency to veer in the opposite direction, or, usually easier to do, he finishes the stroke with the paddle flat against the side of the canoe astern of himself. There he can use the paddle as a rudder to control direction. In the same manner, the stern paddler can use the paddle as a rudder if he wants to make a turn towards the side on which he is paddling. If he wants to turn in the opposite direction, he uses a sweep stroke, starting forward of himself close to the gunwale, sweeping the paddle in a curve as far away from the hull as his arms will reach, and finishing aft, pushing the water across the stern. The bow paddler can help by paddling hard on the side opposite the direction of the turn. It's a good idea to avoid becoming a one-sided canoeist — early habits are difficult to break later! — and learn right from the start to paddle equally well on both sides. It makes you a more versatile canoeist and reduces fatigue and the risk of muscle spasms.

It is important to know that on moving water the canoe must be propelled faster than the current to remain maneuverable. If you simply drift with the current, you are likely to run into the banks and overhanging vegetation at every bend. In fast whitewater, however, the faster-than-current paddling (barreling) can be extremely dangerous. By trying to steer around a rock at high speed, you can easily hit it sideways, and be done in. Experienced whitewater canoeists know how to arrest the movement of the canoe in midstream in relation to the banks and set it over sideways to avoid an obstacle straight ahead of them. This is strictly for the experts and should not be attempted even by relatively advanced amateurs who are beginning to feel their oats. No matter how well you have learned to handle a canoe, your first outing on difficult whitewater should be in the company of an experienced whitewater canoeist.

How to Paddle Safely

Canoeing is as safe as bicycling, once you have found your balance, know how to propel and steer your conveyance, and use it only on terrain suitable for its design.

Unfortunately, canoeing accidents are numerous, including many fatal ones. Most of them happen to ignorant beginners or irresponsible and daredevil half-wits. Statistics developed by the U.S. Coast Guard some years ago showed that among all pleasure crafts canoes have the highest rate of fatal accidents. Should Ralph Nader decide to focus on these statistics he might lobby for a Federal law requiring that every canoe be equipped with outriggers as well as balloons that automatically inflate when it hits a rock. Since this would spoil the fun for everybody, beginners would be wise to observe a few voluntary safety rules. Even an ordinary spill, with your clothes and paddles drifting downstream, and your camera and watch coming to rest on the bottom of a murky river, can be disconcerting.

In all of my 45 years or so of canoeing I took one spill (and I am reaching for my maple paddle to touch wood as I write this). We had beached the bow of the canoe on a sandy river bank, and my companion, a rather heavy-set person got up to get out without holding on to the gunwales. She lost her balance and tipped the canoe over, landing on the dry sand. I, who had busied myself with gathering our picnic things from the bottom of the canoe, landed in the water. I spent most of the picnic break carefully peeling dollar bills, identification cards, and credit cards out of my wallet and draping them over bushes to dry.

At the beginning of the same trip, another couple in our party — absolute beginners who had insisted on coming along in spite of warnings — ran their canoe into a tree trunk lying halfway across the river. Instead of holding on to the tree, they leaned away from it upstream, and swamped the canoe. The husband, hip-deep in water, shouted at me anxiously and angrily, because I had not immediately jumped overboard, fully dressed, to rescue him and his wife (which, in view of my subsequent spill, would not have made any difference). Instead, I assessed the situation, saw no immediate danger to life, stripped to my bathing trunks and waded into the water to pull their canoe ashore and help them collect their drifting belongings. The keys to their apartment and car had sunk to the bottom of the brown water stained by cedar roots, and it was a miracle that by raking his naked feet over the river bottom the husband found the keys again.

A little further along, the husband of the third couple on this trip lost his balance trying to avoid overhanging branches. Instead of clinging to the canoe, gallant Frenchman that he was, he let himself fall overboard, and his wife floated on safely in the upright canoe.

All this happened on the Grade A (flat water) Wading River in the Pine Barrens of New Jersey, a real beginners' playground; not a riffle anywhere along the entire course! There are good reasons for caution and respect for the elements on any type of water.

Here are 16 general safety hints:

1. *Always grab both gunwales with your hands when getting into or out of a canoe or moving about in it.*

25

2. *Implant both legs firmly close to or against the sides of the boat,* ready at all times to counteract a sudden lurch to one side. When the water gets difficult, *slip to your knees immediately* to lower the center of gravity.

3. *Never shift from one side of your seat to the other or make other sudden moves without alerting your partner;* he or she may move in the same direction at the same moment.

4. *Never overload a canoe.* The gunwale at midship should be at least 6″ above the water; better more.

5. *Always wear a life jacket that supports your head* when on deep or difficult water. Children and non-swimmers should wear a life jacket at all times. Use only U.S. Coast Guard-approved life jackets.

6. *Never travel in a single canoe on medium-to-difficult waters and on very cold water.* Two boats is the minimum. The safety code of the American Whitewater Affiliation requires a minimum of three canoes on difficult waters. They must remain in sight of each other, but never so close as to risk crowding on riffles and rapids.

7. *If you spill, hold on to your boat.* No matter what material it is made of, it will float and support you. In a river stay on the upstream side of your boat to avoid being crushed against an obstacle on the downstream side. If you can't maneuver your boat ashore, wait for help.

8. *In cold water, however, make a dash for the shore immediately* and leave your boat to take care of itself, if necessary; or for others to rescue it. Water at 32°F. can kill you in 15 minutes, and 35° to 45° water is hardly less lethal. Change into dry clothes immediately if available; otherwise, get warm between blankets, or by lighting a fire, with the help of other members of your party. *Never go on cold water (anything less than 50°) with a single canoe. Two people alone spilling in cold water, with no help in sight, are quickly doomed.*

9. *Pack all your gear and other belongings in waterproof bags,* even when paddling on smooth water. Valuables, such as cameras, watches, and wallets, are best protected separately in small, tough, plastic bags obtainable at any dime store, and tied to a thwart. Large duffels with spare clothes, camping equipment, etc., are best stored loose to float on their own in a spill rather than impede the salvage of the canoe.

10. *Never run fast water unless you feel confident about it.* If in doubt, when approaching fast water, go ashore and appraise it first, or watch other canoeists go down. If still not entirely confident, portage. Sometimes you can "line" a boat through difficult waters, guiding it from ashore with a rope attached to both ends. But this needs some experience. *Unknown water that "roars" should at all times be inspected from the shore first if you can't see it in its entirety from the boat.* In riffles and mild rapids, keep your canoe parallel to the current at all times. Head for the point of the V's pointing downstream. Avoid V's pointing upstream. There's a rock under the point. *Never attempt difficult white-*

*water unless accompanied by a skilled whitewater canoeist or you are
fully trained yourself in whitewater canoeing.*

11. *Beware of overhanging branches, fallen trees, log jams, and low
bridges even on smooth rivers.* If these obstacles are too low for your
canoe to pass under and you drift against them, your boat can get
swamped or sucked underneath. If you are up against such an obstacle,
lean towards it and try to maneuver your boat around it. Never lean
upstream, away from the obstacle. It is a sure way to swamp your boat.

12. *When moving swiftly with the current, don't hold on to overhanging branches or bridge supports — in fact, don't hold on to anything stationary while your boat is moving fast.* If the obstacle is high
enough for your boat to pass underneath but would chop your head off,
duck straight forward or slip to the bottom of the boat.

13. *Never run a dam, no matter how low and easy it looks.* If you
swamp on the other side, a strong backflow will push you towards the
dam below the surface. Innumerable people have drowned this way.

14. *If your bow gets stuck on a submerged rock or stump, you may
often get off by letting the canoe swing around in the current and re-
verse the direction of paddling, the bow paddler becoming the stern
paddler.* If lack of space or other obstacles prevent a swing, the bow
paddler should carefully creep backwards, with both hands on the gunwales, until the bow floats free.

15. *On large lakes and on the open sea, always paddle close to shore.*
Shore winds often arise very suddenly and carry you far out in the open
water and pitched waves, sometimes never to return!

16. *If you carry a canoe on the top of your car, be very thorough in
securing it.* Use at least two strong straps to fasten it to both sides of the
car and two strong ropes to tie one end to the front bumper and the
other to the rear bumper. At 55 mph, with a 50 mph diagonal cross-
wind, you have a force of over 100 mph that can blow the canoe off the
roof, endangering other traffic.

Water Ratings

The American Whitewater Affiliation has adopted the Standard International River Classification system that rates the degree of difficulty of
whitewater on a scale from I to VI as follows:

I Easy.
II Moderately difficult, with some small riffles and rapids
and/or other minor obstacles.
III Medium difficult, with high-wave rapids, rocks, eddies,
and other obstacles.

27

IV Difficult — only for experienced whitewater canoeists; long rapids, powerful waves, boils, eddies; course difficult to recognize; spray covers essential.

V Extremely difficult, same as IV only more so.

VI Death trap, even for the greatest experts.

These ratings can be very misleading. In heavy floods, even a Grade I river can be extremely dangerous. In fact, all rivers are dangerous in flood stage. In very dry weather, when a river is low, even a beginner may negotiate a Grade IV river. He may have to "walk" his canoe over sections that in normal water require spray covers and extreme skill.

What is even more misleading is the fact that some rivers, including the Delaware, are rated according to different criteria by local authorities, probably with the good intention of making beginners cautious. However, if such a beginner has successfully run Skinner's Falls on the Delaware, rated VI by the Delaware River Basin Commission, but perhaps deserving no more than a III in low to medium water by the International Classification standards, he may blithely consider himself an accomplished whitewater canoeist and promptly break his neck on another river rated VI. Yet, the Delaware River is never without its dangers. Its waters, in most sections, are very swift and powerful. Even on a smooth stretch, a fidgety beginner taking a spill can easily drown if he wears no life jacket.

Flat or still water is often rated by these categories:

A From standing still to water moving up to 2½ miles an hour.

B Water moving bteween 2½ and 4½ miles an hour.

C Water moving faster than 4½ miles an hour.

Because of the difficulty of rating rivers at all times, no ratings have been used in this book except for some general observations on whether a river is smooth or of the whitewater type. The best way to find out about river conditions at any given time is to ask people in the know on the spot. Most operators of canoe liveries are happy to provide this information even to those who are not customers.

A canoeist inexperienced with whitewater should never attempt to run a river section rated III and higher by the International Classification unless accompanied by an expert whitewater canoeist or he has looked carefully to see that the water flow is so low as to reduce difficulty.

Preserving and Saving the Waterways

It is distressing for a nature lover to find beer cans, paper, broken glass, and other debris left on a picturesque picnic spot. In fact, it is difficult to understand how some people who canoe can be so insensitive to their surroundings and to those who share their pastime considering that a canoe makes it so easy to carry litter away to a trash can at most take-out points.

On principle, I don't bury fresh litter. A popular picnic stop would soon become a thinly disguised garbage dump if everyone were to bury his litter. Scratch the surface a bit, and you'll find yourself sitting on rusting soda cans. Canoeing clubs, Scouts, and local canoe liveries are frequently active in litter clean-up campaigns, and they are worth supporting in their efforts.

Even more formidable opponents than the litterers are the forces that encroach on nature and destroy waterways on a grand scale — residential developers, commercial, industrial, and mining interests, the recreation "industry", local communities, and state and Federal government agencies.

Fortunately, the defenders of nature have developed by far the strongest lobby of any group of individuals from different walks of life banded together in a common cause. (I sometimes wish that individual taxpayers with no access to loopholes would organize themselves as well.) The outdoor lobby includes millions of individuals who will write ardent letters to politicians at the slightest provocation, as well as practically all outdoor organizations, most prominent among them the Appalachian Mountain Club and the Sierra Club. The American Canoe Association lobbies actively on behalf of its members and member organizations, and regional canoe clubs often take up causes at the state and local levels.

These outdoor organizations, in particular the Sierra Club, are often accused of overstating their case and using tricky legal maneuvers to fight their foes. There is some truth to this. In our society, whether one likes it or not, every party to a bargaining session, political controversy, economic deal, and legal action overstates its case, hoping to compromise somewhere in the middle. Our legal system operates on a basis of technical maneuvering, delaying tactics, finesse, and trickery — to the deplorable extent that obvious criminals, especially in higher places, often get off scot-free. Thus, for the outdoor lobby to be effective at the bargaining table and in the legal theater, it must play the game by the prevailing rules.

And I feel their cause is just. We have arrived at a point in history where there is practically no excuse for encroaching on a single additional acre of nature. Anyone visiting the Yellowstone or Yosemite parks, hiking up the mountain trails of the Rockies, or paddling a canoe on the Boundary Waters of Minnesota is likely to come back convinced that what we have left of nature may not be enough for the increasing number of people who feel the need to go back to nature to live and maintain their sanity.

We have enough residential and industrial slums, wrecked scenery

29

along railroad tracks and highways, and abandoned farmlands gone to seed for all the industrial and residential development needed in the foreseeable future for a population whose growth rate has slowed down considerably. Let us use these devastated acres first, before we touch another patch of nature, and let us reclaim some of these areas for nature, as is already happening in a few isolated cases where paper mills and other industrial plants have reduced the pollution levels of some streams.

The cause will be better served if we recognize that there are legitimate economic problems to be dealt with uniformly at the national level. An industrial plant required to stop pollution in one state can only do so if its competition in other states must comply with the same standards or it will go out of business. Moreover, we must realize that pollution control is expensive and that we, as nature lovers, along with everyone else, must pay for it without grumbling about the inflationary rise in the price of our toilet paper.

In general, however, it can be stated that with rare exceptions *there is no excuse for*

1. Destroying one more spot of "nature" to build residential developments or industrial parks;

2. Drying up another swamp or tidal marsh;

3. Constructing yet another dam.

The destruction of swamps, often for "health" reasons, was one of our greatest follies. They are the indispensable regulators of water tables and, together with the wetlands and tidal marshes, the germinating ground for much of our animal life cycle on land and in the water. A swamp holds rain water and releases it slowly during dry spells. A river deprived of its regulator will flood after rains and dry up in dry spells. The flooding is aggravated in densely populated areas, where the woods, fields, and meadows that normally soak up rainwater have been replaced by pavements for streets, highways, driveways, and parking lots of shopping centers and industrial parks. When it rains, the water, rather than seeping into the ground, simply rushes off into the nearest river. The engineering geniuses who created the floods by drying up swamps then find further employment by building dams to stop the floods.

Dams, at one time, had their place in a rapidly growing country to prevent natural flooding of populated areas, such as those of the Ohio-Missouri-Mississippi river system, to provide a water supply for flour mills and early industrial machinery, to create navigable rivers, and, in a few noteworthy cases, such as the Tennessee Valley, to generate inexpensive power.

However, by now far more dams have been built than could be justified by the common weal. What few people except naturalists and nature lovers realize is the fact that the natural flow of rivers, including the seasonal flooding of flood plains, is absolutely essential for the sustenance of animal and plant life. Flood plains produce lush meadows and farmland through the rich deposits carried by the waters. They are an important regulator of water flow. Yet, too often they are exploited for easily built residential and industrial developments. When these developments flood at regular intervals, a hue and cry goes out for flood control dams and Federal disaster help. The real solution is, of course, to zone flood plains for nature only and prevent all construction on them. It's much less costly for the taxpayer, too.

But this is not the way the U.S. Army Corps of Engineers sees it. Dam building seems to have become an atavistic pastime for them. Their efforts are greatly supported by pork barreling politicians who count their achievements by the amount of Federal tax money they can get for their districts "to create jobs" irrespective of the ultimate usefulness of the projects. And they find allies in that sector of the recreation industry that sees better customers in motor boat owners than in canoeists and bird watchers.

Some major dam building projects have been scuttled recently, including one on the Buffalo River in Arkansas and one on the Delaware River, but throughout the United States far more proposals for dams are on the books of the U.S. Army Corps of Engineers than dams already built!

If you want to help preserve nature, join one of the outdoor organizations and clubs. If you are not cut out to be a public fighter, spokesman, or letter writer, tell your friends about your feelings and contribute to those who are keen to fight on your behalf.

One final word: Treat nature like your own mother, which she is. Don't rip branches off trees; collect firewood on the ground. Don't pluck flowers by the bushel. In most states and national forests and parks all plants are protected, and you may be fined if caught picking them. Above all, don't burn nature. If you light a fire, watch it at all times and extinguish the last ember before you leave.

What Canoe Clubs Do

There are a great many canoe clubs throughout the country, but it is not always easy to find out what a particular club does. Many of the local clubs seem to be loose affiliations of ardent canoeists who have little time for organization and correspondence. They are often headed by a president or a secretary who changes every year and with him or her the official address of the club changes. Club activities may vary with the energy and available time of the secretary. These activities may include group outings for members, clean-up operations on streams and rivers, lobbying at local and state levels for conservation and against dams, instruction for beginners, and opportunities for social mingling.

31

The most active clubs are those interested in whitewater canoeing and racing. They have national and regional meetings to arrange races, set standards and rules, and organize other whitewater events.

Most of the active canoe clubs are affiliated with the American Canoe Association, which also has opened its doors to kayakers and rafters. Organized into regional divisions, the Association, on request, will send its latest directory of canoe clubs. The American Canoe Association is a member of the International Canoe Federation and the United States Olympic Committee, and arranges for U.S. participation in international canoeing events and the Olympic Games. Whitewater and wilderness purists are organized in the American Whitewater Affiliation.

Two leading outdoor organizations, the Sierra Club and the Appalachian Mountain Club, have canoeing chapters in various sectors of the country which arrange group trips, provide canoeing instruction, and are active in conservation movements. On request, they will provide information on their canoeing activities and a list of regional chapters.

Here are the key addresses: American Canoe Association, 4260 East Evans Avenue, Denver, Colorado 80222 / American Whitewater Affiliation, Box 1584, San Bruno, California 94066 / Appalachian Mountain Club, 5 Joy Street, Boston, Massachusetts 02108 / Sierra Club, 1050 Mills Tower, San Francisco, California 94104 / United States Canoe Association, Inc., P.O. Box 9, Winamec, Indiana 46996.

Are You Trespassing?

Trespassing is often a moot point for canoeists. If you paddle down a narrow river running through the middle of someone's property, are you trespassing or not? In most states a stream that has been officially declared a fishing stream is open to the public, but the banks above the high water mark, unless they are in state or Federal parks and forests, remain private property, and access should be sought only from official boat ramps and public roads or with the permission of the owner. If challenged while paddling on a stream, a canoeist is wise to apologize, claim ignorance, and promise to paddle out of the owner's domain as fast as possible. No canoeist should camp or picnic on property clearly marked or recognizable as private. There are usually enough public sandbanks or islands on a river for this purpose. Many state and Federal parks allow camping only in designated areas and by permit. By the same token, a canoeist should be careful not to portage through private property. For instance, tow paths along old canals, such as the Delaware Canal and the Chesapeake and Ohio Canal, are public parks all along the way on one side of the canal, but the opposite bank is mostly private property.

Frequent trespassing and excessive littering have caused some states to impose restrictive regulations for paddling on their lakes and streams or to develop safety rules without consulting the canoeing interests. At the Federal level, river management plans and running regulations are often developed which, in the words of the American Canoe Association, "do not treat the people who wish to run the river on their own with fairness. There is, in many cases, a tilt in favor of the business interests of the commercial river running operators."

Canoeists feeling discriminated against or wishing to support activities to counteract such developments should contact the American Canoe Association.

Some states require that canoes be registered. If you bring in your own canoe from another state and see license plates on the local canoes it is wise to ask whether you need a registration and where you can get one.

Using this Book

Canoeable waters are legion, and while every effort has been made to list the important ones in each state, it is impossible to know them all. Many have not been fully explored or publicized, and others are being regained by eager clubs and canoe liveries which are clearing fallen trees and other debris from potentially attractive streams.

This book tries to make it easy for canoeists to locate the key canoeing waters wherever they may be. All rivers of a state or region are listed alphabetically and keyed on the maps by number. References to local road numbers and names are given to help the reader locate the river on his road maps. Detailed maps of many of the waterways are available from local liveries and other information sources listed at the end of each chapter. These local maps usually include river ratings, distances, put-in and take-out points, portages, campsites, and local sights. Because of the great variation in river ratings, dependent as they are on seasonal water conditions and personal opinion, this book does not provide river ratings, except to mention when a river has difficult whitewater sections or other danger spots. When no such mention is made, it can be assumed that a river is suitable for family canoeing. *However, for the first trip on an unfamiliar river it is always wise to ask locally about difficulties and water conditions before setting out.*

Listed mileages and travel times should always be taken with a grain of salt. Authorities often disagree widely on mileages. The time needed to paddle a given number of miles varies greatly with the speed of the current, prevailing winds, the skill of the canoeists, and the stops along the way. Three miles per hour on a medium-fast river is making good time. Travel times given out by local authorities or canoe liveries usually allow for the slowest, most inept paddler. In most cases, I have found that I can paddle leisurely in two hours a course that is rated for three.

Every effort has been made in this book to give an indication of mileage for the rivers listed. Even so, canoeists are urged to raise any questions they have with the livery operators listed in this book.

Where rental services are available on, or close to, a listed waterway the listing has a cross-reference to the community in which the service is located. Rental locations are listed alphabetically by community. If no rental service is included under a waterway listing, none could be identified nearby. However, liveries in the same state that rent for car-top carrying should make it possible to travel such waterways with a rented canoe.

A few words on assessing the information presented in this book are in order. Every effort has been made to make it easy for readers to locate each waterway quickly. To do this, maps have been drawn especially for this book and each waterway description usually contains the names of access points and route numbers. These route numbers refer primarily to the towns mentioned as access points. This has been done because road maps do not show many of the waterways described here and if you find the towns and roads you will know where the river is. Where no routes are given, these towns are on local roads.

As for the "best canoeing months" category, I have included here the professional opinions of the livery operators. The recommended months are a matter of personal opinion and the reader will find that, in some cases, one rental operator will list a time period that is different from another operator's in the same town or same area. Also, in many cases different rental operators within the same town or area might provide canoes for different waterways and their recommendations for the "best canoeing months" would take this into account.

"Transportation" is a category which, when answered "yes", means that shuttle service is provided, taking canoeists and canoes to put-in points and/or picking canoeists and canoes up at a take-out point. A "yes" for car-top carriers indicates that the livery rents canoes which canoeists can secure to the tops of their cars for canoeing streams that may be some distance from the rental point. A "yes" answer under campsites indicates that campsites — ranging from primitive to comfortable — are available, whether at the rental base or on public or private lands along the riverways.

One last word, this about spelling. The names of towns and waterways have been checked very carefully against a number of sources. But these sources do not always agree on the proper spelling of these names, so I've used the spelling that was corroborated by a majority of the sources. And finally, while every care has been taken to check the information given in this book, neither the author nor the publisher can be held responsible for inaccuracies or for accidents resulting from the use of this book as a guide.

Rental Services

Rental services, liveries, and outfitters have done an outstanding job in furthering the cause of canoeing. Many of the owners and operators of these services are ardent canoeists themselves and are among the happy few who can make their hobby their business. When not too busy with an influx of customers on a weekend, most of them are glad to counsel canoeists, provide them with information on local waterways, and give canoeing lessons. They are the best sources of information on local water conditions. Before venturing into any given area to rent a canoe or to use your own, it is wise to phone a rental service shortly before departure to find out about the water conditions. This is particularly important after heavy rains, when a river may have become too dangerous, or in dry spells when it may no longer be passable. The U.S. Weather Bureau in a given area may also be able to provide information on water levels of local rivers.

When planning to rent, it is always advisable to make a reservation in advance, but especially so on weekends in the most popular season — usually spring.

Most canoe rentals that provide transportation to put-in and/or take-out points for their customers will also make this service available to canoe owners. It's worth phoning a service if you anticipate problems getting back to your own car from a take-out point.

When renting a canoe, look carefully at the contract you are signing— are you fully responsible for any damage to the canoe or for total loss and is insurance protection provided by the rental service? It's worth paying an extra charge for insurance.

The season of the vast majority of liveries is relatively short. We have indicated those which are open all year. Where a livery only indicated the best canoeing months it is, as a rule, open one or more months before and after the best canoeing months time period.

All information on canoe rental services and outfitters provided in this book has been taken from questionnaires filled out by these services. Every effort has been made to interpret and evaluate questionnaires correctly, but no guarantee can be given that every listing is correct in all its detail. Human error, both in filling in the questionnaires and in transcribing the information may have slipped in here or there. The publisher and author welcome your corrections and comments.

Rental services listed as "unconfirmed" are those which have not responded to two written requests for information, but are listed as being active in a number of other information sources.

PART ONE

THE NORTHEAST

•

MAINE

MAINE IS CONSIDERED a canoeist's paradise. Probably no other state has so great a variety of canoeing waters, ranging from small ponds to large interlocking chains of lakes; from gently meandering brooks to turbulent, cascading streams; from rocky creeks to deep and wide rivers emptying into the sea. The Maine coast itself, with thousands of inlets, estuaries, channels, and islands offers a seemingly endless network of waterways on which a canoeist can travel for weeks without having to retrace his wake.

Because of its low population density (30 persons per square mile), Maine, like no other state, can give the visitor a true feeling of remoteness—of having left the hustle and noise of city and highway far behind and of getting into wilderness at its most serene. This is particularly true of the North Maine Woods, the northwest section of the state, bordering on Canada, with millions of acres of forests, interspersed with thousands of lakes, streams, and rivers, and accessible only from rough forestry roads, most of them private and requiring a permit to be traveled.

Here, at the northernmost tip of the United States, are two of the best known canoeing waters—the Allagash Wilderness Waterway and the St. John River. The banks of the Allagash are protected for 500 feet on either side to preserve the "natural beauty, character, and habitat of a unique area." The Waterway is an interconnected system of lakes, streams, and ponds with a great deal of scenic variety, and without excessive difficulties for the canoeist of average skill. It tends to be crowded at the peak season.

The St. John, on the other hand, is a wild, exciting river, recommended only for experts or for moderately experienced canoeists traveling with guides. Ardent wilderness canoeists love the river for its continuity — over 100 miles of fast, varied river flow without portage, testing the ingenuity and skill of the paddler all along the way. Like so many other unspoiled rivers throughout the country, the St. John has become the target of the itchy, dam-building fingers of the U.S. Army Corps of Engineers.

In addition to these two waterways, there are hundreds of other forest lakes and streams in Maine for canoeing. Only a fraction could be included in this book, but additional ones can be discovered by inquiring and obtaining maps locally.

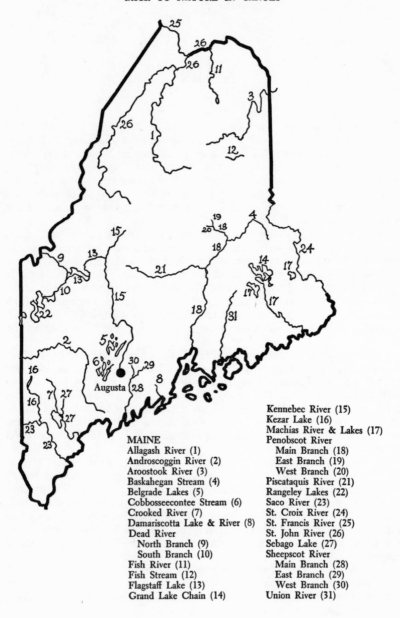

MAINE
Allagash River (1)
Androscoggin River (2)
Aroostook River (3)
Baskahegan Stream (4)
Belgrade Lakes (5)
Cobbosseecontee Stream (6)
Crooked River (7)
Damariscotta Lake & River (8)
Dead River
  North Branch (9)
  South Branch (10)
Fish River (11)
Fish Stream (12)
Flagstaff Lake (13)
Grand Lake Chain (14)

Kennebec River (15)
Kezar Lake (16)
Machias River & Lakes (17)
Penobscot River
  Main Branch (18)
  East Branch (19)
  West Branch (20)
Piscataquis River (21)
Rangeley Lakes (22)
Saco River (23)
St. Croix River (24)
St. Francis River (25)
St. John River (26)
Sebago Lake (27)
Sheepscot River
  Main Branch (28)
  East Branch (29)
  West Branch (30)
Union River (31)

40

Local advice is essential before going on any of the Maine waterways for the first time. Water conditions can vary greatly with the season and the difficulty of a river can change overnight. Many rivers have water that might be too shallow for canoeing during the summer or dry spells.

Many of the Maine canoeing trips require overnight camping, often in remote wilderness areas. Thus, a canoeist using these waters should either be a seasoned wilderness camper or should use the services of a wilderness outfitter and guide. Information on camping permits and campsites should be obtained in advance from the Maine Publicity Bureau or the Maine Forest Service (addresses are at the end of this chapter). Information on private access roads is available from the Paper Industry Information Office (see the end of this chapter).

Fly-in service for canoeists and equipment is available at Greenville, Millinocket, Jackman, and at commercial airports.

Maine Waters

Allagash Wilderness Waterway

The most popular canoe trail in Maine is the Allagash Wilderness Waterway, consisting of a series of interconnecting lakes and streams along the path of the Allagash River, a distance of about 100 miles from Telos Lake in the south to the town of Allagash in the north. A usual starting point is Telos Lake, accessible from Patten on Routes 11–159, via Grand Lake Road and Baxter State Park, or from Millinocket on Route 11, via the Great Northern Paper Co. Road, a private road open to the pubic (closed in winter). The official end of the waterway is at West Twin Brook, 5 miles south of the town of Allagash, just about at the Canadian border and situated at the confluence of the Allagash River and St. John River. A shorter trip can begin at Umsaskis Lake or Long Lake — about 42 miles to the town of Allagash — accessible from Ashland, on Route 11, via American Realty Road, a private road. Longer trips start at North East Carry on Moosehead Lake, from a private road that is open to the public off Routes 5–16. Many round trips are possible, including a popular circuit via Black Pond, the Caucomgomac Lakes, and Allagash Lake. Rentals: Allagash, Augusta, Fairfield, Fort Kent, Greenville, Millinocket, and St. Francis.

Androscoggin River

The Androscoggin begins in New Hampshire and enters Maine near Gilead. Gilead on Route 2 to Bethel on Route 26: 9 miles / Bethel to Rumford on Route 2: 22 miles, a beautiful stretch / Rumford to Livermore Falls on Route 4: 24 miles, still pleasant / Livermore Falls to Brunswick on Route 1: 52 miles of rural countryside / Tidal waters below Brunswick; polluted in the Auburn-Lewiston area / Rentals: North Jay.

41

Aroostook River

Chase Lake, accessible by rough road from Ashland on Route 11, or from Millinocket Lake (north of Baxter State Park), accessible from Grand Lake Road off Route 159 at Shin Pond to Oxbow: about 25 miles, some difficulties, high water needed in the upper reaches / Oxbow to Ashland: 28 miles of smooth waters / Ashland to the confluence with the St. John River: 62 miles, broad and shallow. Rentals: Allagash, Greenville, Millinocket, St. Francis, and Springfield.

Baskahegan Stream

Baskahegan Lake near Brookton on Route 1 to Mattawamkeag River at South Bancroft: 24 miles, some rapids / South Bancroft on the Mattawamkeag to the town of Mattawamkeag on Route 2 and on the Penobscot River: 26 miles. Rentals: Millinocket and Springfield.

Belgrade Lakes

Popular circular trip of some 35 miles, beginning at the town of Belgrade Lakes on Route 27 or Clements Camp on East Pond on Route 137, via North Pond, Great Meadow Stream, Great Pond, Long Pond, Ingham Stream, Belgrade Stream, and the Messalonskee Lake to Oakland on Route 23 — a number of portages. Rentals: Belgrade Lakes and North Jay.

Cobbosseecontee Stream and chain of lakes

Torsey Lake off Route 41 north of Kents Hill to Lake Maranacook: 4 miles / Through the lake to Mill Stream outlet near Winthrop on Routes 41–133: 5 miles / From this point through Annabessacook Lake: 4 miles / lake to Wilson Stream outlet for connection to Belgrade Lakes or to Juggernot Stream connecting with Cobbosseecontee Lake: 2 miles / lake to Cobbosseecontee Stream outlet: 6 miles / outlet through Pleasant Pond: 11 miles / Pleasant Pond to Gardiner on Route 201 on the Kennebec River: 6 miles / Many portages on this canoe trail, much smooth water, and the trip can be made in both directions. Rentals: Rangeley.

Crooked River

Songo Pond off Route 5 to North Waterford on Route 35: 10 miles, in high water only, some rapids / North Waterford to East Waterford on Route 118: 11 miles, steep rapids / East Waterford to Sebago Lake: 40 miles, more rapids.

Damariscotta Lake and River

50-mile round trip through smooth and tidal waters which can be started at any point. Jefferson on Routes 32–126 to town of Damariscotta on Route 1: 11 miles / Damariscotta to South Bristol on Route 129: 16 miles, tidal water / Pemaquid River north of South Bristol to Bristol on Routes 129–130 and Pemaquid Pond: 20 miles / Connect with portage via Muscongus Bay back into Damariscotta Lake and River. Rentals: Jefferson.

Dead River
North Branch: Arnold Pond on Route 27 at the Canadian border to Chain Lakes (also called Chain of Ponds): 5 miles, canoeable at high water only / through the Chain Lakes, an easy and popular trip of about 6 miles / Chain Lakes to Flagstaff Lake: 15 miles. Rentals: Rangeley.

South Branch: Dallas school on Route 16 to Flagstaff Lake: 20 miles, canoeable at high water only, difficult near Dallas. Rentals: Rangeley.

Main Branch: see Flagstaff Lake.

Fish River
Fish River Lake on private road east of town of Portage on Route 11 to Portage: 25 miles / Portage to St. John River at Fort Kent on Route 1: 45 miles with many intermediate starting points. Rentals: Allagash.

Fish Stream
Patten on Route 11 to Island Falls on Route 2: 12 miles, a pleasant 1-day trip without portages, possible to extend the trip by continuing down through Mattawamkeag Lake and the West Branch of the Mattawamkeag River. Rentals: Millinocket.

Flagstaff Lake and Main Branch of the Dead River
The lake is artificial and offers excellent canoeing. It is accessible from Flagstaff Lake campground off Route 27. The lake is drained by the Main Branch of the Dead River which offers 22 miles of very difficult canoeing from Flagstaff Lake to town of The Forks on Route 201 and on the Kennebec River. Rentals: Greenville, Jackman, and Rangeley.

Grand Lake Chain
Some 70 miles of lake canoeing beginning either near Springfield on Route 6 or Princeton on Route 1; connection 7 miles below Princeton with St. Croix River. From Lower Syslodobsis Lake to Fourth Machias Lake: 1½ miles portage / Third Machias Lake connects with Machias River which flows into the Atlantic Ocean at Machias Bay. Rentals: Springfield.

Kennebec River
Moosehead Lake East Outlet at Moosehead on Routes 6–15 or from near Rockwood on Routes 6–15 via Indian Pond to The Forks on Route 201: 24 miles with many difficulties / The Forks to Augusta on I–95: 88 miles, many dams and other obstructions / Tidal waters below Augusta. Rentals: Greenville.

Kezar Lake
North Lovell town dock on Route 5 to Kezar Lake outlet: 8 miles / Outlet to Saco River: 10 miles. Rentals: Kezar Falls.

Long Lake
See Sebago Lake.

Machias River and Lakes
An intricate system of lakes and rivers allowing up to 100 miles of

canoeing with some rapids and many portages. A number of access points, including Big Lake near Princeton on Route 1, Sabao Lake accessible via a private road off Route 9, and Nicatous Lake accessible via a private road off Route 188 at Saponac. The main canoeing trail ends near Whitneyville on Route 1A and the river feeds into Machias Bay on the Atlantic below Whitneyville. Rentals: Springfield.

Ossipee River
See New Hampshire.

Pemaquid River
See Damariscotta River.

Penobscot River
Main Branch: Formed at the junction of the East and West Branches at Medway on Routes 11–157 to Bangor on I-95: 70 miles, mostly smooth, dammed water / Tidal waters below Bangor.

East Branch: Telos Lake off a private road west of Baxter State Park to Grand Lake Matagamon dam: 24 miles, canoeable in spring or after rains / Grand Lake Matagamon accessible from a private road in Baxter State Park off Route 159 to Medway off I-95: 50 miles, some falls to be portaged.

West Branch: Big Eddy on a private road 3 miles below Ripogenus Dam northwest of Millinocket on Route 11 to Millinocket Landing: 32 miles, scenic, some difficulties. Rentals for Main, East, and West Branches: Fairfield, Greenville, and Millinocket.

Piscataquis River
Blanchard off Routes 6–15 to Guilford on the same road: 13 miles, some rapids / Guilford to Howland off I-95 and the Penobscot River: 50 miles, mostly smooth, some rapids.

Presumpscot River
See Sebago Lake.

Rangeley Lakes
Accessible from Routes 4, 16, and 17; excellent canoeing on the following lakes — Rangeley. Cupsuptic, Mooselookmeguntic, Upper Richardson, Lower Richardson, and Umbagog. Umbagog Lake is partially in New Hampshire. Rentals: Rangeley, Maine, and, in New Hampshire — Center Conway, Errol, Milan, and North Conway.

Saco River
See New Hampshire for the Saco above Fryeburg, Maine. Fryeburg on Route 302 to Biddeford on Routes 1 and I-95: about 70 miles, mostly pleasant, some portages and minor rapids. Rentals: Fryeburg and Kezar Falls.

St. Croix River
Orient at the northern end of Grand Lake on Route 122 to Vanceboro on Route 6: 36 miles / Vanceboro to Calais on Route 1: 53 miles, very difficult / Tidal waters with strong currents below Calais, feeding into Passamaquoddy Bay. Rentals: Springfield.

St. Francis River

Accessible only from Canada at Estcourt on Route 51. Estcourt to confluence with St. John River (*see also* Allagash Wilderness Waterway above): 56 miles, upper reaches canoeable only at high water, mostly easy, the St. Francis River forms a portion of the United States-Canada border and it also flows through Beau Lake. Rentals: St. Francis.

St. John River

A great wilderness river recommended only for experts or non-experts traveling with guides. Access to the St. John River is difficult. One approach is from North East Carry on Moosehead Lake accessible from a private road off Routes 6–15; portages and poling before the main river is reached. Or from Baker Lake, accessible from a rough logging road off Routes 6–15 or from Daaquam in Canada on Route 24. Baker Lake to junction with the Allagash River: about 120 miles. Rentals: Allagash, Fairfield, Greenville, Jackman, Millinocket, St. Francis, and Springfield. Fly-in service is available from Greenville.

Sebago Lake

Harrison on Route 117 on north end of Long Lake through Sebago Lake and down the Presumpscot River to Portland on Route 1: about 50 miles of lake and easy river canoeing with portages. A round trip is possible from Harrison with a 5-mile portage to Bolster Mills on the Crooked River.

Sheepscot River

West Branch: Palermo on Route 3 to junction with the East Branch: 17 miles, canoeable in high water, one bad rapid.

East Branch: West of Route 220 near Center Montville to junction with the West Branch: 18 miles, some rapids.

Main Branch: Junction of East and West Branches to Wiscasset on Route 1: 25 miles, mostly smooth; tidal below Wiscasset. Rentals: Jefferson.

Union River

Brandy Pond on private road off Route 9 at Beddington to Amherst on Routes 8–181: 21 miles, passes through Great Pond / Amherst to Ellsworth on Route 1: 24 miles, passes through Graham Lake, fairly easy at high water early in the season; tidal below Ellsworth.

Maine Rentals

Allagash

Allagash Outfitters (Wilmer Hafford), Box 149, Allagash, Me. 04774; telephone: 207–398–3277 / Waters: Allagash and St. John Rivers and other waterways / Trips: a few days to several weeks, guides available / Best canoeing months: mid-May to end of September / Campsites: yes

/ Transportation: yes / Car-top carriers: yes / Complete outfitters providing camping equipment and food.

Chester McBreairty, Box 134, Allagash, Me. 04774; telephone: 207–398–3197 / Unconfirmed.

Augusta

Frederick W. King, Route 5, 16 Woodside Road, Augusta, Me. 04330; telephone: 207–623–4429 / Guided canoe trips only; King conducts regularly scheduled trips on the Allagash River for up to 5 people, providing canoes, equipment, and food.

Belgrade Lakes

Great Pond Marina (David M. Webster), RD, Belgrade Lakes, Me. 04918; telephone: 207–495–2213 / Waters: chain of nearby lakes and streams / Trips: 1 day or more / Best canoeing months: May to mid-October / Campsites: yes / Transportation: yes / Car-top carriers: yes.

Brewer

Twin City Marine & Camping Headquarters, 99 South Main Street, Brewer, Me. 04412; telephone: 207–989–6397 / Waters: nearby waters / Trips: 1 day or more / Best canoeing months: April and May / Campsites: no / Transportation: no / Car-top carriers: yes.

Fairfield

Gilpatrick's Guide Service, RFD 1, Fairfield, Me. 04937; telephone: 207–453–6959 / Waters: West Branch of the Penobscot, Allagash, and St. John Rivers and other waterways / Trips: guided canoe trips only, up to 1 month / Best canoeing months: July and August / Campsites: yes / Transportation: yes / Car-top carriers: no / Camping equipment provided.

Fort Kent

Pierre Z. Freeman, 47 West Main Street, Fort Kent, Me. 04743; telephone: 207–834–5505 / Unconfirmed.

Fryeburg

Saco Bound/Northern Waters, see Center Conway, New Hampshire.

Saco River Canoe & Kayak Company, Fryeburg, Me. 04037; telephone: 207–935–2369 / Unconfirmed.

Greenville

Allagash Wilderness Outfitters (Rick and Judy Givens), Frost Pond, Star Route 76, Greenville, Me. 04441; telephone: none / Waters: Allagash River, upper West Branch of the Penobscot River, St. John River, and other northern Maine waters / Trips: 2 days and longer / Best canoeing months: mid-June to mid-September / Campsites: yes / Transportation: yes / Car-top carriers: yes / Complete outfitters providing camping equipment and food.

Folsom's Air Service, Moosehead Lake, Greenville, Me. 04441; telephone: 207–695–2821 / Air lift service / Waters: lakes in Maine and Canada / Trips: various / Best canoeing months: May-October /

Campsites: yes, accessible by plane / Transportation: yes, by plane / Car-top carriers: no / Housekeeping cabins and camps.

Jackman

Smith Hardware Inc., P.O. Box 278, Jackman, Me. 04945; telephone: 207–668–5151 / Waters: Allagash and St. John Rivers and nearby lakes / Trips: 1 day to several weeks / Best canoeing months: June-September / Campsites: yes / Transportation: yes / Car-top carriers: no response.

Jefferson

Damariscotta Lake Farm's Lakeside Marina (George M. Cleaves, Sr.), Box 89 B, Jefferson, Me. 04348; telephone: 207–549–5252 or 549–9253 / Waters: Damariscotta Lake and River and Sheepscot River and nearby lakes / Trips: a few hours to several days / Best canoeing months: May-October / Campsites: yes / Transportation: yes / Car-top carriers: yes.

Kezar Falls

Tip-A-Canoe Adventures at Kezar Falls Kampground (Phil M. Young), Route 25, Box C, Kezar Falls, Me. 04047; telephone: 207–625–3256 / Waters: Saco and Ossipee Rivers, Kezar Lake, and many other nearby waters / Trips: 1 or more days, guides available / Best canoeing months: May-October / Campsites: yes / Transportation: yes / Car-top carriers: yes / Camping equipment and travel trailers for rent.

Millinocket

Smith Pond Camping (Bud and Elaine Dionne), P.O. Box 34, Millinocket, Me. 04462; telephone: summer — 207–723–4400; winter — 207–723–9036 / Waters: Allagash Wilderness Waterway, St. John River, and other Maine rivers and lakes / Trips: 1 day or more / Best canoeing months: late spring and early fall / Campsites: yes / Transportation: yes / Car-top carriers: yes.

North Jay

Moose Horn Trading Post, Route 4, North Jay, Me. 04262; telephone: 207–645–2057 / Waters: nearby rivers and lakes / Trips: 1 day to several days / Best canoeing months: June-September / Campsites: yes / Transportation: yes / Car-top carriers: yes.

Rangeley

Davis Marine, Main Street, Rangeley, Me. 04970; telephone: 207–864–3451 / Waters: Rangeley Lakes area and elsewhere / Trips: any length of time / Best canoeing months: June-September / Campsites: yes / Transportation: no / Car-top carriers: yes.

Raymond

Taylor's Marina, Raymond, Me. 04071; telephone: 207–655–4949 / Unconfirmed.

St. Francis

Pelletier's Campground (Edwin A. Pelletier), Box 7, St. Francis, Me.

04774; telephone: 207–398–3187 / Waters: St. Francis, St. John, and Allagash Rivers and other waterways / Trips: 1 to several days / Best canoeing months: May-June / Campsites: yes / Transportation: yes / Car-top carriers: yes / Guided group tours, motel, camping and tenting grounds.

Sangerville

Halls' Trading Post, Pleasant Avenue, Sangerville, Me. 04970; telephone: 207–876–3920 / Unconfirmed.

Springfield

Maine Wilderness Canoe Basin (Capt. Carl Selin), Pleasant Lake, Springfield, Me. 04487; telephone: 207–989–3636, ext. 631 / Waters: Pleasant Lake and Grand Lake Chain and St. Croix, Machias, St. John, Baskahegan Stream, Mattawamkeag River, and other waterways / Trips: 1 day to 1 month, guides available / Best canoeing months: May-October / Campsites: yes / Transportation: yes / Car-top carriers: yes / Complete camping outfitters, camp facilities and housekeeping cabins at base, shelter cabins and deluxe tent cabins along routes / Open all year.

Sources of Information

Allagash Wilderness Waterway, Maine Bureau of Parks and Recreation (Augusta, Me. 04330), n.d., brochure, free. Descriptive and with a useful map.

A.M.C. New England Canoeing Guide, Appalachian Mountain Club (5 Joy Street, Boston, Mass. 02108), 1971, 600 pp., $5.00. Very detailed description of all canoeable waterways in the six New England states with three maps and ratings for type of water and attractiveness of scenery.

Canoeing in Maine, Maine Department of Economic Development (State House, Augusta, Me. 04330), n.d., brochure, free.

Maine campsite information is available from Maine Forest Service (State Office Building, Augusta, Me. 04330).

Maine fishing and hunting information is available from Maine Department of Inland Fisheries and Game (State House, Augusta, Me. 04330).

Maine tourist information is available from Maine Publicity Bureau (Gateway Circle, Portland, Me. 04102).

North Maine Woods: Guide Map, Regulations, and Information, North Maine Woods (Box 1113, Bangor, Me. 04401), n.d., brochure, supplements provided with updated materials, free.

Private road use permit information is available from Paper Industry Information Office (133 State Street, Augusta, Me. 04330).

Thomas, Eben, *No Horns Blowing*, Hallowell Printing Co. (145 Water Street, Hallowell, Me. 04347), 1975, 134 pp., $3.95. Description of 10 Maine canoe routes and some general information.

•

NEW HAMPSHIRE and VERMONT

EXCEPT FOR THE CONNECTICUT RIVER, which forms the entire boundary between the two states and separates them neatly from each other, New Hampshire and Vermont share no rivers. The only excuse for pooling them in this chapter is their common attraction for vacationers — the kindred beauty of their forests, mountains, and streams, relatively unspoiled by man. Easterners go to these states in the summer to enjoy their cool, fresh air, and Canadians come south perhaps to get a little warmer.

The two largest forest tracts are the White Mountain National Forest in New Hampshire and the Green Mountain National Forest in Vermont. Clear, fast streams run down their slopes and through their valleys and gorges — a delight to the trout fisherman. The canoeist is more limited in their use. Many of them are too small or too rough to be canoeable, and those that are can usually be navigated only in the spring or after heavy rains. Also, the whitewater enthusiast finds more opportunities for his sport than the flat-water nature lover. Nevertheless, even the roughest streams usually have stretches of smooth water, and there are well over 1,000 lakes and ponds in these two New England states for quiet paddling.

The Connecticut River is one of the grandest long-distance canoeing routes in the country — some 250 miles from the headwaters in New Hampshire to the Massachusetts border, and about 150 miles from Massachusetts to Long Island Sound. In its upper reaches the river is tricky during the spring flood waters, but usually from May onwards most of the river is relatively safe for the average canoeist, and there is enough water throughout the year.

Northeastern New Hampshire offers some wilderness canoeing trails, some of them leading into Maine.

Northwestern Vermont is farmland, with good flat water canoeing on pleasant meandering streams or on the numerous bays or inlets of Lake Champlain.

Some pleasant tidewater canoeing can be found along the 18-mile Atlantic coast of New Hampshire.

New Hampshire Waters

Ammonoosuc River
Bretton Woods on Route 302 to Twin Mountain on Route 3: 7 miles, fast but easy / Twin Mountain to town of Pierce Bridge on Route 302: 7 miles with rapids / Pierce Bridge to Littleton on Route 302: 11 miles, smooth waters and rapids / Littleton to Woodsville on Route 302: 22 miles, mostly smooth but with some rapids.

Androscoggin River
Starts at the outlet of Umbagog Lake on Route 16 near Errol; dam controlled. Errol to Berlin on Route 16: 35 miles, some rapids, dangerous at high water. *See also* Maine. Rentals: Center Conway, Errol, Milan, and North Conway.

Baker River
Warren on Routes 25–118 to West Rumney on Route 25: 12 miles, very difficult / West Rumney to Plymouth west of I–93: 16 miles, recommended for spring canoeing and after rains, relatively easy. Rentals: Ashland and West Thornton.

Bearcamp River
Scenic river, good only at high water. Bearcamp Pond off Route 25 to Bennet Corners: 3 miles, easy / Bennet Corners to Whittier on Route 25–113: 4 miles, rapids / Whittier to Ossipee Lake: 9 miles, mostly flat. Rentals: Center Conway and North Conway.

Blackwater River
East Salisbury, Massachusetts, from Route 1 bridge to Hampton, New Hampshire, on Route 1: 8 miles of pleasant tidewater canoeing.

Cocheco River
Farmington off Route 11 to Rochester on Route 202: 10 miles, pleasant and fairly easy / waters below Rochester are polluted and dammed / waters below Dover are tidal.

Connecticut Lakes
Pleasant canoeing on these three lakes at the headwaters of the Connecticut River as well as nearby Lake Francis (sometimes called the Fourth Lake), all accessible from Route 3, north of Pittsburg. Rivers linking some of the lakes may be impassable in spots.

Connecticut River
Canoeable from the First Lake off Route 3 north of Pittsburg all the way to Long Island Sound, about 400 miles. The upper section has some whitewater and there are about 16 dams along the way. See the end of this chapter for information about the *Connecticut River Guide*, which is recommended. *See also* Connecticut. Rentals: Hanover and Sunapee.

Contoocook River
Cheshire Pond on Route 202 to Peterborough on Route 202: 7 miles, moderate whitewater / Peterborough to Hillsboro on Route 202: 24 miles, mostly flat and with power dams / Hillsboro to Henniker on

NEW HAMPSHIRE
Ammonoosuc River (1)
Androscoggin River (2)
Baker River (3)
Bearcamp River (4)
Blackwater River (5)
Cocheco River (6)
Connecticut Lakes (7)
Connecticut River (8)
Contoocook River (9)
Great Bay (10)
Lake Winnipesaukee (11)
Magalloway River (12)
Merrimack River (13)
Newfound Lake (14)
Ossipee Lake & River (15)
Pemigewasset River (16)
Rangeley Lakes (17)
Saco River (18)
Squam Lake & Little
   Squam Lake (19)
Sugar River (20)
Sunapee Lake (21)
Suncook River (22)
Swift River (23)

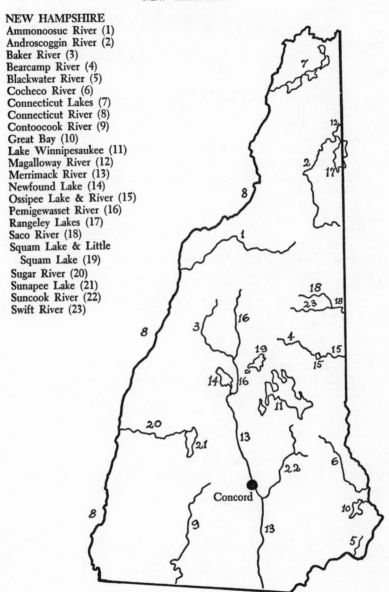

Route 202: 8 miles, rapids / Henniker to Penacook on Route 3–4: 25 miles, backed-up water and mostly flat.

Great Bay

Excellent tidewater canoeing near Dover on Routes 4–16–108 and good canoeing on several of the feeder rivers.

Lake Winnipesaukee

Accessible from Routes 11–28–109, populated, Lake Winnipesaukee offers varied canoeing on the lake itself, tributary lakes, bays, and feeder rivers. Rentals: Wolfeboro.

Magalloway River

From Aziscohos Dam on Route 16 in Maine, one can canoe upstream for about 20 miles on Aziscohos Lake and about 20 miles downstream to Umbagog Lake on the New Hampshire-Maine border. Scenic wilderness is what one can see; the waters are mostly easy with exception of a few rapids. Rentals: Errol.

Merrimack River

Formed by the confluence of the Pemigewasset and Winnipesaukee Rivers at Franklin on Route 3. Franklin to Nashua on Route 3: 62 miles, canoeable all year, mostly uninteresting flat water, several dams, and polluted in the lower stretch.

Newfound Lake

Located between East Hebron and Bristol on Route 3A, Newfound Lake offers excellent lake canoeing as well as the lake's feeders, the Fowler and Cockermouth Rivers. Rentals: Bristol.

Ossipee Lake and Ossipee River

The lake is in New Hampshire but the river also runs into Maine. The lake canoeing is pleasant, accessible from Routes 16 and 25. The river offers 16 miles of canoeing from the Route 153 bridge at Effingham Falls in New Hampshire to the confluence of the Saco River in Maine, the water is mostly smooth with some rapids. Rentals: Center Conway and North Conway.

Pemigewasset River

North Woodstock on Route 3 to Plymouth west of I–93: 27 miles, dangerous at Livermore Falls a few miles above Plymouth / Plymouth to dam at Bristol on Route 104: 17 miles of smooth water, slack water at the lower end / Bristol Dam to Franklin on Route 3: 17 miles, some rapids. Rentals: Ashland and West Thornton.

Rangeley Lakes

Accessible from Routes 16 and 26, excellent lake and river canoeing in New Hampshire and Maine. In New Hampshire, canoeing is on Umbagog Lake; in Maine on Rangeley Lake, the Cupsuptic River, Mooselookmeguntic Lake, and the Upper and Lower Richardson Lakes. Rentals: Center Conway, Errol, Milan, and North Conway in New Hampshire and Rangeley in Maine.

Saco River

Above Bartlett on Routes 302–16A extremely difficult. Bartlett to North Conway on Route 16–302: 11 miles, mostly whitewater / North Conway to Fryeburg, Maine, and Route 302: 20 miles, smooth water and rapids. Good canoeing only at high water. For the Saco River below Fryeburg, *see* Maine. Rentals: Center Conway, Errol, Milan, North Conway, and Raymond.

Squam Lake and Little Squam Lake

Pleasant lake canoeing on Routes 3–113, the lakes drain into the Pemigewasset River with its rapids and dams. Rentals: Ashland.

Sugar River

Sunapee Lake on Route 11 to the Connecticut River: 25 miles, industrialized, dammed, irregular flow, but some pleasant stretches. Rentals: Georges Mills and Sunapee.

Sunapee Lake

Scenic lake canoeing accessible from Route 11. Rentals: Georges Mills and Sunapee.

Suncook River

Pittsfield on Route 28 to North Chichester on Route 28: 6 miles, much whitewater / North Chichester to town of Short Falls east of Route 28: 7 miles, mostly flat water / Short Falls to the Merrimack River: 9 miles, flat.

Swift River

Passaconaway Campground on Route 112 to the Saco River at Conway on Route 16: 17 miles, very difficult with some impassable spots. Rentals: Center Conway.

New Hampshire Rentals

Ashland

Riveredge Inc. Marina, RFD 1, Ashland, N.H. 03217; telephone 603–968–4411 / Waters: Squam Lakes and its feeders, Pemigewasset and Baker Rivers / Trips: 2 days or more / Best canoeing months: June-October / Campsites: yes / Transportation: no / Car-top carriers: yes.

Bristol

Alexandria Boat Shop (Peter Brown), RFD 1, Bristol, N.H. 03222; telephone: 603–744–3647 or 744–5163 / Waters: Newfound Lake / Trips: several hours to 2 days / Best canoeing months: May-September / Campsites: yes / Transportation: yes / Car-top carriers: yes.

Center Conway

Saco Bound/Northern Waters, located 2 miles east of Center Conway on Route 302 (mailing address: P.O., Fryeburg, Maine 04037);

telephone: 603–447–2177 / Waters: Saco, Swift, Bearcamp, Ossipee, and Androscoggin Rivers and Rangeley Lakes and other waters /Trips: 2 or more days, guides available / Best canoeing months: April-October / Campsites: yes / Transportation: yes / Car-top carriers: yes / Second location at Errol, N.H. / Complete outfitters / Instruction in whitewater canoeing and kayaking is also available.

Derry

Derry Marine, Route 28 S, Derry, N.H. 03038; telephone 603–434–4433 / Unconfirmed.

Dublin

Norman B. Wight, Box 105, Dublin, N.H. 03444; telephone: 603–563–6581 / Waters: northern Maine rivers / Trips: 7–28 days with guides only / Best canoeing months: June-October / Complete outfitters.

Errol

Brown Owl Camps (Harry F. Ashley), R.F.D., Errol, N.H. 03579; telephone: 603–586–4414 / Unconfirmed.

Saco Bound/Northern Waters, *see* Center Conway.

Georges Mills

Sargents Lakeshore Cottages and Marina, Box 417, Georges Mills, N.H. 03751; telephone: 603–763–5032 / Waters: Sugar River and Sunapee Lake / Trips: up to 1 day / Best canoeing months: July-September / Campsites: no / Transportation: no / Car-top carriers: no.

Hanover

Ledyard Canoe Club of Dartmouth, Robinson Hall, Hanover, N.H. 03755; telephone: 603–646–2753 / Waters: Connecticut River / Trips: several hours to several days / Best canoeing months: May-October / Campsites: yes / Transportation: no / Car-top carriers: yes, but not to whitewaters.

Holderness

Squam Boats, Inc., R.F.D., Holderness, N.H. 03245; telephone: 603–968–7721 / Unconfirmed.

Laconia

Goodhue Enterprises, Route 3, Weirs Boulevard, Laconia, N.H. 03246; telephone: 603–524–0982 / Unconfirmed.

Milan

Scotlyn Yard, Inc., Milan, N.H. (mailing address: R.F.D. 1, Berlin, N.H. 03570); telephone: 603–449–3333 / Waters: Rangeley Lakes, Androscoggin River, Saco River, and other northern New Hampshire waters / Trips: 2–5 days / Best canoeing months: April-October / Campsites: yes / Transportation: yes / Car-top carriers: yes / Affiliated with Gralyn Sports Center in North Conway.

North Conway

Canoe King of New England, Gralyn Sports Center, South Main

Street, North Conway, N.H. 03860; telephone: 603–356–5546 / Waters: nearby lakes and rivers including Rangeley Lakes and the Androscoggin, Bearcamp, Ossipee, and Saco Rivers / Trips: up to 5 days, guides available / Best canoeing months: early spring for whitewater, July-August for flat water / Campsites: yes / Transportation: yes / Car-top carriers: yes / Affiliated with Scotlyn Yard, Inc. in Milan.

Raymond

OutDoors Unlimited Inc. (Bill Carney), Harriman Road, Raymond, N.H. 03077; telephone: 603–895–3493 / Waters: Saco River and other New Hampshire waterways / Trips: 1–3 days on the Saco River for up to 14 people including all equipment and food, guides available / Best canoeing months: July-September / Campsites: yes / Transportation: yes / Car-top carriers: yes / Also rents camping equipment.

Sunapee

Osborne's Marine Inc., Main Street, Sunapee Harbor, P.O. Box 356, Sunapee, N.H. 03782; telephone: 603–763–2611 / Waters: Sunapee Lake, Connecticut River, Suger River, and other nearby waters / Trips: up to 1 day / Best canoeing months: June-October / Campsites: no / Transportation: no / Car-top carriers: no.

West Thornton

White Mountain Canoe Co., 93 Motel, U.S. 3, West Thornton, N.H. 03285; telephone: 603–726–3534 / Waters: Baker and Pemigewasset Rivers / Trips: up to 2 days / Best canoeing months: April-August / Campsites: yes / Transportation: yes, by special arrangement / Car-top carriers: yes.

Wolfeboro

Winnipesaukee Motor Craft Co., Route 109, Wolfeboro, N.H. 03894; telephone: 603–569–1220 / Waters: Lake Winnipesaukee / Trips: up to 1 day / Best canoeing months: June-October / Campsites: no / Transportation: no / Car-top carriers: no.

Vermont Waters

Arrowhead Mountain Lake

Accessible from Route 7 near East Georgia, the lake offers 4 miles of smooth canoeing, a possible take-out point for Lamoille River trips. Rentals: Fairfax.

Batten Kill

Manchester on Route 7 to Arlington on Route 7: 11 miles, mostly smooth at high water / Arlington to Middle Falls, New York, on Route 29: 30 miles, not recommended below Middle Falls.

Black River (Orleans County)

Albany on Route 14 to Route 58 bridge at Irasburg: 14 miles, pleasant

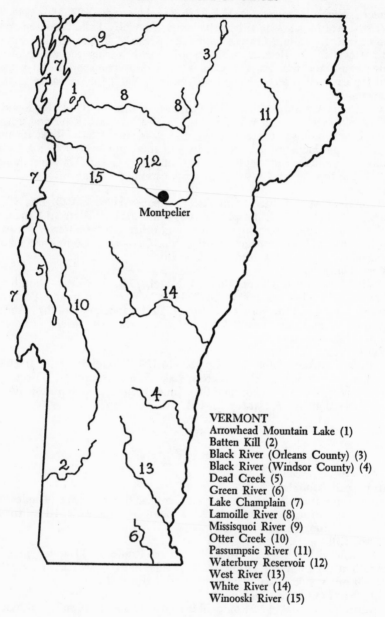

Montpelier

VERMONT
Arrowhead Mountain Lake (1)
Batten Kill (2)
Black River (Orleans County) (3)
Black River (Windsor County) (4)
Dead Creek (5)
Green River (6)
Lake Champlain (7)
Lamoille River (8)
Missisquoi River (9)
Otter Creek (10)
Passumpsic River (11)
Waterbury Reservoir (12)
West River (13)
White River (14)
Winooski River (15)

canoeing / Irasburg, below the gorge, to above Coventry on Route 5: 6 miles, impassable rapids / Coventry to Newport on Route 5: 8 miles, flat water. Rentals: Burlington.

Black River (Windsor County)

Excellent for the family canoeist are the Black River Lakes near Tyson on Route 100. The canoeing is very pleasant. The river itself is an exit at Reservoir Pond to the Connecticut River, 32 miles of complicated waters with rapids, dams, portages, but some smooth stretches.

Dead Creek

From a dike 1 mile south of Route 17 to Otter Creek near Vergennes on Route 22A is Dead Creek, a marshland creek about 10 miles long which relies for its water level on the water level of Lake Champlain. Rentals: Burlington and Fairfax.

Green River

From town of Green River near Brattleboro off Route 5 or 9 to Greenfield, Massachusetts, on I–91: a scenic stretch of 21 miles. Rentals: Fairfax.

Lake Champlain

Good canoeing in the smaller bays and feeder streams. The lake is 110 miles long but has considerable commercial and motor boat traffic. Rentals: Burlington and Fairfax.

Lamoille River

Hardwick Lake at Route 12B to Morrisville at Route 100: 15 miles / Morrisville to Johnson on Route 15: 10 miles / Johnson to Jeffersonville on Route 15: 13 miles / Jeffersonville to the falls at Fairfax on Route 104: 14 miles / Fairfax to Lake Champlain: 20 miles. Mostly easy canoeing, a scenic run, best at high water. Rentals: Burlington, Fairfax, and Stowe.

Missisquoi River

North Troy on Route 105 to East Richford on Route 105A: 12 miles; these towns are on the United States-Canadian border and the 12-mile stretch is almost entirely in Canada; canoeists must report to Canadian Customs at Highwater and to U.S. Customs at East Richford / East Richford to Lake Champlain: 65 miles, scenic and mostly easy canoeing at high water. Rentals: Fairfax.

Otter Creek

Danby on Route 7 to Lake Champlain: about 100 miles; an excellent, smooth, scenic trip with many intermediate access points especially suggested for spring and after rains. Rentals: Brandon and Burlington.

Passumpsic River

Route 114 bridge 2 miles south of Lyndon Center at the confluence of the East and West Branches of the Passumpsic River to the Connecticut River: 22 miles, mostly slack, dammed water / a few miles of swift canoeing at high water is found on the East and West Branches above the Route 114 bridge.

Waterbury Reservoir

Pleasant lake canoeing near Waterbury on Route 100. Rentals: Fairfax and Stowe.

West River

South Londonderry on Route 100 to East Jamaica on Route 30–100: 13 miles, a slalom race track / East Jamaica to West Townshend flood control dam on Route 30: 1 mile / West Townshend to Brattleboro off I–91: 21 miles, mostly smooth.

White River

Granville on Route 100 to Rochester on Route 100: 8 miles, recommended only at high water / Rochester to Bethel and bridge on Route 107: 20 miles, partly whitewater and rapids / Bethel to Connecticut River: 28 miles, some difficult spots. The White River has three branches, all of which have stretches which can be canoed. Some difficulty may be encountered on the First Branch, in the 9-mile stretch from Chelsea on Route 110 to Tunbridge on Route 110 and from Tunbridge to the main river, a stretch of 17 miles. The Second Branch has a good 10-mile stretch from East Randolphe on Route 14 to North Royalton on Route 14. A 16-mile stretch paralleling a railroad line is on the Third Branch, from Braintree on Route 12A to Bethel on Route 107, recommended only in high water. Rentals: Brandon, Burlington, and Fairfax.

Winooski River

Marshfield on Route 2 to Plainfield on Route 2: 9 miles, some whitewater / Plainfield to Montpelier on Route 2: 14 miles, some rapids / Montpelier to the falls at Bolton on Route 2: 15 miles, easy canoeing most of the year / Bolton to Essex Junction on Route 15: 19 miles, large dam / Essex Junction to Lake Champlain: 17 miles, mostly smooth. Rentals: Burlington, Fairfax, and Stowe.

Vermont Rentals

Bennington

De Marco Sporting Goods, 200 North Side Drive, Bennington, Vt. 05201; telephone: 802–442–5330 / Unconfirmed.

Brandon

Eddy's Marine and Sport Center, Route 7, Brandon, Vt. 05733; telephone: 802–247–6320 / Waters: Otter Creek, White River, and other nearby waters / Trips: 1–2 days / Best canoeing months: April-October / Campsites: yes / Transportation: no / Car-top carriers: yes.

Burlington

Canoe Imports Inc., 74 South Willard Street, Burlington, Vt. 05401;

telephone: 802–862–2146 / Waters: anywhere / Trips: 1 or more days / Best canoeing months: June-August / Campsites: yes / Transportation: no / Car-top carriers: yes, for flat waters only.

Fairfax

Mead Rent-A-Canoe (Alan and Gretchen Mead), R.F.D. 2, River Road, Fairfax, Vt. 05454; telephone: 802–849–6819 / Waters: Lamoille, Missisquoi, White, and Winooski Rivers, Arrowhead Mountain Lake, Lake Champlain, Green River Reservoir, Dead Creek, and Waterbury Reservoir / Trips: 1 or more days, guides available / Best canoeing months: June-September / Campsites: yes / Transportation: yes / Car-top carriers: yes / Also rents camping equipment.

Newport

Canoes Unlimited, 187 Elm Street, Newport, Vt. 05855; telephone: 802–334–8888 / Unconfirmed.

North Hero

Tudhope Marine Co., Inc., U.S. Route 2, North Hero, Vt. 05474; telephone: 802–372–5545 / Unconfirmed.

Stowe

Stowe Canoe Company, Route 100, Stowe, Vt. 05672; telephone: 802–253–7398 / Waters: Lamoille and Winooski Rivers, Waterbury Reservoir, and other nearby waters / Trips: 1–4 days / Best canoeing months: April-October / Campsites: yes / Transportation: no / Cartop carriers: yes / Manufactures, sells, and rents canoes and accessories.

Woodstock

Woodstock Sports, 30 Central Street, Woodstock, Vt. 05091; telephone: 802–457–1568 / Unconfirmed.

Sources of Information

A.M.C. *New England Canoeing Guide*, Appalachian Mountain Club (5 Joy Street, Boston, Mass. 02108), 1971, 600 pp., $5.00. Very detailed description of all canoeable waterways in the six New England states, three area maps with ratings of the waters and attractiveness of scenery.

Connecticut River Guide, Connecticut River Watershed Council (125 Combs Road, Easthampton, Mass. 01027), n.d., 82 pp., $4.50. Detailed description of the entire river with three maps.

Canoeing on the Connecticut River, Vermont Division of Recreation (Montpelier, Vt. 05602), 1964, 21 pp., free. Somewhat out of date; needs additional checking along the way.

New Hampshire bulletins on canoeing, state parks, and other recreational facilities are available from New Hampshire Department of Resources and Economic Development (P.O. Box 856, State House Annex,

Concord, N.H. 03301). Information on fishing and hunting is available from New Hampshire Fish and Game Department (34 Bridge Street, Concord, N.H. 03301).

New England Power Company (20 Turnpike Road, Westboro, Mass. 01581) maintains campsites on the Connecticut River and provides general information.

Summer Canoeing and Kayaking in the White Mountains of New Hampshire, White Mountain Region Association (Box K, Lancaster, N.H. 03584), n.d., 24 pp., free.

Vermont fishing and hunting information is available from Vermont Agency of Environmental Conservation, Fish and Game Department (Montpelier, Vt. 05602).

Vermont tourist information is available from Greater Vermont Association (Box 37, Montpelier, Vt. 05602) and Vermont Development Agency (Montpelier, Vt. 05602).

•

CONNECTICUT, MASSACHUSETTS, and RHODE ISLAND

THE HEARTLANDS OF NEW ENGLAND have undergone many scenic changes in the three-and-one-half centuries since the landing of the Pilgrims at Plymouth Rock. Virgin forests became farmlands, rivers turned into industrial sewers, tangled second growth replaced abandoned farms and lumbered forests; urban sprawl proliferated factories, offices, gas stations, shopping centers, subdivisions, and the manicured gardens of suburbia; marshes were drained and valleys flooded to create reservoirs. Most of the rivers are dammed, often at short intervals, and sluggish water has replaced many rippling runs.

There is little left to take a canoeist back to nature as it once was, but enough river stretches and secluded ponds remain to provide pleasant paddling through quiet waters or down some riffles and rapids.

Some of the most satisfying scenery is in northwestern Connecticut and in the Berkshire Mountains — the watershed of the Housatonic River. The Berkshires, where the Housatonic begins, are richly wooded, benign mountains. The river then winds its way through farmland and meadows, and a canoeist may sometimes have to paddle around lethargic cows cooling off in the water. The most popular stretch of the river is in Connecticut, between Falls Village and Kent, where it threads its way

60

between steep, wooded banks. A race track in early spring, when the water is high, this portion is a pleasant family run at other times, with just enough excitement to tickle the sense of adventure, yet without serious danger to the cautious.

The Farmington River, which joins the Connecticut River at Windsor, Connecticut, was called "Tunxis" by the Indians, meaning "the beautiful river that ripples through the hills." Badly destroyed and polluted in the early stages of industrial development, it has regained some of its natural charms and is now a favorite whitewater course, with some smooth stretches.

Canoeists who enjoy the open vistas of wide rivers can float the Connecticut River on its entire length through Massachusetts and Connecticut, or they can start even higher upstream in Vermont and New Hampshire.

The Concord and Charles Rivers, at the outskirts of Boston, carry the canoeist over much historical ground. Walden Pond, near the town of Concord, where Thoreau contemplated nature, is now a state park with picnic tables and rental boats.

Rhode Island has made efforts to preserve some nature within its limited boundaries, including at least three canoeable rivers.

Finally, there is some fine canoeing in the bays, salt water marshes, and tidal inlets of Cape Cod and some other coastal areas.

Connecticut Waters

Bantam and Shepaug Rivers
Litchfield at Route 25 bridge to Washington Depot on Route 109: 15 miles with some whitewater / Washington Depot to Lake Lillinonah (a dammed section of the Housatonic River): 13 miles, more whitewater, watch for Roxbury Falls, 1 mile above the lake. Rentals: New Milford and West Simsbury.

Colebrook Impoundment
Some sources refer to this body of water as Colebrook River Lake. The lake follows the river bed from Connecticut into Massachusetts. It is a lake of 1,000 acres north of Winsted on Route 8 and is scenic.

Connecticut River
About 150 miles of canoeable waters from the northern border of Massachusetts with Vermont and New Hampshire through Connecticut into Long Island Sound. Several dams and minor rapids. *See also* New Hampshire. Rentals: Clinton, Newington, and West Simsbury.

Farmington River
Primarily a Connecticut river with a short stretch in Massachusetts. Otis, Massachusetts, on Route 23 to the Connecticut River at Windsor,

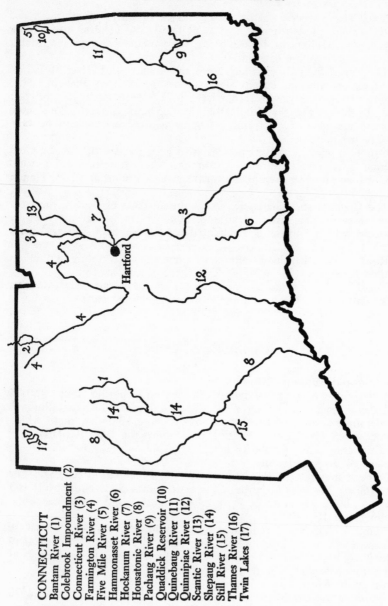

CONNECTICUT
Bantam River (1)
Colebrook Impoundment (2)
Connecticut River (3)
Farmington River (4)
Five Mile River (5)
Hammonasset River (6)
Hockanum River (7)
Housatonic River (8)
Pachang River (9)
Quaddick Reservoir (10)
Quinebaug River (11)
Quinnipiac River (12)
Scantic River (13)
Shepaug River (14)
Still River (15)
Thames River (16)
Twin Lakes (17)

Connecticut, on Route 159: about 80 miles with much whitewater and some smooth stretches. Use *Farmington River and Watershed Guide* (*see* sources at end of chapter) and ask locally for water conditions. Rentals: Newington and West Simsbury.

Five Mile River and Quaddick Reservoir

Begins in Massachusetts but mostly in Connecticut. Lake Webster on Routes 52–16 in Massachusetts to Quaddick Reservoir in Connecticut: 7 miles, portages, high water needed / Quaddick Reservoir to Ballouville: 8 miles / Ballouville to Danielson on Route 12: 7 miles / Danielson to the Quinebaug River via portage.

Hammonasset River

From below the reservoir at Summer Hill Road off Route 80 to Hammonasset Beach State Park near Clinton on Route 1: an 8-mile stretch suggested only when there is adequate water release from the reservoir. Rentals: Clinton.

Hockanum River

Talcottville on Route 30 to the Connecticut River at East Hartford on I-84: 11 miles, several dams / above Talcottville canoeable only at high water.

Housatonic River

Begins in Massachusetts but is primarily a Connecticut River. Lenox, Massachusetts, on Route 7 to Stockbridge, Massachusetts, on Route 7: 12 miles / Stockbridge to Great Barrington, Massachusetts, on Route 7–23: 13 miles / Great Barrington to Falls Village, Connecticut, on Route 126: 25 miles with intermediate access points / Falls Village to Kent on Route 7: 21 miles, the most scenic and popular stretch, watch for dangerous rapids at high water near West Cornwall / Kent to New Milford on Route 202: 17 miles, much whitewater / below New Milford: dammed lake or tidal waters. Rentals: Falls Village, Newington, New Milford, and West Simsbury.

Pachaug River

Begins at Beach Pond on Route 165, at the Rhode Island-Connecticut border, and runs through a string of ponds until it reaches the Quinebaug River, a 15-mile stretch with some dams, slight current, and easy paddling in both directions. From Jewett City, Connecticut, on Route 12, portage is possible to Aspinook Pond and the Quinebaug River system.

Quinebaug and Thames Rivers

The Quinebaug begins in Massachusetts but is primarily a Connecticut river; the Thames is entirely in Connecticut. The Quinebaug is canoeable from Mashapaug Pond, 11 miles upstream from the dam at East Brimfield, Massachusetts, on Route 9. The Quinebaug joins the Shetucket River at Norwich, Connecticut, on Route 2 to form the Thames River. Between East Brimfield and Norwich is a stretch of about 70 miles with many dams and access points. The Thames below Norwich is tidal.

Quinnipiac River

Hanover Pond near Meriden on Route 15 to North Haven on Route 22: 10 miles / tidal waters below North Haven.

Scantic River

North Somers on Route 83 to Hazardville on Route 190: 9 miles / Hazardville to the Connecticut River: 11 miles, no hazards, a few dams.

Still River

From 3 miles north of Danbury on Route 7 to town of Still River off Route 7–202 above the dam: 10 miles, much marshland. Rentals: New Milford.

Twin Lakes

Near Salisbury off Route 44: 562 acres of lake canoeing in undeveloped country. Rentals: Salisbury.

Connecticut Rentals

Clinton

Needle Loft, 180 West Main Street, Clinton, Conn. 06413; telephone: 203–669–8065 / Waters: Hammonasset and Connecticut Rivers / Trips: 1 day to the Hammonasset and 1 day or more to the Connecticut River / Best canoeing months: May-October / Campsites: no / Transportation: no / Car-top carriers: yes / Open all year.

Falls Village

Riverrun Outfitters (Mark Caliendo), Main Street, Route 126, Falls Village, Conn. 06031; telephone: 203–824–5579 / Waters: Housatonic River / Trips: 1–2 days, guides available / Best canoeing months: April-June / Campsites: yes / Transportation: yes / Car-top carriers: yes / Also rents camping equipment and offers canoe instruction and guided wilderness tours into many other areas.

Mansfield

Mead Rent-A-Canoe (Dave Meikle), 35 Brookside Lane, Mansfield, Conn. 06250; telephone: 203–429–5310 / Unconfirmed.

Monroe

Boyce Town and Country Marine, 126 Main Street, Route 25, Monroe, Conn. 06468; telephone: 203–268–0839 / Unconfirmed.

Newington

Taylor Rental Center, 111 Pane Road, Newington, Conn. 06111; telephone: 203–667–2216 / Waters: Connecticut, Farmington, and Housatonic Rivers / Trips: 1–2 days / Best canoeing months: spring / Campsites: yes / Transportation: no / Car-top carriers: yes.

New Milford

Lakes End Marina, Grove Street, New Milford, Conn. 06776; telephone: 203–354–8155 / Waters: Lake Lillinonah on the Housatonic River and the Still River / Trips: up to 1 day / Best canoeing months: April-October / Campsites: no / Transportation: no /Car-top carriers: no.

Marineland, Inc., 120 Old Town Park Road, New Milford, Conn. 06776; telephone: 203–354–3929 / Waters: Housatonic, Bantam, and Shepaug Rivers and other nearby waters / Best canoeing months: March-November / Trips: up to 2 days / Campsites: yes / Transportation: no / Car-top carriers: yes / Open all year.

Rockville

Gessay's Sports Center, East Main and Prospect Streets, Rockville, Conn. 06066; telephone: 203–875–5780 / Unconfirmed.

Salisbury

O'Hara's Trading Post, Twin Lakes Road, Salisbury, Conn. 06068; telephone: 203–824–7583 / Waters: Twin Lakes and other nearby waters / Trips: up to 1 day / Best canoeing months: April-October / Campsites: no / Transportation: no / Car-top carriers: no.

Stratford

Olsen Marine Co., Inc., 76 Ferry Boulevard, Stratford, Conn. 06497; telephone: 203–375–5841 / Unconfirmed.

West Simsbury

Great World (Culver A. Modisette), 250 Farms Village Road, West Simsbury, Conn. 06092; telephone: 203–658–4461 / Waters: Bantam, Connecticut, Farmington, Housatonic, Shepaug, and (in Massachusetts) Westfield River and other nearby waters / Trips: 1 or more days / Best canoeing months: May-October / Campsites: yes / Transportation: yes, by prearrangement / Car-top carriers: yes.

Massachusetts Waters

Charles River
Factory Pond at Bellingham on Route 140 to the dam at Watertown on Route 20: 60 miles, much meandering, the most scenic section is the 20-mile stretch between Medfield and Dedham, both on Route 109. Motorboats are permitted below the Watertown dam. Rentals: Auburndale, Belmont, Cambridge, Needham, Stow, and Worcester.

Colebrook Impoundment
See Connecticut.

Concord and Assabet Rivers
Concord on Route 62 at Lowell Road bridge to the Merrimack River:

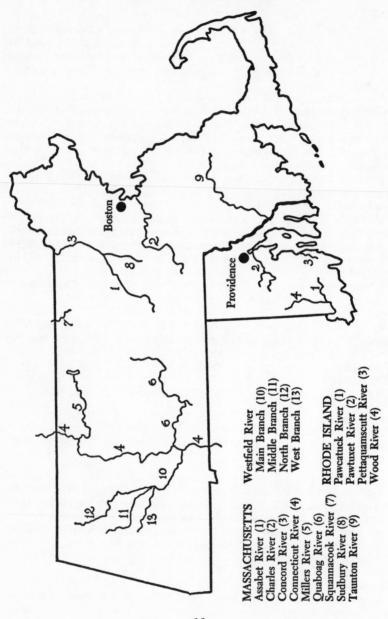

MASSACHUSETTS
Assabet River (1)
Charles River (2)
Concord River (3)
Connecticut River (4)
Millers River (5)
Quaboag River (6)
Squannacook River (7)
Sudbury River (8)
Taunton River (9)

Westfield River
Main Branch (10)
Middle Branch (11)
North Branch (12)
West Branch (13)

RHODE ISLAND
Pawcatuck River (1)
Pawtuxet River (2)
Pettaquamscutt River (3)
Wood River (4)

20 miles of the Concord River, no longer what it was in Thoreau's day / Concord to Westboro on Route 30: 32 miles of industrial scenery is to be seen on the Assabet River. Rentals: Belmont, Concord, Leominster, and Stow.

Connecticut River
See Connecticut and New Hampshire.

Millers River
Hydeville bridge on a side road to South Royalston on Route 68: 5 miles of smooth waters, scenic / South Royalston to Athol on Route 32: 8 miles, mostly whitewater / Athol to Erving on Route 2: 11 miles, flat, several dams / Erving to Millers Falls on Route 63: 6 miles, whitewater / Millers Falls to the Connecticut River: 2 miles with 3 dams. Rentals: Worcester.

Quaboag River
East Brookfield on Route 9 to West Warren on Route 67: 17 miles, flat / West Warren to Blanchardville: 8 miles, whitewater / Blanchardville to Three Rivers: 5 miles, smooth. At Three Rivers the Quaboag joins the Swift and Ware Rivers to form the Chicopee River which flows for 14 miles of smooth waters with many dams and portages into the Connecticut River. Rentals: Worcester.

Squannacook River
West Townsend on Route 123 to West Groton on Route 225: 10 miles with several dams and mild rapids. Rentals: Leominster and Worcester.

Sudbury River
Framingham Center on Route 135 to Saxonville off Route 126: 3 miles / Saxonville to Concord on Route 62: 17 miles, Walden Pond is on this stretch; less than a mile below Saxonville is the outlet from Lake Cochituate (permit required to canoe the lake). Rentals: Belmont and Concord.

Taunton River
Monponset Pond on Route 58 to Matfield River: 11 miles, scenic / Paper Mill Village on Route 104 to Taunton on Route 44: 20 miles, with tidal waters below Taunton.

Westfield River
North Branch: Cummington on Route 9 to Huntington on Route 20 and the Main Branch: 32 miles, much of it whitewater.

Middle Branch: Smiths Hollow off Route 143 to the flood control dam at the town of North Branch: 12 miles, rapid but not necessarily dangerous, canoeable only at high water.

West Branch: Southwest of Middlefield to Huntington on Route 20 on the Main Branch: 12 miles of difficult race track, canoeable by experts only.

Main Branch: Huntington on Route 20 to the Connecticut River: 21 miles, industrialized, polluted. Rentals: Worcester.

Massachusetts Rentals

Andover
Moor and Mountain, 63 Park Street, Andover, Mass. 01810; telephone: 617–475–3665 / Unconfirmed.

Auburn
See Leominster.

Auburndale
Charles River Canoe Service (Ed Bourgeois), 2401 Commonwealth Avenue, Auburndale, Mass. 02166; telephone: 617–527–9885 / Waters: Charles River and other waterways in the Boston area / Trips: 1 or more days, guides available / Best canoeing months: April-October / Campsites: yes / Transportation: yes, for groups only / Car-top carriers: yes / Instruction offered.

Belmont
Canoe Adventures Northeast, 8 Cherry Street, Belmont, Mass. 02178; telephone: 617–484–6571 / Waters: Concord River, Charles River, Lake Cochituate, Sudbury River, and other local waters / Trips: 2 or more days, guides available / Best canoeing months: March-November / Campsites: no / Transportation: no / Car-top carriers: yes, and trailers / Equips groups for wilderness and whitewater canoeing expeditions in New England and Canada and also rents camping equipment; canoeing training program available.

Cambridge
Cambridge Canoe Rental/Backpacker's Country, 50 Boylston Street, Cambridge, Mass. 02138; telephone: 617–868–7464 / Waters: Charles River and other nearby rivers / Trips: 1 day / Best canoeing months: June-September / Campsites: no / Transportation: no / Car-top carriers: yes / Also rents camping equipment, skis, and kayaks.

Concord
South Bridge Boat House, Route 62 (Main Street), Concord, Mass. 01742; telephone: 617–369–9438 / Waters: Assabet, Concord, and Sudbury Rivers / Trips: 1 day / Best canoeing months: spring-fall / Campsites: yes / Transportation: no / Car-top carriers: yes, but not for whitewater canoeing.

Falmouth
Taylor Rental Center, 626 Main Street, Falmouth, Mass. 02540; telephone: 617–548–8809 / Unconfirmed.

Fitchburg
Dandi Rental Sales Service, 535 Water Street, Fitchburg, Mass. 01420; telephone: 617–345–7703 / Unconfirmed.
See also Leominster.

Gardner
See Leominster.

Ipswich
Foote Brothers, Topsfield Road, Ipswich, Mass. 01938; telephone: 617–356–9771 / Unconfirmed.

Leominster
A & G Rental, Inc., 195 Mill Street, Leominster, Mass. 01453; telephone: 617–537–9793 / Waters: Concord and Squannacook Rivers and many other nearby waters / Trips: 1 or more days / Best canoeing months: March-November / Campsites: yes / Transportation: no / Car-top carriers: yes / Also rents camping equipment. Other stores: A & G Rental, 345 Summer Street, Fitchburg, Mass. 01420; A & G Rental, 22 Union Square, Gardner, Mass. 01440; Webster Square Rentals, 561 Park Avenue, Worcester, Mass. 01600; Greendale Rentals, 290 West Boylston Street, Worcester, Mass. 01603; Auburn Rentals, 690 Southbridge Street, Auburn, Mass. 01501; Natick Diversified Rentals, 38 South Main Street, Natick, Mass. 01760.

Natick
See Leominster.

Needham
Needham YMCA Canoe Center, Fisher Street, Needham, Mass. 02197; telephone: 617–444–6400 / Waters: Charles River / Trips: 1 day, guides available / Best canoeing months: April-October / Campsites: yes / Transportation: no / Car-top carriers: yes.

Newbury
Fernald's Marine, Route 1, Newbury, Mass. 01950; telephone: 617–465–0312 / Unconfirmed.

North Grafton
Ruby Marine Inc., Route 122–140, North Grafton, Mass. 01536; telephone: 617–839–5341 / Unconfirmed.

Orleans
Goose Hummock Shop, Route 6A, Orleans, Mass. 02653; telephone: 617–255–0455 / Unconfirmed.

Salem
Jimmy's Marine Service, 278 Derby, Salem, Mass. 01970; telephone: 617–766–7717/ Unconfirmed.

Salem Willows Boat Livery, Salem Willows, Salem, Mass. 01970; telephone: 617–765–6996 / Unconfirmed.

Southwick
Elmer's Sport and Bait Shop, Point Grove Road, Southwick, Mass. 01077; telephone: 413–569–5331 / Unconfirmed.

Sanders Boat Livery, Inc., Congamond Road, Southwick, Mass. 01077; telephone: 413–569–9080 / Unconfirmed.

Stow
Car Top Boats, Inc. (Scott R. Bickford), Gleasondale Industrial Park, Route 62, Stow, Mass. 01775; telephone: 617–568–8701 / Waters: Assabet River, Concord River, Charles River, and other area waterways /

Trips: 1 day / Best canoeing months: early spring and fall / Campsites: no / Transportation: yes, only for Assabet River / Car-top carriers: yes / Also rents kayaks / Open all year.

Sturbridge
Rent-A-Canoe (J. W. Hicks), Apple Hill Road, Sturbridge, Mass. 01566; telephone: 617–347–3827 / Unconfirmed.

Westfield
Lambert's Trailer and Marine Sales, Route 202, Westfield, Mass. 01085; telephone: 413–533–6336 / Unconfirmed.

Worcester
Great Canadian (John G. Berg), 45 Water Street (exit 122S off I-290), Worcester, Mass. 01604; telephone: 617–755–5237 / Waters: Charles, Quaboag, Millers, Squannacook, and Westfield Rivers, and other nearby lakes and rivers / Trips: 1 or more days / Best canoeing months: March-October / Campsites: yes / Transportation: no / Car-top carriers: yes / Open all year.

See also Leominster.

Rhode Island Waters

Pawcatuck River
Liberty bridge to Usquepaug on Route 138: 5 miles / Usquepaug to Kenyon on Route 2: 8 miles / Kenyon to Bradford on Route 91: 13 miles / Bradford to Watch Hill on Little Narragansett Bay: 17 miles, waters are tidal below Westerly. Rentals: East Greenwich, Narragansett, and Warwick.

Pawtuxet River
River Point on Route 115 to Pawtuxet on Route 1A: 11 miles. Rentals: Warwick.

Pettaquamscutt River
Middle Bridge Road in Narragansett for 6 miles upriver to Gilbert Stuart Road and 2 miles downriver under Route 1A bridge to the river's mouth, tidal waters. Rentals: Narragansett.

Wood River
Escoheag Hill north of Route 165 to Pawcatuck River near Alton on Route 91: 20 miles. Rentals: East Greenwich, Narragansett, and Warwick.

Rhode Island Rentals

East Greenwich
Fin & Feather Lodge, Ltd., 95 Frenchtown Road, East Greenwich, R.I., 02818; telephone: 401–884–4432 / Waters: Pawcatuck and Wood

Rivers, coastal waters, and nearby lakes / Trips: 1 or more days / Best canoeing months: May-October / Campsites: yes / Transportation: yes, 4 or more canoes only / Car-top carriers: yes / Open all year.
Narragansett
Middlebridge, Inc. (Helen and Bob Eddy), R.R. 2, Box 711, Narragansett, R.I. 02882; telephone: 401–783–2903 / Waters: Pawcatuck, Narrow (Pettaquamscutt), and Wood Rivers / Trips: up to 1 day / Best canoeing months: June-September / Campsites: yes / Transportation: no / Car-top carriers: yes / Cottages and many other facilities available.
Wakefield
Steadman's Boat Livery and Campground, Tuckerton Road, Wakefield, R.I. 02879; telephone: 401–789–1503 / Unconfirmed.
Warwick
Canoes, Inc., 1245 Jefferson Boulevard, Warwick, R.I. 02886; telephone: 401–738–0880 / Waters: Wood River (Arcadia Park), Pawcatuck River, Pawtuxet River, and other nearby waters / Trips: 1–2 days / Best canoeing months: April, May, September, and October / Campsites: yes / Transportation: no / Car-top carriers: yes.

Sources of Information

A.M.C. *New England Canoeing Guide,* Appalachian Mountain Club (5 Joy Street, Boston, Mass. 02108), 1971, 600 pp., $5.00. Very detailed description of all canoeable waterways in the six New England states, three area maps with ratings of the waters and attractiveness of the scenery.

Connecticut Canoeing Guide, Connecticut Department of Environmental Protection (State Office Building, Hartford, Conn. 06115), free brochure. Precise and useful publication listing canoeable lakes and rivers and offering some general hints on canoeing.

Connecticut fishing and hunting information is available from Connecticut Department of Environmental Protection (State Office Building, Hartford, Conn. 06115).

Connecticut River Guide, Connecticut River Watershed Council (125 Combs Road, Easthampton, Mass. 01027), n.d., 82 pp., $4.50. A detailed description of the entire river with three maps.

Connecticut tourist information is available from Connecticut Department of Commerce (210 Washington Street, Hartford, Conn. 06106).

Farmington River and Watershed Guide, Farmington River Watershed Association (195 West Main Street, Avon, Conn. 06001), 1974, 60 pp., $2.50. Detailed description of the area with a map.

Massachusetts fishing and hunting information is available from Mass-

71

achusetts Department of Natural Resources, Division of Fisheries and Game (State Office Building, 100 Cambridge Street, Boston, Mass. 02202).

Pawtucket River and Wood River, Rhode Island Department of Natural Resources (Veterans Memorial Building, Providence, R.I. 02903), a free publication. Describes canoeing on these two waterways.

Rhode Island fishing and hunting information is available from Rhode Island Department of Natural Resources (Veterans Memorial Building, Providence, R.I. 02903).

Rhode Island tourist information is available from Rhode Island Department of Economic Development (1 Weybosset Hill, Prvidence, R.I. 02903.

Westfield River information is available from Westfield River Watershed Association (P.O. Box 232, Huntington, Mass. 01050).

●

NEW YORK

NEW YORK HAS AT LEAST FIVE DISTINCT REGIONS — New York City and its suburbs clustered around the rocky island of Manhattan; sandy Long Island, jutting some 100 miles out into the Atlantic Ocean as if wanting to turn its back on the rest of the state; the Catskill Mountains west of the lower Hudson River, a weekend and vacation playground; the extensive upstate agricultural and industrial regions stretching to Lake Erie and including the Finger Lakes; and the empty wilderness of the Adirondacks in the north.

From a canoeing point of view, New York City has little to offer even though canoeists have paddled the choppy waters of the Hudson and East Rivers for publicity purposes. Long Island with its vast housing tracts has, surprisingly, at least three small streams for leisurely paddling — the Nissequogue, Carmans, and Peconic Rivers. The Catskill streams are too seasonal and too steep for reliable family canoeing. That leaves the upstate region and the Adirondacks, which amply compensate for what is lacking in the south.

For the family canoeist the Adirondacks are the most rewarding. Several chains of interconnected lakes and streams offer excellent flat water from the snow melting season until the leaves turn in the fall in the beautiful north woods characterized by an abundance of white birch. The northern boundary of the state is formed by the Thousand Island section of the St. Lawrence River, which has many secluded and protected areas ideal for canoeists.

Many rivers in the southern tier of upstate New York have beautiful scenery. They forge their way through glacial moraines, canyons, and gently rolling agricultural lands and meadows, but their water levels may only be adequate in the spring and after prolonged spells of rain.

A unique feature of New York is the intact system of the Erie Barge Canal, connecting Lake Erie via the Hudson River with the Atlantic Ocean at New York City and with the St. Lawrence River via Lake Champlain. There is also a branch to Lake Ontario. On most sections of the canal a canoeist must share the waters with slow moving barges and pleasure craft, but an attractive stretch of feeder canal near Syracuse is all his own. The Mohawk River parallels the canal over its entire lower course and canoeists use it interchangeably with the canal for round trips.

All of the rivers of the Hudson, Delaware, and Susquehanna watersheds are extraordinarily well documented in the three volumes by Walter F. Burmeister entitled *Appalachian Waters* (listed at the end of the chapter). Information on the rivers flowing north into Lake Erie, Lake Ontario, and the St. Lawrence River is more sketchy, and the interested canoeist might do some scouting on his own.

New York Waters

Adirondack Canoe Routes

Many days of lake canoeing with interconnecting rivers and portages. Here are some of the main routes: Old Forge on Route 28 through Fulton Chain of Lakes, Raquette Lake, Marion River, and Blue Mountain Lake on Route 30: 37 miles / Raquette Lake on Route 28 via Forked Lake, Long Lake, Raquette River, and the town of Axton near Coreys on Route 3 to Tupper Lake on Route 3: 60 miles / Axton to Upper Saranac Lake on Route 30: 15 miles / Axton through Middle Saranac Lake (Round Lake) to Ampersand Dock on Lower Saranac Lake: 17 miles / Axton via Saranac River and Oseetah Lake to town of Saranac Lake on Route 3: 25 miles / Town of Saranac Inn on Route 30 after about 7 portages one can reach Lake Kushaqua and Loon Lake on Route 99 via town of Paul Smiths on Route 192 and Rainbow Lake: about 20 miles / Shorter round trips are possible from Fish Creek Bay on Upper Saranac Lake to Follensby Pond. Rentals: Blue Mountain Lake, Inlet, Long Lake, Mayfield, Old Forge, Raquette Lake, Saranac Lake, and Tupper Lake — these are all names of towns.

Allegheny River and Reservoir

The Allegheny River enters New York from Pennsylvania and then goes back to Pennsylvania. Portville, New York, on Route 305 to Olean on Route 17: about 10 miles, canoeable only in spring and high water /

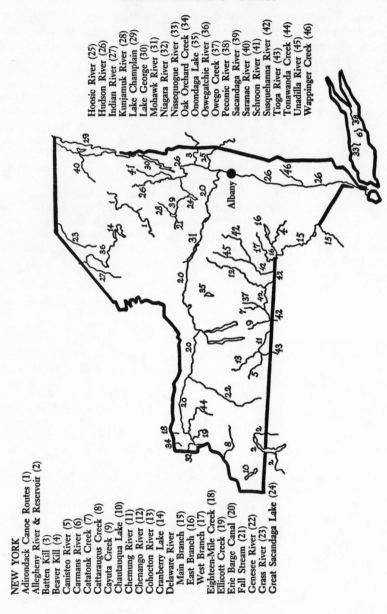

NEW YORK
Adirondack Canoe Routes (1)
Allegheny River & Reservoir (2)
Batten Kill (3)
Beaver Kill (4)
Canisteo River (5)
Carmans River (6)
Catatonk Creek (7)
Cattaraugus Creek (8)
Cayuta Creek (9)
Chautauqua Lake (10)
Chemung River (11)
Chenango River (12)
Cohocton River (13)
Cranberry Lake (14)
Delaware River
  Main Branch (15)
  East Branch (16)
  West Branch (17)
Eighteen-Mile Creek (18)
Ellicott Creek (19)
Erie Barge Canal (20)
Fall Stream (21)
Genesee River (22)
Grass River (23)
Great Sacandaga Lake (24)

Hoosic River (25)
Hudson River (26)
Indian River (27)
Kunjamuk River (28)
Lake Champlain (29)
Lake George (30)
Mohawk River (31)
Niagara River (32)
Nissequogue River (33)
Oak Orchard Creek (34)
Onondaga Lake (35)
Oswegatchie River (36)
Owego Creek (37)
Peconic River (38)
Sacandaga River (39)
Saranac River (40)
Schroon River (41)
Susquehanna River (42)
Tioga River (43)
Tonawanda Creek (44)
Unadilla River (45)
Wappinger Creek (46)

74

Olean to Salamanca on Route 17: 23 miles, smooth / Salamanca through Allegheny Reservoir to Kinzua Dam in Pennsylvania: about 50 miles / *See also* Pennsylvania. Rentals: Lakewood.

Batten Kill
Arlington, Vermont, on Route 313 to bridge at Shushan, New York, east of Route 22: 17 miles / Shushan to Middle Falls dam below Battenville on Route 29: 15 miles / below falls several additional dams and whitewater to junction with the Hudson River: 12 miles / *See also* Vermont.

Beaver Kill
Route 17 at Roscoe to East Branch on Routes 17–30 and junction with the East Branch of the Delaware River: 17 miles, canoeable in spring and high water only, above Roscoe mostly whitewater canoeable only in high water. Rentals: Downsville.

Blue Mountain Lake
See Adirondack Canoe Routes.

Canisteo River
Bridge 2 miles northwest of town of Canisteo on Route 36 to Adrian on Route 119: 10 miles / Adrian to Cameron on Routes 10–119: 11 miles / Cameron to Rathbone on Route 432: 9 miles / Rathbone to Addison on Route 17: 8 miles / Addison to Erwins at Routes 15–17 and junction with the Tioga River: 7 miles, canoeable in spring and high water only.

Carmans River
A Long Island river. North of Southhaven County Park at Yaphank on Route 21 or from south of the park to Great South Bay, the river is canoeable in short stretches only and the park is at present closed to canoeists. Rentals: Brookhaven.

Catatonk Creek
Bridge on dirt road north of Route 96 east of Spencer to dam at Candor off Route 96: 12 miles / dam to junction with the Owego River north of town of Owego on Routes 38–96: 11 miles, scenic, easy whitewater, canoeable in spring and high water only.

Cattaraugus Creek
Route 16 at Yorkshire to Lake Erie at Irving on Route 5: 44 miles, very scenic, through Cattaraugus Indian Reservation, some easy stretches but much hazardous whitewater, requires careful scouting.

Cayuta Creek
Route 224 at town of Cayuta to Route 3 near Van Etten: 12 miles / Van Etten to Sayre, Pennsylvania, and junction with the Susquehanna River: 18 miles, easy whitewater, scenic, canoeable in spring and high water only.

Chautauqua Lake
A 17-mile-long lake, accessible from Routes 394 and 17. Rentals: Lakewood.

Chemung River

Formed by junction of the Tioga and Cohocton Rivers west of Corning on Route 17. Junction to backwater of power plant storage pool: 6 miles / backwater to dam: 3 miles / dam to Elmira storage pool dam: 12 miles / Elmira dam to Wellsburg Road bridge off Route 427: about 7 miles / Wellsburg to Athens, Pennsylvania, and junction with the Susquehanna River: 20 miles.

Chenango River

Randalsville bridge off Route 12B south of Hamilton on Route 12B to Sherburne on Route 80: 15 miles / Sherburne to Norwich on Route 23: 16 miles / Norwich to Oxford on Route 35: 13 miles / Oxford to Greene on Route 41: 20 miles / Greene to Binghamton dam: 23 miles, 1 mile below dam is junction with the Susquehanna River, canoeable in spring and high water only. Rentals: Binghamton.

Cohocton River

Route 15 at Wallace to Kanona on Route 35: 10 miles / Kanona to Bath on Route 54: 5 miles / Bath to Campbell on Route 333: 13 miles / Campbell to west of Corning on Route 17 and junction with the Tioga River: 10 miles.

Cranberry Lake

About 2 days of smooth water canoeing, including Cranberry Lake inlet, accessible from Route 3 and town of Cranberry Lake. Rentals: Cranberry Lake.

Delaware River

Main Branch: Hancock and Route 97 bridge to Port Jervis on Route 6: about 90 miles, many intermediate access points, several whitewater stretches at Skinner's Falls and above Port Jervis. For detailed description of the river, *see* Pennsylvania. Rentals: Barryville, Callicoon, Downsville, Narrowsburg, Pond Eddy, Port Jervis, and Sparrowbush. *See also* New Jersey and Pennsylvania.

East Branch: Halcottsville on Route 30 to backwater of Pepacton Reservoir and bridge below Margaretville off Route 28: about 10 miles, canoeable in high water only / below reservoir on Route 30 at Downsville to Harvard bridge on Route 30: about 15 miles / Harvard to town of East Branch on Route 17 and junction with the Beaver Kill: 4 miles / East Branch to Fishs Eddy on Route 28: 5 miles / Fishs Eddy to junction with the West Branch near Hancock: 12 miles. Rentals: Downsville.

West Branch: Canoeable in spring and high water only. Hobart on Route 10 to South Kortright off Route 10: 5 miles / South Kortright to Bloomville on Route 10: 6 miles / Bloomville to Delhi on Route 28: 10 miles / Delhi to De Lancey on Route 2: 8 miles / De Lancey to Walton on Route 206: 12 miles / Walton to backwater of Cannonsville Reservoir at Route 10 bridge: 8 miles / Route 10 below reservoir to Route 17: 5 miles / Route 17 to Hale Eddy on Route 17: 6 miles /

Hale Eddy to junction with the East Branch near Hancock: 12 miles. Rentals: Downsville.

Eighteen-Mile Creek

Route 104 bridge to Olcott on Route 18 and Lake Ontario: about 10 miles, some difficult and some shallow spots. Rentals: Olcott.

Ellicott Creek

Route 324 northeast of Buffalo to east of Tonawanda on Route 265 and junction with the Tonawanda Creek: 13 miles, some difficult spots. Rentals: Amherst.

Erie Barge Canal

The famous Erie Canal stretches from Buffalo to Troy on the Hudson River, about 340 miles, during which it connects at Montezuma on Route 31 with Cayuga Lake and Seneca Lake, at Waterford on Route 32 is the Champlain Canal which connects with Lake Champlain and the St. Lawrence River in Canada, and near Syracuse is the Oswego Canal which connects the Erie Canal with Lake Ontario. Smooth paddling on the canal but canoeists are competing with power boats and barges; near Syracuse is an attractive feeder canal. Rentals: Amherst, Liverpool, Olcott, Romulus, Webster, and West Monroe.

Fall Stream

Route 8 east of Hoffmeister through Piseco Lake upstream into Fall Stream: about 22 miles, return possible; no access to the upper reaches of Fall Stream and Fall Lake; the 22-mile stretch is scenic. Another route is possible from Piseco Lake outlet through the West Branch of the Sacandaga River to junction with the Main Branch of the Sacandaga River: about 20 miles, difficult whitewater.

Forked Lake

See Adirondack Canoe Routes.

Fulton Chain of Lakes

See Adirondack Canoe Routes.

Genesee River

Route 17 at Wellsville to Belmont on Route 19: 12 miles / Belmont to Belfast on Route 19: 15 miles / Belfast to Fillmore on Route 19: 17 miles / Fillmore to Portageville on Routes 19A and 436: 5 miles; much whitewater all the way from Wellsville with some easier sections closer to Portageville / the stretch below Portageville through the canyon in Letchworth State Park is not canoeable / mostly flat water below the canyon from the Mount Morris flood control dam / Route 36 at Mount Morris to Route 63 at Geneseo: 13 miles / Route 63 to Route 20 at Avon: 20 miles / Route 20 to the Erie Canal at Rochester: 30 miles. Rentals: Webster.

Grass River

Canton on Route 11 to St. Lawrence River near Louisville on Route 39: about 35 miles, a few difficult rapids and impassable ledges in the lower course.

77

Great Sacandaga Lake

Accessible from Route 30 north of Amsterdam, the lake has about 320 miles of shoreline with many secluded inlets and islands and is suitable for canoeing. Rentals: Mayfield.

Hoosic River

Canoeable in spring and high water only. Cheshire Reservoir dam on Route 8 in Massachusetts to North Adams, Massachusetts, on Route 2: 13 miles / North Adams, Massachusetts, to North Pownal, Vermont, dam on Route 346: 15 miles / North Pownal, Vermont, to North Petersburg, New York, and junction with the Little Hoosic River on Route 22: 6 miles / junction to town of Hoosick Falls on Route 22: 8 miles, portage falls / Hoosick Falls to dam at town of Valley Falls on Route 67: 18 miles / dam to junction with the Hudson River: 11 miles, mostly whitewater.

Hudson River

From its source in Sanford Lake in the Adirondacks to the town of The Glen on Route 28: about 70 miles, mostly whitewater, canoeable in spring and high water only / The Glen to Thurman Station on Route 418 just below junction with the Schroon River: 10 miles, mostly whitewater / Route 418 to Corinth Dam: about 22 miles, fairly easy / short stretch of whitewater below Corinth Dam to backwater of Palmer Dam and on to above Glens Falls on Route 9: 20 miles / Glens Falls to Fort Edward on Route 197: 9 miles, whitewater / Fort Edward to dam at Thomson on Route 4: 13 miles / Thomson to Stillwater on Route 67: 15 miles, whitewater for about 1 mile below Thomson dam / Stillwater to Troy and junction with the Mohawk River on Route 4: 15 miles / Troy to Albany: 10 miles / Albany to the George Washington Bridge in New York City: about 160 miles, high tides and winds below Albany. Rentals: Mayfield and Poughkeepsie.

Indian River

Antwerp on Routes 11–26 to Philadelphia dam on Routes 26–411: 7 miles, some whitewater / Philadelphia to Theresa on Route 411: 15 miles / Theresa to backwater of Black Lake below Rossie on Routes 2–185: about 30 miles, below Black Lake is junction with the Oswegatchie River.

Kunjamuk River

About 15 miles upstream from junction with the Sacandaga River near Route 8 at Speculator is very scenic flat water. The headwaters can be reached via a forest service road and portage from the town of Speculator.

Lake Champlain

About 125 miles from the southern tip of Champlain Canal near Whitehall on Route 4 to the lake's outlet at the Canadian border. It connects at Ticonderoga on Route 22 with Lake George. Lake Champlain offers some very pleasant canoeing in its narrow stretches and

78

inlets. Rentals: Bolton Landing in New York, and Burlington and Fairfax in Vermont.

Lake George

Town of Lake George on Route 9 to Ticonderoga exit into Lake Champlain: about 32 miles, popular "wilderness" island camping in The Narrows section, offering some protection from power boats. A return to a point close to the starting point is possible by entering Lake Champlain and turning south into Champlain Canal, finishing at the Route 4 bridge near Whitehall, a total distance from town of Lake George to Whitehall is about 90 miles. Rentals: Bolton Landing and Mayfield.

Lake Kushaqua

See Adirondack Canoe Routes.

Long Lake

See Adirondack Canoe Routes.

Loon Lake

See Adirondack Canoe Routes.

Mohawk River

Delta Lake on Route 46 to Route 49 at Rome: 7 miles, some whitewater / below Route 49 canoeists use the Erie Canal most of the way to the Hudson River, about 130 miles, with an occasional switch to the Mohawk River when water conditions permit and attractive scenery calls for the switch; many intermediate access points. Rentals: Mayfield.

Niagara River

Canoeable from Lewiston on Route 185 to Youngstown: 6 miles, forming a portion of the United States-Canadian border. Rentals: Olcott.

Nissequogue River

A Long Island river. Route 25 at Smithtown to Long Island Sound: about 6 miles. Rentals: Brookhaven and Smithtown.

Oak Orchard Creek

An attractive creek a few miles near Olcott. Rentals: Olcott.

Onondaga Lake

A lake 4 miles long near Syracuse used for short outings. Rentals: Liverpool.

Oseetah Lake

See Adirondack Canoe Routes.

Oswegatchie River

From 5 miles west of Wanakena off Route 3 to Cranberry Lake: 15 miles, smooth, sometimes called Cranberry Lake Inlet / Cranberry Lake outlet to Newton Falls dam: 10 miles / Canoeing below the dam is not recommended due to irregular release of water from the dam. Rentals: Cranberry Lake.

Owego Creek

East Branch: Route 79 at Richford to Owego Dam near Owego on Routes 96–38: about 25 miles, scenic, easy whitewater, canoeable in spring and high water only.

Peconic River

A Long Island river, from Peconic River County Park north of Manorville to Great Peconic Bay east of Riverhead on Route 25: about 11 miles. Rentals: Brookhaven.

Piseco Lake and Outlet

See Fall Stream.

Rainbow Lake

See Adirondack Canoe Routes.

Raquette Lake and Raquette River

See Adirondack Canoe Routes.

Sacandaga River

Outlet of Lake Pleasant at Speculator on Routes 8–30 to Wells on Route 30: 16 miles, mostly whitewater / Wells to Northville on Route 4 and Great Sacandaga Lake: 20 miles / Northville through the lake to the dam at Conklingville on Routes 4–7: 30 miles / dam to Hadley on Route 9N and junction with the Hudson River: 5 miles, whitewater. For West Branch, *see* Fall Stream.

Saranac Lakes

See Adirondack Canoe Routes.

Saranac River

Town of Loon Lake on Route 99 to Lake Champlain at Plattsburgh: about 40 miles, mixed whitewater and flat water.

Schroon River

Canoeable in spring and high water only. Sharp Bridge Campsite off Route 9 south of Underwood to North Hudson on Route 9: 16 miles / North Hudson to Route 73 at Severance: 10 miles / Route 73 to Schroon Lake at town of Schroon Lake on Route 9: 6 miles, the lake is 12 miles long / Schroon Lake exit to town of Brant Lake on Route 8: 7 miles / Brant Lake to dam at Warrensburg on Route 9: 23 miles, stretches of dangerous whitewater / dam to junction with the Hudson River: 4 miles, difficult whitewater.

Susquehanna River

North Branch: Dam at Cooperstown on Routes 28–80 to Route 166 east of Milford: 15 miles / Milford to backwater of Goodyear Lake at Portlandville on Route 28: 8 miles / Portlandville to Goodyear Lake dam: 3 miles / dam to Oneonta dam at Route 23: 9 miles / Oneonta to Otego on Route 7: 12 miles / Otego to Sidney at Route 8 bridge: 18 miles / Sidney to Afton on Route 41: 12 miles / Afton to Windsor on Route 17: 22 miles / Windsor to dam at Oakland, Pennsylvania, on Route 171: 13 miles / Oakland, Pennsylvania, to Rockbottom Dam at Binghamton, New York: 25 miles / Rockbottom Dam via center dam to lower dam at Binghamton: 5 miles / lower dam to Apalachin on Route 17 and junction with the Apalachin Creek: 12 miles / Apalachin to Owego on Route 96: 10 miles / Owego to Route 17 slightly north of the Pennsylvania state line: 18 miles. *See also* Pennsylvania. Rentals: Binghamton.

Tioga River

Lawrenceville, Pennsylvania, on Route 15 to west of Corning, New York, on Route 17 and junction with the Cohocton River: 15 miles. *See also* Pennsylvania.

Tonawanda Creek

Attica on Route 98 to Alexander on Rcute 20: 5 miles, swift, relatively smooth / Alexander to Route 93 bridge: 40 miles, difficult, many portages, rapids / Route 93 bridge to west of Millersport on Route 78 and the Erie Canal: 30 miles, smoother than previous stretch, some portages / Millersport to Niagara River at Tonawanda on Routes 384 and 265: 14 miles, smooth. Rentals: Amherst.

Tupper Lake

See Adirondack Canoe Routes.

Unadilla River

Unadilla Forks on Route 19 to West Edmeston dam on Route 18: 12 miles / dam to New Berlin on Routes 13–80: 17 miles / New Berlin to Mount Upton on Route 51: 22 miles / Mount Upton to junction with the Susquehanna River near Sidney on Route 8: 12 miles, canoeable until late spring and in high water.

Wappinger Creek

Pleasant Valley dam off Route 44 near Rochdale to the dam at the town of Red Oaks Mill above Route 376 bridge: about 10 miles / dam to Wappinger Lake near town of Wappingers Falls on Route 9: 6 miles, whitewater / for the next three miles, until junction with the Hudson River, Wappinger Creek is tidal backwater. Rentals: Poughkeepsie.

New York Rentals

Amherst

Wolf's Boat House (R. Hess and R. Sullivan), 327 South Ellicott Creek Road, Amherst, N.Y. 14150; telephone: 716–691–9331 and 716–834–7930 / Waters: Tonawanda Creek, Ellicott Creek, and Erie Barge Canal / Trips: 1 or more days / Best canoeing months: May-September / Campsites: yes / Transportation: no / Car-top carriers: yes.

Barryville

Bob Lander's Canoe Rental and Campgrounds, *see* Narrowsburg.

Kittatinny Canoes Inc., *see* Dingman's Ferry, Pennsylvania.

Binghamton

Eureka Camping Center, 625 Conklin Road, Binghamton, N.Y. 13902; telephone: 607–723–4179 / Waters: Susquehanna and Chenango Rivers / Trips: 1 or more days / Best canoeing months: April-Labor Day / Campsites: no / Transportation: no / Car-top carriers: yes / Also rents camping equipment.

Blue Mountain Lake

Blue Mountain Lake Boat Livery, Inc., Blue Mountain Lake, N.Y. 12812; telephone: 518–352–7351 / Waters: Adirondack Canoe Routes / Trips: 1 or more days / Best canoeing months: May-October / Campsites: yes / Transportation: yes / Car-top carriers: yes.

Griffins Boat Livery, Blue Mountain Lake, N.Y. 12812; telephone: 518–352–7331 / Waters: Adirondack Canoe Routes / Trips: 1 or more days / Best canoeing months: May-October / Campsites: yes / Transportation: yes / Car-top carriers: no response.

Bolton Landing

Lamb Bros. Inc., Main Street, Bolton Landing, N.Y. 12814; telephone: 518–644–5411 / Waters: Lake George and Lake Champlain / Trips: several hours to several days / Best canoeing months: May-October / Campsites: yes /Transportation: no / Car-top carriers: no response.

Port Jerry, Lakeshore Drive, Bolton Landing, N.Y. 12814; telephone: 518–644–3311 / Waters: Lake George and Lake Champlain / Trips: several hours to 4 days or longer / Best canoeing months: May-October / Campsites: yes / Transportation: no / Car-top carriers: no / Housekeeping cottages available / Also rents camping equipment.

Brookhaven

Bob's Long Island Canoe Rentals (Bob Bergoffen), 3 Carol Place, Brookhaven, N.Y. 11719; telephone: 516–286–8140 / Waters: Carmans, Peconic, and Nissequogue Rivers / Trips: up to 1 day / Best canoeing months: September-November, guides available / Campsites: no / Transportation: yes / Car-top carriers: yes / Also rents camping equipment and conducts guided canoe trips on the Delaware River, in the Adirondacks, in southern New Jersey, and other areas.

Callicoon

Bob Lander's Canoe Rental and Campgrounds, see Narrowsburg.

Upper Delaware Outdoor Recreations Inc., Box 188, Callicoon, N.Y. 12723; telephone: 800–942–0116 — toll free in New York State, or 914–887–5344 from out of state / Waters: Delaware River / Trips: 1 or more days, guides available / Campsites: yes / Transportation: yes, for canoes only, canoeists must provide their own transportation / Car-top carriers: yes.

Chestertown

Loon Lake Marina, Marina Road, Chestertown, N.Y. 12817; telephone: 518–494–3410 / Unconfirmed.

Cleveland

Pack & Paddle Outfitters, Oneida Lake, Cleveland, N.Y. 13042; telephone: 315–675–3687 / Unconfirmed.

Cranberry Lake

Camper's Village Marina, Route 3, Cranberry Lake, N.Y. 12927; telephone: 315–848–3669 / Waters: Cranberry Lake, Oswegatchie River, and other area waterways / Trips: 1 or more days / Best canoeing months: May-October / Campsites: yes / Transportation: yes / Car-top carriers: yes / Also rents camping equipment.

Mountain View Marina (Edgar Beckman), Cranberry Lake, N.Y. 12927; telephone: 315–848–2121 / Unconfirmed.

Downsville

Pepacton Sport Center, Main Street, Downsville, N.Y. 13755; telephone 607–363–7368 / Waters: Delaware River and Beaver Kill / Trips: 1 or more days / Best canoeing months: April-June, October, and November / Campsites: yes / Transportation: yes /Car-top carriers: yes / Good source for maps and information on water conditions / Also rents camping equipment / Open all year.

East Rockaway

Buzz-Arina, Inc., 140 Williamson Street, East Rockaway, N.Y. 11518; telephone: 516–599–5383 / Unconfirmed.

Edmeston

A.W. Rollins, Edmeston, N.Y. 13335; telephone: 607–965–8692 / Unconfirmed.

Elmira

Benson, Jessup & Knapp, Inc., 809 Pennsylvania Avenue, Elmira, N.Y. 14904; telephone: 607–737–2124 / Unconfirmed.

Fayetteville

Syracuse Yacht Sales, Lyndon Corners, Fayetteville, N.Y. 13066; telephone: 315–446–2731 / Unconfirmed.

Fishers Landing

H. Chalk & Son, Inc., Fishers Landing, N.Y. 13641; telephone: 315–686–5622 / Unconfirmed.

Geneva

Roy's Marina, Inc., R.D. 1, Geneva, N.Y. 14456; telephone: 315–789–9488 or 789–3449 / Unconfirmed.

Hankins

Frank and Marge McBride, Hankins House Route 97, Hankins, N.Y. 12741; telephone: 914–887–4423 / Unconfirmed.

Inlet

Inlet Marina, South Shore Road, Inlet, N.Y. 13360; telephone: 315–357–3883 / Waters: Adirondack Canoe Routes / Trips: 1 or more days / Best canoeing months: May-June, September-October; July and August are good but crowded / Campsites: yes / Transportation: yes / Car-top carriers: yes.

Lakewood

Maple Bay Marina, Inc., P.O. Box 256, Lakewood, N.Y. 14750; telephone: 716–763–8367 / Waters: Chautauqua Lake and Kinzua

Dam area in Pennsylvania / Trips: up to 1 day / Best canoeing months: April-October / Campsites: yes / Transportation: no / Car-top carriers: no response.

Liverpool

Liverpool Sport Center, 125 First Street, Liverpool, N.Y. 13088; telephone: 315–457–2290 / Waters: Onondaga Lake, Erie Canal, and other state waterways / Best canoeing months: May-October / Campsites: yes / Transportation: no / Car-top carriers: yes / Also rents camping equipment.

Long Lake

Camp Hilary (Joe and Dixie LeBlanc), Route 28N, Deerland Road, Long Lake, N.Y. 12847; telephone: 518–624–2233 / Waters: Long Lake / Trips: 1 or more days / Best canoeing months: May-October / Campsites: yes / Transportation: yes / Car-top carriers: yes / Housekeeping cottages available.

Emerson's Boat Livery, Inc., Deerland Road, Long Lake, N.Y. 12847; telephone: 518–624–4596 / Waters: Long Lake and other nearby waters / Trips: 1–5 days / Best canoeing months: May-October / Campsites: yes / Transportation: yes, for canoes only, canoeists must provide their own transportation / Car-top carriers: yes.

Lowville

The Stillwater Shop (Paul Jacobs), Lowville, N.Y. 13367; telephone: 315–357–4943 / Unconfirmed.

Mayfield

Sacandaga Marine, Inc., Route 30 and School Street "At the Dome", Mayfield, N.Y. 12117; telephone: 518–961–6021 or 961–6023 / Waters: Great Sacandaga Lake, Lake George, Hudson River, Mohawk River, Long Lake, Saranac Lake, Tupper Lake, and Raquette River / Trips: 3 hours to 1 week, guides available / Best canoeing months: May-October / Campsites: yes / Transportation: yes / Car-top carriers: yes / Also offers group camping and canoeing trips and rents camping equipment.

Naples

West River Marine, Inc., Route 245, R.D. 1, Naples, N.Y. 14512; telephone: 315–394–6286 / Unconfirmed.

Narrowsburg

Bob Lander's Canoe Rental and Campgrounds, Narrowsburg, N.Y. 12764; telephone: 914–252–7101 / Waters: Delaware River / Trips: 3 hours to 5 days / Best canoeing months: May-July / Campsites: yes / Transportation: yes / Car-top carriers: no / Operates 2 campsites and 5 canoe bases on the Delaware River / Also rents camping equipment / Arranges packaged canoe vacations / Motel and housekeeping units on premises.

Skip Feagles Canoe & Boat Rental, Route 97, Narrowsburg, N.Y. 12764; telephone: 914–252–7373 / Waters: Delaware River / Trips:

2 or more days / Best canoeing months: May-June / Campsites: yes / Transportation: yes / Car-top carriers: yes.
Norwich
Hodges Marine Sales, Inc., R.D. 3, Route 12, Norwich, N.Y. 13815; telephone: 607–334–3361 / Unconfirmed.
Olcott
McDonough Marine, 5852 Main Street, Olcott, N.Y. 14126; telephone: 716–778–7048 / Waters: Erie Canal, Niagara River, Oak Orchard Creek, Eighteen-Mile Creek / Trips: several hours to several days / Best canoeing months: April-November / Campsites: yes / Transportation: no / Car-top carriers: yes / Open all year.
Old Forge
Palmer Point Boats, Fourth Lake (Eagle Bay), Old Forge, N.Y. 13420; telephone: 315–357–5594 / Waters: Adirondack Canoe Routes / Trips: several hours to several days / Best canoeing months: July-September / Campsites: yes / Transportation: no / Car-top carriers:
Rivett's Boat Livery, Old Forge, N.Y. 13420; telephone: 315–369–3123 / Waters: Adirondack Canoe Routes / Trips: 1 or more days / Best canoeing months: May-October / Campsites: yes / Transportation: yes / Car-top carriers: yes.
Penn Yan
Hopkins Marine Inc., 100 East Lake Road, Penn Yan, N.Y. 14527; telephone: 518–563–0330 / Unconfirmed.
Pilot Knob
Pilot Knob Boat Shop, Pilot Knob, N.Y. 12844; telephone: 518–656–9981 / Unconfirmed.
Plattsburgh
Janco's Northern Sports, R.D. 3, Box 90, Plattsburgh, N.Y. 12901; telephone: 518–563–0330 / Unconfirmed.
Pond Eddy
Jerry's Three River Canoe Corp., Pond Eddy, N.Y. 12770; telephone: 914–956–6078 / Waters: Delaware River / Trips: 2 or more days / Best canoeing months: May-June / Campsites: yes / Transportation: yes / Car-top carriers: yes.
Port Jervis
White Water Rentals, Inc., R.D. 3, Box 6, Port Jervis, N.Y. 12771; telephone: 914–856–7031 or 914–956–6075 / Waters: Delaware River / Trips: 1 or more days / Best canoeing months: May-July / Campsites: yes / Transportation: yes, for canoes only, canoeists must have their own transportation / Car-top carriers: yes.
Poughkeepsie
Arlington Sporting Goods Inc., 794 Main Street, Poughkeepsie, N.Y. 12603; telephone: 914–471–3055 / Waters: Wappinger Creek and Hudson River / Trips: up to 1 day / Best canoeing months: April-

May / Campsites: no / Transportation: no / Car-top carriers: yes / Open all year.

Raquette Lake

Birds Boat Livery, Raquette Lake, N.Y. 13436; telephone: 315–354–4441 / Waters: Adirondack Canoe Routes / Trips: 1 or more days / Best canoeing months: July-October / Campsites: yes / Transportation: yes / Car-top carriers: yes.

Raquette Lake Marina, Inc., Box 37, Raquette Lake, N.Y. 13436; telephone: 315–354–4361 / Waters: Adirondack Canoe Routes / Trips: 1 or more days / Best canoeing months: June-October / Campsites: yes / Transportation: yes / Car-top carriers: yes.

Rochester

Black Creek Marina, 20 Black Creek Road, Rochester, N.Y. 14623; telephone: 716–464–8210 / Unconfirmed.

Romulus

Lakeside Cottage Court Marina & Campsite, R.D. 1, East Lake Road, Romulus, N.Y. 14541; telephone: 315–585–6619 / Waters: Seneca Lake and Erie Canal / Trips: 1 or more days / Best canoeing months: April-October / Campsites: yes / Transportation: no / Car-top carriers: no.

Sabael

John Monthony, Sabael, N.Y. 12864; telephone: 518–648–3852 / Unconfirmed.

Saranac Inn

Hickock Boat Livery, Stockade Trading Post, Saranac Inn, N.Y. 12982; telephone: 518–891–0480 / Unconfirmed.

Saranac Lake

Ampersand Bay Boat Club (Walt Emmons) P.O. Box 547, Ampersand Bay Road, Saranac Lake, N.Y. 12983; telephone: 518–891–3001 and 891–9869 / Waters: Adirondack Canoe Routes / Trips: 1 or more days / Best canoeing months: May-November / Campsites: yes / Transportation: no / Car-top carriers: yes / Motel rooms and housekeeping cottages available.

Swiss Marine Inc., 7 Duprey Street, Saranac Lake, N.Y. 12983; telephone: 518–891–2130 / Waters: Adirondack Canoe Routes / Trips: 1 or more days / Best canoeing months: May-October / Campsites: yes / Transportation: yes / Car-top carriers: yes.

Smithtown

Cycle and Sea, Inc., Route 25A and Rose Street, Smithtown, N.Y. 11787; telephone: 516–265–5552 / Waters: Nissequogue River / Trips: up to 1 day / Best canoeing months: April-September / Campsites: yes / Transportation: yes, for groups only / Car-top carriers: yes.

Sparrowbush

Curt's Canoe Rentals (Curtis Kanitz), Route 97, Sparrowbush, N.Y. 12780; telephone: 914–856–5024 / Waters: Delaware River / Trips:

1–14 days and longer / Best canoeing months: April-October / Camp-sites: yes / Transportation: yes / Car-top carriers: yes / Also rents rubber rafts and camping equipment.

Tupper Lake

McDonalds Boat Livery, Moody Road, Tupper Lake, N.Y. 12986; telephone: 315–359–9060 / Waters: Adirondack Canoe Routes / Trips: 1 or more days / Best canoeing months: July-October / Camp-sites: yes / Transportation: yes / Car-top carriers: yes.

Webster

Taylor Rental Center, 150 Orchard Street, Webster, N.Y. 14580; tele-phone: 716–872–2770 / Waters: Erie Canal, Finger Lakes, Genesee River, and other upstate waterways / Best canoeing months: spring to early fall / Campsites: yes / Transportation: no / Car-top carriers: yes / Also rents camping equipment.

West Monroe

Wheeler Canoe Sales (Al Wheeler), County Route 84, West Mon-roe, N.Y. 13167; telephone: 315–668–3725 / Waters: waterways within a 100-mile radius of West Monroe, near Syracuse / Trips: any length / Best canoeing months: June-September / Campsites: yes / Trans-portation: no / Car-top carriers: yes.

Sources of Information

Adirondack Canoe Routes, New York Department of Environmental Conservation, Division of Lands and Forests (Albany, N.Y. 12233), an 8-page free brochure with detailed descriptions and a simple map.

Barge Canal System and Connecting Waterways, New York Depart-ment of Transportation (Albany, N.Y. 12233).

Burmeister, Walter F. *Appalachian Waters 2: The Hudson and its Tributaries,* Appalachian Books (Box 249, Oakton, Va. 22124), 1974, 488 pp., $7.50. Excellent, detailed descriptions of the rivers with diffi-culty ratings and seasonal water levels; no maps. *See also* Pennsylvania sources of information.

Canoe Trips, New York Department of Environmental Conservation (Albany, N.Y. 12233), a free, 4-page brochure with brief listings of the main canoe trips in the state.

Delaware River map set, *see* Pennsylvania sources of information.

New York fishing and hunting information is available from New York Department of Environmental Conservation, Division of Fish and Wildlife (50 Wolf Road, Albany, N.Y. 12233).

New York tourist information is available from New York Depart-ment of Commerce, Travel Bureau (99 Washington Avenue, Albany, N.Y. 12245).

PENNSYLVANIA

THE RECTANGULAR SHAPE of the Keystone State belies its undulating scenery. Seven ridges of the Appalachian Mountain chain, like waves following one another, run diagonally across the state. A plateau in the north is furrowed by deep valleys, including the "Grand Canyon of Pennsylvania" cut out by Pine Creek, a dramatically beautiful if somewhat wild canoeing stream. Much of the forest land, while not wilderness, is remote and thinly settled. The population centers are at both ends of the state — Philadelphia in the east, with the rich farmlands of the Pennsylvania Dutch close by, and Pittsburgh in the west, the Gateway to the Plains.

Three large and fairly unfettered rivers grace the state. The Delaware River, forming the entire eastern border of Pennsylvania, is canoeable and free flowing all the way from the northeastern corner of the state to Philadelphia — more than 200 miles. Most canoeists stop at Trenton, New Jersey, where the river becomes tidal.

The Susquehanna River has two parts—the North Branch coming from New York State, and the West Branch, from the forests of western Pennsylvania. That they ever found each other, as well as a way to the sea across seven mountain ranges, is a geographical wonder and a scenic delight. Of the two branches, the West Branch has the greater canoeing appeal. It flows through rugged gorges and canyons and immense stretches of quiet forests. Its fast moving and occasional white waters are rarely so rough that a family canoeist could not enjoy them. The most popular section is between Clearfield and Williamsport. For the North Branch, a state brochure recommends the section from Wysox to Tunkhannock.

The upper Allegheny River, together with some Indian reservation lands, was drowned by the U.S. Army Corps of Engineers some years ago when they built the controversial Kinzua Dam. But below the dam, for at least as far as the famous horseshoe bend at East Brady, the winding river has a swift current and pleasant wooded banks. Of course, a canoeist so inclined could continue down the Allegheny River the few thousand miles to New Orleans via the Ohio and Mississippi Rivers.

A number of the tributaries of the Allegheny River are enticing, including Tionesta Creek, French Creek, and the Clarion River. In Cook Forest State Park at Cooksburg, the Clarion passes one of the few stands of virgin timber left in the entire eastern United States — white pine, hemlock, and beech trees.

88

The Youghiogheny River, unpronounceable to all but the initiated, with its famous waterfall at Ohiopyle, has become the playground of rubber rafters.

Innumerable mountain streams — far too many to do justice to in this book — offer exciting, scenic, spring-time canoeing. Anyone interested in details is referred to the excellent sources listed at the end of this chapter.

Pennsylvania Waters

Allegheny Reservoir
Above Kinzua Dam on Route 59 east of Warren, about 90 miles of shoreline, power boats permitted. Rentals: Clarendon and Oil City.

Allegheny River
Kinzua Dam on Route 59 east of Warren to Warren: 10 miles / Warren to Irvine on Route 62: 10 miles / Irvine to Tidioute on Route 127: 25 miles / Tidioute to Tionesta on Route 36: 17 miles / Tionesta to Oil City on Route 62: 25 miles / Oil City to Franklin on Route 62: 10 miles / Franklin to Emlenton on Route 208: 42 miles / Emlenton to East Brady on Route 68: 22 miles / East Brady to Kittanning on Route 422: 25 miles / Kittanning to Freeport on Route 356: 20 miles / Freeport to junction with the Monongahela River at Pittsburgh: 30 miles. The river is dammed at regular intervals from East Brady downstream. Rentals: Clarendon, Oil City, and Wilkinsburg.

Aughwick Creek
Maddensville on Route 475 to junction with the Juniata River southeast of Mount Union on Route 747: about 30 miles, canoeable in spring and high water only.

Bald Eagle Creek
Canoeable in spring and high water only. Port Matilda bridge off Route 220 to Route 322 bridge west of town of State College: 4 miles / Route 322 to Route 144 at Bellefonte: 18 miles / Route 144 to backwater of Blanchard Lake near Mount Eagle: 7 miles / backwater to Blanchard Dam: 9 miles / dam to junction with the West Branch of the Susquehanna River at Lock Haven on Route 220: 17 miles, one dam portage. Rentals: Milesburg.

Beaver River
New Castle on Route 422 to Beaver Falls on the Ohio River: about 30 miles, some polluted stretches, dammed backwater above Beaver Falls has power boats. Rentals: Wilkinsburg.

Black Moshannon Lake
A 250-acre lake in Black Moshannon State Park on Route 504 east of Philipsburg; power boats on the lake. *See also* Moshannon Creek. Rentals: Philipsburg.

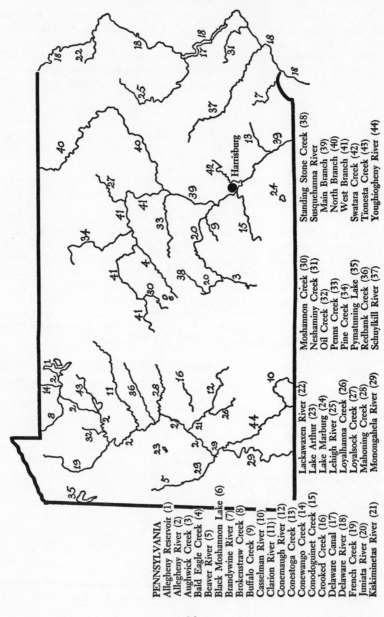

PENNSYLVANIA
Allegheny Reservoir (1)
Allegheny River (2)
Aughwick Creek (3)
Bald Eagle Creek (4)
Beaver River (5)
Black Moshannon Lake (6)
Brandywine River (7)
Brokenstraw Creek (8)
Buffalo Creek (9)
Casselman River (10)
Clarion River (11)
Conemaugh River (12)
Conestoga Creek (13)
Conewango Creek (14)
Conodoguinet Creek (15)
Crooked Creek (16)
Delaware Canal (17)
Delaware River (18)
French Creek (19)
Juniata River (20)
Kiskiminetas River (21)

Lackawaxen River (22)
Lake Arthur (23)
Lake Marburg (24)
Lehigh River (25)
Loyalhanna Creek (26)
Loyalsock Creek (27)
Mahoning Creek (28)
Monongahela River (29)

Moshannon Creek (30)
Neshaminy Creek (31)
Oil Creek (32)
Penns Creek (33)
Pine Creek (34)
Pymatuning Lake (35)
Redbank Creek (36)
Schuylkill River (37)

Standing Stone Creek (38)
Susquehanna River
  Main Branch (39)
  North Branch (40)
  West Branch (41)
Swatara Creek (42)
Tionesta Creek (43)
Yonghiogheny River (44)

Harrisburg

Brandywine River

Route 162 at Embreeville to junction with the Main Branch below Route 842 bridge southwest of West Chester on Route 842: 12 miles / junction to Route 52 at Lenape: 1½ miles / Route 52 to Rockland Dam near Wilmington, Delaware: about 15 miles, dangerous whitewater below the dam at Rockland. Rentals: Exton.

Brokenstraw Creek

Town of Spring Creek on Route 77 to Garland on Route 27: 10 miles / Garland to Youngsville on Routes 6–27: 12 miles / Youngsville to junction with the Allegheny River at Irvine on Route 62: 6 miles, fast, relatively easy whitewater, canoeable in spring or after rains. Rentals: Clarendon.

Buffalo Creek

Bridge on a dirt road off Route 849 southeast of Ickesburg to junction with the Juniata River at Newport on Route 34: about 20 miles.

Casselman River

Route 40 at Grantsville, Maryland, to Salisbury, Pennsylvania, on Route 699: 7 miles / Salisbury to Garrett on Routes 219–653: 15 miles / Garrett to confluence with the Youghiogheny River at the town of Confluence on Route 281: about 30 miles, whitewater.

Clarion River

Ridgway on Routes 219–949 to Clear Creek State Park off Route 949: 30 miles / park to Cook Forest at Cooksburg on Route 36: 12 miles / Cooksburg to the town of Clarion on Route 322: 20 miles, the last 6 miles of which are in Clarion Reservoir which has motor boats / Piney Dam below the reservoir to Callensburg on Route 58: 15 miles / Callensburg to junction with the Allegheny River north of Parker on Route 368: 17 miles. Rentals: Oil City.

Conemaugh River

Johnstown on Route 271 to New Florence on Route 711: 13 miles, scenic but polluted water, 2 dams to be portaged / New Florence to Blairsville above backwater of Conemaugh River Lake on Routes 22–217: 15 miles / lake dam to Saltsburg on Route 286 and junction with the Loyalhanna River: 6 miles.

Conestoga Creek

Canoeable in spring and high water only. Route 772 at Brownstown to dam at Lancaster near Route 462: 10 miles / Lancaster to junction with the Susquehanna River north of Pequea on Route 324: about 25 miles.

Conewango Creek

Frewsburg, New York, on Route 62 to Russell, Pennsylvania, on Route 957: 12 miles / Russell to the junction with the Allegheny River at Warren on Route 62: 10 miles. Rentals: Clarendon.

Conodoguinet Creek

Canoeable in spring and high water only. Near Shippensburg on

91

Route 533 to dam at Carlisle on I–76: about 40 miles, mild white-water / dam to junction with the Susquehanna River at Harrisburg on Route 11–15: about 40 miles, it meanders.

Crooked Creek

Creekside on Routes 110–954 to Shelocta on Route 156: 10 miles / Shelocta to Girty north of Route 156: 12 miles, backwater of Crooked Creek Lake in Crooked Creek State Park, a 350-acre lake which allows power boats of unlimited horsepower.

Delaware Canal

Parallels the Delaware River from Easton to New Hope, a stretch of about 40 miles, which permits round trips by going downstream on the river and upstream on the canal. Rentals: Point Pleasant and Washington Crossing.

Delaware River

Hancock, New York, at Pennsylvania Route 191 to Callicoon (on Route 97 in New York) bridge: 31 miles, easy / Callicoon to Lackawaxen, Pennsylvania, on Route 590 and junction with the Lackawaxen River: 28 miles, intermediate whitewater, rapids at Skinner's Falls are extremely dangerous at high water / Lackawaxen to Pond Eddy bridge (the bridge spans the Delaware from Pond Eddy, New York, to Pond Eddy, Pennsylvania): 17 miles, intermediate whitewater near Pond Eddy / Pond Eddy to Port Jervis, New York, on Routes 6–209: 15 miles / Port Jervis to Milford, Pennsylvania, on Routes 206–209: 9 miles / Milford to Dingman's Ferry on Route 739: 8 miles / Dingman's Ferry to Bushkill on Route 209 and junction with Bushkill Creek: 13 miles / Bushkill to Delaware Water Gap on I–80: 18 miles / Delaware Water Gap to Belvidere, New Jersey, off Route 46: 15 miles / Belvidere to Easton, Pennsylvania, on Route 22: 15 miles / Easton to Riegelsville, Pennsylvania, on Route 611: 10 miles / Riegelsville to Frenchtown, New Jersey, bridge on Route 12: 10 miles / Frenchtown to Point Pleasant, Pennsylvania, on Route 32: 8 miles / Point Pleasant to New Hope on Route 202: 9 miles / New Hope to Trenton, New Jersey: 17 miles, intermediate whitewater at Wells Falls and Scudders Falls, below Trenton to Delaware Bay is 150 miles of tidal waters. Rentals: Dingman's Ferry, Exton, Pocono Pines, Point Pleasant, Portland, Stroudsburg, and Washington Crossing; see also New Jersey and New York.

French Creek

Meadville on Routes 6–322 to Cochranton on Route 173: 15 miles / Cochranton to Utica off Route 322: 12 miles / Utica to Franklin on Route 322 and junction with the Allegheny River: 10 miles. Rentals: Oil City.

Juniata River

Warrior Ridge Reservoir dam north of Huntington on Route 26 to Route 829 bridge southeast of Huntingdon: 10 miles / Route 829 to Mount Union on Route 522: 8 miles / Mount Union to McVeytown bridge on Routes 22–103: 21 miles / McVeytown to Routes 103–333 at Lewistown: 17 miles / Lewistown to Route 35 at Mifflintown: 14 miles / Mifflintown to Millerstown on Route 17: 18 miles / Millerstown to junction with the Susquehanna River near Duncannon on Routes 11–15: 20 miles.

Kiskiminetas River

Saltsburg on Route 286 to Salina off Route 819: 7 miles, below Salina the river offers industrial scenery and pollution until it meets the Allegheny River at Schenley near Route 66.

Lackawaxen River

Difficult whitewater above Honesdale on Route 6. Honesdale to Hawley on Route 6: 10 miles, intermediate whitewater / Hawley to junction with the Delaware River: 17 miles, difficult whitewater depending on water release from power dam at Lake Wallenpaupack.

Lake Arthur

A 3,200-acre lake in Moraine State Park northwest of Butler on Route 422. Power boats of up to 10 h.p. are permitted on the lake. Rentals: Portersville.

Lake Marburg

A 1,300-acre lake in Codorus State Park on Route 216 east of Hanover. The lake has 26 miles of shoreline but power boats of up to 10 h.p. are permitted. Rentals: Hanover.

Lehigh River

Canoeable in spring and high water only, most of the course is light to intermediate whitewater. I-380 at northwest corner of Tobyhanna State Park to Francis E. Walter Reservoir and Dam southeast of Wilkes-Barre: about 25 miles / reservoir to town of Jim Thorpe on Route 903: 36 miles / Jim Thorpe to Northampton on Route 329: 25 miles / Northampton to junction with the Delaware River at Easton on Route 22: about 25 miles, passes through the industrial centers of Allentown and Bethlehem. Rentals: Pocono Pines.

Loyalhanna Creek

Ligonier on Route 30 to Kingston Dam above Latrobe on Route 981: 10 miles, intermediate whitewater / dam to Loyalhanna Lake above Saltsburg on Route 286: 15 miles.

Loyalsock Creek

Lopez on Route 487 to Forksville on Route 87: about 20 miles, heavy whitewater / Forksville to junction with the West Branch of the Susquehanna River south of Montoursville on Route 220: 36 miles, intermediate whitewater.

Mahoning Creek

Punxsutawney on Routes 36–119 to Valier north of Route 210: 10 miles / Valier to Route 839 and backwater of Mahoning Creek Lake: 15 miles / Eddyville below the lake to junction with the Allegheny River north of Templeton: about 25 miles.

93

Monongahela River

East of Fairmont, West Virginia, on Route 250 to Pittsburgh and junction with the Allegheny River: about 150 miles, dammed, slack water, commercial traffic, industrial scenery; at Pittsburgh the confluence of the Monongahela and Allegheny Rivers forms the Ohio River which is also dammed, polluted, and has much commercial traffic.

Moshannon Creek

Canoeable in spring and high water only. Winburne south of I-80 to junction with the West Branch of the Susquehanna River: 25 miles, intermediate whitewater.

Neshaminy Creek

Route 611 at Edison south of Doylestown to Route 332 west of Newtown: 18 miles / Route 332 to Route 13 above junction with the Delaware River near Bristol: 17 miles, many intermediate access points, suburban scenery, canoeable in spring and high waters only. Rentals: Washington Crossing.

Oil Creek

Centerville on Route 8 to Titusville on Route 27: 20 miles, canoeable in high water only / Titusville to Rouseville on Route 8: 15 miles; not recommended through Oil City to junction with the Allegheny River. Rentals: Oil City.

Penns Creek

Canoeable in spring and high water only. Near Spring Mills on Route 45 to Coburn south of Routes 45–445 at Millheim: 7 miles / Coburn to Route 235 at Glen Iron: 24 miles / Glen Iron to Route 204 at New Berlin: 14 miles / Route 204 to junction with the Susquehanna River at Selinsgrove on Routes 11–15: 18 miles. Rentals: Milesburg.

Pine Creek

Galeton on Routes 6–144 to Ansonia on Route 6: 16 miles, intermediate whitewater / Ansonia to Tiadaghton through "Grand Canyon of Pennsylvania": about 10 miles, whitewater / Tiadaghton to Blackwell on Route 414: about 10 miles, mild whitewater / Blackwell to Waterville on Route 44: 27 miles / Waterville to junction with the West Branch of the Susquehanna River: 13 miles.

Pymatuning Lake

On Pennsylvania-Ohio border, northwest of Jamestown, Pennsylvania, on Routes 58–322. It has an area of 16,000 acres with many shallow parts and inlets suitable for canoeing even through power boats of up to 10 h.p. are permitted. Rentals: Linesville.

Redbank Creek

Brookville on Route 322 to New Bethlehem on Routes 28–66: about 30 miles, canoeable in high water only / New Bethlehem to junction with the Allegheny River southeast of East Brady: 22 miles.

Schuylkill River

Upper course is canoeable in spring and high water only; much coal mining along its course, much pollution. Pottsville on Route 61 to Hamburg on Route I-78: about 25 miles / Hamburg to Reading on Route 422: about 25 miles / Reading to Pottstown on Route 100: 22 miles / dammed water below Pottstown to Philadelphia: about 50 miles.

Standing Stone Creek

Canoeable in spring and high water only. Route 305 at McAlevys Fort to junction with the Juniata River at Huntingdon on Route 26: about 20 miles.

Susquehanna River

Main Branch: Junction of North and West Branches at Northumberland on Route 11 to Halifax on Routes 147–225: 40 miles / Halifax to Harrisburg: 25 miles / Harrisburg to Columbia on Route 462: about 35 miles, less scenic than upper stretches, several dams / Columbia to Holtwood Dam above Route 372: 18 miles, one portage / dam to tidewater at Havre de Grace, Maryland, on Route 40: 30 miles. Rentals: Wormleysburg.

North Branch: For upper section *see* New York. New York border above Sayre, Pennsylvania, on Route 199 to Wysox on Route 187: 27 miles / Wysox to Laceyville on Routes 6–367: 29 miles / Laceyville to Tunkhannock on Route 29: 25 miles / Tunkhannock to town of Falls on Route 92: 12 miles / Route 92 to Routes 11–239 at Shickshinny: about 40 miles, unattractive, industrial scenery, polluted / Shickshinny to Route 487 at Bloomsburg: 25 miles / Bloomsburg to Northumberland on Route 11 and junction with the West Branch: 25 miles. Rentals: Pocono Pines and Wormleysburg.

West Branch: Upper course is canoeable in spring and high water only. Route 322 bridge at Clearfield to Frenchville Station bridge south of Route 879: 28 miles, portage at Clearfield Dam / Frenchville Station to Karthaus on Route 879: 17 miles, watch for rapids / Karthaus to junction with the Sinnemahoning Creek at Keating off Route 120: about 30 miles / Keating to Renovo on Route 144: 14 miles / Renovo to Lock Haven dam on Route 664: 30 miles / Lock Haven to Williamsport on Route 220: 32 miles / Williamsport to junction with the North Branch at Northumberland on Route 11: about 40 miles. Rentals: Milesburg and Wormleysburg.

Swatara Creek

Canoeable in spring and high water only. Pine Grove on Route 443 to Route 72 at Lickdale: about 20 miles / Route 72 to Route 934 at Harpers Tavern: about 15 miles / Route 934 to Route 39 above dam west of Hershey: about 15 miles / dam to Middletown on Route 230 and junction with the Susquehanna River: about 20 miles, 2 dam portages.

Tionesta Creek

Barnes on Routes 666–948 in Allegheny National Forest to Lynch on Route 666: 6 miles / Lynch to Kellettville on Route 666: 15 miles /

Kellettville to Tionesta Creek Reservoir: 15 miles. Rentals: Clarendon and Oil City.

Youghiogheny River

Town of Confluence on Route 281 below Youghiogheny River Reservoir to Ohiopyle on Route 381: 12 miles, intermediate whitewater, caution required when approaching the falls / Ohiopyle to Stewarton: 7 miles, difficult whitewater / Stewarton to South Connellsville above dam: 7 miles, intermediate whitewater, portage through Connellsville / Connellsville to Perryopolis on Route 51: 14 miles, flat water / Perryopolis to McKeesport on Route 148 and junction with the Monongahela River: 34 miles. Rentals: Wilkinsburg.

Pennsylvania Rentals

Addison

Yough Lake Marina, Youghiogheny Reservoir, Addison, Pa. 15411; telephone: 814-395-3423 / Unconfirmed.

Clarendon

Allegheny Outfitters, 19 South Main Street, Clarendon, Pa. 16313; telephone: 814-726-1232 / Waters: Allegheny River and Reservoir, Tionesta Creek, Conewango Creek, Brokenstraw Creek, and nearby waters / Trips: several hours to 3 days / Best canoeing months: April-October / Campsites: yes / Transportation: yes / Car-top carriers: yes / Also rents camping equipment and rafts / Open all year.

Clearfield

See Philipsburg.

Cooksburg

Cook Riverside Cabins, Cook Forest State Park, Cooksburg, Pa. 16217; telephone: 814-744-8300 / Unconfirmed.

Dingman's Ferry

Kittatinny Canoes Inc. (Frank and Ruth Jones), Silver Lake Road Dingman's Ferry, Pa. 18328; telephone: 717-828-2700 / Waters: Delaware River / Trips: 1 or more days / Best canoeing months: May-October / Campsites: yes / Transportation: yes / Car-top carriers: yes / Second canoe base at Barryville, New York / Housekeeping cabins available.

Easton

Pasch Marine Service, North Delaware Drive, Easton, Pa. 18042; telephone: 215-258-7754 / Unconfirmed.

Erie

Presque Isle Sports, 3214 West Lake Road, Erie, Pa. 16505; telephone: 814-833-5312 / Unconfirmed.

Lou Stefan's Lagoon Boat Livery, Presque Isle State Park, Erie, Pa.

16505; telephone: 814–838–1771 / Waters: Presque Isle Bay and state park lagoons / Trips: up to 1 day / Best canoeing months: May-October / Campsites: yes / Transportation: no / Car-top carriers: yes.

Exton
Paul Wick's Ski Shop, 403 North Pottstown Park (Route 100), Exton, Pa. 19341; telephone: 215–363–1893 / Waters: Brandywine and Delaware Rivers / Trips: 1 or more days / Best canoeing months: May-October / Campsites: yes / Transportation: no / Car-top carriers: yes / Open all year.

Hanover
Watko Marina, R.D. #3, Coadorus State Park, Hanover, Pa. 17331; telephone: 717–632–2628 / Waters: Lake Marburg / Trips: up to 1 day / Best canoeing months: April-November / Campsites: yes / Transportation: no / Car-top carriers: yes, on weekdays only.

Hawley
Baker's Marine Co., Lake Wallenpaupack, Hawley, Pa. 18428; telephone: 717–226–4602 / Unconfirmed.

Hummelstown
Woodrow W. Behney, R.D. 4, Box 320, Hummelstown, Pa. 17036; telephone: 717–566–2327 / Unconfirmed.

Indiana
Outdoor Specialists, 307 South 13th Street, Indiana, Pa. 15701; telephone: 412–465–2987 / Unconfirmed.

Jeannette
Central Service Station, 10–12 South Second Street, Jeannette, Pa. 15644; telephone: 412–523–5581 / Unconfirmed.

Lancaster
Conestoga Marine & Cyclery, 1361 Manheim Pike, Lancaster, Pa. 17601; telephone: 717–394–9861 / Unconfirmed.

Linesville
Louis P. Stefan, Whispering Trails Campground, R.D. 2, Linesville, Pa. 16424; telephone: 215–643–1529 / Unconfirmed.

Uniservice, Inc.-Causeway Boat Marina, Espyville Station, Linesville, Pa. 16424; telephone: 412–927–2009 / Waters: Pymatuning Lake / Trips: 1–7 days / Best canoeing months: April-September / Campsites: yes / Transportation: no / Car-top carriers: no.

Manorville
Hileman's Boat Service, Manorville, Pa. 16238; telephone: 412–762–8771 / Unconfirmed.

Milanville
James O. Card-Cushetunk Campground, Box 3, Milanville, Pa. 18443; telephone: 717–729–7984 / Unconfirmed.

Milesburg
Milesburg Boat and Trailer Sales, Route 144–220, Milesburg, Pa. 16853; telephone: 814–355–1511 / Waters: Bald Eagle Creek, Susque-

hanna River, and Penns Creek / Trips: up to 1 day / Best canoeing months: April-October / Campsites: yes / Transportation: no / Car-top carriers: yes / Open all year.

Mill Run

A House of Canoeing, Laurel Highlands River Tours, Route 381, Box 86, Mill Run, Pa. 15464; telephone: 412–455–3703 / Unconfirmed.

Milton

Robbins Marine, Milton, Pa. 17847; telephone: 717–524–2415 / Unconfirmed.

Minisink Hills

Chamberlain's Canoes, Inc. (Jim and Judy Chamberlain), Minisink Hills, Pa. (mailing address: 1527 Spruce Street, Stroudsburg, Pa. 18360); telephone: 717–421–9816 / Waters: Delaware River / Trips: 1 or more days / Best canoeing months: May-October / Campsites: yes / Transportation: yes / Car-top carriers: yes.

Oakmont

See Wilkinsburg.

Oil City

Oil City Canoe Sales (Walt Pilenski), Route 62N, R.D. 2, Oil City, Pa. 16301; telephone: 814–645–7981 / Waters: Allegheny and Clarion Rivers, Kinzua Dam area, French Creek, Tionesta Creek, Oil Creek, Two-Mile Run Lake, and Sugar Lake / Trips: 1 or more days / Best canoeing months: May-September / Campsites: yes / Transportation: yes / Car-top carriers: yes / Open all year.

Philipsburg

Jeff's Boats, Black Moshannon State Park, Philipsburg, Pa. 16836; telephone: 814–765–6725 / Waters: Black Moshannon Lake / Trips: up to 1 day / Best canoeing months: May-October / Campsites: yes / Transportation: no / Car-top carriers: no.

Pocono Pines

The Pocono Boathouse, Box 127, Pocono Pines, Pa. 18350; telephone: 717–646–2728 / Waters: Delaware, Susquehanna, and Lehigh Rivers / Trips: 1–2 days / Best canoeing months: June-September / Campsites: yes / Transportation: no / Car-top carriers: yes.

Point Pleasant

Point Pleasant Canoe Rental & Sales (Tom and Marie McBrien), Box 6, Point Pleasant, Pa. 18950; telephone: 215–297–8400 and 297–8949 / Waters: Delaware River and Canal and Roosevelt State Park / Trips: several hours to several days / Best canoeing months: May-October / Campsites: yes / Transportation: yes / Car-top carriers: yes / Also rents camping equipment.

Portersville

Uniservice Inc.-Lake Arthur Marina, Moraine State Park, R.D. 1, Portersville, Pa. 16051; telephone: 412–368–8663 / Waters: Lake Arthur / Trips: up to 1 day / Best canoeing months: April 15-October

15 / Campsites: under development / Transportation: no / Car-top carriers: no.

Portland

Port and Land Sports Shop, P.O. Box 124, Portland, Pa. 18351; telephone: 717–897–5244 / Waters: Delaware River and nearby lakes / Trips: 1 or more days / Best canoeing months: April-October / Campsites: yes / Transportation: yes / Car-top carriers: yes / Open all year.

Reading

Wolf's Equipment & Rental Co., 208 Revere Boulevard, Reading, Pa. 19609; telephone: 215–777–7908 / Unconfirmed.

Richboro

Samuel M. Bryan, 3032 Second Street Pike, Richboro, Pa. 18954; telephone: 215–598–3206 / Unconfirmed.

Slippery Rock

See Wilkinsburg.

Springfield

Paul Wick's Ski Shops, Inc., 321 West Woodland Avenue, Springfield, Pa. 19064; telephone: 215–543–5445 / See Exton.

Stroudsburg

See Minisink Hills.

Turtle Creek

Valley Buick Inc. Trailer Center, 629 Brown Avenue Extension, Turtle Creek, Pa. 15145; telephone: 412–823–5858 / Unconfirmed.

Washington Crossing

Dauber Canoe & Kayak, Taylorsville Road, P.O. Box 59, Washington Crossing, Pa. 18977; telephone: 215–493–5959 / Waters: Delaware River, Delaware Canal in Pennsylvania and the Delaware and Raritan Canal in New Jersey, Neshaminy Creek, and nearby lakes / Trips: 1 or more days, guides available / Best canoeing months: April-October / Campsites: yes / Transportation: yes / Car-top carriers: yes / Also rents camping equipment and kayaks / Arranges guided wilderness trips to northern Quebec and other areas / Open all year.

West Conshohocken

John Wright Boats Inc., 1000 New DeHaven Street, West Conshohocken, Pa. 19428; telephone: 215–825–6610 / Unconfirmed.

Wilkinsburg

Canoe Kayak & Sailing Craft (Douglas Ettinger), 701 Wood Street, Wilkinsburg, Pa. 15221; telephone: 412–371–4802 / Waters: Allegheny, Youghiogheny, and Beaver Rivers and tributaries and other waters in western Pennsylvania / Trips: 1 or more days, guides available / Best canoeing months: April-June / Campsites: yes / Transportation: yes / Car-top carriers: yes / Arranges group trips and special events / Has other locations in Oakmont and Slippery Rock / Reservations required / Sailing and canoeing instruction.

Wormleysburg
Harrisburg Seaplane Base Inc., 333 South Front Street, Wormleysburg, Pa. 17043; telephone: 717–232–6759 / Waters: Susquehanna River / Trips: 1 or more days / Best canoeing months: February-October / Campsites: no / Transportation: yes / Car-top carriers: no / Open all year.
York
Sports World, R.D. 11, Hellam Branch, York, Pa. 17406; telephone: 717–757–6111 / Unconfirmed.

Sources of Information

Burmeister, Walter F. *Appalachian Waters 1: The Delaware and its Tributaries*, Appalachian Books (Box 249, Oakton, Va. 22124), 1974, 282 pp., $6.95. Excellent, detailed descriptions of the rivers with difficulty ratings and seasonal water levels; no maps.

————*Appalachian Waters 3: The Susquehanna and its Tributaries*, Appalachian Books (Box 249, Oakton, Va. 22124), 1975, 608 pp., $8.25. Excellent, detailed descriptions of the rivers with difficulty ratings and seasonal water levels; no maps.

Canoe Country Pennsylvania Style, Pennsylvania Department of Commerce, Travel Development Bureau (431 South Office Building, Harrisburg, Pa. 17120), an excellent, free brochure showing main canoeing rivers with difficulty ratings.

Canoeing Streams of the Upper Ohio Basin, an excellent multicolor map showing locations and ratings of rivers compiled by Thomas L. Gray (11121 Dewey Road, Kensington, Md. 20795).

Delaware River map set, Delaware River Basin Commission (P.O. Box 360, Trenton, N.J. 08603), $2.00. Ten detailed maps of the river from Hancock, N.Y., to Trenton with recommended canoe courses, access points, and difficulties.

Pennsylvania fishing information is available from Pennsylvania Fish Commission (P.O. Box 1673, Harrisburg, Pa. 17120).

Pennsylvania tourist information is available from Pennsylvania Department of Commerce, Travel Development Bureau (431 South Office Building, Harrisburg, Pa. 17120).

Select Rivers of Central Pennsylvania, Penn State Outing Club, Canoe Division (60 Recreation Building, University Park, Pa. 16802), 4th ed., 1974, 44 pp., 75¢. Detailed river descriptions and ratings; no maps.

Spindt, Katherine M. and Mary Shaw, eds. *Canoeing Guide to Western Pennsylvania and Northern West Virginia*, Pittsburgh Council, American Youth Hostels Inc. (6300 Fifth Avenue, Pittsburgh, Pa. 15232), 1975, 164 pp., $2.00. Detailed river descriptions and area maps.

NEW JERSEY

PROBABLY NO STATE in the Union originally had a greater diversity of scenery within such a relatively small area — 7,500 square miles — than New Jersey. Much of it has been destroyed by man, but enough remains to give the nature lover at least a sampling of the extraordinary beauty that once was.

A rocky, wooded mountain range, part of the Appalachians, covers the northwest. Eastward this drops off into rolling country, covered with countless lakes left by the last ice age. This was once followed by extensive, lush marshland, reaching right to the doorstep of New York City, but it is now covered with garbage and industrial debris. The cliffs of the Palisades along the Hudson River, in the northeast section of the state, have remained fairly intact as one of the most dramatic river banks in the country. To the south of New York City are 100 miles of long, narrow barrier beaches, greatly overdeveloped; only one of these, Island Beach, has been taken over by the state for a park and has remained in its natural state.

Inland and parallel to the coast are the Pine Barrens — this strange piece of wilderness of scrubby pines and oaks growing on meager, sandy soil — which has survived, albeit in a much diminished size, in its virgin state so very close to the largest population centers in the country. Residential and industrial developers continue to encroach on this easily destroyed bit of nature, but at least one section is reasonably well protected — the Wharton State Forest, midway between Philadelphia and Atlantic City. This tract includes a quartet of unspoiled small canoeing rivers of exceptional beauty — the Batsto, Mullica, Oswego, and Wading Rivers — their clean waters stained brown by the roots of cedars lining their banks.

On its western border, New Jersey shares with Pennsylvania the Delaware, a grandiose, free-flowing, fast river which cuts its course through wooded hills most of the way, offering several days of some of the best canoeing in the United States.

Most of the smaller rivers in the more populated areas of New Jersey have suffered badly from dams, residential and industrial developments, pollution, and filled-in swamps and marshes. Having lost their natural life cycle, most of them tend to veer between the extremes of floods and droughts.

Except for the Delaware and the Passaic Rivers, the canoeing trips in New Jersey are mainly one-day outings.

New Jersey Waters

Batsto River
Hampton Furnace on Hampton Road off Route 206 to town of Batsto on Route 542: 20 miles all of which is within Wharton State Forest — a previously used launching spot at Lower Forge is now closed to cars / The Mullica River tidal estuary is below Batsto. Rentals: Green Bank, Hammonton, Lebanon, Sweetwater, and Vincentown.

Cedar Creek
Double Trouble State Forest off Pinewald-Keswick Road (Route 530) to the dam east of Route 9: 7 miles / In high water, a trip can begin higher up, at Dover Forge, off Route 530, or at the dam at Bamber, about 2½ miles above Pinewald-Keswick Road, on Lacey Road, but these sections have many obstructions. This creek is scheduled to be a part of a Federal Green Acres project. Rentals: Bayville and Toms River.

Delaware and Raritan Canal
The canal begins at Raven Rock 5 miles north of Lambertville on Route 29 and runs south to a point below Scudders Falls, where it turns and heads northeast towards Princeton, Kingston, and Zarephath. The canal measures about 60 miles of generally scenic, smooth water. It is not navigable for a short stretch south of Scudders Falls. On the stretch which is navigable from above Scudders Falls to East Millstone on Route 514 is 18 miles of pleasant canoeing, 4 miles from East Millstone to Zarephath east of Route 533 at Manville and about 9 miles from Zarephath to New Brunswick on Route 527. Zarephath to New Brunswick has industrial scenery. Portages into the Millstone River at several points or from feeder sections into the Delaware, which permit round trips without transportation. Rentals: East Millstone, Kingston, and Titusville.

Delaware River
Hancock, New York, to Trenton, New Jersey: about 200 miles, some whitewater above Port Jervis, New York, many intermediate access points, tidal waters below Trenton / North of Trenton, at Lambertville on Route 29, is a connection to the Delaware and Raritan Canal. The Delaware is especially scenic and one can also easily paddle the Delaware Canal on the Pennsylvania side. See Pennsylvania for a full description of the river and *see* New York for the upper reaches. Rentals: Belvidere, Cranford, East Millstone, Jefferson, Lebanon, and Titusville (*see also* Pennsylvania and New York).

Great Egg Harbor River
Penny Pot on Route 322 to Weymouth Furnace on Route 559: 8 miles / Penny Pot to Winding River Campground on Route 559: 10 miles / The river is canoeable above Penny Pot only after rains and is often obstructed / Below Mays Landing are tidal waters. Rentals: Mays Landing.

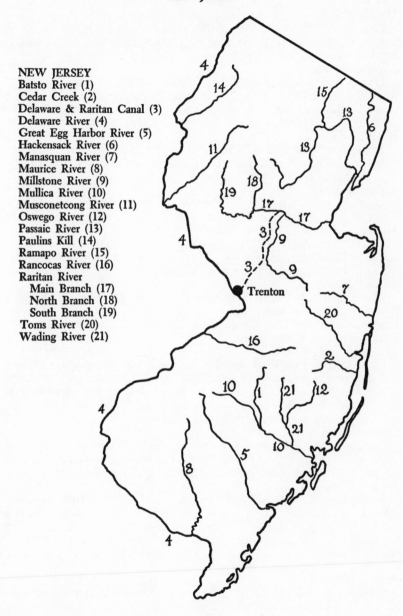

NEW JERSEY
Batsto River (1)
Cedar Creek (2)
Delaware & Raritan Canal (3)
Delaware River (4)
Great Egg Harbor River (5)
Hackensack River (6)
Manasquan River (7)
Maurice River (8)
Millstone River (9)
Mullica River (10)
Musconetcong River (11)
Oswego River (12)
Passaic River (13)
Paulins Kill (14)
Ramapo River (15)
Rancocas River (16)
Raritan River
    Main Branch (17)
    North Branch (18)
    South Branch (19)
Toms River (20)
Wading River (21)

Hackensack River

New Bridge on Route 503 to the tidal waters: 15 miles, industrial scenery for the most part, but good canoeing and excellent bird watching in the Hackensack Meadows.

Manasquan River

Howell Park to Allaire State Park: about 6 miles / or near Route 547 to Allaire State Park: about 2½ miles / Upper course of the river is canoeable from Route 9 after rains and it is often obstructed. Rentals: Brick Town and Toms River.

Maurice River

Malaga on Routes 40–47 to Millville on Route 47: about 20 miles, very scenic, the river goes through Willow Grove Lake and Union Lake. Rentals: Millville.

Millstone River

Cranbury off Route 130 to Princeton off Route 1: 8 miles, through Carnegie Lake / portage 3 miles to Route 27 / Route 27 via town of Millstone to town of Bound Brook on Route 28 on the Raritan River: 12 miles. The river parallels the Delaware and Raritan Canal from Carnegie Lake and the portages allow for round trips without transportation. Rentals: East Millstone and Kingston.

Mullica River

Atsion on Route 206 to Batsto on Route 542: 16 miles, all of which is within Wharton State Forest / Below Batsto is the tidal estuary. Rentals: Gloucester City, Green Bank, Hammonton, Jefferson, Lebanon, Sweetwater, and Vincentown.

Musconetcong River

Canoeable only on short stretches, primarily near Stanhope on Route 206 and nearby Waterloo Village, Stephens State Park, and remnants of the Morris Canal, for which it once provided water. Some canoeing is also possible between Asbury and the Delaware River, about 11 miles, but this section is interrupted by many fish dams.

Oswego River

Oswego Lake off Route 563 to Harrisville Pond dam on Route 563 Spur: about 10 miles, partly in state forest lands, too shallow in prolonged dry weather. Rentals: Green Bank, Jenkins, and Lebanon.

Passaic River

Millington off Route 512 to Singac on Route 23: more than 90 miles, canoeable only in good water, many intermediate access points, especially scenic on the upper reaches but the river floods easily and is shallow in dry spells. The Great Swamp National Wildlife Refuge, above Millington on Route 512, is now closed to canoeists. Rentals: Berkeley Heights, Cranford, and Pompton Plains.

Paulins Kill

Stillwater on Route 521 to Columbia on Route 46 on the Delaware River: 20 miles, several dams, some sections are too shallow in dry weather.

Ramapo River

South of Suffern, New York, near the junction of Routes 202 and 17 to the dam at Pompton on Route 202: about 30 miles, swift, and sometimes tricky waters in spring and after heavy rains; the river flows through the two Pompton Lakes. In high water the trip can be started from Route 17, in New York, between Tuxedo and Sloatsburg. Residential scenery below Pompton. Rentals: Pompton Plains.

Rancocas River

Browns Mills on Route 545 to Mount Holly on Route 537: about 15 miles, very scenic, tidal waters below Mount Holly. Intermediate access at Pemberton on Route 530 midway between Browns Mills and Mount Holly. Rentals: Gloucester City.

Raritan River

South Branch: High Bridge on Route 513 or Clinton on I–78 and Route 513 to Flemington Junction on Route 523: 12 miles / Flemington Junction to off Route 202 near Three Bridges: 4 miles / Three Bridges to junction with the North Branch below Route 567 bridge: 11 miles.

North Branch: Far Hills on Route 512 to junction with the South Branch: about 15 miles.

Main Branch: Route 567 bridge to Manville on Route 533: about 7 miles, the Millstone River joins the Raritan at Manville. It is possible to canoe all the way from the Raritan to the Delaware River by going up the Millstone, making a portage to the Delaware and Raritan Canal, and from the Canal into the Delaware River. The upper reaches of the North and South Branches are too shallow for canoeing in dry spells. Rentals: East Millstone and Lebanon.

Toms River

Route 528 bridge at Bowman's Mill, near Cassville, to Toms River bus terminal: about 25 miles with intermediate access points at Holmansville off Route 527, Whitesville on Route 547, and the Route 70 bridge. Waters are tidal below the town of Toms River. Rentals: Brick Town and Toms River.

Wading River

Speedwell on Route 563 to Evans Bridge on Route 563: about 9 miles / or Speedwell to Bodine's Field off Route 563: about 12 miles / Within Wharton State Forest. Rentals: Gloucester City, Green Bank, Jefferson, Jenkins, and Lebanon.

New Jersey Rentals

Avalon

Morgan's Wharf, 589 24th Street, Avalon, N.J. 08202; telephone: 609–967–3980 / Waters: back bay waters / Trips: up to 1 day / Best canoeing months: June-October / Campsites: no / Transportation: no / Car-top carriers: no.

Bayville

Cedar Creek Campground, 1052 Route 9, Bayville, N.J. 08721; telephone: 201–269–1413 / Waters: Cedar Creek / Trips: up to 1 day / Best canoeing months: early spring to late fall / Campsites: no / Transportation: yes / Car-top carriers: yes / Open all year.

Belvidere

Stanley's Marine & Sports Shop, Route 46, Box 478, Belvidere, N.J. 07823; telephone: 201–475–2540 / Waters: Delaware River and other nearby waters / Trips: 1 day or longer / Best canoeing months: April until late fall / Campsites: yes / Transportation: no / Car-top carriers: yes.

Berkeley Heights

Explorer Post 68 (Frank Schade), 96 Old Farm Road, Berkeley Heights, N.J. 07922; telephone: 201–322–1676 / Waters: Passaic River / Trips: up to 2 days / Best canoeing months: April-November / Campsites: no / Transportation: by special arrangement / Car-top carriers: yes, also trailers for rent / Open all year.

Brick Town

Jersey Paddler, 900 Route 70, Laurelton Circle, Brick Town, N.J. 08723; telephone: 201–892–3785 / Waters: Toms River and Manasquan River / Trips: 1–2 days / Best canoeing months: spring to fall / Campsites: yes / Transportation: no / Car-top carriers yes / Open all year.

Cranford

Cranford Boat and Canoe Company, 250 Springfield Avenue, Cranford, N.J. 07016; telephone: 201–272–6991 / Waters: Delaware, Passaic, and other waterways / Trips: several hours to several days / Best canoeing months: March-November / Campsites: yes / Transportation: no / Car-top carriers: yes / Open all year.

East Millstone

Canal Canoe Rental, Route 514 (Amwell Road), East Millstone, N.J. 08873; telephone: 201–873–2161 / Waters: Delaware, Millstone, and Raritan Rivers and the Delaware and Raritan Canal / Trips: several hours to several days / Best canoeing months: March-November / Campsites: yes / Transportation: yes / Car-top carriers: yes.

Gloucester City

M & E Marine Supply Co., Route 130 at Klemm Avenue, Gloucester City, N.J. (mailing address: P.O. Box 601, Camden, N.J. 08101); telephone: 609–456–5454 / Waters: Mullica, Rancocas, and Wading Rivers / Trips: 1–2 days / Best canoeing months: April, June, September, and October / Campsites: yes / Transportation: no / Car-top carriers: yes.

Green Bank

Bel Haven Lake (Bill Bell), Route 542, Green Bank, N.J. (mailing address: R.D. 2, Egg Harbor, N.J. 08215); telephone: 609–965–2031 or 965–2205 / Waters: Batsto, Mullica, Oswego, and Wading Rivers / Trips: 1–2 days / Best canoeing months: March-June, September-November / Campsites: yes / Transportation: yes / Car-top carriers: yes / Camping and trailer park on premises / Open all year.

Mullica River Boat Basin, Route 542, Green Bank, N.J. (mailing address: R.D. 2, Egg Harbor, N.J. 08215); telephone: 609–965–2120 / Waters: Mullica and Wading Rivers / Trips: 1–2 days / Best canoeing months: April-June, September, and October / Campsites: yes / Transportation: yes / Car-top carriers: yes.

Hammonton

Paradise Lakes Campground (Lou Neirle), Route 206, P.O. Box 46, Hammonton, N.J. 08037; telephone: 609–561–7095 / Waters: Batsto and Mullica Rivers / Trips: 1 hour to 2 days / Best canoeing months: April-June, September, and October / Campsites: yes / Transportation: yes / Car-top carriers: yes.

Jefferson

Oscar Jenkins Co., Route 45, Jefferson, N.J. (mailing address: Mullica Hill, N.J. 08062); telephone: 609–478–2800 and 609–468–4600 / Waters: Delaware, Mullica, and Wading Rivers / Trips: 1–2 days / Best canoeing months: May-September / Campsites: no / Transportation: no / Car-top carriers: yes.

Jenkins

Mick's Canoe Rental, Route 563, Jenkins, N.J. (mailing address: Chatsworth, N.J. 08019); telephone: 609–726–1380 / Waters: Oswego River and East and West Branches of the Wading River / Trips: 2 hours to 2 days / Best canoeing months: spring and fall / Campsites: yes / Transportation: yes / Car-top carriers: no response.

Kingston

Bernard's Boat Rental, Route 27, Kingston, N.J. 08528; telephone: 609–924–9418 / Waters: Millstone River and Delaware and Raritan Canal / Trips: up to 1 day / Best canoeing months: June-September / Campsites: yes / Transportation: yes / Car-top carriers: yes.

Lebanon

South Branch Canoe Cruises (Peter Buell and Jay Langley), P.O. Box 173, Lebanon, N.J. 08833; telephone: 201–782–9700 / Waters: South Branch of the Raritan River, all sections of the Delaware River, and the Batsto, Mullica, Oswego, and Wading Rivers; out of state waters include the Lehigh, Shenandoah, and Susquehanna Rivers / Trips: 1–3 days with canoes, camping equipment, and food provided / Best canoeing months: spring and fall / Campsites: yes / Transportation: yes / Car-top carriers: yes / Canoes rented upon availability, check first /

Instruction on canoeing and kayaking is offered / Open all year.

Mays Landing

Lenape Park Recreation Center, Box 57, Park Road, Mays Landing, N.J. 08330; telephone: 609–625–1191 or 625–2021 / Waters: Great Egg Harbor River / Trips: 5–12 hours / Best canoeing months: May-June, September, and October / Campsites: yes / Transportation: yes but minimum of 3 canoes / Car-top carriers: yes.

Winding River Campground, R.D. 2, Box 246, Mays Landing, N.J. 08330; telephone: 609–625–3191 / Waters: Great Egg Harbor River / Trips: 1–2 days / Best canoeing months: April-October / Campsites: no / Transportation: yes / Car-top carriers: yes.

Millville

Dick's Canoes, 14 East Vine Street, Millville, N.J. 08332; telephone: 609–825–1000 / Waters: Maurice River / Trips: 1–2 days / Best canoeing months: spring and late fall / Campsites: yes / Transportation: yes / Car-top carriers: yes.

Pompton Plains

Rentals Unlimited, 444 Route 23, Pompton Plains, N.J. 07444; telephone: 201–839–3201 / Waters: Passaic, Pompton, and Ramapo Rivers / Trips: up to 1 day / Best canoeing months: June-September / Campsites: no / Transportation: no / Car-top carriers: yes / Also rents camping equipment / Open all year.

Sweetwater

Mullica River Marina, Route 563, Sweetwater, N.J. 08037; telephone: 609–561–4337 / Waters: Batsto and Mullica Rivers / Trips: 1–2 days / Best canoeing months: spring and fall / Campsites: yes / Transportation: yes / Car-top carriers: no.

Titusville

Abbott's Marine Center, Route 29 (River Road), Titusville, N.J. 08560; telephone: 609–737–3446 / Waters: Delaware River and Delaware and Raritan Canal / Trips: up to several days / Best canoeing months: June-September / Campsites: yes / Transportation: yes / Car-top carriers: yes.

Toms River

Albocondo Campground (Hugh and Jean Clayton), 1480 Whitesville Road, Toms River, N.J. 08753; telephone: 201–349–4079 / Waters: Toms River and Cedar Creek / Trips: 1–2 days / Best canoeing months: spring to fall / Campsites: yes / Transportation: yes, but only for 6 or more canoes / Car-top carriers: yes / Open all year.

Pineland Canoes, R.D. 2, Box 451 O, Route 527, Toms River, N.J. 08753; telephone: 201–364–0389 or 201–892–8811 / Waters: Toms River, Manasquan River, and Cedar Creek / Trips: 1–3 days / Best canoeing months: May, June, September, and October / Campsites: yes / Transportation: yes, only to Toms River / Car-top carriers: yes.

108

Vincentown

Adams Canoe Rental, Lake Drive Atsion, Vincentown, N.J. 08088; telephone: 609–268–0189 / Waters: Batsto and Mullica Rivers / Trips: 1–2 days / Best canoeing months: April, May, and September / Campsites: yes / Transportation: yes / Car-top carriers: yes.

Sources of Information

Canoeing in New Jersey, New Jersey Department of Community Affairs (363 West State Street, Trenton, N.J. 08625), 1974, 26 pp., free. Out of print when this list was compiled but the Department of Community Affairs indicated it is planning to reprint this pamphlet.

Cawley, James and Margaret. *Exploring the Little Rivers of New Jersey,* Rutgers University Press (New Brunswick, N.J.), 1971, 252 pp., $2.75. A classic, if somewhat outdated.

Delaware River Basin Commission (P.O. Box 360, Trenton, N.J. 08603) publishes a set of 10 excellent maps of the Delaware River from Hancock, New York, to Trenton, New Jersey, including the best channel for canoeing. The set costs $2.00. The Commission also offers a free brochure, *Shooting Rapids on the Upper Delaware.*

McPhee, John. *The Pine Barrens,* Farrar, Straus & Giroux (New York, N.Y.), 1968, 157 pp., $4.50. A beautifully written account of the New Jersey pinelands, its history, people, economy, rivers, etc.

Meyer, Joan and Bill. *Canoe Trails of the Jersey Shore,* Specialty Press Inc. (Ocean, N.J. 07712), 1974, 73 pp., $2.95.

New Jersey fishing and hunting information is available from the New Jersey Department of Environmental Protection, Division of Fish and Game (Labor and Industry Building, P.O. Box 1809, Trenton, N.J. 08625).

New Jersey tourist information is available from New Jersey Department of Labor and Industry, Division of Economic Development, State Promotion Section (P.O. Box 400, Trenton, N.J. 08625).

Pine Barrens Canoeing, Eastwoods Press (421 Hudson Street, New York, N.Y. 10014), to be published.

PART TWO

THE SOUTHEAST

•

VIRGINIA, WEST VIRGINIA, MARYLAND, DELAWARE, and DISTRICT OF COLUMBIA

READING THE PROLIFIC LITERATURE on the canoeing waters of Virginia, West Virginia, and Maryland, one gets the impression that the authors recognize only the whitewaters. This apparent bias is largely explained by the topography of these states. They straddle several ranges of the Appalachian Mountains, including the Blue Ridge with its famous Skyline Drive, the Shenandoah Mountains, and the Allegheny Mountains. In between run lovely valleys and fast streams, the best known among them the lush Shenandoah Valley with the Shenandoah River and its branches, flowing north to join the Potomac River.

Streams also run off these mountains towards the east, south, and west, trying to find their ways out of the winding valleys and through gaps in the wooded ranges. Moreover, the rolling Piedmont Plateau, sloping from the mountains toward the ocean, has an abrupt ledge on its eastern side, the Fall Line, ranging from Baltimore past Washington, D.C., Fredericksburg, and Richmond to Petersburg and creating in the process striking waterfalls for the rivers trying to get to the sea, including such well-known dramatic ones as the Great Falls of the Potomac River outside Washington and the James River Falls at Richmond, or intimate, picturesque ones such as the falls of the Little River north of Richmond.

Most of the whitewater streams have stretches of flat water, often long ones, and the family canoeist can enjoy many of the scenic pleasures that the Appalachian rivers have to offer. The waterways selected for this chapter are of the flat or mixed whitewater-flat variety. Additional "pure" whitewater streams can be found in the books listed at the end of this chapter. These river guides should be consulted for any river that contains sections of whitewater to avoid sudden surprises. The books not only describe every danger point but also list the seasonal water conditions — an important piece of information since most of the Appalachian rivers become to shallow for canoeing at different times from spring on.

113

There seem to be few canoeable flat water rivers in these states even though the coastal areas below the plateau ledge offer the appropriate terrain. Apparently, many of the coastal rivers are obstructed by fallen trees and dense vegetation. Exceptions are the Pamunkey River and the lower course of the Mattaponi River, which join to form the York River estuary.

Bird watchers and other nature lovers canoe on the flat waters of the Dismal Swamp on and around Lake Drummond south of Norfolk.

There are only two canoeable inland waterways in Delaware — a scenic 5-mile creek leading from Trap Pond State Park to Laurel and the Brandywine River above the rapids north of Wilmington. Shallow back-bays and narrow tidewater inlets inaccessible to power boats can be found in the Chesapeake Bay and other coastal waters.

Virginia Waters

Cedar Creek
Route 55 above town of Star Tannery to Stephens Fort bridge on Route 628 near Marlboro: 10 miles / Route 628 to Route 635 east of Strasburg above junction with the Shenandoah River: 14 miles, dangerous rapids at the end of the trip. Cedar Creek recommended for spring canoeing only.

James River
The river runs for some 300 miles from its headwaters near the town of Eagle Rock on Route 43 in Jefferson National Forest in the Appalachians to the tidal waters below Richmond, where it flows into Chesapeake Bay and the Atlantic Ocean. There are many dangerous as well as placid and wide stretches on the James River. Popular whitewater runs are above Snowden on Route 501 and The Falls at Richmond. A scenic stretch with minor rapids but a stretch requiring careful navigation in tricky waters is downstream of Scottsville on Routes 6–20. There are innumerable access points along the river.

Lake Drummond
In the Dismal Swamp, a good-sized lake with connecting canals to the west of Route 17 south of Norfolk. A bird watcher's paradise.

Little River
Route 685 off Route 1 at Doswell to Route 688: 3 miles, via beautiful but dangerous falls which must be portaged / Route 688 to Route 1: 4 miles, minor rapids / below Route 1 to junction with the North Anna River: about 8 miles, the obstructions have reportedly been cleared. Not to be confused with a river of the same name in the southwestern part of the state. Rentals: Doswell.

Mattaponi River
Route 360 at Aylett to tidewater below Walkerton: about 20 miles,

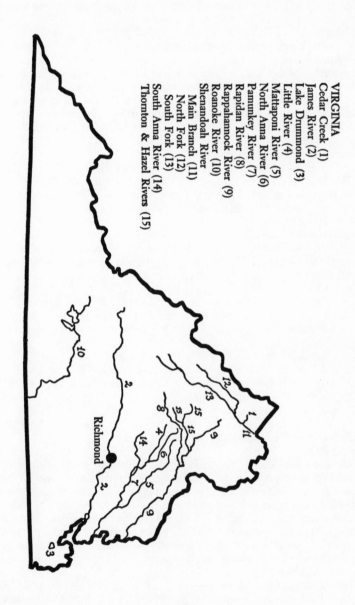

VIRGINIA
Cedar Creek (1)
James River (2)
Lake Drummond (3)
Little River (4)
Mattaponi River (5)
North Anna River (6)
Pamunkey River (7)
Rapidan River (8)
Rappahannock River (9)
Roanoke River (10)
Shenandoah River
   Main Branch (11)
   North Fork (12)
   South Fork (13)
South Anna River (14)
Thornton & Hazel Rivers (15)

Richmond

scenic, much wildlife / above Route 360 the river has many obstructions.

New River

See West Virginia and North Carolina.

North Anna River

Smith Mill bridge below Lake Anna to Route 1 south of the town of Carmel Church: about 25 miles, portage 6 miles below Smith Mill and 1½ miles above Route 1 (North Anna Falls), otherwise an easy stretch / Route 1 to junction with the South Anna River: 10 miles. Pamunkey River begins at junction of North and South Anna Rivers. Rentals: Doswell.

Pamunkey River

Junction of North and South Anna Rivers east of Gum Tree on Route 1 to Route 301 north of Hanover: 12 miles / Route 301 to Route 360 northeast of Richmond: 25 miles, scenic, much wildlife / Route 360 to tidal waters: about 25 miles. Rentals: Doswell.

Potomac River

The Potomac River flows through Virginia, West Virginia, and Maryland. For the Main Branch of the Potomac *see* Maryland. For the North and South Branches *see* West Virginia. Virginia rentals are listed in the Maryland entry.

Rapidan River

Route 29 north of Ruckersville to Madison Mills on Route 15: 18 miles / Route 15 to junction with the Rappahannock River 10 miles above Fredericksburg: about 50 miles, 2–3 difficult rapids, rated unattractive.

Rappahannock River

Route 211 west of Warrenton to Remington on Routes 15–29: 18 miles, canoeable in high water only / Remington to Kelleys Ford: about 6 miles, fairly difficult rapids especially in high water / Kelleys Ford to the dam above Fredericksburg: 30 miles, smooth, some wilderness, no intermediate access. Dangerous rapids below the dam; tidewater about 15 miles below Fredericksburg. Rentals: Oakton.

Roanoke River

Elliston on Routes 11–460 to Roanoke: 26 miles, some whitewater / Roanoke to Smith Mountain Lake south of Route 24: about 20 miles, polluted / can canoe through Smith Mountain Lake to dam and short portage into Leesville Lake and through this lake to the dam at Leesville on Route 43: about 30 miles / Route 43 to Staunton River State Park on Route 344 at tidewater: about 100 miles, relatively few access points, this stretch is sometimes called the Staunton River. The Roanoke River is recommended for canoeing in the spring.

Shenandoah River

Main Branch: Formed by the confluence of the South and North Forks at Riverton on Route 55, north of Front Royal. Riverton to

Routes 17–50: 19 miles / Routes 17–50 to Route 7: 15 miles, scenic / Route 7 to Route 9 at Bloomery, West Virginia: 14 miles / Bloomery to Harpers Ferry, West Virginia, and junction with the Potomac River: 10 miles, rapids and famous "staircase" for advanced whitewater experts only. Rentals: Berryville, Front Royal, and Oakton.

North Fork: The North Fork can be run in its entirety only in spring or after heavy rains. Above Mount Jackson are whitewaters. Mount Jackson bridge 3 miles below town off Route 11 to Edinburg on Route 672 about 2 miles below town: 12 miles / Edinburg to Stonewall Mill on Route 663: 20 miles / Stonewall Mill to junction with the South Fork at Riverton on Route 55: 42 miles, much meandering. Rentals: Berryville and Front Royal.

South Fork: Formed by the confluence of the South and North Rivers at Port Republic on Route 685. Route 685 to Elkton on Route 340: 18 miles, some difficulties / Elkton to town of Shenandoah on Route 340: 6 miles / Shenandoah to Newport on Routes 340 and 685: 14 miles / Newport to Route 211 west of Luray: 10 miles / Route 211 to Bixler Bridge on Route 675: 7 miles / Bixler Bridge to Burners Ford on Route 664 off Route 340: 20 miles, scenic, minor rapids, difficult in high water / Burners Ford to Karo Landing off Route 340 north of Bentonville: 17 miles / Karo Landing to junction with the North Fork at Riverton on Route 55: 10 miles. Rentals: Berryville, Front Royal, Luray, and Oakton.

South Anna River

Route 673 at Casco off Route 33 to Route 54 northwest of Ashland: 12 miles, several falls, called a "beginner's whitewater" / Route 54 to Route 1: 10 miles, minor rapids / Route 1 to Route 738 above junction with the North Anna River: 7 miles. Pamunkey River begins at junction of North and South Anna Rivers. Rentals: Doswell.

Thornton and Hazel Rivers

Canoeable in high water only. Fletcher's Mill at Sperryville off Route 211 to Monumental Mills at junction with Hazel River: 20 miles, one falls at the beginning and a minor rapids / confluence to Remington on Routes 15–29 and junction with the Rappahannock River: 15 miles, smooth.

Virginia Rentals

Berryville

Spring Valley Canoe Base (John Shaffer), Route 2, Box 175, Berryville, Va. 22611; telephone: 703–955–3631 / Waters: Shenandoah River, Potomac River, and other rivers in Virginia, West Virginia, and

Maryland / Trips: 1 or more days / Best canoeing months: all year / Campsites: yes / Transportation: yes / Car-top carriers: yes / Open all year.

Charlottesville

Blue Ridge Mountain Sports, 1417 Emmet Street, Charlottesville, Va. 22901; telephone: 804–977–4400 / Waters: anywhere / Trips: 1 or more days / Best canoeing months: spring to fall / Campsites: yes / Transportation: no / Car-top carriers: yes / Also rents camping equipment / Open all year.

Doswell

Little River Leisure Enterprises (Chuck and Nancy Martin), P.O. Box 83, Doswell, Va. 23047; telephone: 804–227–3401 / Waters: Little, North Anna, South Anna, and Pamunkey Rivers / Trips: a few hours to 3 days / Best canoeing months: spring and fall / Campsites: yes / Transportation: yes / Car-top carriers: yes.

Fredericksburg

Sport Center Marine, 3425 Jefferson Davis Boulevard, Fredericksburg, Va. 22401; telephone: 804–373–2555 / Unconfirmed.

Front Royal

Three Springs Campground (KOA Campground) (Don Roberts), P.O. Box 274, Front Royal, Va. 22630; telephone: 703–635–2741 / Waters: Shenandoah River and other rivers in Virginia and West Virginia / Trips: 1 or more days / Best canoeing months: April-October / Campsites: yes / Transportation: no / Car-top carriers: yes / Open all year.

Luray

Shenandoah River Outfitters, R.D. 3, Luray, Va. 22845; telephone: 703–745–4159 / Waters: South Fork of the Shenandoah River / Trips: 1–3 days, guides available / Best canoeing months: April-October / Campsites: yes / Transportation: yes / Car-top carriers: yes / Also rents camping equipment and provides completely outfitted canoe trips for groups up to 100 persons / Open all year.

Oakton

Canoe Center Matacia Outfitters (Louis J. Matacia), P.O. Box 32, Oakton, Va. 22124; telephone 703–560–8993 / Waters: Shenandoah, Potomac, and Rappahannock Rivers, Chesapeake and Ohio Canal, and whitewaters in Maryland, Virginia, Pennsylvania, and West Virginia / Trips: 1 or more days, guides available / Best canoeing months: any time / Campsites: yes / Transportation: no / Car-top carriers: yes / Arranges guided whitewater trips into many areas and also offers canoeing instruction / Open all year.

Virginia Beach

Camping Servicecenter, 4975 Holland Road, Virginia Beach, Va. 23462; telephone: 804–499–4356 / Unconfirmed.

118

West Virginia Waters

Cacapon River

Wardensville on Route 259 to town of Capon Bridge on Route 50: about 30 miles / Capon Bridge to town of Forks of Cacapon on Route 45: 12 miles, scenic, several falls of medium difficulty / Forks of Cacapon to Largent on Route 9: 18 miles, scenic / Largent to town of Great Cacapon on Route 9 and junction with the Potomac River: 21 miles, canoeable in spring or high water only. Rentals: Capon Bridge.

Cheat River

Main Branch: Parsons on Route 219 to Rowlesburg on Route 72: 35 miles, this is the only flat stretch of the Cheat River, scenic, some minor rapids / Rowlesburg to Route 73 on Cheat Lake east of Morgantown: about 35 miles, varying degrees of difficulty but most of the whitewater is difficult.

Dry Fork: Gandy Creek above Route 33 to Wayside Park on Route 32: about 5 miles, difficult whitewater below Route 33 / park to Jenningston and junction with the Glady Fork: 7 miles, easier whitewater except in high water / Jenningston to Parsons and junction with the Shavers Fork: 12 miles, difficult whitewater.

Glady Fork: Route 33 bridge southwest of Harman to junction with the Dry Fork near Elk on Route 72: 17 miles, scenic, a "beginner's whitewater" in spring.

Laurel Fork: Route 33 near Wymer to Jenningston just below junction with the Dry Fork: 13 miles, scenic, difficult whitewater in high water but too shallow in low water.

Shavers Fork: Town of Cheat Bridge on Route 250 to Bemis: about 25 miles, whitewater, varying degrees of difficulty / Bemis to Route 33 east of Elkins: 14 miles, difficult whitewater / Route 33 to Parsons: 22 miles, scenic, fast, not very difficult. Rentals: Albright.

Greenbrier River

Durbin on Route 250 to Cass on Route 3: 17 miles, fast, some rapids / Cass to Marlinton on Route 39: 27 miles, slower, easier rapids / Marlinton to Denmar on Route 20 off Route 219: 17 miles, swift, minor rapids / Denmar to Renick on Route 219: 18 miles, very dangerous in high water / Renick to Anthony on Route 21: 15 miles, scenic, slower, one dangerous rapids / Anthony to Ronceverte on Route 219: 18 miles, fairly slow, occasional rapids / Ronceverte to Alderson on Routes 3–12: about 20 miles, powerful whitewater for the experts only / Alderson to Talcott on Routes 3–12: 14 miles, mostly flat water / Talcott to junction with the New River near Hinton on Route 20: about 15 miles, the end of this chapter. Rentals: Thurmond.

New River

The New River enters Virginia from North Carolina south of Inde-

WEST VIRGINIA
Cacapon River (1)
Cheat River
Main Branch (2)
Dry Fork (3)
Glady Fork (4)
Laurel Fork (5)
Shavers Fork (6)
Greenbrier River (7)
New River (8)
North River (9)
Potomac River
North Branch (10)
South Branch (11)
Tygart River (12)

Charleston

pendence on Routes 21–221 and flows for about 180 miles through Virginia. The longest stretch of the New River is in West Virginia. It can be entered in West Virginia at the mouth of Bluestone Lake near Glen Lyn on Route 460. Canoeists can paddle through the lake. From the exit of the lake to Kanawha Falls on Route 61 is a 60-mile stretch with many impoundments, many rapids, and also stretches of flat water in scenic settings. For more details, see Randy Carter's book listed at the end of this chapter. Rentals: Thurmond.

North River

Route 50 west of the town of Capon Bridge to town of Forks of Cacapon on Route 45 and the last bridge before junction with the Cacapon River: 24 miles, scenic, canoeable in spring only. Rentals: Capon Bridge.

Potomac River

North Branch: Very dangerous whitewater, usual put-in point is Gormania on Routes 50–560. The North Branch forms part of the West Virginia-Maryland border.

South Branch: Canoeable in spring and high water only; some minor difficulties will be found. Petersburg on Route 220 to Route 220 bridge below Moorefield: 17 miles / Moorefield to Romney to Route 50: 24 miles / Romney to junction with the North Branch of the Potomac: 34 miles. For the Main Branch, *see* Maryland. Rentals: Berryville and Oakton in Virginia and Capon Bridge in West Virginia.

Tygart River

Elkins on Routes 219–250 to Norton on Routes 33–250: 12 miles, flat, minor rapids / Norton to mouth of Buckhannon River near Carrolton off Route 119: 18 miles, dangerous whitewater / river mouth to Philippi on Route 250: 6 miles, minor rapids / Philippi to Tygart Lake State Park: about 10 miles, via Arden falls, the first 6 miles are flat, the next 4 miles are dangerous whitewater / Lake Tygart dam near Grafton to Hammond: 10 miles, dangerous whitewater, danger at Valley Falls / Hammond to Fairmont on Route 79: 10 miles, flat.

West Virginia Rentals

Albright

Cheat Canyon Expeditions, Box 194, Albright, W. Va. 26519; telephone: 412–465–2987 / Waters: Cheat River / Trips: guided whitewater raft trips only / Best months: spring and summer / Campsites: yes / Transportation: yes / Car-top carriers: no. Address off-season correspondence to Cheat Canyon Expeditions, 1286 Washington Street, Indiana, Pa. 15701 / Also rents camping equipment.

Capon Bridge

Wolford's Grocery (Mervin and Opal Wolford), Capon Bridge, W. Va. 26711; telephone: 304–856–2750 / Waters: Cacapon River, North River, and South Branch of the Potomac River / Trips: 1 hour-2 days with guides only / Best canoeing months: spring and summer / Campsites: no / Transportation: yes / Car-top carriers: no.

Harpers Ferry

Blue Ridge Outfitters (KOA Campground), Harpers Ferry, W. Va. 25425; telephone: 304–725–3444 / Unconfirmed.

Morgantown

Sunset Beach Marina, Inc., Cheat Lake, Box 93A, Route 6, Morgantown, W. Va. 26505; telephone: 304–292–5818 / Unconfirmed.

Thurmond

Wildwater Expeditions Unlimited, Inc., P.O. Box 55, Thurmond, W. Va. 25936 / Waters: New River, Greenbrier River, and other area waterways / Trips: 1–2 days or longer by previous arrangement, guided whitewater raft trips only / Best months: June-October / Campsites: yes / Transportation: yes / Car-top carriers: no.

Maryland Waters

Assateague National Seashore

Overnight canoe trail system on bayside of Assateague Island reached via Route 611 south of Ocean City on Route 50.

Chesapeake and Ohio Canal

The canal runs for 162 miles. The tow path along its entire course is a public park for hiking, bicycles, and camping. Canoeists do not paddle the entire course of the canal and tend to limit themselves to a few isolated stretches, such as the stretch from the Georgetown part of Washington D.C. for about 20 miles with portages around locks to Seneca, Maryland, and the 7-mile stretch from Oldtown, Maryland, on Route 51 southeast of Cumberland to Town Creek. Rentals: Washington, D.C., La Vale, Maryland, and Oakton, Virginia.

Gunpowder River

Dam at exit of Prettyboy Reservoir about 3 miles north of Route 137 to Falls Road: 2 miles, dangerous whitewater / Falls Road to Phoenix above Loch Raven Reservoir: 15 miles, fine in low and medium water but dangerous in high water / Loch Raven Reservoir is closed to canoes / Cromwell Bridge below Loch Raven Reservoir to Route 1 (Bel Air Road): 6 miles, minor riffles / below Route 1 to tidewater at Route 40: about 4 miles, dangerous whitewater. Rentals: Cockeysville and Ellicott City.

Monocacy River

Route 355 southeast of Frederick to Route 28 just above junction with the Potomac River: 12 miles, one dam and minor riffles.

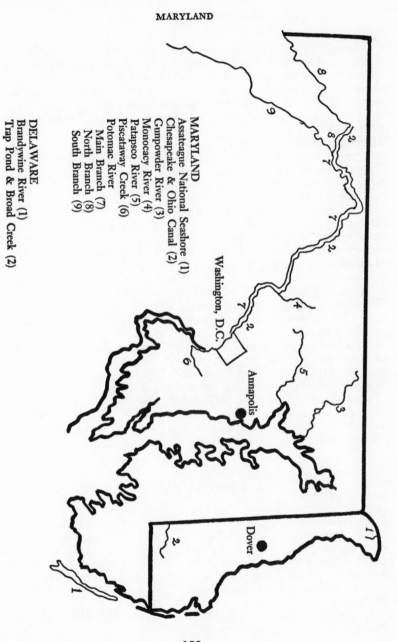

MARYLAND

MARYLAND
Assateague National Seashore (1)
Chesapeake & Ohio Canal (2)
Gunpowder River (3)
Monocacy River (4)
Patapsco River (5)
Piscataway Creek (6)
Potomac River
  Main Branch (7)
  North Branch (8)
  South Branch (9)

DELAWARE
Brandywine River (1)
Trap Pond & Broad Creek (2)

Washington, D.C.

Annapolis

Dover

123

Patapsco River

Sykesville near Route 32 west of Baltimore to Marriotsville Road: 5 miles, minor rapids / Marriotsville Road to Woodstock on Route 125: 3 miles, dangerous falls and rapids / Woodstock to Hollfield above Union Dam: 5 miles, easy canoeing, dangerous whitewaters below this point. Sykesville is on the South Branch which joins the North Branch near Woodstock to form the Main Branch. Rentals: Cockeysville and Ellicott City.

Piscataway Creek

A small tributary of the Potomac River opposite Mount Vernon, Virginia, on the Maryland side. Town of Piscataway on Route 223 to tidewater: about 3 miles. Rentals: Oxon Hill.

Potomac River

Junction of South and North Branches (*see* West Virginia) east of Oldtown, Maryland, on Route 51 to Paw Paw, West Virginia, on Route 9: 10 miles / Paw Paw, West Virginia, to Little Orleans, Maryland: 20 miles / Little Orleans to Hancock on Routes 144 and I–70: 15 miles / Hancock to Williamsport on Route 68: 30 miles, railroad traffic parallels the river / Williamsport to dam 1 mile above Harpers Ferry, West Virginia, and junction with the Shenandoah River: 40 miles / dam to Knoxville, Maryland, below Harpers Ferry, West Virginia: 5 miles, dangerous whitewater / Knoxville to Point of Rocks on Route 15: 11 miles / Point of Rocks to Whites Ferry on Route 107: 14 miles / Whites Ferry to Seneca on Route 112: 14 miles / Seneca to Great Falls of the Potomac dam: 9 miles, difficult, inexperienced canoers should portage into the Chesapeake and Ohio Canal / The Potomac River is not canoeable below the dam and across the falls; the stretch from the Great Falls to Washington, D.C., is for those who are absolutely expert in whitewater canoeing. Below Washington, D.C., the waters are tidal. Rentals: La Vale and Oxon Hill in Maryland, Berryville and Oakton in Virginia, and Washington, D.C.

Maryland Rentals

Cockeysville

Suburban Sales and Rental Center, Inc., 11023 York Road, Box 404, Cockeysville, Md. 21030; telephone: 301–666–2122 / Waters: Gunpowder and Patapsco Rivers / Trips: no response / Best canoeing months: early spring and fall / Campsites: yes / Transportation: no / Car-top carriers: yes / Open all year.

Darlington

Glen Cover Marina, Inc., Route 2, Darlington, Md. 21034; telephone: 301–457–5260 / Unconfirmed.

Edgewater
Pier 7-South River, Route 2, Edgewater, Md. 21037; telephone: 301–956–2288 / Unconfirmed.
Ellicott City
Appalachian Outfitters (Bill Robinson), Box 44, Ellicott City, Md. 21043; telephone: 301–465–7227 or 465–7228 / Waters: anywhere within the region / Trips: 1 or more days / Best canoeing months: December-April for whitewater and May-October for flat water /Campsites: yes / Transportation: no / Car-top carriers: yes / Also rents kayaks and camping equipment / Primarily a backpacking outfitter / Open all year.
Knoxville
River & Trail Outfitters, Box 246, Valley Road, Knoxville, Md. 21758; telephone: 301–834–9950 / Unconfirmed.
La Vale
Cycles & Things, 1231 National Highway, La Vale, Md. 21502; telephone: 301–729–2525 / Waters: Potomac River, and Chesapeake and Ohio Canal, and other area waterways / Trips: 1 or more days / Best canoeing months: spring and fall / Campsites: yes / Transportation: no / Car-top carriers: yes / Open all year.
Oxon Hill
Capital Sailboat Agency, Inc., Fort Washington Marina, Oxon Hill, Md. 20022; telephone: 301–292–2227 or 292–1301 / Waters: Potomac River and Piscataway Creek / Trips: 1 hour to several days / Best canoeing months: April-June, September, and October / Campsites: yes / Transportation: no / Car-top carriers: yes.

Delaware Waters

Brandywine River
Lenape, Pennsylvania, on Route 52 to Rockland, Delaware: about 15 miles / Rockland to Wilmington: about 5 miles, dangerous rapids.
Trap Pond and Broad Creek
Trap Pond State Park west of Laurel on Route 13 to Laurel: about 5 miles, scenic. Rentals: Laurel.

Delaware Rentals

Laurel
Trap Pond State Park, Route 2, Box 331, Laurel, Del. 19956; telephone: 302–875–5153 / Waters: Trap Pond and feeder swamp /

Trips: up to half a day / Best canoeing months: Memorial Day to Labor Day / Campsites: no / Transportation: no / Car-top carriers: no, canoes rented only for paddling from the base.

Washington, D.C. Rentals

Fletcher's Boat House, Chesapeake and Ohio Canal Mile 3, Washington, D.C. 20007; telephone: 202–244–0461 / Waters: Chesapeake and Ohio Canal / Trips: by the hour / Best canoeing months: spring to fall / Campsites: no / Transportation: no / Car-top carriers: no, canoes rented only for paddling from base.

Harry T. Thompson Boating Center (John A. Bardon), Virginia Avenue and Rock Creek Parkway N.W., Washington, D.C. 20037; telephone: 202–333–4861 or 333–9711 / Waters: Potomac River / Trips: 1 or more days / Best canoeing months: spring and fall / Campsites: no / Transportation: no / Car-top carriers: yes.

Sources of Information

Baltimore Trail Book, Appalachian Books (Box 248, Oakton, Va. 22124), $3.00. Mostly hiking, some canoe trails.

Burrell, Robert G. and Paul C. Davidson. *Wild Water West Virginia,* McClain Printing Co. (212 Main Street, Parsons, W. Va. 26287), 1972, 160 pp., $5.00. Description of some 50 rivers most of which are whitewater.

Canoeing Guide to Western Pennsylvania and Northern West Virginia, Pittsburgh Council, American Youth Hostels, Inc. (6300 Fifth Avenue, Pittsburgh, Pa. 15232), 1975, 164 pp., $2.50. Slanted towards whitewater canoeing but several flat water rivers are included.

Carter, Randy. *Canoeing Whitewater River Guide,* Appalachian Books (Box 248, Oakton, Va. 22124), 1974, 267 pp., $5.00. Covers Virginia, eastern West Virginia, North Carolina, and the Great Smoky Mountain Area.

Corbett, H. Roger, Jr. and Louis J. Matacia. *Blue Ridge Voyages, Vol. 1: One- and Two-Day River Cruises in Maryland, Virginia, and West Virginia,* Blue Ridge Voyageurs (P.O. Box 32, Oakton, Va. 22124), 1973, 83 pp., $3.50.

————*Blue Ridge Voyages, Vol. 2,* Blue Ridge Voyageurs (P.O. Box 32, Oakton, Va. 22124), out of print, reprint expected. An additional 10 canoe trips within 160 miles of Washington, D.C.

————*Blue Ridge Voyages, Vol. 3: One-Day River Cruises in Virginia and West Virginia,* Blue Ridge Voyageurs (P.O. Box 32, Oakton, Va. 22124), 1972, 116 pp., $3.50.

See also Matacia, Louis J.

Delaware fishing and hunting information is available from Delaware Division of Fish and Wildlife (William Penn Street, Dover, Del. 19901).

Delaware tourist information is available from Delaware State Visitors Service (45 The Green, Dover, Del. 19901).

Maryland fishing and hunting information is available from Maryland Fish and Wildlife Administration (State Office Building, P.O. Box 231, Annapolis, Md. 21401).

Maryland tourist information is available from Maryland Department of Economic and Community Development, Tourist Division (2525 Riva Road, Annapolis, Md. 21401).

Matacia, Louis J. and Owen S. Cecil III. *Blue Ridge Voyages, Vol. 4: An Illustrated Canoe Log of the Shenandoah River and its South Fork,* Blue Ridge Voyageurs (P.O. Box 32, Oakton, Va. 22124), 1974, 171 pp., $6.95.

Robinson, William M., Jr. *Central Maryland Trips, Maryland-Pennsylvania Countryside Canoe Trails,* Appalachian Books (Box 248, Oakton, Va. 22124), 1974, 34 pp., $1.00.

Virginia fishing and hunting information is available from Virginia Commission of Game and Inland Fisheries (P.O. Box 11104, Richmond, Va. 23230).

Virginia tourist information is available from Virginia State Travel Service (6 North 6th Street, Richmond, Va. 23219).

West Virginia fishing and hunting information is available from West Virginia Department of Natural Resources (Capital Building, Charleston, W. Va. 25305).

West Virginia tourist information is available from West Virginia Department of Commerce, Travel Development Division (State Capital, Charleston, W. Va. 25305).

●

THE CAROLINAS

THE CAROLINAS HAVE THE DUBIOUS DISTINCTION of being the source of the *"Deliverance* syndrome" — the urge to prove one's manhood by senselessly risking one's neck canoeing on an uncanoeable river. The river scenes for the movie *Deliverance,* which depicts the confrontation of four suburban men with nature, were filmed on the Chattooga River which rises in North Carolina and forms the border between South Carolina and Georgia before being impounded in Tugaloo Lake.

As a result of the movie, innumerable incompetents went on the Chattooga and other wildwater rivers, caused innumerable accidents, and gave canoeing a bad name among the authorities who came to fish for the bodies and mend the broken limbs. In some areas, authorities are making efforts to ban certain rivers to canoeists altogether, competent or not.

Anyone who saw the film could not fail to recognize the Chattooga as an unusual survivor of remote and wild virgin nature. Its very remoteness and wildness saved it from the deadening hands of commercialism and the U.S. Army Corps of Engineers. But only a short stretch is suitable for contemplative family canoeing. Most of the course is for whitewater stars and rubber rafters only.

Whitewater enthusiasts share some of the responsibility for the Chattooga's dangerous halo. A South Carolina canoe club member with whom I spoke wanted to be sure that the river be identified with his state rather than North Carolina, which apparently gets some unjustified credit for harboring the source of the river and the uncanoeable upper course.

When driving from the north to Florida via the Carolinas, a traveller gets intriguing glimpses from highway bridges of quiet rivers lined with cypress, swamp oaks, and dangling vines draped with Spanish moss. If he is a canoeist he is tempted to stop and put in to explore these enticing waterways.

Published information from official sources on the waters of North and South Carolina is very sketchy and the mileages given in this chapter are only estimates. But from what I have seen of them, the rivers are well worth exploring, in addition to the streams of the popular Blue Ridge and Smoky Mountains, where car traffic is, unfortunately, bumper to bumper during the tourist season.

And a word of caution: if you like wine with your picnic, plan and search for it well ahead of the need. The Carolina liquor laws defy understanding by the uninitiated.

North Carolina Waters

Black River

Formed by junction of Great Coharie Creek and Six Run Creek east of Garland on Route 411 to Route 53: about 30 miles / Route 53 to junction with Cape Fear River west of Route 42 and tidal water above Wilmington on Route 421: about 20 miles.

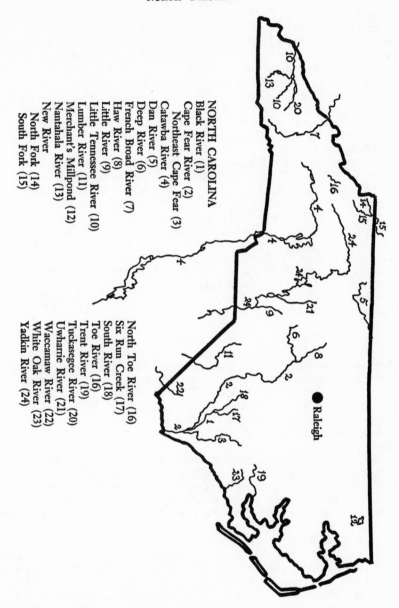

NORTH CAROLINA

Black River (1)
Cape Fear River (2)
Northeast Cape Fear (3)
Catawba River (4)
Dan River (5)
Deep River (6)
French Broad River (7)
Haw River (8)
Little River (9)
Little Tennessee River (10)
Lumber River (11)
Merchant's Millpond (12)
Nantahala River (13)
New River
North Fork (14)
South Fork (15)

North Toe River (16)
Six Run Creek (17)
South River (18)
Toe River (16)
Trent River (19)
Tuckasegee River (20)
Uwharrie River (21)
Waccamaw River (22)
White Oak River (23)
Yadkin River (24)

Cape Fear River

Formed by junction of Deep River and Haw River at Haywood off Route 1 southwest of Raleigh to Route 42 northeast of Sanford: 5 miles / Route 42 to tidal water at Wilmington on Route 421: about 145 miles, many intermediate access points, via Fayetteville on I-95 and Bladen Lakes State Forest on Route 701.

Northeast Cape Fear River: Route 41 at Chinquapin to Route 53 northeast of Burgaw: about 40 miles / Route 53 to Route 210 east of town of Rocky Point: about 20 miles / Route 210 to tidal waters above Wilmington on Route 421: about 20 miles.

Catawba River

County Road 1234 off I-40 (Parker Padgett Road exit) to Route 221 north of Marion: 12 miles / a few miles below Route 221 is backwater of Lake James / Lake James exit west of Glen Alpine on Route 70 to Route 18 at Morganton: 16 miles, water level depends on release from dam / at Morganton is backwater of Lake Rhodhiss, river continues through innumerable impoundments into South Carolina and is renamed the Wateree River (*see* South Carolina) after it exits from Fishing Creek Pond near Route 47 and flows to the Atlantic Ocean via Lake Marion and Lake Moultrie. It is called the Cooper River (*see* South Carolina) on the stretch from Lake Moultrie to the Atlantic Ocean.

Chattooga River

See South Carolina.

Dan River

Jessup's Mill on Route 1432 off Route 89 via Route 1413 north of Francisco to Route 704 east of Francisco: 10 miles / Route 704 to Danbury on Route 89: about 25 miles, 2 intermediate access points on Route 89 / Danbury to Route 311 northeast of town of Walnut Cove: about 20 miles / Route 311 to Route 704 at Madison: about 20 miles / Madison to Eden on Route 87: about 30 miles / Eden to Danville, Virginia, on Route 58: 40 miles / river ends in John H. Kerr Reservoir below Danville in Virginia.

Deep River

Above Route 42 at Coleridge is whitewater and the river is too shallow for canoeing in dry spells. Route 42 to Route 22 at Highfalls: about 35 miles / Route 22 to Route 42 at Carbonton: about 25 miles / Carbonton to Route 421 about 7 miles northwest of Sanford: 12 miles / Route 421 to junction with the Haw River at Haywood near Route 1: about 20 miles.

French Broad River

U.S. 64 at Rosman to Route 276 at Brevard: about 20 miles / Route 276 to Route 64 at Etowah: about 20 miles / Route 64 to power dam on Route 191 north of Asheville: about 35 miles / Asheville to Hot Springs on Routes 25-70: about 40 miles, dangerous whitewater / Hot Springs and junction with the Pigeon River in Tennessee above backwater of Douglas Lake: about 40 miles, easier whitewater, most of this stretch is in Tennessee. Rentals: Arden.

Haw River

Above Routes 15–501 south of Chapel Hill the Haw River is too low in dry spells. Routes 15–501 to Route 1: about 15 miles, whitewater which can be very dangerous in high water / Route 1 to junction with the Deep River to form the Cape Fear River: about 4 miles.

Little River

Route 24–27 east of Troy to Route 731 east of Mt. Gilead: about 20 miles, flows through Uwharrie National Forest / Route 731 to junction with the Pee Dee River: 15 miles.

Little Tennessee River

Route 28 at Iotla to Lost Bridge on Route 28: 12 miles, easy whitewater / Lost Bridge to Route 19 at Fontana Lake: 15 miles, in Nantahala National Forest, dangerous whitewater especially near Fontana Lake / for river below Fontana Lake, *see* Tennessee. Rentals: Arden and Bryson City.

Lumber River

Boardman on Routes 74–130 via Fair Bluff on Routes 76–904 to junction with the Little Pee Dee River in South Carolina: about 40 miles.

Merchant's Millpond

Off Route 158 at Gatesville is this scenic swamp area with much wildlife, canoe this area only with an experienced guide.

Nantahala River

Route 64 at Rainbow Springs to Nantahala Lake entry: 10 miles, easy whitewater / Nantahala Lake is 5 miles long and offers pleasant lake canoeing, the river is not canoeable immediately below exit from the lake / Nantahala powerhouse at Beechertown on Route 19 to Wesser on Route 19: 8 miles, popular but very dangerous whitewater racecourse. The river flows through Nantahala National Forest. Rentals: Arden and Bryson City.

New River

North Fork: Ashland on Route 88 to Route 88 bridge west of Clifton: 14 miles / Clifton to Route 194 at Warrensville: 10 miles / Route 194 to Route 16 near Crumpler: 15 miles / Route 16 to junction with the South Fork: 10 miles / the upper course of the North Fork is canoeable in high water only.

South Fork: Route 421 east of Boone to County Road 1347 near Todd: 18 miles, canoeable in high water only / Todd to Fleetwood off Route 221: 10 miles / Fleetwood to Route 163: 17 miles / Route 163 to Routes 16–88 east of Jefferson: 14 miles / Routes 16–88 to Route 221 west of Scottville: 15 miles / Route 221 to Mouth of Wilson, Virginia, on Route 58: 15 miles. Rentals: Blowing Rock.

North Toe River and Toe River

Spear on Route 19E to Ingalls on Route 19E: about 6 miles, easy whitewater / Ingalls to Route 80 below Penland: about 20 miles, some difficulties at broken dams / Route 80 past confluence with the South Toe River to Route 197 at town of Red Hill: 17 miles, some difficulties above and below confluence with South Toe River / Route 197 to junction with the Cane River: about 12 miles.

Six Run Creek

Route 24 east of Clinton to junction with the Black River east of Garland on Route 411: about 30 miles.

South River

Route 242 south of Roseboro to junction with the Black River off Route 210 west of Atkinson on Route 53: about 30 miles.

Trent River

Route 258 south of Kinston to Route 58 west of Trenton: about 30 miles / Route 58 to Trenton: about 10 miles / Trenton to Route 17 at Pollocksville: 15 miles / Route 17 to tidal waters at Trent Woods off Route 17: about 20 miles, flows along Croatan National Forest.

Tuckasegee River

Route 107 at town of Tuckasegee to Cullowhee dam on Route 107: 10 miles, some difficult whitewater / dam to Dillsboro dam on Routes 19A–441: 11 miles, easy whitewater / dam to Barkers Creek Bridge on Route 19A: 5 miles, dangerous whitewater / bridge to Whittier on Route 19A: 8 miles, easy whitewater / Whittier to Bryson City on Route 19: 10 miles, dangerous whitewater. Rentals: Arden and Bryson City.

Uwharrie River

Route 49 west of Asheboro to Route 109 at town of Uwharrie in Uwharrie National Forest: about 30 miles, too shallow in dry spells / Route 109 to Lake Tillery: 7 miles.

Waccamaw River

See South Carolina.

White Oak River

Route 17 at Maysville to tidal waters: 20 miles, flows along Croatan National Forest, scenic.

Yadkin River

Route 268 at Patterson to W. Kerr Scott Reservoir west of Wilkesboro on Route 421: about 30 miles / the reservoir is about 5 miles long and is scenic / reservoir exit to Elkin on Route 21: about 30 miles / Elkin to Siloam: about 30 miles / Siloam to Route 67 east of East Bend: about 20 miles, a number of rapids, dangerous in medium and high water / Route 67 to Route 421 west of Winston-Salem: 15 miles / Route 421 to Route 158 southwest of Winston-Salem: 20 miles / Route 158 to Route 64 west of Lexington: 25 miles, dangerous dam at

Tanglewood Park / Route 64 to junction with the South Fork of the Yadkin River and backwater of High Rock Lake: 30 miles / emerging from its impoundments, the Yadkin River becomes the Pee Dee River and then flows into South Carolina.

North Carolina Rentals

Arden
Balsam Quarter Tac, Inc., Route 1, Long Shoals Road, Arden, N.C. 28704; telephone: 704–684–8445 or 684–7652 / Waters: French Broad, Nantahala, Little Tennessee, Tuckasegee, and Chattooga Rivers and other waterways, many with whitewater / Trips: 1 or more days / Best canoeing months: April-October / Campsites: yes / Transportation: no / Car-top carriers: yes / Also rents rafts / Open all year.

Blowing Rock
Appalachian Outfitters of Carolina, Route 1, Box 88D, Blowing Rock, N.C. 28605; telephone: 704–295–3123 or 295–3751 / Waters: South Fork of the New River, with guides only / Trips: 1 or more days / Best canoeing months: April-June / Campsites: yes / Transportation: yes / Car-top carriers: no.

Bryson City
Nantahala Outdoor Center (Payson and Aurelia Kennedy), Star Route, Box 68, Bryson City, N.C. 28713; telephone: 704–488–6406 / Waters: Nantahala, Little Tennessee, Chattooga, and Tuckasegee Rivers, Fontana Lake, and other Carolina waterways, many with whitewater / Trips: 1 or more days, guides available / Best canoeing months: good all year, high water from January to June, low water from August to November / Campsites: yes / Transportation: yes, by special arrangement / Car-top carriers: yes / Complete outfitters for camping / Also rents kayaks and offers instruction for whitewater canoeing and kayaking / Rafting / Year-round lodgings and housekeeping units / Open all year.

Greensboro
Blue Ridge Mountain Sports, 1507 Spring Garden Street, Greensboro, N.C. 27403; telephone: 919–275–8115 / Waters: nearby waterways / Trips: 1 or more days / Best canoeing months: good all year / Campsites: yes / Transportation: no / Car-top carriers: yes / Also rents camping equipment / Open all year.

Mill Spring
Silver Creek Camping Park & Canoe Livery, Silver Creek Road, Route 2, Box 37, Mill Spring, N.C. 28756; telephone: 704–488–8302 /Unconfirmed.

Winston-Salem
   Tommy McNabb-Rent-A-Canoe, 5531 Pinebrook Lane, Winston-Salem, N.C. 27105; telephone: 919–767–4752 / Unconfirmed.
   Pack 'n Paddle/The Paddle Shop, 4240 Kernersville Road, Winston-Salem, N.C. 27107; telephone: 919–784–7422 / Unconfirmed.

South Carolina Waters

Ashley River
   Route 165 northwest of Charleston to tidal waters: about 20 miles.
Black River
   Route 52 at Kingstree to Route 377 south of Kingstree: 10 miles / Route 377 to Route 41 north of Andrews: 30 miles / Route 41 to Route 51 northwest of Georgetown: 20 miles / Route 51 to Route 701 north of Georgetown: 20 miles / Route 701 to Winyah Bay at Georgetown on Route 17: 10 miles.
Broad River
   Route 29 east of Gaffney to junction with the Saluda River at Columbia on Route 126: about 160 miles, flows through Sumter National Forest and Parr Reservoir.
Chattooga River
   This is the river seen in the film *Deliverance*. Burells Ford off Route 107 north of Walhalla on Route 28 to backwater of Tugaloo Lake off Routes 23–441 in Georgia: about 35 miles, exciting and often dangerous whitewater / A somewhat easier stretch with what has been described as an "exciting ledge" good for beginning whitewater canoeists runs from Route 28 to Earls Ford, accessible from Whetstone Road off Route 28, a 9-mile stretch. Rentals: Arden and Bryson City in North Carolina, and for rafters at Long Creek, South Carolina.
Combahee River
   Can be paddled upstream in slow current from Route Alternate 17 northeast of Yemassee at junction of the Salkehatchie and Little Salkehatchie Rivers: about 10 miles / and downstream from Route Alternate 17 to Route 17 and tidal water: about 40 miles, 20 miles to Route 17, 20 miles to tidal water.
Congaree River
   Columbia on Route 126 to Lake Marion below Route 601: about 60 miles, power boat traffic.
Cooper River
   Drains Lake Moultrie to Atlantic Ocean at Charleston on Route 17: about 50 miles, wide with power boats, but several side creeks allow for quiet canoeing and nature watching in Francis Marion National Forest. *See* Catawba River in North Carolina.

134

SOUTH CAROLINA

SOUTH CAROLINA
Ashley River (1)
Black River (2)
Broad River (3)
Chattooga River (4)
Combahee River (5)
Congaree River (6)
Cooper River (7)
Edisto River
Main Branch (8)
North Fork (9)
South Fork (10)
Four Hole Swamp (11)
Little Pee Dee River (12)
Pee Dee River (13)
Saluda River (14)
Santee River (15)
Waccamaw River (16)
Wateree River (17)

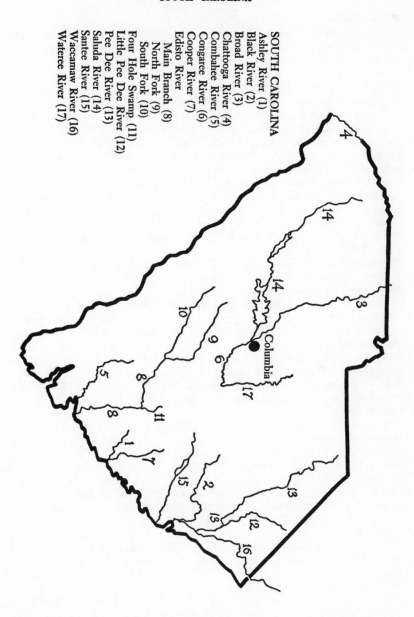

Edisto River

Main Branch: Formed by confluence of North and South Forks above Route 78 southwest of Branchville, the Main Branch is wider than either of the forks and power boats use the lower course. Route 78 to Route 21 south of Branchville: 12 miles / Route 21 to Route 15 at Canadys: 25 miles / Route 15 to Route 61 west of Givhans: 30 miles / Route 61 to Route 17 at Jacksonboro: about 40 miles, tidal waters below Route 17.

North Fork: Route 215 south of Pelion to Route 3: 12 miles / Route 3 to Route 394 southeast of town of North 10 miles / Route 394 to Route 321 south of town of North: 5 miles /Route 321 to Orangeburg on Route 301: 30 miles / Orangeburg to junction with the South Fork west of Branchville on Route 78: about 30 miles.

South Fork: Route 113 north of Williston to Route 39 southwest of Springfield: 10 miles / Route 39 to Route 3 south of Springfield: 5 miles / Route 3 to Route 321 at Sweden: 20 miles / Route 321 to Route 301 north of Bamberg: 15 miles / Route 301 to junction with the North Fork west of Branchville on Route 78: 20 miles.

Four Hole Swamp

Junction of Routes 78 and 178 northwest of Charleston to junction with the Edisto River: 12 miles, fast water, scenic.

Little Pee Dee River

Route 9 east of Dillon to junction with the Lumber River east of Mullins below Route 76 bridge: about 30 miles / Mullins to junction with the Pee Dee River above Route 701: about 60 miles.

Pee Dee River

Route 15 southwest of Bennettsville to tidal waters and Winyah Bay near Georgetown on Route 17: about 150 miles, crosses Routes 34 northeast of Darlington, Route 301 east of Florence, Route 378 north of Kingsburg, and Route 701 below junction with the Little Pee Dee River.

Saluda River

Various access points southeast of Greenville on I–85 to Lake Greenwood backwater near town of Ware Shoals on Route 25: about 35 miles, canoeable in high water only, whitewater stretches / Lake Greenwood exit to Lake Murray: about 25 miles, flow depends on water release from Lake Greenwood / Lake Murray is about 25 miles long / Lake Murray exit to confluence with the Broad River at Columbia on Route 126: about 10 miles, dangerous falls on this stretch, confluence of Saluda and Broad Rivers forms the Congaree River.

Santee River

Lake Marion along Francis Marion National Forest to tidewater: about 100 miles, power boat traffic, scenic side trips are possible into the forest.

Waccamaw River

Old Dock, North Carolina, on Route 130 below Lake Waccamaw in North Carolina to Route 9 in South Carolina southeast of Longs: about

50 miles / Route 9 to tidal waters of Winyah Bay near Georgetown on Route 17: about 70 miles, interconnecting channels with the Pee Dee River in the lower reaches.

Wateree River
Connects Wateree Lake north of Camden on Routes 1–601 with Lake Marion: about 100 miles, power boat traffic. *See* Catawba River in North Carolina.

South Carolina Rentals

Long Creek
Nantahala Outdoor Center, Chattooga Outpost, Long Creek, S.C. 29658; telephone: 803–647–9014 / primarily for rafting trips on the Chattooga River. *See* Bryson City, North Carolina.

Seneca
Harris Sporting Goods, Inc., Seneca, S.C. 29678; telephone: 803–882–3291 / Unconfirmed.

Sources of Information

Benner, Bob. *Carolina Whitewater: A Canoeist's Guide to Western North Carolina*, Pisgah Providers (P.O. Box 101, Morganton, N.C. 28655, 1976, 142 pp., $4.00. Detailed descriptions of rivers, most of which are difficult whitewater, a few are easy whitewater, no flat water river descriptions.

Kissner, J. *Fabulous Folbot Holidays*, Folbot Corp. (Stark Industrial Park, Charleston, S.C. 29405), n.d., 308 pp., $2.75. A general guide about kayaking with useful information on Carolinas waterways and other parts of the country and abroad.

Little Tennessee Valley Canoe Trails, Tennessee Valley Authority (301 West Cumberland Avenue, Knoxville, Tenn. 37902), a free publication with maps on 6 Smoky Mountain canoe streams, mostly whitewater.

North Carolina fishing and hunting information is available from North Carolina Wildlife Resources Commission (P.O. Box 2919, Raleigh, N.C. 27602).

North Carolina tourist information is available from North Carolina Department of Natural and Economic Resources, Travel Development Section (Raleigh, N.C. 27611).

South Carolina fishing and hunting information is available from South Carolina Wildlife Resources Department (Box 167, Columbia, S.C. 29202).

South Carolina tourist information is available from South Carolina

Department of Parks, Recreation, and Tourism, Inquiry Division (Box 71, Columbia, S.C. 29202).

Trails and Streams of North Carolina, North Carolina Department of Natural and Economic Resources, Travel Development Section (Raleigh, N.C. 27611), a free 20-page brochure.

•

GEORGIA

GEORGIA'S CLAIM TO FLAT WATER CANOEING FAME is the Okefenokee Swamp at the southern edge of the state. One of the most exotic wilderness and wildlife areas in the nation, it has become a popular tourist attraction — but as with so many things for which demand exceeds supply, canoeing in the swamp has become rationed. You have to apply for a permit before you can go in. This assures you of some privacy with nature.

To enjoy the swamp fully involves overnight camping, preferably with an insect repellent and a staunch heart that isn't rattled by lethargic alligators, mysterious animal noises at night, and mice scurrying through the tent. However, the luxuriant intimacy of the waterways, the great variety of water birds and of subtropical aquatic vegetation, and the feeling of complete remoteness amply compensate for minor inconveniences. Those who don't want to camp out can find overnight facilities at the Stephen Foster entrance to the park and can take a short day trip by canoe or party boat.

Tourist authorities have begun to publicize the scenic attractions of a few other flat water rivers in southern Georgia, notably the Satilla and Alapaha Rivers. Reportedly other coastal rivers offer similar scenic flat water pleasures in remote wilderness areas, including the Canoochee and the Ogeechee Rivers, but no information is available on them. Canoe club members in Georgia all seem to be whitewater fans who don't look downstream beyond the last rapid.

As this book went to press, the Sierra Club chapter in Georgia was working on a guide to flat water rivers, and anyone wanting to investigate Georgia flat waters may want to check with the club about the guide's progress.

Georgia Waters

Alapaha River

Route 135 near Willacoochee to Route 168 east of Nashville: 20 miles / Route 168 to Routes 122–129 east of Lakeland: 18 miles / Lakeland to Route 84 west of Stockton: 18 miles / Route 84 to Route

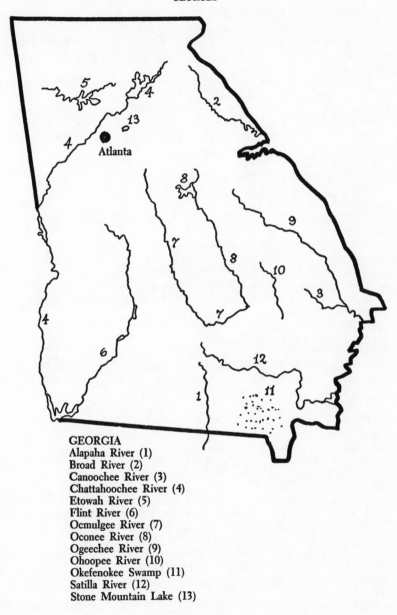

GEORGIA
Alapaha River (1)
Broad River (2)
Canoochee River (3)
Chattahoochee River (4)
Etowah River (5)
Flint River (6)
Ocmulgee River (7)
Oconee River (8)
Ogeechee River (9)
Ohoopee River (10)
Okefenokee Swamp (11)
Satilla River (12)
Stone Mountain Lake (13)

187 west of Mayday 12 miles / Route 187 to Route 94 at Statenville: 15 miles, end of the official canoe trail, some minor rapids / Route 94 to junction with the Suwannee River in Florida: about 30 miles. Rentals: Branford, Florida.

Broad River

Route 29 southwest of Franklin Springs to Route 172 southwest of Bowman: 15 miles / Route 172 to Route 72 west of Oglesby: 20 miles / Route 72 to Route 77 south of Elberton 15 miles / Route 77 to Route 17 south of Bell: 12 miles / Bell to Clark Hill Reservoir: 10 miles, passes through Nancy Hart State Park / Some easy to intermediate whitewater in the upper course.

Canoochee River

Route 46 west of Metter to junction with the Ogeechee River above Route 17 southwest of Savannah: about 60 miles.

Chattahoochee River

Difficult whitewater above Sidney Lanier Lake. Below the lake are some difficult rapids but then the water is mostly smooth via Atlanta, where it is polluted, to West Point Reservoir on the Alabama state line. Below West Point Reservoir the river forms the boundary with Alabama and has two more major impoundments — Lake Harding and Lake Eufaula — before it reaches the Florida Panhandle at Lake Seminole. The stretch from Sidney Lanier Lake to Lake Seminole is about 350 miles long. Rentals: Buford.

Chattooga River

See North and South Carolina.

Etowah River

Whitewater above Route 52 at Jay. Route 52 to Allatoona Lake at Canton to Route 20 about 50 miles, minor rapids / lake exit to junction with the Oostanaula River at Rome on Route 27: 40 miles.

Flint River

Route 18 east of Woodbury to Route 80 east of Carsonville: about 50 miles, scenic but difficult whitewater / Route 80 to Blackshear Lake on Route 280: about 100 miles, mostly flat water, many intermediate access points / Blackshear Lake via Albany to Lake Seminole on the Florida Panhandle: about 150 miles.

Ocmulgee River

Jackson Lake on Route 16 east of Jackson via Macon to the junction with the Oconee River northeast of Hazlehurst on Route 221 forming the Altamaha River; no detailed information available.

Oconee River

Sinclair Lake north of Milledgeville on Route 441 to junction with the Ocmulgee River northeast of Hazlehurst on Route 221, this confluence forms the Altamaha River; no detailed information available.

Ogeechee River

Route 221 west of Louisville to junction with the Canoochee River above Route 17 west of Savannah; no detailed information available.

Ohoopee River

Route 80 west of Swainsboro to junction with the Altamaha River on Route 178 east of town of Altamaha; no detailed information available.

Okefenokee Swamp

A system of 13 designated canoe trails for trips of 1–6 days from 3 access points: 1. Kingfisher Landing Entrance off Routes 1–23 between Waycross and Folkston; 2. Suwannee Canal Entrance off Route 121 south of Folkston; 3. Stephen Foster Entrance on Route 177 off Route 441 at Fargo. Canoeing permit is required, see rentals section for more information. Rentals: Folkston.

St. Marys River

See Florida.

Satilla River

Route 82 northeast of Waycross to Route 15–121 north of Hoboken: 24 miles / Route 15–121 to Route 301 south of Hortense: 30 miles / Route 301 to Route 84 at Atkinson 25 miles / Route 84 to Route 252 at Burnt Fort: 45 miles / Route 252 to Route 17 at Woodbine: 35 miles, tidal estuary below Woodbine.

Sidney Lanier Lake

See Chattahoochee River.

Stone Mountain Lake

A good-sized lake near Atlanta. Rentals: Stone Mountain.

Suwannee River

See Florida.

Withlacoochee River

See Florida.

Georgia Rentals

Acworth

Ponderosa Parks-Atlanta North, U.S. 41, West Kemp Road, Acworth, Ga. 30101; telephone: 404–970–4042 / Unconfirmed.

Buford

Lanier Island Rental, Box 356, Buford, Ga. 30518; telephone: 404–945–6731, 945–6732, or 945–6733 / Waters: Sidney Lanier Lake and many other nearby waterways / Trips: several hours to several days / Best canoeing months: April-September / Campsites: yes / Transportation: no / Car-top carriers: yes / Also rents housekeeping cabins, houseboats, sailboats, paddle boats, and pontoon boats.

Folkston

Okefenokee National Wildlife Refuge, Suwannee Canal Recreation Area (Harry Johnson, concessioner), Route 2, Folkston, Ga. 31537; telephone: 912–496–7156 / Waters: Okefenokee Swamp / Trips: 1–6 days / Best canoeing months: all year / Campsites: yes / Transportation: no / Car-top carriers: yes / Access to canoe trails is only by reservation and permit through Okefenokee National Wildlife Refuge, P.O. Box 117, 411 Pendleton Street, Waycross, Ga. 31501; telephone: 921–283–2580 / Also rents camping equipment /Open all year.

Stone Mountain

Riverboat Activity-Stone Mountain Park (Max Lindholm), P.O. Box 778, Stone Mountain, Ga. 30083; telephone 404–469–9831 / Waters: Stone Mountain Lake / Trips: up to 1 day / Best canoeing months: June-August / Campsites: yes / Transportation: no / Also rents rowboats and sailboats / Open all year.

Sources of Information

Georgia fishing and hunting information is available from Georgia Department of Natural Resources (Trinity-Washington Building, 270 Washington Street S.W., Atlanta, Ga. 30334).

Georgia tourist information is available from Georgia Department of Community Development, Tourist Division (P.O. Box 38097, Atlanta, Ga. 30334) and, for the waterways of southern Georgia, Coastal Plain Area Tourist Council (P.O. Box 1223, Valdosta, Ga. 31601).

•

FLORIDA

ANYONE DEPLORING THE RUIN of Florida's scenery by the epidemic of beach resorts, retirement colonies, industrial sites, amusement parks, power boats, and other manifestations of sun-loving seekers of leisure or work can take consolation in the fact that some of the state's most enticing scenery, vegetation, and animal life have been preserved in its rivers and swamps. As this book went to press, the Florida Department of Natural Resources had designated 32 river sections as wilderness canoe trails, and additional trails are planned.

Because of Florida's pancake flatness, practically all of the rivers have flat water, allowing lovers of nature and leisure to observe the scenery rather than the rocks, eddies, and haystacks. There are a few exceptions, such as the shoals of the Suwannee River, which originates in the Okefenokee Swamp in Georgia as a small, intimate stream and ends as a wide, busy river at the Gulf of Mexico. But all such rapids can be easily portaged.

A vacationing canoeist can tour the state by canoe from the extreme northwestern corner of the Panhandle, where the swift, spring-fed, and remote Perdido River forms the state line with Alabama, to the 100-mile Everglades Wilderness Waterway, through mangrove swamps, to the southernmost tip of the peninsula at Flamingo.

In the Panhandle, a canoeist will find many other attractive waterways heading for the Gulf of Mexico, including the popular Ochlockonee River, which winds its way through a dense forest of pines, cypress, oak, gum, maple, and birch, and the Econfina and Wacissa Rivers, whose crystal-clear waters have cut their way through limestone canyons.

Going further east he can sample some of the rivers coming from Georgia, such as the Withlacoochee (not to be confused with a river of the same name in central Florida) and the Alapaha Rivers, which join the Suwannee River in an extensive canoe trail network. Newly added to the network is another tributary of the Suwannee further downstream, the Santa Fe River, which is joined by one of the most popular canoeing streams in the state, the Ichetucknee River, with its pure spring water flowing over fine bleached sand and its banks lined with cypress and willows.

The Ocala National Forest has several short and picturesque canoeing streams, and to the south of the forest two tributaries of the St. Johns River are very scenic — the Wekiva River near Sanford and the Econlockhatchee River east of Orlando.

What better sylvan pleasures are imaginable than floating down a river named Peace to a town named Arcadia? The Peace River, canoeable for several days from west of Tampa through a dense, subtropical forest with no evidence of human settlement, truly lives up to its name.

Some slow-moving rivers, as well as swamp waterways such as those found in the Everglades, can be easily canoed in both directions thereby eliminating the need for shuttle service. However, such still waters often lack a clearly defined course, and it is easy to get lost on them. So caution is advisable.

Florida is a bird watcher's paradise. And fishermen don't have to exaggerate to impress listeners when talking about their catch.

Florida Waters

Alafia River
Alderman Ford County Park on Route 39 south of Plant City on Route 92 to northwest of Lithia on Route 640: 8 miles / Route 640 to Bell Shoals Road east of Riverview on Route 301: 5 miles.
Alapaha River
See Georgia.

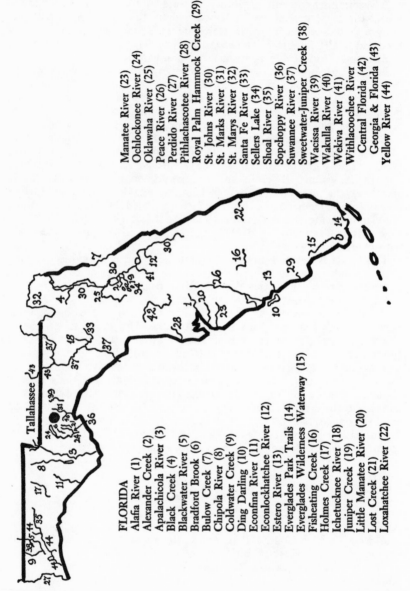

Manatee River (23)
Ochlockonee River (24)
Oklawaha River (25)
Peace River (26)
Perdido River (27)
Pithlachascotee River (28)
Royal Palm Hammock Creek (29)
St. Johns River (30)
St. Marks River (31)
St. Marys River (32)
Santa Fe River (33)
Sellers Lake (34)
Shoal River (35)
Sopchoppy River (36)
Suwannee River (37)
Sweetwater-Juniper Creek (38)
Wacissa River (39)
Wakulla River (40)
Wekiva River (41)
Withlacoochee River
Central Florida (42)
Georgia & Florida (43)
Yellow River (44)

FLORIDA
Alafia River (1)
Alexander Creek (2)
Apalachicola River (3)
Black Creek (4)
Blackwater River (5)
Bradford Brook (6)
Bulow Creek (7)
Chipola River (8)
Coldwater Creek (9)
Ding Darling (10)
Econfina River (11)
Econlockhatchee River (12)
Estero River (13)
Everglades Park Trails (14)
Everglades Wilderness Waterway (15)
Fisheating Creek (16)
Holmes Creek (17)
Ichetucknee River (18)
Juniper Creek (19)
Little Manatee River (20)
Lost Creek (21)
Loxahatchee River (22)

144

Alexander Creek

Alexander Springs Recreation Area on Route 445 in Ocala National Forest to Horseshoe Mud Landing on the St. Johns River: 13 miles. Rentals: Ocala, Sanford, and Silver Springs.

Apalachicola River

Route 90 below dam of Lake Seminole on the Georgia-Florida border to the Gulf of Mexico at the town of Apalachicola on Route 98: about 120 miles, commercial traffic and power boats.

Black Creek

Route 16 west of town of Penney Farms to Route 209 north of Penney Farms: 10 miles / Route 209 to Route 17 at St. Johns River: 7 miles.

Blackwater River

Route 180 west of Escambia Farms below Alabama state line to Route 2 bridge: 5 miles / Route 2 to Route 4 northwest of Baker: 12 miles / Route 4 to forest road northwest of Holt on Route 90: 15 miles, flows through Blackwater River State Forest / forest road to Blackwater River State Park north of Route 90: 8 miles / park to junction with the Coldwater Creek: about 10 miles. Rentals: Milton.

Bradford Brook

In chain of lakes southwest of Tallahassee between Routes 263 and 371, high water needed to canoe connecting channels in the chain of lakes, portage at other times. Rentals: Tallahassee.

Bulow Creek

Bulow Plantation Ruins off Route 5A, upstream 3 miles (no access) and downstream 6 miles to Route 201 and junction with the Intracoastal Waterway north of Ormond on Route A1A.

Chipola River

Florida Caverns State Park off Route 167 north of Marianna to Route 278 between Routes 71 and 73 south of Marianna: about 20 miles / Route 278 to Route 274 east of Chason: 8 miles, rapids, portage recommended / Route 274 to Route 20 east of Clarksville: 10 miles / Clarksville to Route 71 above Dead Lake: 13 miles. Rentals: Tallahassee.

Coldwater Creek

Route 4 west of Munson in Blackwater River State Forest to Berrydale Beach and junction with the West Fork of Coldwater Creek on Route 87 south of Berrydale: about 12 miles / Route 87 to Route 191 northeast of Milton: about 9 miles / Route 191 to junction with the Blackwater River: 4 miles. Rentals: Milton.

Ding Darling Wildlife Sanctuary

On Sanibel Island, a 2-hour marked canoe trail that is a bird watcher's dream. Rentals: Sanibel Island.

Econfina River

Route 167 at Betts north of junction with Route 231 to rural road west of Route 231 at Fountain: 9 miles / rural road to Route 388 at Bennett: 11 miles, tidewater a few miles below Bennett.

145

Econlockhatchee River

Route 50 about 9 miles east of Orlando to Route 419 southeast of Oviedo: about 10 miles / Route 419 to Route 46 below junction with the St. Johns River: about 20 miles, may be too shallow in dry season above Route 419.

Estero River

Route 41 at town of Estero to Estero Bay: 4 miles, canoes can cross the bay to Carl E. Johnson County Park on Route 865.

Everglades National Park Trails

Four trails in the vicinity of the town of Flamingo at the end of the park road, guided tours offered by park rangers, canoe rentals are available at Flamingo with advance reservations placed with the ranger station.

Everglades Wilderness Waterway

Everglades City on Route 29 to Flamingo at the end of Everglades National Park Road: about 100 miles, for small power boats and canoes. Rentals: Chokoloskee Island.

Fisheating Creek

Ingram Crossing Camp Area in Fisheating Creek Wildlife Management Area north of Route 74 and west of Palmdale on Route 27 to Burnt Bridge off Route 74: 9 miles / Burnt Bridge to Fisheating Creek Campground on Route 27 south of Palmdale: 7 miles, marked trail / Route 27 to Lake Okeechobee near Lakeport on Route 78: about 25 miles, stream is unmarked on this stretch. Rentals: Palmdale.

Holmes Creek

Route 79 at Vernon to Route 284 west of New Hope on Route 79: about 20 miles, joins the Choctawhatchee River about 5 miles below Route 284.

Ichetucknee River

Route 238 in Ichetucknee Springs State Park northeast of Branford on Route 129 to Route 27 east of Branford: 4 miles, this section is spring fed and crystal clear / Route 27 to junction with the Santa Fe River: 2 miles, canoeists can continue down the Santa Fe to the Suwannee River. Rentals: Branford.

Juniper Creek

Juniper Springs Recreation Area off Route 40 in Ocala National Forest to Juniper Wayside Park on Route 19: 7 miles. Rentals: Ocala and Silver Springs.

Little Manatee River

Route 674 east of Wimauma to Route 301 south of Sun City Center on Route 674: about 7 miles.

Lost Creek

Apalachicola National Forest Highway 13 northwest of Crawfordville on Route 369, this is a short but winding canoe trail best in June to September at high water; no published mileages. Rentals: Tallahassee.

146

Loxahatchee River
Route 706 east of Jupiter to Jonathan Dickinson State Park west of Route 1 north of Jupiter: 12 miles.

Manatee River
Routes 64–675 to tidal waters east of Bradenton: about 7 miles, then flows into the Gulf of Mexico.

Ochlockonee River
Route 20 below Lake Talquin west of Bloxham on Route 267 to Pine Creek Landing below junction with Telogia Creek off Route 375: 16 miles / Pine Creek Landing to Lower Langston Landing off Route 67: 14 miles / Lower Langston Landing to Mack Landing off Route 375: 10 miles / Mack Landing to Wood Lake off Route 299: 15 miles / Wood Lake to Route 319: 15 miles, wide fluctuation of water levels depending on release of water from dams. A long stretch of the Ochlockonee River flows through Apalachicola National Forest. Rentals: Tallahassee.

Oklawaha River
Sharps Ferry on Route 60C south of Route 40 in Ocala National Forest to Wayside Park at Route 40: 3 miles / Route 40 to Route 316 at Lake Oklawaha: 17 miles / Rodman Dam at exit of Lake Oklawaha to Route 19: 3 miles / Route 19 to junction with the St. Johns River: 3 miles. Rentals: Ocala and Silver Springs.

Peace River
Route 60 at Bartow to Route 98 east of Fort Meade: 22 miles / Route 98 to bridge east of Bowling Green on Route 17: 12 miles / Bowling Green to Route 64A at Wauchula: 8 miles / Route 64A to Route 17 at Zolfo Springs: 7 miles / Zolfo Springs to boat ramp west of Gardner on Route 17: 23 miles / Gardner to Brownville bridge west of Route 17: 6 miles / Brownville to west of Arcadia on Route 70: 11 miles / Arcadia to Route 760 west of Nocatee: 9 miles / Nocatee to Route 761 at Fort Ogden: 17 miles / below Fort Ogden the Peace River flows into Charlotte Harbor and the Gulf of Mexico. Rentals: Arcadia.

Perdido River
Forming the Alabama-Florida state line. West of Pineville, Florida, on Route 99A to Alabama Route 112 west of Muscogee, Florida: about 20 miles / Alabama Route 112 to Route 90 northwest of Pensacola: about 15 miles, from this point it flows into Perdido Bay and the Gulf of Mexico.

Pithlachascotee River
Canoeable from about 5 miles above New Port Richey on Route 19.

Royal Palm Hammock Creek
A 13-mile loop in Collier Seminole State Park on Routes 41–92 at town of Royal Palm Hammock.

St. Johns River

About 250 miles from swamps west of Melbourne on Route 1, the river parallels the Atlantic Coast through Lake Poinsett, Lake Harney, Lake Monroe, Lake Dexter, and Lake George to the mouth of the river east of Jacksonville. Lake Poinsett to Lake Harney: about 35 miles / Lake Harney to Lake Monroe: about 18 miles / Lake Monroe to Lake Dexter: about 25 miles / Lake Dexter to Lake George: about 8 miles / Lake George to the Atlantic Ocean: more than 100 miles. The river is wide and has power boat traffic from Lake George to the Atlantic Ocean, and canoeists have a better time above Lake Harney. Rentals: Sanford.

St. Marks River

Natural Bridge Historical Memorial off Route 363 south of Tallahassee to junction with the Wakulla River south of town of St. Marks on Route 363: about 15 miles. Rentals: Tallahassee.

St. Marys River

Main Branch: Forming the Georgia-Florida state line, from bridge at state line on Route 121 north of Macclenny, Florida, on Route 90 to Georgia Route 94 east of Saint George, Georgia: 26 miles / Route 94 to Traders Hill Park off Georgia Routes 23–121: 33 miles / park to Route 1 at Boulogne, Florida: 4 miles, trail ends at Camp Pickney Park 1 mile below Route 1 / trail's end to the Atlantic Ocean: about 40 miles.

Santa Fe River

Routes 41–441 north of High Springs to Route 47 at Fort White: 14 miles / Route 47 to Route 129 south of Branford: about 12 miles / Route 129 to junction with the Suwannee River: 3 miles. Rentals: Branford and Ocala.

Sellers Lake-Farles Prairie Chain of Lakes

In Ocala National Forest off Route 19, extensive lake and channel canoeing in the high water of June through October.

Shoal River

Route 285 at Dorcas northeast of Crestview to Route 90 east of Crestview: 16 miles / Route 90 to Route 85 south of Crestview: 8 miles / Route 85 to junction with the Yellow River near Route 10 southwest of Crestview and near Eglin Air Force Base: 6 miles. Rentals: Milton.

Sopchoppy River

A new, short canoe trail in Apalachicola National Forest at Sopchoppy on Route 319 southwest of Tallahassee, no mileages published. Rentals: Tallahassee.

Suwannee River

Begins in Georgia at Lem Griffis Hunting and Fishing Camp on Route 177 northeast of Fargo, Georgia, to Route 441 at Fargo: 13 miles / Route 441 to Florida Route 6 bridge: 26 miles / Route 6 to White

Springs Landing on Route 41: 25 miles, some whitewater shoals to be portaged / Route 41 to Route 129 at town of Suwannee Springs: 20 miles / Route 129 to Suwannee River State Park on Route 90: 22 miles, junction with the Withlacoochee River and end of official canoe trail / Many canoeists continue from Route 90 to Route 250 at town of Dowling Park: about 15 miles / Route 250 to Route 51 at Luraville: about 15 miles / Luraville to Branford on Route 27: about 24 miles / Below Branford the river widens and there is power boat traffic for the approximately 100 miles to the Gulf of Mexico. Rentals: Branford and Ocala.

Sweetwater-Juniper Creek

Forest road off Route 191 south of Munson on Route 4 to Blackwater River State Park and junction with the Blackwater River north of Route 90: about 12 miles. Rentals: Milton.

Wacissa River

Route 59 at town of Wacissa Springs east of Tallahassee to Route 98 east of Newport: 15 miles. Rentals: Tallahassee.

Wakulla River

Town of Wakulla Springs off Route 61 south of Tallahassee to junction with the St. Marks River south of town of St. Marks on Route 363: about 10 miles. Rentals: Tallahassee.

Wekiva River

Wekiva Springs State Park north of Orlando off Route 436 to Route 46 west of Sanford: 9 miles / Route 46 to junction with the St. Johns River: 6 miles. Between Route 46 and St. Johns River junction is the Little Wekiva River which is canoeable from about 5 miles upstream to its junction with the Wekiva River. Rentals: Sanford.

Withlacoochee River (Central Florida)

Coulter Hammock Recreation Area on Lacoochee Park Road east of Lacoochee on Route 575 to Route 98 east of town of Spring Lake: 11 miles / Route 98 to town of Silver Lake on I-75: 7 miles / Silver Lake to Route 476 at Nobleton: 10 miles / Route 476 to Route 48 west of Bushnell: 9 miles / Route 48 to Route 44 at Rutland: 15 miles / Route 44 to Route 200: 17 miles / Route 200 to Route 41 and Lake Rousseau reservoir: 15 miles / Rentals: Lake Panasoffkee, Ocala, and Silver Springs.

Withlacoochee River (Georgia and Florida)

Georgia Route 94 northwest of Valdosta, Georgia, to Route 84 west of Valdosta: 8 miles / Route 84 to Rocky Ford Road west of Clyatt-ville, Georgia, on Route 31: 12 miles / Rocky Ford Road to Georgia-Florida state line on Florida Route 145 and Georgia Route 31: 4 miles / state line to Route 6 at town of Blue Springs, Florida: 20 miles / Route 6 to junction with the Suwannee River State Park at Ellaville on Route 90: 12 miles. Rentals: Branford.

Yellow River
Route 2 at Oak Grove to Route 90 west of Crestview: 16 miles /
Route 90 to junction with the Shoal River south of I–10: 6 miles
/ junction to Route 189 south of Holt: 8 miles / Route 189 to Route
87: 20 miles / Route 87 to Pensacola Bay on the Gulf of Mexico: 8
miles. Rentals: Milton.

Florida Rentals

Arcadia
Canoe Outpost (Tex and Donna Stout), Route 2, Box 301, Arcadia,
Fla. 33821; telephone: 813–494–1215 / Waters: Peace River / Trips:
several hours to 8 days, guides available / Best canoeing months: all
year / Campsites: yes / Transportation: yes / Car-top carriers: no /
Also conducts guided trips to the Everglades, Okefenokee Swamp, and
Boundary Waters Canoe Area in Minnesota / Open all year.

Branford
Canoe Outpost (Glenda Gibbs), P.O. Box 473, Branford, Fla. 32008;
telephone: 904–935–1226 / Waters: Suwannee, Santa Fe, Ichetucknee,
Withlacoochee, and Alapaha Rivers / Trips: 1 or more days, guides
available / Best canoeing months: all year / Campsites: yes / Transportation: yes / Car-top carriers: no / Also rents camping equipment
/ Open all year.

Chokoloskee Island
Anglers Motel and Marina (Arvid and Stanley Brown), Chokoloskee
Island, Fla. 33925; telephone: 813–695–2881 / Waters: Everglades
Wilderness Waterway and other Everglades and bay waters /   Trips:
several hours to several days / Best canoeing months: November-April
/ Campsites: yes / Transportation: yes, for 5 or more canoes / Car-
top carriers: yes / Open all year.

Gainesville
Taylor Rental Center, 4308 Northwest 13th Street, Gainesville, Fla.
33538; telephone: 904–748–2237 / Waters: Withlacoochee River /
Trips: up to 1 day / Best canoeing months: October-April, summers
also good but it rains for a part of each day / Campsites: yes / Transportation: no / Car-top carriers: no.

Lake Panasoffkee
Campers World (Olmen Family), Route 1, Lake Panasoffkee, Fla.
33538; telephone: 904–748–2237 / Waters: Withlacoochee River /
Trips: up to 1 day / Best canoeing months: October-April, summers also
good but it rains for a part of each day / Campsites: yes / Transportation: no / Car-top carriers no.

Milton

Bob's Canoe Rental & Sales, Inc., Route 8, Box 34, Milton, Fla. 32570; telephone: 904–623–5457 / Waters: Blackwater, Yellow, and Shoal Rivers and Coldwater, Sweetwater, and Juniper Creeks / Trips: several hours to several days / Best canoeing months: April-November / Campsites: yes / Transportation: yes / Car-top carriers: no / Open all year.

Ocala

John's Canoe Rental (John and Chris Peileke), mailing address only: 829 Northeast 12th Terrace, Ocala, Fla. 32670; telephone: 904–629–7346 / Waters: Santa Fe, Suwannee, Oklawaha, and Withlacoochee Rivers and Juniper Creek, and other area waterways / Trips: 1 or more days / Best canoeing months: all year / Campsites: yes / Transportation: yes / Car-top carriers: yes / Open all year.

Orlando

Barrett's Marine, 4503 North Orange Blossom Trail, Sanford, Fla. 32771; telephone: 305–295–0117 / Waters: Lake Fairview / Trips: up to 1 day / Best canoeing months: summer / Campsites: no / Transportation: no / Car-top carriers: yes / Open all year.

Palmdale

Lykes Fisheating Creek Campgrounds, P.O. Box 100, Palmdale, Fla. 33944; telephone: 813–675–1852 / Waters: Fisheating Creek / Trips: up to 2 days / Best canoeing months: all year / Campsites: yes / Transportation: yes / Car-top carriers: no.

St. Petersburg

Bill Jackson Inc., 1100 Fourth Street South, St. Petersburg, Fla. 33701; telephone: 813–896–8634 / Unconfirmed.

Sanford

Barrett's Marine, 4503 North Orange Blossom Trail, Sanford, Fla. 32771; telephone: 305–321–0900 / Waters: Lake Monroe / Trips: several hours to several days / Best canoeing months: summer / Campsites: no / Transportation: no / Car-top carriers: yes / Open all year.

Wekiva Landing Canoe Club (Katie Moncrief), Wekiva Park Drive, Route 1, Box 184, Sanford, Fla. 32771; telephone: 305–322–4470 / Waters: Wekiva River, St. Johns River, Lake Monroe, Lake Jessup, and other nearby waters / Trips: several hours to several days / Best canoeing months: all year / Campsites: yes / Transportation: yes / Car-top carriers: yes / Owner writes: "A canoeist is able to leave Wekiva Landing and, without portaging, reach Maine." / Also organizes group tours for which guides are available / Open all year.

Sanibel Island

Tarpon Bay Marina, Tarpon Bay Road, Sanibel Island, Fla. 33957; telephone: 813–472–3196 / Waters: Back bays and inlets / Trips: 1 or more days / Best canoeing months: all year / Campsites: no / Transportation: no / Car-top carriers: yes / Open all year.

Silver Springs

Juniper Springs Recreational Services (Shirley and Harry Fleury), Route 1, Box 651, Silver Springs, Fla. 32688; telephone: 904–236–2808 / Waters: Juniper Creek and many nearby waterways / Trips: up to 4 hours / Best canoeing months: all year / Campsites: no / Transportation: yes, but limited / Car-top carriers: no / Open all year.

Tallahassee

Warriors Canoe Livery, 565 East Tennessee Street, Tallahassee, Fla. 32301; telephone: 904–222–6976 / Waters: Wacissa, Wakulla, Ochlockonee, St. Marks, and Sopchoppy Rivers and Lakes Jackson and Talquin and other nearby waterways / Trips: 1 or more days / Best canoeing months: March and April / Campsites: yes / Transportation: no / Car-top carriers: yes / Open all year.

Trenton

Otter Springs Campground, Trenton, Fla. 32693; telephone: 904–463–2696 / Unconfirmed.

Sources of Information

Canoeing — Your Apachicola, Oscecola, and Ocala National Forests, U.S. Department of Agriculture, Forest Service (Southern Region, P.O. Box 1050, Tallahassee, Fla. 32302), a free brochure.

Florida Canoe Trail Guide, Florida Department of Natural Resources, Division of Recreation and Parks (Larson Building, Tallahassee, Fla. 32304), a free booklet with descriptions and maps of trails.

Florida fishing and hunting information is available from Florida Game and Fresh Water Fish Commission (620 South Meridian, Tallahassee, Fla. 32304).

Florida News Bureau, Florida Department of Commerce (410 D Collins, Tallahassee, Fla. 32304) is a source of up-to-date news on all outdoor recreation, including canoeing, in the state. Write to the Outdoors Editor.

Florida tourist information is available from Florida Department of Commerce, Direct Mail Section (107 West Gaines Street, Tallahassee, Fla. 32304).

Florida Trail Association (4410 Northwest 18th Place, Gainesville, Fla. 32605) is a good general source of information. The Association sponsors canoe trips for members.

Truesdell, William G. *Guide to the Wilderness Waterway of the Everglades National Park,* University of Miami Press (Drawer 9088, Coral Gables, Fla. 33124), 1975, 64 pp., $2.50. Description with 27 detail maps of the trail from Everglades City to Flamingo.

KENTUCKY and TENNESSEE

WHETHER OR NOT THEY LIKE IT in Kentucky and Tennessee, the two states are often joined together on maps. This can be justified topographically. Both states are bounded by Appalachian mountain ranges in the east which slope towards the plains in the west. Both have another natural boundary in the west in the Ohio and Mississippi Rivers; and in the case of Kentucky, the Ohio River also forms a natural boundary in the north. Both states have an unusually large number of man-made lakes which generate the largest amount of hydroelectric power in the country and provide hard-working waterways for commercial traffic and a profusion of playgrounds for motorized pleasure boats.

There are subtle scenic differences between the two states. Kentucky's eastern section has more ruggedness, more canyons, more cuts, including the Cumberland Gap, and more wilderness than Tennessee. Except for the Great Smoky Mountains, a spectacular tourist attraction which it shares with North Carolina, Tennessee is populated and industrialized in the eastern section between Knoxville and Chattanooga. In its central region Kentucky has soft limestone formations which created some of the most extensive and attractive caves in the world, including the famous Mammoth Cave. The Green River nearby offers a very scenic canoeing trip.

Tennessee has some of its best wilderness in its west, in the swamps drained by the Hatchie River. And its most popular canoeing stream, the Buffalo River, is found southwest of Nashville.

Except for the heavily impounded Cumberland and Tennessee Rivers, the two states share practically no canoeable rivers.

Kentucky's waterways recommended for quiet water paddling, in addition to the Green River, are the middle section of the Red River, the upper portions of the Rockcastle River, Elkhorn Creek, and the Licking River. Tennessee authorities recommend the Elk, Harpeth, and Clinch Rivers for "amateur canoeists."

In neither state is canoeing as well publicized and commercialized as in neighboring states to the east, west, and north. Published information is scanty and does not always seem reliable. Canoe liveries are few in number but these few are especially helpful with information. Because of the lack of published information and the extreme changes that can

153

occur in water conditions of the free-flowing rivers within a very short time, it is worth consulting canoe rental operators and other local authorities when going on a river for the first time. Several of the rivers get too shallow in dry weather. Others have dangerous whitewaters in their upper reaches. Some have been polluted by strip mining, some are obstructed. But most of them flow through unusually attractive scenery, ranging from wooded mountain valleys and blue grass country to swamp wilderness, and it is well worth the effort to explore them.

One word of warning: If you canoe above the famous Cumberland Falls, be very careful not to go over them. It would be your last trip.

Kentucky Waters

Barren River and Lake
Barren Lake is a narrow, 10,000-acre lake between Routes 31E and 252 southwest of Glasgow. The Barren River is canoeable from the dam at Route 252 to Bowling Green on Route 31W: about 30 miles / Bowling Green to junction with the Green River near Woodbury on Route 263: about 30 miles.

Big Sandy River
Levisa Fork: Dam at Millard on Route 460 to junction with the Tug Fork on Routes 3 and 37: about 90 miles, many intermediate access points, reportedly scenic.

Main Fork: Junction of Levisa and Tug Forks to junction with the Ohio River forming the border between Kentucky and West Virginia: about 20 miles.

Buck Creek
Route 80 about 2 miles east of Shopville to Route 769, 9 miles southeast of Somerset: about 25 miles. Rentals: London.

Cumberland River and Lake
Lake Cumberland: North arm from west of Somerset on Route 80 and south arm from Burnside on Route 27 to the dam at Route 127, a total of about 100 miles of lake canoeing with narrow inlets and side arms for pleasant paddling and fishing. Rentals: London.

Main Branch: Route 204 at Red Bird near Williamsburg on I–75 and Route 92 to Cumberland Falls: 15 miles, very scenic, some pollution, exercise great caution when approaching the falls / below the falls is dangerous whitewater almost to the backwater of Lake Cumberland near Burnside on Route 27 and junction with the Big South Fork: 30 miles / Lake Cumberland to junction with the Ohio River at Paducah on Route 60: about 400 miles, passes through Nashville, Tennessee, many

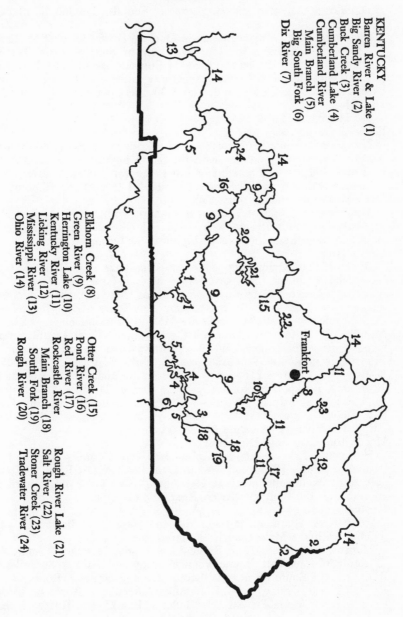

KENTUCKY

Barren River & Lake (1)
Big Sandy River (2)
Buck Creek (3)
Cumberland Lake (4)
Cumberland River
Main Branch (5)
Big South Fork (6)
Dix River (7)

Elkhorn Creek (8)
Green River (9)
Herrington Lake (10)
Kentucky River (11)
Licking River (12)
Mississippi River (13)
Ohio River (14)

Otter Creek (15)
Pond River (16)
Red River (17)
Rockcastle River
Main Branch (18)
South Fork (19)
Rough River (20)

Rough River Lake (21)
Salt River (22)
Stoner Creek (23)
Tradewater River (24)

155

impoundments, limited canoeing appeal. Rentals: London, Kentucky, and Nashville, Tennessee.

Big South Fork: Whitewater above Oneida, Tennessee, west of Route 27. Oneida, Tennessee, to Route 92 west of Stearns, Kentucky: 30 miles, very scenic / Stearns to General Burnside Island State Park and junction with the Main Branch (sometimes called the North Fork) and backwater of Lake Cumberland: about 30 miles. Rentals: London.

Dix River

See Herrington Lake.

Elkhorn Creek

North Fork: Route 1262 northeast of Woodlake on Route 460 northwest of Lexington to junction with the South Fork at Forks of Elkhorn on Route 460 east of Frankfort: 8 miles, canoeable in high water only.

South Fork: Moores Hill Road off Route 421 to Forks of Elkhorn: 16 miles, canoeable in high water only.

Main Branch: Forks of Elkhorn to junction with the Kentucky River at Route 127 south of Swallowfield: 12 miles, scenic. Rentals for both forks and Main Branch: Forks of Elkhorn and Lexington.

Green River

Route 198 at Middleburg to Green River Lake near Route 551 at Neatsville: 40 miles, the lake is 8,360 acres in area and is about 30 miles long / lake dam at Route 55 south of Campbellsville to Greensburg on Route 68: 30 miles / Greensburg to Route 31E north of Canmer: 36 miles / Route 31E to Route 31W at Munfordville: 14 miles / Munfordville to ferry in Mammoth Cave National Park: 32 miles, very scenic / ferry to Routes 259–70 at Brownsville: 15 miles, scenic / Brownsville to Route 79 at Aberdeen: 28 miles / Aberdeen to Routes 70–369 at Rochester: 21 miles / Rochester to Route 62 at Rockport: 20 miles / Rockport to Route 431 at Livermore: 28 miles / Livermore to Route 56 at Sebree: 37 miles / Sebree to Route 54 at Bluff City near Hebbardsville: 36 miles / Route 54 to junction with the Ohio River at Henderson on Route 41: 35 miles.

Herrington Lake and Dix River

Herrington Lake is 1,860 acres in area and 35 miles long and is located at Routes 27–34 northeast of Danville. The Dix River is canoeable from its impoundment at Herrington Lake for 7 miles until it empties into the Kentucky River. Rentals: Lexington.

Kentucky River

South Fork: Route 11 at Booneville to Route 52 at Beattyville and junction with the Main Branch: 12 miles, some rapids.

Main Branch: Route 52 to Route 89 at Irvine: 38 miles / Route 89 to Route 627 at Fort Boonesborough State Park: about 50 miles / Route 627 to Route 68 near Wilmore: about 50 miles / Route 68 to Route 62 near Tyrone, west of Versailles: 26 miles / Route 62 to St. Clair Street bridge in Frankfort: 26 miles / Frankfort to Route 22 near

Gratz: 39 miles / Gratz to junction with the Ohio River at Carrollton on Route 36: about 35 miles. Rentals: Camp Nelson and Lexington.

Licking River

Route 460 southeast of West Liberty to Cave Run Lake on Route 1274: about 40 miles / through lake to dam above town of Farmers on Route 60: about 30 miles / Farmers to Falmouth on Route 22: about 100 miles / Falmouth to Newport on Route 27 and junction with the Ohio River on the Kentucky side at Cincinnati: 45 miles. Rentals: Lexington.

Mississippi River

Forms the boundary between Kentucky and Missouri for about 60 miles. Much commercial traffic on this grandiose, wide river.

Ohio River

Forms the northern boundary of Kentucky from Catlettsburg on Route 23 to junction with the Mississippi River at Cairo on Route 51, a stretch of about 600 miles, scenic in many sections, wide, much commercial traffic.

Otter Creek

Route 60 at Grahampton east of Garrett to Otter Creek Park on the Ohio River south of Louisville on Route 31W–60: 12 miles. Rentals: New Albany, Indiana.

Pond River

Route 62 east of Nortonville to junction with the Green River on Route 138 west of Calhoun: 36 miles.

Red River

Route 746 at Spradlin bridge about 6 miles north of Campton on Route 15 to Route 715 bridge north of Pine Ridge: 9 miles, whitewater / Route 715 to Route 77 north of Slade: 8 miles, smooth / Route 77 to Route 213 north of Stanton: 21 miles / Stanton to junction with the Kentucky River below Route 89: about 20 miles. Rentals: Lexington.

Rockcastle River

Main Branch: Route 89 south of McKee to Route 25 near Livingston: 25 miles / Route 25 to Route 80 west of London: 12 miles / Route 80 to Bee Rock Campground on Route 192: 17 miles, some whitewater / Route 192 to backwater of Cumberland River impoundment at Burnside on Route 27: about 30 miles, scenic in upper course. Rentals: London.

South Fork: Route 30 southwest of Annville to junction with the Main Branch at Route 89 northeast of Livingston: 5 miles. Rentals: London.

Rough River and Rough River Lake

The lake is about 5,000 acres in area and is narrow. The river is canoeable from Route 79 at Axtel to Hartford on Route 231: about 30 miles, passes through Rough River Falls below the lake's dam / Hart-

157

ford to junction with the Green River at Livermore on Route 43: about 30 miles.

Salt River

Route 44 at Taylorsville to Route 31E south of Mount Washington: 25 miles / Route 31E to Route 61 at Shepherdsville: 15 miles / Shepherdsville to junction with the Ohio River at West Point on Route 31W: 25 miles.

Stoner Creek

Spears Mill Road off Route 627 south of Paris to Route 68 at Paris: 13 miles. Rentals: Lexington.

Tradewater River

Route 120 at Belleville west of Providence on Route 293 to junction with the Ohio River near Caseyville on Route 1508: about 40 miles.

Kentucky Rentals

Camp Nelson

Sage Kentucky River Canoe Livery, *see* Lexington.

Forks of Elkhorn

Sage Ekhorn Outpost Canoe Livery, *see* Lexington.

Lexington

Sage, 209 East High Street, Lexington, Ky. 40507; telephone: 606–255–1547 / Waters: Elkhorn and Stoner Creeks and Kentucky, Red, Dix, and Licking Rivers and Herrington Lake / Trips: 1–9 days, guides available; in addition to local trips, Sage offers trips to the Louisiana bayous, Canada, and Cape Hatteras in North Carolina / Best canoeing months: all year for flat water, October-June for whitewater / Campsites: yes / Transportation: yes / Car-top carriers: yes / Also rents kayaks and camping equipment / Instruction for canoeing, kayaking, climbing, sailing, and wilderness survival / Branch locations at Forks of Elkhorn and Camp Nelson / Open all year.

London

Rockcastle Adventures (Jim and Chris Stamm), Box 662, London, Ky. 40741; telephone: 606–864–9407 / Waters: Rockcastle and Cumberland Rivers, Buck Creek, Cumberland Lake, and other nearby waters / Trips: 1 or more days, guides available / Best canoeing months: April-June / Campsites: yes / Transportation: yes / Car-top carriers: yes / No trips for less than 2 canoes.

Louisville

Viking Canoe and Mountaineering Center, 2006 Marilee Drive, Louisville, Ky. 04272; telephone: 502–361–8051 / Unconfirmed.

Tennessee Waters

Buffalo River

Henryville bridge 4½ miles southwest of Summertown on Routes 20–43 to Natchez Trace Parkway: 15 miles / parkway to North Riverside on County Road 6196: 11 miles / North Riverside to Route 13 south of junction with Route 48 near Flatwoods: 18 miles / Route 13 to Flatwoods on Route 13 west of the town: 14 miles / Flatwoods to Linden on Routes 20–100: 18 miles / Linden to Lobelville on Route 13: 20 miles / Lobelville to mouth of river: 30 miles. Rentals: Flatwoods, Lawrenceburg, Nashville, and Waynesboro.

Caney Fork River

Route 70 west of Crossville to backwater of impoundment at Route 111 south of Sparta: about 30 miles / impoundment to Carthage on Route 70N and junction with the Cumberland River: about 20 miles. Rentals: Nashville.

Clear Creek

Route 127 at Clarkrange to Lilly Bridge and junction with the Obed River: 30 miles, mostly whitewater.

Clinch River

Arrives in Tennessee from Virginia, where it is primarily a whitewater river. Northeast of Kyles Ford on Route 70 to Route 31 near Sneedville: about 20 miles / Route 31 to Route 25E: 25 miles, rural, minor rapids; a few miles below Route 25E is backwater of Norris Lake, and the Clinch River continues below the lake through further impoundments to join the Tennessee River at Kingston on Route 70.

Collins River

Route 56 south of McMinnville to backwater of Caney Fork River impoundment at McMinnville: about 15 miles, smooth canoeing. Rentals: Nashville.

Cumberland River

See Kentucky.

Daddy's Creek

Route 127 at Big Lick south of Crossville to Route 70 east of Crossville: 20 miles, minor rapids / Route 70 to Devil's Breakfast Table and junction with the Obed River: 18 miles, whitewater.

Duck River

Route 41 northwest of Manchester to Normandy off Route 41A: 22 miles / Normandy to Shelbyville on Route 231: 25 miles / Route 231 to Route 31A: 30 miles / Route 31A to Pottsville on Route 431: 20 miles / Pottsville to Columbia on Route 31: 40 miles / Columbia to Williamsport on Route 50: 20 miles / Williamsport to second Route 50 crossing at Natchez Trace Parkway: 15 miles / parkway to Centerville on Routes 50–100: 25 miles / Centerville to I–40 at town of

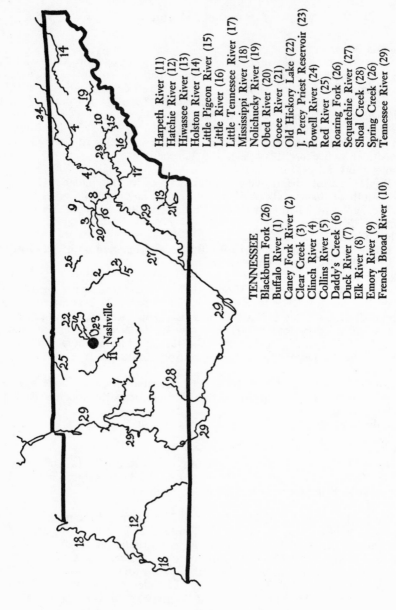

Harpeth River (11)
Hatchie River (12)
Hiwassee River (13)
Holston River (14)
Little Pigeon River (15)
Little River (16)
Little Tennessee River (17)
Mississippi River (18)
Nolichucky River (19)
Obed River (20)
Ocoee River (21)
Old Hickory Lake (22)
J. Percy Priest Reservoir (23)
Powell River (24)
Red River (25)
Roaring Fork (26)
Sequatchie River (27)
Shoal Creek (28)
Spring Creek (26)
Tennessee River (29)

TENNESSEE
Blackburn Fork (26)
Buffalo River (1)
Caney Fork River (2)
Clear Creek (3)
Clinch River (4)
Collins River (5)
Daddy's Creek (6)
Duck River (7)
Elk River (8)
Emory River (9)
French Broad River (10)

Only: 40 miles / I–40 to mouth of river: 30 miles. Rentals: Chapel Hill, Flatwoods, and Nashville.

Elk River

Route 50 west of Winchester below Tims Ford Lake to backwater of Tennessee River impoundment at Route 99 northwest of Athens, Alabama: about 100 miles, slow, rural, other access points at Routes 64 and 231, east and south of Fayetteville, and I–65 and Route 7 near Elkton.

Emory River

Canoeable in high water only from about 11 miles above Route 27 bridge at Wartburg, relatively smooth but unattractive / Route 27 to Routes 27–61 at Harriman: 21 miles, dangerous whitewater for the first 14 miles, then smooth but with minor rapids; below Harriman is backwater of the Tennessee River.

French Broad River

Douglas Lake east of Knoxville to junction with the Tennessee River in Knoxville: about 15 miles.

Harpeth River

Route 31 or 431 north of Franklin to Riverview Drive in Pegram off Route 70: about 30 miles / Pegram to Route 49 near Bellsburg just above Cheatham Lake, impoundment of Cumberland River: about 30 miles. Rentals: Nashville.

Hatchie River

Route 57 at Pocahontas to junction with the Mississippi River about 35 miles north of Memphis: about 200 miles, slow, through swamp and wilderness areas with many intermediate access points including Route 18 north of Bolivar, Route 76 south of Brownsville, and Route 51 south of Ripley.

Hiwassee River

Power dam at North Carolina state line at Farner on Route 68 to Route 411 near Delano: about 20 miles, mostly whitewater / Route 411 to Route 11 at Charleston: about 20 miles, smooth. Rentals: Delano.

Holston River

The North Fork and South Fork, rising in Virginia, join at Kingsport, Tennessee, on Route 11W. Route 11W to Route 66 at Rogersville: about 40 miles, backwater of Cherokee Lake.

Little Pigeon River

Knoxville metropolitan area river, from Route 411 to junction with the French Broad River: about 10 miles.

Little River

Knoxville metropolitan area river, south of the city, from Route 411 to junction with the Tennessee River: about 15 miles.

Little Tennessee River

Tallassee on Route 129 to Route 411 at Niles Ferry: 15 miles / Route 411 to Lenoir City and Watts Bar Lake: 20 miles. Canoe it while you can, for a dam is scheduled to wreck this waterway in 1977.

Mississippi River

The Mississippi River forms Tennessee's western border, shared with Arkansas and Missouri, for about 175 miles. The grandiose, wide river has much commercial traffic.

Nolichucky River

Routes 81 or 107 near Embreeville to Davy Crockett Lake on Route 70: about 30 miles / lake to backwater of Douglas Lake south of Morristown on Route 11E: about 30 miles.

Obed River

Route 127 north of Crossville to junction with the Emory River southwest of Wartburg on Routes 27–62: 34 miles, dangerous whitewater.

Ocoee River

Lake Ocoee at Parksville on Route 64 to junction with the Hiwassee River near Benton on Route 411: about 15 miles.

Old Hickory Lake

Impoundment of Cumberland River at Nashville, motor boats. Rentals: Nashville.

J. Percy Priest Reservoir

Artificial lake of 652,000 acres near Nashville, motor boats. Rentals: Nashville.

Powell River

Route 70 south of Jonesville, Virginia, to Route 25E south of town of Cumberland Gap: about 70 miles, several intermediate access points, may be too shallow in the upper reaches in dry spells / Route 25E to backwater of Norris Lake: about 20 miles, rural scenery, slow.

Red River

Route 161 at Kentucky border northwest of Springfield and below the junction of the North and South Forks to the junction with the Cumberland River at Clarksville on Route 41A: about 35 miles, slow, rural scenery. Rentals: Nashville.

Roaring Fork, Spring Creek, and Blackburn Fork

Route 136 north of Cookeville to the Cumberland River impoundment near Gainesboro: about 20 miles, a favorite whitewater run.

Sequatchie River

Route 30 at Pikeville to junction with the Tennessee River at South Pittsburg on Route 72: about 80 miles, rural, slow, shallow in upper stretches in dry spells, other access points at Route 127 near Dunlap and Route 27 near Whitwell.

Shoal Creek

At Davy Crockett State Park near Lawrenceburg on Route 64 is a 2-hour round trip to the old power dam. The river continues to Iron City near the Alabama border and backwater of the Tennessee River: about 50 miles. Rentals: Lawrenceburg.

Tennessee River

Begins at confluence of the Holston and French Broad Rivers at Knoxville, the river is harnessed all along its 650-mile course to its junction with the Ohio River at Paducah, Kentucky, on Route 60 after a swing through Alabama. The Tennessee River is a commercial waterway rather than a float stream, but it nevertheless has many backwaters and inlets on its numerous impoundments that offer canoeing opportunities. Rentals: Nashville.

Tennessee Rentals

Chapel Hill
Voyageur Canoe Livery, division of Voyageurs of America Family Canoeing, P.O. Box 178, Chapel Hill, Tenn. 37034; telephone: 615–364–2254 or call headquarters in Bruce, Wisconsin: 715–868–6565 or 868–9245 / Waters: Duck River / Trips: several hours to several days / Best canoeing months: May-October / Campsites: yes / Transportation: yes / Car-top carriers: yes.

Delano
Hiwassee Float Service, Inc. (H.C. Sartin), Highway 411, Delano, Tenn. 37325; telephone: 615–263–5581 / Waters: Hiwassee River / Trips: 1–2 days, guides available / Best canoeing months: April-October / Campsites: yes / Transportation: yes / Car-top carriers: yes.

Flatwoods
Buffalo River Canoe Rental Co., Flatwoods, Tenn. 38458; telephone: 615–589–2755 or mobile phones 589–5526 and 589–5527; or in Memphis at 2080 Goodhaven Drive, Memphis, Tenn. 38116; telephone: 901–398–8885 / Waters: Buffalo River and Duck River / Trips: 1 to several days / Best canoeing months: April-October / Campsites: yes / Transportation: yes / Car-top carriers: yes.

Knoxville
Concord Boat Dock, c/o Athletic House, Alcoa Highway, Knoxville, Tenn. 37920; telephone: 615–966–8138 / Unconfirmed.

Lawrenceburg
Davy Crockett Canoe Livery, Inc., Davy Crockett State Park, Highway 64 West, Box 306, Lawrenceburg, Tenn. 38464; telephone: 615–762–3895 (evenings) / Waters: Buffalo River and Shoal Creek / Trips: several hours to several days, guides available / Best canoeing months: April-September / Campsites: yes / Transportation: yes / Car-top carriers: yes.

Memphis
Buffalo River Canoe Rental Co., *see* Flatwoods.

Nashville
Chad's Apache Camping Center, 336 Welch Road, Nashville, Tenn. 37211; telephone: 615–833–0254 / Unconfirmed.

Elm Hill Marina, P.O. Box 17097, Nashville, Tenn. 37217; telephone: 615–889–5363 / Waters: J. Percy Priest Reservoir, Duck River, and Old Hickory Lake / Trips: 1 or more days / Best canoeing months: all year / Campsites: yes / Transportation: no / Car-top carriers: yes / Also rents pontoon boats, and sailboats / Open all year.

Morris Rent-All Center, Inc., 3609 Nolensville Road, Nashville, Tenn. 37211; telephone: 615–833–1000 / Waters: Cumberland, Collins, Harpeth, Red, Tennessee, Buffalo, Duck, and Caney Fork Rivers and other Tennessee waterways / Trips: 1 or more days / Best canoeing months: May-July / Campsites: yes / Transportation: yes / Car-top carriers: yes / Also rents camping equipment / Open all year.

Waynesboro

Buffalo Shoals (Resort) Inc., Box 4, Waynesboro, Tenn. 38485; telephone: 615–722–3960 or 722–5675 / Waters: Buffalo River / Trips: 1 or more days / Best canoeing months: May-October / Campsites: yes / Transportation: yes / Car-top carriers: yes / Open all year.

Sources of Information

Canoeing in Kentucky, Kentucky Department of Public Information (Capitol Annex, Frankfort, Ky. 40601), a free information sheet.

Canoeing in Tennessee, Tennessee Tourism Development Division (Andrew Jackson Building, Nashville, Tenn. 37219), a free folder.

Kentucky fishing and hunting information is available from Kentucky Department of Fish and Wildlife Resources (Capital Plaza, Frankfort, Ky. 40601).

Kentucky tourist information is available from Kentucky Department of Public Information (Capitol Annex, Frankfort, Ky. 40601).

Mid-South River Guide, Bluff City Canoe Club (P.O. Box 5423, Memphis, Tenn. 38104), $1.00 A description of the Buffalo River and rivers in adjacent states.

Principal Floatable Streams in Tennessee, Tennessee Division of Planning and Development, Department of Conservation (26111 West End Avenue, Nashville, Tenn. 37203), a free information sheet.

Sage, School of the Outdoors (209 East High Street, Lexington, Ky. 40507) is preparing an extensive guide to Kentucky rivers.

Tennessee fishing and hunting information is available from Tennessee Wildlife Resources Agency (Ellington Center, Nashville, Tenn. 37220).

Tennessee tourist information is available from Tennessee Tourism Development Division (Andrew Jackson Building, Nashville, Tenn. 37219).

LOUISIANA, MISSISSIPPI, and ALABAMA

BAYOU . . . A SILENT PIROGUE ON SLUGGISH WATERS, floats of purple water hyacinths, swampgrass along a labyrinth of secret channels, gnarled oaks and bald cypress bedecked with Spanish moss, herons, pelicans, ibises, and flocks of noisy ducks dipping their beaks into the water, and blobs of alligator eyes popping up from underneath . . .

It is a canoeing world of subtle mood and mystery. You can drift and dream and watch. No worries, except perhaps to lose your way. And not to let your hand, trailing in the water, accidentally caress a water moccasin.

Bayous arise in flat coastal areas where the river water is backed up by shellbeach ridges, shallow seas, and sluggish tides. And a subtropical sun spurs a luxuriant vegetation. Bayous, stretching along the coast of the Gulf of Mexico, are particularly prevalent in Louisiana and Mississippi on both sides of the Mississippi Delta, most notable among them the Atchafalaya Basin, Bayou Teche, Bogue Chitto, and the Pearl River swamp.

However, the uninitiated should be aware that the Gulf Coast population uses the word "bayou" not only for a coastal swamp but also for what the Pennsylvanians call a "creek". So if you try the Kisatchie Bayou or the Saline Bayou in Kisatchie National Forest, don't expect swamps, but small, fast streams with sand bottoms seen through clear, shallow water.

Canoeing information is only beginning to be assembled in Louisiana and is particularly unorganized in Mississippi and Alabama. The State of Louisiana in 1970 set aside segments of 31 free-flowing rivers and streams to be protected, but there still seems to be controversy about the Act, and the State has not published any information on the streams. The Louisiana information which has been assembled for this chapter comes from private sources.

Information on Mississippi and Alabama is even more sketchy — in declining degree. Mississippi canoe country is closer in character to Louisiana than to Alabama. Waterways in Alabama are widely channelized into three commercial waterways — the Tennessee River in the north, the Warrior-Tombigbee Rivers system in the west, and the Alabama

165

River system in the east, leaving very few free-flowing rivers. The U.S. Army Corps of Engineers is now at work connecting the Tennessee River with the Tombigbee. And that will cost the taxpayers at least $1.6 billion.

The lack of rental services in the three states confirms the impression of a still undeveloped canoeing culture. So for the most part, an enterprising canoeist is left to his own devices and word-of-mouth information from fellow canoeists.

Louisiana Waters

Amite River

Route 10 west of Darlington near the Mississippi border to Route 37–448 at Grangeville: 15 miles, the most popular stretch / Grangeville to Denham Springs on Route 190: about 25 miles / Denham Springs to Lake Maurepas: about 40 miles / Lake Maurepas to Lake Pontchartrain near New Orleans: about 7 miles. Rentals: New Orleans.

Atchafalaya River

Junction of Red River and Old River at Simmesport on Route 1 to Melville on Route 10: about 30 miles / Melville to Route 190 at town of Krotz Springs: 15 miles / Route 190 to junction with the Upper Grand River east of Lafayette on Route 167: 25 miles / junction to Charenton off Route 90: about 30 miles, passes through Grand Lake, short portage to Bayou Teche from Charenton / Charenton to Morgan City on Route 90: about 25 miles, passes through Six Mile Lake / tidal waters below Morgan City to the Gulf of Mexico at Atchafalaya Bay south of Route 90. In its lower section, near the bay, the Atchafalaya River becomes a complex bayou system with interconnecting waterways to other bayous. Guides are recommended for this area. Rentals: Lafayette and New Orleans.

Bayou La Branche

U.S. 61 west of New Orleans to Lake Pontchartrain: about 6 miles.

Bayou Teche

Route 190 between Opelousas and Point Barre to Arnaudville on Route 31: 25 miles / Arnaudville to town of Breaux Bridge on Routes 31–347: 20 miles / Breaux Bridge to St. Martinville on Route 31: 15 miles / St. Martinville to New Iberia on Route 90: 10 miles / New Iberia to Jeanerette on Route 90: 20 miles / Jeanerette to Franklin on Route 90: 15 miles / Franklin to Patterson on Route 90: 10 miles / Patterson to confluence with the Atchafalaya River at Morgan City on Route 90: 10 miles. Rentals: Lafayette and New Orleans.

Bogue Chitto River

Route 98 northwest of Tylertown, Mississippi, to Route 48 west of

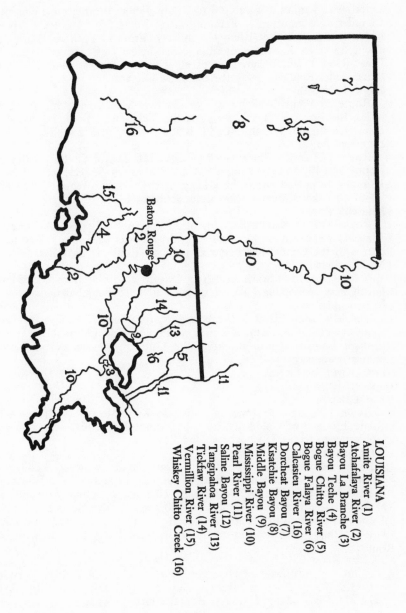

LOUISIANA
Amite River (1)
Atchafalaya River (2)
Bayou La Branche (3)
Bayou Teche (4)
Bogue Chitto River (5)
Bogue Falaya River (6)
Calcasieu River (16)
Dorcheat Bayou (7)
Kisatchie Bayou (8)
Middle Bayou (9)
Mississippi River (10)
Pearl River (11)
Saline Bayou (12)
Tangipahoa River (13)
Tickfaw River (14)
Vermillion River (15)
Whiskey Chitto Creek (16)

Tylertown: 5 miles / Route 48 to Route 438 at Warnerton, Louisiana: 15 miles / Warnerton to Franklinton on Route 25: 15 miles / Franklinton to Route 437 at Enon: 15 miles / Enon to Bush on Route 21: about 15 miles / river ends at a canal below Bush, beyond canal is Pearl River Basin, a labyrinth of sloughs and bayous canoeable with guides only. Rentals: Lafayette and New Orleans.

Bogue Falaya River

Route 25 about 6 miles north of Covington to Covington: about 10 miles, the Bogue Falaya River joins the Tchefuncte River immediately below Covington, but this stretch is too shallow in dry spells.

Dorcheat Bayou

Route 157 east of Springhill to Route 160 east of Cotton Valley on Route 53: 13 miles / Route 160 to Routes 79–80 east of Minden: 18 miles, through swamps, knowledge of the course is required / Route 79–80 to Lake Bistineau a few miles south of I–20: 10 miles.

Kisatchie Bayou

Route 117 in Kisatchie National Forest to Route 337 at Longleaf Trail: 15 miles, scenic, too shallow in dry weather / Route 337 to junction with the Cane River below Cypress on Route 1: 25 miles.

Middle Bayou

A scenic bayou network near New Orleans accessible from U.S. 51 on North Pass connecting Lake Maurepas and Lake Pontchartrain.

Mississippi River

The Mississippi River is the boundary, for about 250 miles, between Louisiana and Mississippi. The river continues for an additional 300 miles through Louisiana until it enters the Gulf of Mexico. A busy commercial waterway.

Pearl River and Swamp

See Mississippi.

Saline Bayou

Route 126 south of town of Saline in Kisatchie National Forest to Route 156 east of Goldonna: 20 miles, canoeable in high water only / Goldonna to Saline Lake: about 10 miles.

Tangipahoa River

Osyka, Mississippi, on Route 51 to Route 38 at Kentwood, Louisiana: 12 miles, other access points in high water between I–55 and Route 51 / Kentwood to Route 440 at Bolivar: 10 miles / Bolivar to Route 16 at Amite: 15 miles / Amite to Route 40 east of Independence: 12 miles / Independence to Route 190 at Robert: 15 miles / Route 190 to Lake Pontchartrain: 15 miles, power boats. Rentals: Lafayette and New Orleans.

Tickfaw River

Route 442 northwest of Hammond to Route 190 at Holden: 8 miles / Route 190 to Route 42 west of Springfield: 8 miles / Route 42 to Lake Maurepas: about 15 miles. Rentals: New Orleans.

Vermillion River
Surrey Street or Route 90 in Lafayette to Route 92: 15 miles, populated stretch, some pollution / Route 92 to Route 14 at Erath: 15 miles / Erath to Vermillion Bay at the Gulf of Mexico south of Route 331: about 25 miles. Rentals: Lafayette.

Whiskey Chitto Creek and Calcasieu River
Route 26 at Mittie to Route 190 west of Kinder and below confluence with the Calcasieu River: 22 miles / on Calcasieu River, Route 190 to town of Indian Village off Route 383: 7 miles / Indian Village to town of Lake Charles on Route 90: 20 miles, tidal waters below Lake Charles. Rentals: Lafayette.

Louisiana Rentals

Baton Rouge
The Sports Shop, 8055 Airline Highway, Baton Rouge, La. 70815; telephone: 504–927–2613 / Unconfirmed.

Lafayette
Pack and Paddle, 1539 Pinhook Road, Lafayette, La. 70501; telephone: 318–232–5854 / Waters: Whiskey Chitto Creek, Vermillion River, Tangipahoa River, Bogue Chitto River, Atchafalaya River, Bayou Teche, and many other nearby waterways / Trips: 1 or more days, guides available / Best canoeing months: all year / Campsites: yes / Transportation: no / Car-top carriers: yes / Also rents camping equipment / Open all year.

New Orleans
Canoe and Trail Shop, 624 Moss Street, New Orleans, La. 70119; telephone: 504–488–8528 / Waters: in Louisiana — Tangipahoa, Bogue Chitto, Amite, Pearl, Tickfaw, and Atchafalaya Rivers, and Bayou Teche; in Mississippi — Red Creek, Black Creek, Wolf River, Big Biloxi River, Magee's Creek, and other waters / Trips: 1 or more days / Best canoeing months: March, April, September-November / Campsites: yes / Transportation: no / Car-top carriers: yes / Also rents camping equipment / Open all year.

Mississippi Waters

Beaverdam Creek
Spring Branch Recreation Area on Route 308 to junction with Black Creek 2 miles below Route 29: 8 miles, marked canoe trail together with Black Creek.

MISSISSIPPI
Beaverdam Creek (1)
Big Biloxi River (2)
Black Creek (3)
Bogue Chitto River (4)
Leaf River (5)
Magee's Creek (6)
Mississippi River (7)
Pearl River (8)
Red Creek (9)
Strong River (10)
Wolf River (11)

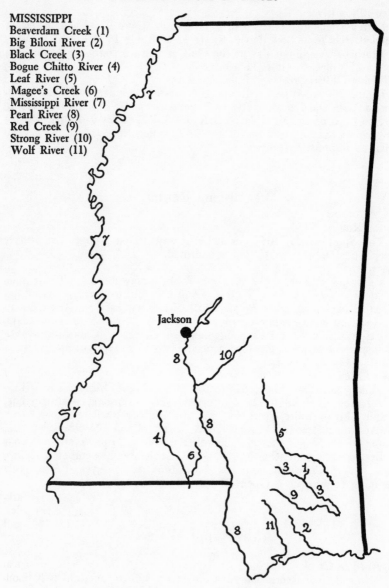

Big Biloxi River

Bridge 2 miles west of Howison off old Route 49 to road west of Saucier off Route 49: 7 miles / Saucier to Route 49 south of Saucier: 6 miles / Route 49 to Three River Bridge east of Lyman on Route 53: 10 miles / bridge to Gulf of Mexico: about 10 miles. Rentals: New Orleans, Louisiana.

Black Creek

Big Creek west of Brooklyn on Route 49: 6 miles / Route 49 to Moody's Landing Recreation Area east of Brooklyn: 6 miles / recreation area to Route 29 at Janice Recreation Area: 10 miles / Route 29 to Cypress Creek Recreation Area off Route 395: 5 miles / recreation area to Fairley Bridge: 6 miles / Fairley Bridge to Old Alexander Bridge 1 mile above Route 26 east of Wiggins: 9 miles, end of officially marked canoe trail / Route 26 to Route 57: about 20 miles / Route 57 to junction with Red Creek and Pascagoula River west of Route 63: about 20 miles. Rentals: New Orleans, Louisiana.

Bogue Chitto River

See Louisiana.

Leaf River

Route 18 east of Raleigh to Route 28 east of Taylorsville: about 20 miles, very scenic, narrow, with chutes, upper stretch may be too shallow in dry spells / the Leaf River continues for about 100 miles via Route 84 west of Laurel, I–59 at Moselle, Route 42 at Hattiesburg, Route 29 north of New Augusta, and Route 15 north of Beaumont to join the Chickasawhay River east of town of Leaf on Route 57 to form the Pascagoula River.

Magee's Creek

Tylertown on Routes 48–98 to junction with Bogue Chitto River 2 miles below Route 27 crossing: about 12 miles, intermediate whitewater in upper course, first 6 miles may be too shallow in dry spells. Rentals: New Orleans, Louisiana.

Mississippi River

The Mississippi River is the State of Mississippi's border, for about 500 miles, with Louisiana and Arkansas. It is a busy commercial waterway.

Pearl River and Swamp

Ross Barnett Reservoir near Jackson on Natchez Trace National Parkway to the Gulf of Mexico northeast of New Orleans: about 150 miles. The Pearl River forms the southeastern border between Mississippi and Louisiana. The lower section, east of Slidell, Louisiana, is a network of channels, bayous, and swamps that are popular with canoeists. But one can get lost easily here and experienced guides and U.S. Geological Survey maps are strongly recommended. Rentals: New Orleans, Louisiana.

171

Red Creek

Perkinston on Route 49 to Route 15: about 12 miles / Route 15 to Vestry: about 10 miles / Vestry to Route 57: about 6 miles / below Route 57 the Red Creek joins the Black Creek and the Pascagoula River. Rentals: New Orleans, Louisiana.

Strong River

Route 18 east of Puckett to Route 49 west of Mendenhall: about 12 miles, too shallow in dry spells / Route 49 to Route 28 west of Pinola: about 15 miles, several rapids / Route 28 to bridge south of Union on Route 28: 10 miles / joins the Pearl River below the bridge, southeast of Georgetown on Route 28.

Tangipahoa River

See Louisiana.

Wolf River

Route 26 east of Poplarville to Hickory Springs southeast of Poplarville: 7 miles / Hickory Springs to Silver Run east of Millard: 12 miles / Silver Run to Sellers on Route 53: 13 miles / Route 53 to unnumbered road southwest of Lizana on Route 53: 12 miles / Lizana to St. Louis Bay and the Gulf of Mexico: about 15 miles, upper course very shallow in dry spells. Rentals: New Orleans, Louisiana.

Mississippi Rentals

None.

Alabama Waters

Cahaba River

U.S. 280 southeast of Birmingham to U.S. 31 south of Birmingham: about 10 miles / Route 31 to county road west of Helena off Route 31: 7 miles / Helena to Piper-West Blocton road bridge: 20 miles / Piper to Centreville on Route 82: 15 miles / Route 82 to Route 183 northeast of Marion on Route 5: about 25 miles / Route 183 to Route 6 west of Suttle: 15 miles / Route 6 to Route 80 west of Selma: 20 miles, below Route 80 is backwater of Millers Ferry Reservoir.

Little River

De Soto State Park off Routes 89–117 to Route 35: about 15 miles / Route 35 to Weiss Reservoir: about 15 miles, passes through the scenic Little River Canyon, some whitewater on this stretch.

Perdido River

See Florida.

Sipsey River

West Fork: Route 60 west of Route 33 in William B. Bankhead National Forest to Route 278 crossing Lewis M. Smith Lake: about 20 miles.

ALABAMA
Cahaba River (1)
Little River (2)
Sipsey River (3)

Alabama Rentals

None.

Sources of Information

Alabama fishing and hunting information is available from Alabama Department of Conservation, Division of Fish and Game (Montgomery, Ala. 36130).

Alabama tourist information is available from Alabama Bureau of Publicity and Information (State Capitol, Montgomery, Ala. 36130).

Canoeing in Louisiana, Lafayette Natural History Museum and Planetarium (637 Girard Park Drive, Lafayette, La. 70501), 1972, 62 pp., $2.00. A guide to 14 canoe trails with maps.

Louisiana fishing and hunting information is available from Louisiana Wildlife and Fisheries Commission (400 Royal Street, New Orleans, La. 70130).

Louisiana tourist information is available from Louisiana Tourist Development Commission (Box 44291, Baton Rouge, La. 70804).

Mississippi fishing and hunting information is available from Mississippi Game and Fish Commission (Box 451, Jackson, Miss. 39205).

Mississippi tourist information is available from Mississippi Agricultural and Industrial Board, Travel Department (P.O. Box 849, Jackson, Miss. 39205).

PART THREE

THE MIDWEST

●

OHIO

WHEN YOU DRIVE from Pennsylvania into Ohio on the Turnpike or another east-west route, leaving the mountain and rolling hill country behind, you feel that you are suddenly entering a different world — the midwest and the vast Great Plains. The country is not entirely pancake flat, there are some undulations; but on the surface it seems dull — densely farmed, densely populated, and, in many spots, heavily industrialized.

What you don't see from the highway are the hidden scenic beauties — the meandering rivers and the tree-lined lakes. Ohio has a surprisingly large number of long, quietly flowing rivers. Many have been ruined by pollution and an excess of dams. In fact, the Cuyahoga River at Cleveland has the unique distinction of having been set on fire by industrial effluent. But enough scenic rivers remain, winding their ways through lush meadows and farmland, dense woods, swamps, and rugged rocklands. The State of Ohio has designated a number of rivers as "scenic" to preserve them in their natural condition. Among them are the Sandusky, Olentangy, Little Miami, Grand, and a part of the Maumee River, as well as the upper reaches of the Cuyahoga River and Beaver Creek.

A watershed divide crosses the state east to west approximately along Route 30. Rivers north flow into Lake Erie while rivers south of the divide flow into the Ohio River. Beautiful forested and rocky countryside is found in the southeastern section of the state near the Ohio River. The river, forming part of the eastern and all of the southern border of the state, has a grandeur and beauty along much of its course, but also commercial barge traffic that discourages canoeing on the Ohio. The Ohio River runs through Pennsylvania, Ohio, Indiana, and Illinois for 981 miles, and more than 400 of these miles form the border of the state.

The State of Ohio has developed a number of recreational lakes, among them the 10 lakes of the Muskingum Watershed Conservation District.

Not all canoeable waterways have been as well recorded and charted in Ohio as in some of the other midwest states, and the enterprising canoeist has ample latitude to do some uncharted exploring of his own.

177

Ohio Waters

Auglaize River
Wapakoneta on Route 33 to Fort Amanda State Memorial on Route 198: 18 miles / Fort Amanda to Fort Jennings on Routes 189 and 190: 35 miles / Fort Jennings to Oakwood on Route 113: 30 miles / Oakwood to the Maumee River at Defiance on Route 66: 18 miles, many intermediate access points. Rentals: Wapakoneta.

Beaver Creek
Beaver Creek State Park off Route 7 to Fredericktown on Route 170: 8 miles, passes through Beaver Creek State Park / Fredericktown to the Ohio River: 10 miles / Designated a "scenic river." Rentals: Fredericktown.

Cuyahoga River
Route 168 at Burton to Route 422 bridge: 10 miles / Or start at River Park south of Burton to Route 422 bridge: 7 miles, some obstacles and riffles / Route 422 to Route 303 southwest of Mantua: 20 miles, pleasant, with intermediate access points at Camp Hi on Abbott Road on Route 82 near Mantua / Route 303 to Rockwell Dam at Kent on Route 5: closed to boats / Rockwell Dam to town of Cuyahoga Falls on Route 5: 14 miles, falls are impassable, reenter at Cuyahoga Street in Akron / Akron to Peninsula on Route 303: 15 miles, or continue on for an additional 8 miles to east of Brecksville on Route 82, this lower run is not especially attractive. Rentals: Akron, Cuyahoga Falls, and Hiram.

Darby Creek
Georgesville on county road southwest of Columbus on I-70 to Orient on Route 762: 12 miles / Orient to Darbyville on Route 316: 12 miles / Darbyville to Circleville on Route 23 at junction with the Scioto River: 15 miles. Rentals: Washington Courthouse.

Deer Creek
Route 56 near Mount Sterling to Deer Creek Lake and State Park: 6 miles / Deer Creek Lake to Scioto River near Route 23: 12 miles. Rentals: Washington Courthouse.

Grand Lake (Lake St. Marys)
Fairly wide lake, about 8 miles long, between Celina on Route 29 and Villa Nova on Route 364, motor boats on the lake. Rentals: Celina and Wapakoneta.

Grand River
Near Farmington on Route 88 to Harpersfield on Route 534: about 40 miles / Harpersfield to Route 2 near Painesville and Lake Erie: about 30 miles, many intermediate access points, not fully charted / Designated a "scenic river." Rentals: Painesville.

Great Miami River
Route 274 near Indian Lake to Sidney on Route 25: 25 miles / Sid-

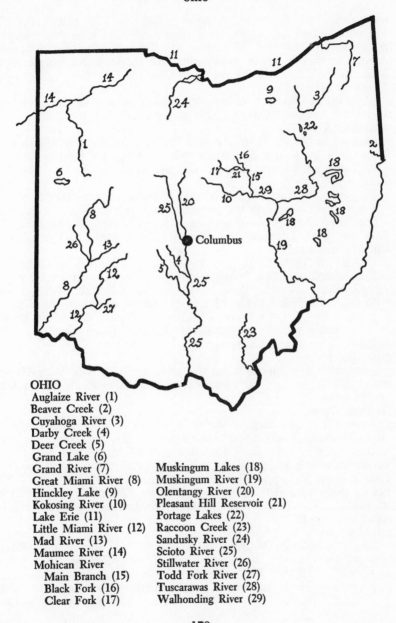

OHIO
Auglaize River (1)
Beaver Creek (2)
Cuyahoga River (3)
Darby Creek (4)
Deer Creek (5)
Grand Lake (6)
Grand River (7)
Great Miami River (8)
Hinckley Lake (9)
Kokosing River (10)
Lake Erie (11)
Little Miami River (12)
Mad River (13)
Maumee River (14)
Mohican River
  Main Branch (15)
  Black Fork (16)
  Clear Fork (17)

Muskingum Lakes (18)
Muskingum River (19)
Olentangy River (20)
Pleasant Hill Reservoir (21)
Portage Lakes (22)
Raccoon Creek (23)
Sandusky River (24)
Scioto River (25)
Stillwater River (26)
Todd Fork River (27)
Tuscarawas River (28)
Walhonding River (29)

179

ney to Piqua on Route 36: 15 miles / Piqua to Troy near Route 25: 15 miles / Troy to Dayton near Route 48: 25 miles / Dayton to Middletown on Route 4: 30 miles / Middletown to the Ohio River: 55 miles. The river is best in its upper reaches, the lower reaches are populated. Rentals: Indian Lake and Tipp City.

Hinckley Lake

In Hinckley Reservation, near Route 303, a part of the Cleveland Metropark System. Rentals: Hinckley.

Kokosing River

Howard on Route 36 to Mohawk Reservoir dam on the Walhonding River: 40 miles, with several intermediate access points. Rentals: Coshocton, Glenmont, Howard, Loudonville, and Walhonding.

Lake Erie

Not very good for canoeing because of its unprotected lake front but it is used for canoeing in the protected bays such as Sandusky Bay and along some of the incoming rivers and creeks such as the Sandusky River and Pipe Creek. Rentals: Painesville, Sandusky, and Vermilion.

Little Miami River

Clifton on Route 72 or John Bryan State Park south of Clifton to Bellbrook on Route 725: 20 miles / Bellbrook to Waynesville on Route 73: 13 miles / Waynesville to Morrow on Route 22: 22 miles, junction with the Todd Fork River / Morrow to Milford on Route 50: 25 miles / Milford to the Ohio River: 13 miles, developed. The Little Miami River is a designated "scenic river." Rentals: Bellbrook, Clarksville, Milford, Morrow, and Oregonia.

Mad River

Joins the Great Miami River at Dayton on I-75. It is canoeable for about 30 miles in high water from near Springfield at Route 40. Rentals: Indian Lake.

Maumee River

Enters Ohio from Indiana. Route 24 west of Antwerp along Route 24 to Defiance on Route 66: about 45 miles / 3 miles below Defiance is Independence Dam State Park; the restored Miami and Erie Canal bypasses the dam and parallels the river for much of the river's course / Independence Dam State Park to Napoleon on Route 6: 15 miles / Napoleon to the dam at Grand Rapids on Route 578 and Providence Park: 20 miles / Grand Rapids to the town of Maumee on Route 24: 22 miles, two rapids.

Mohican River

Black Fork: Canoeable from below Charles Mill Reservoir off Route 603 to junction with the Clear Fork of the Mohican River below Loudonville on Route 3: 9 miles.

Clear Fork: Hemlock Grove Camp in Mohican State Forest to Route 3 bridge and junction with the Black Fork: 4 miles / junction with the

180

Black Fork to junction with the Lake Fork of the Mohican River: 4 miles.

Main Branch: Lake Fork junction with the Main Branch to Brinkhaven on Route 62: 11 miles / Brinkhaven to Mohawk Reservoir dam on the Walhonding River: 18 miles. Rentals: Brinkhaven, Butler, Coshocton, Glenmont, Loudonville, Perrysville, and Walhonding.

Muskingum Lakes

A group of recreational lakes administered by the Muskingum Watershed Conservancy District in New Philadelphia. The group includes Atwood Reservoir on Route 542, Leesville Reservoir on Route 164, Tappan Reservoir on Route 250, Clendening Reservoir on Route 799, Piedmont Reservoir on Route 22, Senecaville Reservoir on Route 313, Wills Creek Reservoir on Route 93, Pleasant Hill Reservoir on Route 95, and Charles Mill Reservoir on Route 30. Rentals: Perrysville.

Muskingum River

Formed by the junction of the Walhonding River and the Tuscarawas River at Coshocton on Route 36. Coshocton to Ellis Dam on Route 666 south of Dresden: 30 miles / Ellis Dam to Zanesville on Route 40: 8 miles / Zanesville to McConnelsville on Route 60: 28 miles / McConnelsville to Stockport on Route 792: 9 miles / Stockport to Beverly on Route 60: 15 miles / Beverly to the Ohio River at Marietta on Route 21: 25 miles. It is a trip of 167 miles from the beginnings of the Clear Fork of the Mohican River through the Muskingum River to the Ohio River at Marietta. Rentals: Brinkhaven, Coshocton, Glenmont, Loudonville, Perrysville, and Walhonding.

Olentangy River

Caledonia on Route 288 to Columbus on Route 33 at junction with the Scioto River: about 45 miles, through Delaware Reservoir, with intermediate access points; designated a "scenic river." Rentals: Caledonia.

Pleasant Hill Reservoir

About 5 miles of lake canoeing on a body of water formed by damming the Clear Fork of the Mohican River. It is accessible from Route 95 near Perrysville. Rentals: Perrysville.

Portage Lakes

A chain of recreational lakes near Akron. Rentals: Akron.

Raccoon Creek

Vales Mills on Route 346 to Vinton on Route 325: 40 miles, can be extended by beginning above Vales Mills if water conditions permit / Vinton to east of town of Rio Grande on Route 35: 15 miles / Rio Grande to the Ohio River: 30 miles. Rentals: Rio Grande.

Sandusky River

Upper Sandusky on Route 67 to Route 103 bridge: 25 miles, shallow water in the upper reaches / Route 103 bridge to Route 224 bridge near Tiffin: 22 miles / Tiffin to Fremont on Route 12: 28 miles, designated a "scenic river" / Fremont to Sandusky Bay: 20 miles. Rentals: Fremont.

Scioto River

Depending on water conditions, begin at Kenton on Routes 31 and 68 or a few miles downstream to Columbus on Route 33 and junction with the Olentangy River: about 40 miles, flows through O'Shaughnessy Reservoir / Columbus to the Ohio River near Portsmouth on Route 23: about 120 miles, canoeable all the way with many portages around dams and many intermediate access points; not charted in detail. Rentals: Caledonia.

Stillwater River

Pleasant Hill on Route 718 to Englewood on old Route 40: 20 miles / Englewood to Dayton on I-75 and junction with the Great Miami River: 15 miles, through built-up populated lands. Rentals: Tipp City.

Todd Fork River

Clarksville on Route 350 to junction with the Little Miami River at Morrow on Route 22: 17 miles, canoeable in high water only. Rentals: Clarksville.

Tuscarawas River

Town of Canal Fulton on Route 93 to Massillon on Route 30: 9 miles / Massillon to Bolivar on Route 212: 21 miles / Route 212 to Route 39 near New Philadelphia: 20 miles / New Philadelphia to Coshocton on Route 36 and the Muskingum River: 40 miles. Rentals: Canal Fulton and Coshocton.

Walhonding River

Formed by junction of the Mohican and Kokosing Rivers. Mohawk Reservoir Dam near Route 36 to Six-Mile Dam near Warsaw on Route 36: 9 miles / dam to junction with the Tuscarawas River to form the Muskingum River at Coshocton on Route 36: 6 miles. Rentals: Brinkhaven, Coshocton, Glenmont, Loudonville, and Walhonding.

Ohio Rentals

Akron

Burch's Landing, 354 Portage Lakes Drive, Akron, Ohio 44319; telephone: 216–644–5711 / Waters: Cuyahoga River, East Reservoir and connecting Portage Lakes / Trips: up to 1 day / Best canoeing months: May-October / Campsites: no / Transportation: no / Car-top carriers: yes.

Bellbrook

Fyffe's Canoe Rental, 2750 Washington Mill Road, Bellbrook, Ohio 45305; telephone: 513–848–4812 / Waters: Little Miami River /Trips:

1 or more days, guides available / Best canoeing months: April-October / Campsites: yes / Transportation: yes / Car-top carriers: yes.
Brinkhaven
Brinkhaven Canoe Livery (David Mapes), Box 277, Brinkhaven, Ohio 43006; telephone: 614–599–7848 or off-season 216–357–6366 (off-season mailing address: 654 Bank Street, Painesville, Ohio 44077) / Waters: Mohican, Walhonding, and Muskingum Rivers / Trips: several hours to two days or more / Best canoeing months: May-October / Campsites: yes / Transportation: yes / Car-top carriers: no / Open daily during June-August, open weekends only during May, September, and October.
Butler
Clearfork Canoe Livery (division of Voyageur Outfitters of America, Inc.), State Route 95, Butler, Ohio 44822; telephone: 419–883–3601 or VOA in Bruce, Wisc.: 715–868–6565 or 868–9245 / Waters: Clear Fork and Black Fork of the Mohican River / Trips: 2 hours to 3 days / Best canoeing months: May-October / Campsites: yes / Transportation: yes / Car-top carriers: yes.
Caledonia
River Bend, 1092 Whetstone River Road South, Caledonia, Ohio 43314; telephone: 614–389–4179 / Waters: Olentangy and Scioto Rivers / Trips: up to 1 day / Best canoeing months: spring to fall / Campsites: on their grounds / Transportation: yes / Car-top carriers: yes / Also rents camping equipment / Open all year.
Canal Fulton
River Run Canoe Livery, Route 93, Canal Fulton, Ohio 44614; telephone: 216–854–3394 / Waters: Tuscarawas River / Trips: 2 hours to 2 days / Best canoeing months: April-October / Campsites: yes / Transportation: yes / Car-top carriers: yes.
Carey
Ronald Vaughn, Hurd Road, Carey, Ohio 43316; telephone: 419–396–6163 / Unconfirmed.
Celina
Northmoor Marina, RR 4, Box 2220, Celina, Ohio 45822; telephone: 419–394–4595 / Unconfirmed.
Chagrin Falls
Zucker Marine Inc., 860 East Washington Street, Chagrin Falls, Ohio 44022; telephone: 216–543–5161 / Unconfirmed.
Cincinnati
Flerlage Marine Inc., 2233 Eastern Avenue, Cincinnati, Ohio 45202; telephone: 513–221–2233 / Unconfirmed.
Clarksville
Scenic Route Campgrounds and Canoe Livery (Harry and Helen Flake), 9388 State Route 350, Clarksville, Ohio 45113; telephone: 513–289–2797 / Waters: Little Miami and Todd Fork Rivers / Trips: 1

hour to 2 or more days / Best canoeing months: April-October / Campsites: yes / Transportation: yes / Car-top carriers: yes / Also rents camping equipment.

Columbus

All Ohio Canoe, 320 South Ardmore Street, Columbus, Ohio 43209; telephone: 614–235–8296 / Unconfirmed.

Coshocton

Three Rivers Canoe Livery (Mike Halco), R.D. #3, Lake Park Road, Coshocton, Ohio 43812; telephone: 614–622–4080 or 216–832–7070 / Waters: Mohican, Kokosing, Walhonding, Tuscarawas, and Muskingum Rivers / Trips: several hours to 5 days or longer / Best canoeing months: May-September / Campsites: yes / Transportation: yes / Car-top carriers: yes / Open daily June-August and weekends only in April, May, and September.

Cuyahoga Falls

Northoga Canoe Livery, 687 Ardella Road, Cuyahoga Falls, Ohio 44223; telephone: 216–928–6096 / Waters: Cuyahoga River / Trips: up to 5 hours / Best canoeing months: April-October / Campsites: yes / Transportation: yes / Car-top carriers: yes / Open Wednesdays, Thursdays, Fridays, weekends and holidays during June-August and weekends and holidays only during April, May, September, and October.

Fairborn

Erhart Sport Center, Inc., 308 West Main Street, Fairborn, Ohio 45324; telephone: 513–878–4314 / Unconfirmed.

Fredericktown

Beaver Creek Canoe Livery, Route 170, Fredericktown, Ohio 43019 (mailing address P.O. Box 2054, East Liverpool, Ohio 43920); telephone: 216–385–8579 / Waters: Beaver Creek / Trips: mainly up to 1 day / Best canoeing months: April-November / Campsites: yes / Transportation: yes / Car-top carriers: no response / Overnight trips can be arranged.

Fremont

Portage Trail Canoe Livery, 1773 South River Road, Fremont, Ohio 43420; telephone 419–334–2988 / Waters: Sandusky River / Trips: up to 2 days / Best canoeing months: May-early July, September-October / Campsites: yes / Transportation: yes / Car-top carriers: yes.

Glenmont

Mohican Wilderness (Ken Wobbecke), The Wally Road, Route 1, Glenmont, Ohio 44628; telephone: 614–599–6741 / Waters: Mohican, Kokosing, Walhonding, and Muskingum Rivers / Trips: several hours to several days, guides available / Best canoeing months: April, May, and October / Campsites: yes / Transportation: yes / Car-top carriers: yes / Housekeeping tents and camping equipment for rent.

Hinckley

Hinckley Lake Boat House (Dennis C. Maier), West Drive, Parkway,

184

Route 1, Hinckley, Ohio 44233; telephone: 216–278–2821 / Waters: Hinckley Lake / Trips: rentals by the hour only / Best canoeing months: April-October / Campsites: no / Transportation: yes / Car-top carriers: no.

Hiram

Camp Hi Canoe Livery (George and Helen Hazlett), 11274 Abbott Road, Hiram, Ohio 44234; telephone: 216–569–7621 / Waters: Cuyahoga River / Trips: up to 2 days / Best canoeing months: April-October / Campsites: yes / Transportation: yes / Car-top carriers: yes.

Howard

Howard Canoe Livery, State Route 36, Howard, Ohio 43028; telephone: 614–599–7056 / Waters: Kokosing River / Trips: 1 hour to 1½ days / Best canoeing months: no response / Campsites: no response / Transportation: yes / Car-top carriers: no response.

Indian Lake

Miami River Canoe Livery, State Route 274, Indian Lake, Ohio (summer mailing address: RR 1, Lewistown, Ohio 43333; winter mailing address: Route 1, Zanesville, Ohio 43360); telephone: 513–843–2935 in summer, 513–355–3297 in winter / Waters: Great Miami and Mad Rivers / Trips: 1½ hours to 10 days / Best canoeing months: May-October / Campsites: yes / Transportation: yes / Car-top carriers: yes.

Loudonville

Black Fork Kayak and Canoe Livery (Larry Rogers), Route 2, Loudonville, Ohio 44842; telephone: 419–994–4354 / Waters: Black Fork, Clear Fork, and Lake Fork of the Mohican River / Trips: 2 hours to 3 days / Best canoeing months: June-August / Campsites: yes / Transportation: no / Car-top carriers: yes.

Loudonville Canoe Livery, 424 West Main Street, Loudonville, Ohio 44842; telephone: 419–994–4561 / Unconfirmed.

Mohican Canoe Livery, R.D. 2, Loudonville, Ohio 44842; telephone: 419–994–4020 / Waters: Mohican, Walhonding, Kokosing, and Muskingum Rivers / Trips: 1–6 days / Best canoeing months: May-October / Campsites: yes / Transportation: yes / Car-top carriers: no.

Mohican Wilderness, The Wally Road, Loudonville, Ohio 44842; telephone: 419–994–3567 / See Glenmont, Ohio.

October Hill Canoe Livery, 424 West Main Street, Loudonville, Ohio 44842; telephone: 419–994–4161 / Waters: Black Fork, Clear Fork, Lake Fork, and Main Branch of the Mohican River / Trips: 1 or more days / Best canoeing months: June-August / Campsites: yes / Transportation: yes / Car-top carriers: yes.

Milford

Miami Canoe Livery (Ross and Genie Terrell), 202 Wooster Pike (U.S. 50), Milford, Ohio 45150; telephone: 513–831–9631 / Waters:

Little Miami River / Trips: 1½ hours to 2 days / Best canoeing months: April-October / Campsites: yes / Transportation: yes / Car-top carriers: yes.

Morrow

Fort Ancient Livery (Bob and June Morgan), Route 350, 2247 Gilmore Road, Morrow, Ohio 45152; telephone: 513-932-7568 / Waters: Little Miami River / Trips: 1½ hours to 2 days / Best canoeing months: April-October / Campsites: yes / Transportation: yes / Car-top carriers: yes.

Oregonia

Little Miami Canoe Livery (division of Voyageur Outfitters of America, Inc.), 5380 Wilmington Road, Oregonia, Ohio 45054; telephone: 513-932-2149 or VOA in Bruce, Wisc.: 715-868-6565 or 868-9245 / Waters: Little Miami River / Trips: 2 hours to 3 days / Best canoeing months: May-October / Campsites: yes / Transportation: yes / Car-top carriers: yes.

Painesville

Lake County Canoes, 81 Elevator Avenue, Paineville, Ohio 44077; telephone: 216-352-7400 / Waters: Grand River and Lake Erie / Trips: up to 2 days / Best canoeing months: April-November / Campsites: yes / Transportation: only for 8 canoes or more / Car-top carriers: yes.

Perrysville

Pleasant Hill Canoe Livery Inc., State Route 39, R.D. 1, Perrysville, Ohio 44864; telephone: 419-938-7777 or 216-659-4831 / Waters: Mohican River system, Muskingum River and Lakes, and Pleasant Hill Lake / Trips: 2 hours to 2 days, longer by special arrangement / Best canoeing months: May-October / Campsites: yes / Transportation: yes / Car-top carriers: no response.

Perrysville Canoe Livery (division of Voyageur Outfitters of America, Inc.), State Route 95, Perrysville, Ohio 44864; telephone: 419-883-3601 or VOA in Bruce, Wisc.: 715-868-6565 or 868-9245 / Waters: Black Fork of the Mohican River to the Ohio River / Trips: several hours to 10 days / Best canoeing months: May-August / Campsites: yes / Transportation: yes / Car-top carriers: yes.

Rio Grande

Raccoon Creek Canoe Livery, P.O. Box 139, Rio Grande, Ohio 45674 – located on Bob Evans Farm; telephone: 614-245-5511 / Waters: Raccoon Creek / Trips: 2 hours to 2 days / Best canoeing months: April-October / Campsites: yes / Transportation: yes / Car-top carriers: no response.

Sandusky

East Bay Marina Inc., 2340 River Avenue, Sandusky, Ohio 44870; telephone: 419-625-4180 / Waters: Sandusky Bay on Lake Erie and

OHIO

nearby waters / Trips: up to 1 day / Best canoeing months: April-September / Campsites: yes / Transportation: yes / Car-top carriers: yes / Also rents camping equipment.

Sheffield Lake
Ohio Canoe Adventures, Inc., 5128 Colorado Avenue, Sheffield Lake, Ohio 44054; telephone: 216–934–5345 / Unconfirmed.

Tipp City
Barefoot Canoes, 3565 West Frederick-Gingham Road, Tipp City, Ohio 45371; telephone: 513–698–4351 / Waters: Stillwater and Great Miami Rivers / Trips: up to 2 days / Best canoeing months: May-September / Campsites: no / Transportation: yes / Car-top carriers: yes.

Vermilion
Romp's Water Port, Inc., 5055 Liberty Avenue, Vermilion, Ohio 44089; telephone: 216–967–4341 or 967–4342 / Waters: Lake Erie / Trips: up to 1 day / Best canoeing months: June-September / Campsites: yes / Transportation: no / Car-top carriers: no.

Walhonding
Campways of Ohio, Inc., Box 38, Walhonding, Ohio 43843: telephone: 614–824–3220 / Waters: Mohican, Muskingum, Walhonding, and Kokosing Rivers / Trips: 1 or more days / Best canoeing months: May-October / Campsites: yes / Transportation: yes / Car-top carriers: no response / Open all year.

Wapakoneta
Sycamore Shores Canoe Livery (James A. Hepp), R.R. 2 Fox Ranch Road (off Route 33, exit 33A), Wapakoneta, Ohio 45895; telephone: 419–738–8237 / Waters: Auglaize River, Grand Lake, and Miami and Erie Canal / Trips: 1 hour to 3 days / Best canoeing months: April-June / Campsites: no / Transportation: yes / Car-top carriers: yes.

Washington Courthouse
Trapper Johns Canoe Livery Inc., Route 5, Washington Courthouse, Ohio 43160; telephone: 614–877–2193 or 869–2622 / Waters: Deer Creek and Darby Creek / Trips: 1 or more days / Best canoeing months: April-October / Campsites: yes / Transportation: yes / Car-top carriers: yes / Open all year.

Youngstown
Trigg's Marine Supply Co., 4174 Market Street, Youngstown, Ohio 44512; telephone: 216–788–8709 / Unconfirmed.

Sources of Information

Boating in Ohio, Publications Center, Ohio Department of Natural Resources, Division of Watercraft (1350 Holly Avenue, Columbus,

187

Ohio 43212), 1974, 58 pp., free. This publication covers law, regulations, and registration for all watercraft in Ohio plus general information on canoeing.

Ohio Canoe Adventures, Ohio Department of Natural Resources, Division of Watercraft (1350 Holly Avenue, Columbus, Ohio 43212), a free brochure with detailed description and maps of 8 Ohio rivers plus several lakes.

Ohio fishing and hunting information is available from Ohio Department of Natural Resources, Division of Wildlife (1500 Dublin Road, Columbus, Ohio 43212).

Ohio's Natural Streams, Ohio Department of Natural Resources, Division of Scenic River Planning (Fountain Square, Columbus, Ohio 43224), a free brochure which describes the state's program for river preservation.

Ohio tourist information is available from the Ohio Department of Economic and Community Development, Publications Center (Box 1001, Columbus, Ohio 43216).

●

INDIANA

WHEN YOU DEAL with Hoosiers, you usually find a pleasant, orderly efficiency in their ways. The same trait applies to their river system. Most rivers cross the state in an orderly northeast to southwesterly direction, to be gathered somewhere along the way by the Wabash River, which then neatly delivers all of the waters into the Ohio River at the southwestern point of the state.

Most Indiana rivers run quietly, making them ideal waterways for family canoeing even though some may have log jams. The most popular rivers are precisely described in a publication of the Indiana Department of Natural Resources (see the end of this chapter). The longer rivers of Indiana, notably the Wabash River and the East and West Forks of the White River, allow a canoeist to spend a two-week vacation on the water, covering a new stretch each day, camping along the way or putting up at the motel closest to each take-out point. Many of the rivers flowing through farmlands are lined with thick vegetation, including a wide variety of beautiful trees — cottonwood, oak, ash, maple, willow, sycamore, tulip, white pine, and hemlock — sometimes interrupted by dramatic limestone bluffs and other rock formations.

The most striking scenery is found in the south, between Bloomington and the Ohio River, where the country becomes hilly, heavily forested, and accentuated by deeply cut valleys. The fall colors in Brown County and the Hoosier National Forest attract dedicated pilgrims each year. The Ohio River itself, forming the southern border of the state for well over 100 miles, winds its way through a narrow, wooded valley. Because of commercial traffic it is rarely canoed.

Canoeing is not yet as heavily commercialized in Indiana as it is in some neighboring states. The state has relatively few canoe liveries, concentrated on the most popular rivers—the Whitewater River, with practically no whitewater, the Sugar Creek, and the rivers that Indiana shares with Michigan at its northern border.

Indiana Waters

Big Pine Creek
Pine Village on Route 26 to junction with the Wabash River near Attica on Route 28: about 25 miles, canoeable in high water only, some whitewater. Rentals: Lafayette and West Lafayette.
Big Walnut Creek
Canoeable in high water only. Putnam-Hendricks County Line Road off Route 236 west of North Salem to Route 36 east of Bainbridge: 15 miles / Route 36 to Route 231 near Greencastle: 15 miles / Greencastle to junction with the Eel River (South) below Cagles Mill Lake: about 20 miles, this stretch is not recommended.
Blue River
Fredericksburg on Route 150 to Milltown on Route 64: 24 miles, some hazards / Milltown to Rothrock Mill dam off Old Mill Road south of Milltown: 13 miles, the dam is dangerous / dam to Harrison Crawford State Forest campground off Route 460: 11 miles / state forest to the Ohio River: 10 miles. Rentals: Fredericksburg and New Albany.
Brookville Lake
A lake of 5,260 acres and 15 miles long formed by damming the East Fork of the Whitewater River at Brookville on Route 52. Rentals: Brookville.
Buck Creek
New Middletown south of Route 460 to the Ohio River above Mauckport on Route 135: about 15 miles, shallow in dry spells. Rentals: New Albany.
Cedar Creek
Tonkel Road Bridge north of Route 1 via Cedarville to junction with the St. Joseph River (Fort Wayne): about 20 miles, a popular float. Rentals: Fort Wayne.

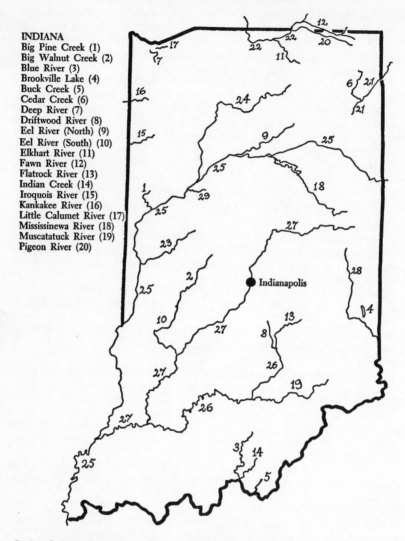

INDIANA
Big Pine Creek (1)
Big Walnut Creek (2)
Blue River (3)
Brookville Lake (4)
Buck Creek (5)
Cedar Creek (6)
Deep River (7)
Driftwood River (8)
Eel River (North) (9)
Eel River (South) (10)
Elkhart River (11)
Fawn River (12)
Flatrock River (13)
Indian Creek (14)
Iroquois River (15)
Kankakee River (16)
Little Calumet River (17)
Mississinewa River (18)
Muscatatuck River (19)
Pigeon River (20)

St. Joseph River (Fort Wayne) (21)
St. Joseph River (South Bend) (22)
Sugar Creek (23)
Tippecanoe River (24)
Wabash River (25)

White River
   East Fork (26)
   West Fork (27)
Whitewater River (28)
Wildcat Creek (29)

Deep River

Arizona Avenue between Routes 51 and 53 south to Gary to junction with the Little Calumet River on Central Avenue: 12 miles, flows through Lake George and over 2 dams / some canoeists continue through the West Branch of the Little Calumet River and Burns Ditch into Lake Michigan. The Deep River is scenic in parts and there is some pollution.

Driftwood River

Formed by the confluence of Sugar Creek and the Big Blue River (not to be confused with the Blue River) near Edinburg on Route 252. Camp Atterbury Road to Millrace Park in Columbus on Route Alternate 31 at the confluence with the Flatrock River: 17 miles.

Eel River (North)

South Whitley on Route 14 to Laketon southwest of North Manchester on Route 114: 20 miles, some pollution / Laketon to Denver where the river is south of Route 16: 22 miles / Denver to Logansport on Route 24 and the junction with the Wabash River: 28 miles. Not to be confused with Eel River (South), a totally different river.

Eel River (South)

Formed by the junction of Big Walnut Creek and Mill Creek below Cagles Mill Lake south of I-70. Junction to Bowling Green on Route 46: 14 miles / Bowling Green to Route 246 west of Martz: 18 miles / Route 246 to junction with the West Fork of the White River at Worthington on Route 231: 20 miles. Not to be confused with Eel River (North), a totally different river.

Elkhart River

South of Route 13 at Millersburg to the dam at Goshen Pond south of Goshen off Route 15: 15 miles / Goshen Pond to Oxbow Park on Route 33: 7 miles / Oxbow Park to Island Park in Elkhart on Route 20 and junction with the St. Joseph River (South Bend): 6 miles. Rentals: Goshen.

Fawn River

Nevada Mills off Route 120 to Greenfield Mills off I-80–90: 10 miles / Greenfield Mills to Fawn River Mill Pond in Michigan south of Michigan Route 12: 14 miles / Fawn River Mill Pond to Star Mill west of Indiana Route 9: 9 miles / Star Mill to Scott on County Road 750 N: 11 miles, some obstacles / Scott to junction with the St. Joseph River (South Bend) near Constantine, Michigan, on Route 131: about 15 miles. Rentals: Goshen and Mongo.

Flatrock River

Route 9 south of Shelbyville to U.S. 31 near Columbus: 23 miles, the Flatrock River joins the Driftwood River at Columbus to form the East Fork of the White River.

Indian Creek

Route 64 west of Georgetown to Corydon on Route 460: about

15 miles / Corydon to the Ohio River south of Harrison Crawford State Forest: about 20 miles. The upper reaches are canoeable in high water only. Rentals: New Albany.

Iroquois River

Route 16 east of Brook to Iroquois, Illinois, on Route 52: about 20 miles, shallow in dry weather / See also Illinois.

Kankakee River

Near Shelby on Route 55 to the Illinois border: about 20 miles, canoeable in high water only / See also Illinois. Rentals: Valparaiso.

Little Calumet River

East Fork is canoeable only in high water. Route 49 north of Chesterton to Samuelson Road Bridge in the city of Portage on Route 20: 10 miles, some canoeists continue through Burns Ditch into Lake Michigan (see also Deep River).

Mississinewa River

Route 67 west of Albany to Matthews on Route 221: 15 miles / Matthews to Gas City on Route 22: 11 miles / Gas City via Marion to Jalapa west of Route 15 and entry to the Mississinewa Reservoir: 15 miles, some industrial scenery, the reservoir is about 20 miles long and motor boats are permitted / Mississinewa Reservoir to the Wabash River east of Peru on Route 24: about 10 miles.

Muscatatuck River

Vernon Fork: Vernon on Route 7 to U.S. 31 north of Uniontown: about 25 miles / U.S. 31 to junction with the East Fork of the Muscatatuck River at Route 39 south of Tampico: 25 miles / Route 39 to Sparksville below junction with the East Fork of the White River: about 25 miles.

Pigeon River

Near Mongo on Route 3 to Route 9 at Howe: 11 miles, some obstacles / Route 9 to Scott on County Road 750N: 10 miles / Scott to junction with the St. Joseph River (South Bend) in Michigan: 15 miles. Rentals: Goshen and Mongo.

St. Joseph River (Fort Wayne)

Rises in Michigan close to the other St. Joseph River (see below) and flows through Ohio arriving in Indiana at Route 249 (Ohio County Road 40 bridge). Route 249 to near Spencerville on Route 1: 17 miles / Spencerville to near Cedarville on Route 1: 12 miles / Cedarville to Fort Wayne near Route 27 and junction with the Maumee River: 12 miles, the Maumee River returns to Ohio. Rentals: Fort Wayne.

St. Joseph River (South Bend)

This river, not to be confused with the St. Joseph River above, enters Indiana from Michigan north of Bristol on Route 120 and returns to Michigan north of South Bend near U.S. 31. Mottville, Michigan, on Route 12 to Bristol, Indiana, on Route 120: 10 miles / Bristol to Elkhart, off Main Street: 10 miles / Elkhart to South Bend Central Park on Route 331: 14 miles, via 2 dams / South Bend to Niles, Michigan, on U.S. 31: 20 miles. *See also* Michigan. Rentals: Goshen.

Sugar Creek

U.S. 136 at Crawfordsville to Shades State Park on Route 234: 16 miles, especially scenic and popular stretch / Route 234 to Turkey Run State Park on County Road 350E off Route 47: 11 miles, especially scenic and popular stretch / state park to the Wabash River: 12 miles. Rentals: Crawfordsville, Lafayette, Rockville, and West Lafayette.

Tippecanoe River

Warsaw on old Route 30 to Route 331 north of town of Tippecanoe: 16 miles / Route 331 to Menominee State Fishing Area on a county road off old Route 31: 14 miles / fishing area to Monterey City Park south of Route 110: 22 miles / Monterey to Tippecanoe River State Park off Route 35: 12 miles / state park to Winamac on Route 14: 15 miles / Winamac to Buffalo on Route 39: 25 miles, below Buffalo the river flows through Lake Shafer and Lake Freeman, both of which have heavy motor boat traffic / Lake Freeman exit off Route 421 to junction with the Wabash River near Americus on Route 25: 20 miles. Rentals: Monterey, Valparaiso, and West Lafayette.

Wabash River

Rises in Ohio and enters Indiana southeast of Decatur; the first 100 miles in Indiana to the city of Wabash is a shallow stretch with many log jams and is canoeable only in high water. Wabash on Route 15 to the Wayne Street Bridge in Peru: 15 miles / Peru to 18th Street Bridge in Logansport: 15 miles / Logansport to Pittsburg on Route 18: 20 miles / Pittsburg to Lafayette on Route 52: 18 miles / Lafayette to Attica on Route 41: 23 miles / Attica to Covington on Route 136: 20 miles / Covington to Route 234 east of Cayuga: about 20 miles / Route 234 to Montezuma on Route 36: 15 miles / Montezuma to Fairbanks Park in Terre Haute on Route 40: 22 miles / Terre Haute to Hutsonville, Illinois, on Route 154: 36 miles, unattractive, some pollution / Hutsonville, Illinois, to Vincennes, Indiana, on Route 50: 45 miles / Vincennes to Mount Carmel, Illinois, on Route 1: about 30 miles / Mount Carmel to New Harmony, Indiana, on Route 460: 20 miles / New Harmony to the Ohio River: 45 miles. Rentals: Lafayette and West Lafayette.

White River

East Fork: Formed by the confluence of the Driftwood River and the Flatrock River at Columbus. Columbus on Route 31A and Route 46 to Rockford on Route 11: 22 miles / Rockford to Route 50 west of Brownstown: 22 miles / Route 50 to Sparksville on Medora Pike: 24 miles / Sparksville to Lawrenceport north of Route 60 at Spring Mill State Park: 13 miles / Lawrenceport to Routes 37–50 south of Bedford: 13 miles / Routes 37–50 to dam at Williams on Route 450: 15 miles, flows through Hoosier National Forest / Williams to Shoals on Route

50: 20 miles / Shoals to Hindostan Falls off Route 550 and southeast of Loogootee: 17 miles, falls are dangerous / Hindostan Falls to Route 231 at Haysville: 18 miles / Haysville to Route 57 just above junction with the West Fork of the White River: 25 miles, see West Fork for continuation to the Wabash River.

West Fork: County Road 1100 W south of Route 32 near the town of Farmland to Tuhey Park in Muncie: 15 miles, shallow, several dams / Muncie to Perkinsville on Route 13 via Anderson: 34 miles, some industrial scenery / Perkinsville to Noblesville on Route 38: 16 miles / Noblesville to Tom Taggart (Riverside) Park in Indianapolis: 25 miles, mostly urban scenery / Indianapolis to Waverly on Route 144: 21 miles / Waverly to Route 39 near Martinsville: 18 miles / Martinsville to Gosport off Route 67: 17 miles / Gosport to Spencer on Route 46: 14 miles / Spencer to Route 157 below junction with the (southern) Eel River near Worthington: 28 miles / Route 157 to Newberry on Route 57: 20 miles / Newberry to Route 358 near Edwardsport: 30 miles / Edwardsport to junction with the East Fork of the White River above Petersburg on Route 57: 30 miles / junction via Petersburg to Hazleton on old Route 41: 27 miles / Hazleton to junction with the Wabash River near Mount Carmel, Illinois, on Route 1: 22 miles.

Whitewater River

West Fork and Main Branch: Near Cambridge City on Route 40 to Connersville on Route 44: 18 miles / Connersville to Laurel Feeder Dam on Route 121: 13 miles / Laurel to Metamora on Route 52: 7 miles / Metamora to Brookville on Route 52: 12 miles, the West Fork joins the East Fork at Brookville to form the Main Branch / Brookville to Cedar Grove on Routes 1 and 52: 9 miles / Cedar Grove to West Harrison near Route 52: 15 miles / West Harrison to junction with the Great Miami River: 15 miles. The old Whitewater Canal can also be canoed for 14 miles; it parallels the river between Laurel and Brookville. A tourist railroad operates on weekends along the river from Connersville to Brookville, providing transportation for canoeists. Rentals: Brookville, Cedar Grove, and Metamora.

Wildcat Creek

Owasco on Route 421 to junction with the Wabash River at Lafayette on Route 52: about 20 miles. Rentals: Lafayette and West Lafayette.

Indiana Rentals

Angola

Elmer's Marine Sales, Route 5-Crooked Lake, Angola, Ind. 46703; telephone: 219–665–5561 / Unconfirmed.

Brookville

Lentz's Canoe Rental, Brookville Marine, 10 West 4th Street, Brookville, Ind. 47012; telephone: 317–647–4773 / Unconfirmed.

Morgan's Brookville Canoe Center & Livery (Wayne and Alice Sawyer), R.R. 2, Blue Creek Road, Brookville, Ind. 47012; telephone: 317–647–4904 / Waters: Whitewater River and Brookville Lake / Trips: 2 hours to several days, guides available / Best canoeing months: May-July and October / Campsites: yes / Transportation: yes / Car-top carriers: no / Complete outfitting for guided group trips.

Whitewater Valley Canoe Rental, Inc. (Ron Ritz), P.O. Box 2, Brookville, Ind. 47012; telephone: 317–647–5434 / Waters: Whitewater River and Canal and Brookville Lake / Trips: 2 hours to 7 days, guides available / Best canoeing months: April-October / Campsites: yes / Transportation: yes / Car-top carriers: yes / Open all year.

Cedar Grove

Tom's Canoe Rental, Box 173, Cedar Grove, Ind. 47016; telephone: 317–647–5310 / Waters: Whitewater River / Trips: several hours to 2 days / Best canoeing months: May-August / Campsites: yes / Transportation: yes / Car-top carriers: no / Also rents kayaks.

Crawfordsville

Bob Clements Canoe Rental and Sales, 911 Wayne Avenue, on Sugar Creek at Route 136 bridge, Crawfordsville, Ind. 47933; telephone: 317–362–9864 or 362–6272 / Waters: Sugar Creek / Trips: 1–2 days / Best canoeing months: April-July / Campsites: yes / Transportation: yes / Car-top carriers: yes / Also rents canoe trailers.

U-Rent-It Center, Inc., 1317 Darlington Avenue, Crawfordsville, Ind., 47933; telephone: 317–362–1104 / Waters: Sugar Creek / Trips: 1 or more days / Best canoeing months: April-June / Campsites: no / Transportation: no / Car-top carriers: yes / Also rents camping equipment.

Fort Wayne

Root's Camp 'n Ski Haus, 6844 North Clinton Street, Fort Wayne, Ind. 46825; telephone: 219–484–2604 / Waters: Cedar Creek and St. Joseph River / Trips: up to 1 day / Best canoeing months: no response / Campsites: no response / Transportation: no / Car-top carriers: yes / Also rents camping equipment.

Fredericksburg

Old Mill Canoe Rental, Fredericksburg, Ind. 47120; telephone: 812–472–3140 / Waters: Blue River / Trips: a few hours to several days / Best canoeing months: April-June and October / Campsites: yes / Transportation: yes / Car-top carriers: yes / Open all year.

Goshen

Oldfather Canoe & Kayak Center, 60390 S.R. 15, Goshen, Ind. 46526; telephone: 219–533–2295 or 533–9461 / Waters: Elkhart, St. Joseph, Pigeon, and Fawn Rivers / Trips: 1 to several days / Best canoeing months: June-September / Campsites: yes / Transportation: yes / Car-top carriers: yes / Also rents kayaks and canoe trailers.

Indianapolis

Marsh Rents, division of U-Rent-It Center, Inc., 2370 Lafayette Road, Indianapolis, Ind. 46222; telephone: 317–636–4466 / Unconfirmed.

Lafayette

Midwest Rentals, Inc., 506 Brown Street, Lafayette, Ind. 47901; telephone: 317–423–5541 / Waters: Wabash River, Wildcat Creek, Big Pine Creek, Sugar Creek, and other area waterways / Trips: several hours to 2 days / Best canoeing months: May-September / Campsites: yes / Transportation: no / Car-top carriers: yes / Also rents camping equipment / Open all year.

Metamora

Whitewater Valley Canoe Rental, Inc., *see* Brookville.

Mongo

Myers Bait & Tackle (Don J. Myers), Box 63, Mongo, Ind. 46771; telephone: 219–367–2369 / Waters: Pigeon and Fawn Rivers / Trips: 1 to several days / Best canoeing months: May-July / Campsites: yes / Transportation: yes / Car-top carriers: yes.

Monterey

Walter M. Kelsey, Monterey, Ind. 46960; telephone: 219–542–2281 or 542–2673 / Waters: Tippecanoe River / Trips: a few hours to several days / Best canoeing: April-September / Campsites: yes / Transportation: yes / Car-top carriers: yes.

New Albany

Sycamore Island, 3241 Corydon Park, New Albany, Ind. 47150; telephone: 812–944–6737 / Waters: Blue and Ohio Rivers and Buck and Indian Creeks and Otter Creek in Kentucky / Trips: 1 to several days / Best canoeing months: spring / Campsites: yes / Transportation: no / Car-top carriers: yes / Open all year.

Richmond

J & J Marine & Sales, 1728 South 9th Street, Richmond, Ind. 47374; telephone: 317–962–3206 / Unconfirmed.

Rockville

Turkey Run Canoe Rental, Inc., 311 West Ohio, Rockville, Ind. 47872; telephone: 812–597–2456 or 812–569–6705 / Waters: Sugar Creek and other area waterways / Trips: 1 hour to 2 days / Best canoeing months: April-June / Campsites: yes / Transportation: yes / Car-top carriers: yes / Also rents kayaks and camping equipment.

Valparaiso

United Rent-All, 906 Calumet Avenue, Valparaiso, Ind. 46383; telephone: 219–464–3594 / Waters: Kankakee and Tippecanoe Rivers and other Indiana waterways / Trips: up to 1 day / Best canoeing months: summer / Campsites: yes / Transportation: no / Car-top carriers: yes / Also rents camping equipment / Open all year.

West Lafayette

Burnham's, P.O. Box 2217, West Lafayette, Ind. 47906 (located on the Wabash River at Brown Street); telephone: 317–743–2136 / Waters: Wabash River, Sugar Creek, Wildcat Creek, Big Pine Creek, and Tippecanoe River / Trips: a few hours to several days / Best canoeing months: March-July / Campsites: yes / Transportation: no / Car-top carriers: yes.

Sources of Information

Indiana Canoe Guide, Indiana Department of Natural Resources (612 State Office Building, Indianapolis, Ind. 46204), n.d., 108 pp., $2.00. Detailed description with maps of 21 Indiana rivers. The Department also sells the U.S. Geological Survey maps for Indiana rivers at 75¢ per map, apply to Map Sales, Room 604, at the address given above.

Indiana fishing and hunting information is available from Indiana Department of Natural Resources (697 State Office Building, Indianapolis, Ind. 46204).

Indiana tourist information is available from Indiana Department of Commerce (Room 336, State House, Indianapolis, Ind. 46204). A camping guide is available free of charge.

●

ILLINOIS

"What? River cruising in Chicago? You must be kidding!"

No, not at all. If you wish, you can canoe within a few miles of the city's famous downtown Loop — on the North Branch of the Chicago River and on the Des Plaines River. The water may not smell like roses but the scenery is pleasant.

From Chicago you can go west and south to find many other canoeable rivers throughout the state. Running through flat farmland, the rivers are ideal for placid family canoeing, with the exception of three whitewater runs — the Big and Little Vermilion and the Mazon. Unfortunately, a number of the calm rivers are polluted to varying degrees. The advice to paddle in high water only should be heeded as much for the dilution of the pollutants as for avoiding scraping bottom.

Large forests with dramatic rock formations cover the extreme south-

197

ern tip of the state between the Ohio and Mississippi Rivers. The 240,000-acre Shawnee National Forest, with beautiful stands of oak, hickory, pine, and cypress, offers a great variety of recreation, including at least three canoeable rivers in addition to the Ohio and Mississippi Rivers.

Illinois has few natural lakes, but it affords canoeists the unique experience of paddling on old, abandoned strip mine ponds. The deep pits left unrestored by the mining companies have filled with clean water and the banks have overgrown with jungle-like vegetation. Kickapoo State Park, along the Middle Fork of the southern Vermilion River near Danville, is built entirely around such lakes, which are used for extensive canoeing trips.

Few Illinois canoe liveries offer transportation (shuttle services) to put-in and take-out points; they are primarily car-top carrier rentals. So the canoeist must make his own shuttle arrangements. Some of the liveries which do not as a rule offer transportation will, on special request, provide shuttle service.

Illinois Waters

Apple River
Canoeable in high water only. Town of Apple River on the Wisconsin border to west of Warren on Route 78: about 20 miles downstream through the dramatic Apple River Canyon. Rentals: Chicago and Rockford.

Big Muddy River
Route 14 at Benton to Route 51 at Carbondale: about 40 miles with some difficulties / Route 51 to Murphysboro on Route 149: 12 miles / Murphysboro to junction with the Ohio River: about 35 miles, designated a scenic canoe trail, runs through Shawnee National Forest, watch out for Rattlesnakes, Copperheads, and Cottonmouths.

Cache River
Route 37 near Karnak to junction with the Ohio River: about 25 miles, runs through an area formerly a cypress swamp, slow progress / above Karnak from Route 37 north of town of Cypress on Route 37: about 15 miles are canoeable only in high water.

Chain o' Lakes
Chain o' Lakes State Park, off Route 12 northwest of Chicago, has a series of lakes including Grass Lake, Fox Lake, Pistakee Lake, Redhead Lake, Wooster Lake, Long Lake, and others. Rentals: Elgin, Evanston, Ingleside, and Libertyville.

Chicago River
North Branch: Skokie Lagoons in Skokie to North Shore Channel at

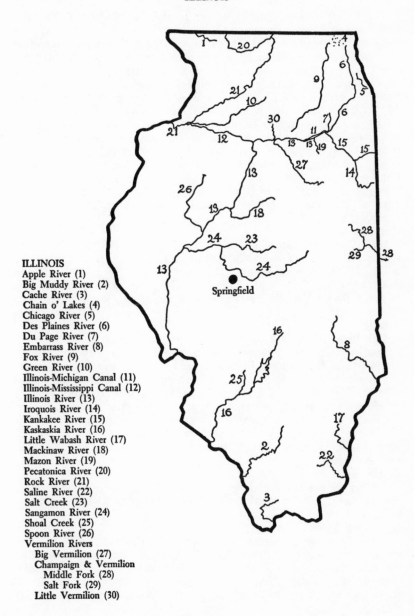

ILLINOIS
Apple River (1)
Big Muddy River (2)
Cache River (3)
Chain o' Lakes (4)
Chicago River (5)
Des Plaines River (6)
Du Page River (7)
Embarrass River (8)
Fox River (9)
Green River (10)
Illinois-Michigan Canal (11)
Illinois-Mississippi Canal (12)
Illinois River (13)
Iroquois River (14)
Kankakee River (15)
Kaskaskia River (16)
Little Wabash River (17)
Mackinaw River (18)
Mazon River (19)
Pecatonica River (20)
Rock River (21)
Saline River (22)
Salt Creek (23)
Sangamon River (24)
Shoal Creek (25)
Spoon River (26)
Vermilion Rivers
    Big Vermilion (27)
    Champaign & Vermilion
        Middle Fork (28)
        Salt Fork (29)
    Little Vermilion (30)

Springfield

Foster Street in Chicago: 17 miles. Rentals: Chicago and Evanston.

Des Plaines River

Wisconsin border near Route 41 to junction with the Kankakee River near Channahon on Route 66, where both rivers form the Illinois River: about 90 miles, canoeable in the upper reaches at high water only, middle and lower stretches are polluted, a popular stretch begins at Libertyville on Route 176 to Dam 2 near junction of Routes 21 and 45: 20 miles; from this point to Willow Springs on I-294: about 15 miles; from this point to Lemont: about 10 miles—watch carefully for dams which must be portaged and which canoeists will not be able to see until they are just about on them. Rentals: Aurora, Chicago, DeKalb, Elgin, Evanston, Fox River Grove, Libertyville, Morris, and Rockford.

Du Page River

Plainfield at junction of Routes 126 and U.S. 30 to Channahon State Park at the Illinois-Michigan Canal: about 18 miles, some scenic stretches, polluted.

Embarrass River

Villa Grove on Route 130 to Route 133 near Oakland: 16 miles / Route 133 to Route 16 at Charleston or Lake Charleston spillway: 20 miles / Charleston to Route 121 near Greenup: 25 miles / Greenup to Newton on Route 130: 20 miles / Newton to junction with the Wabash River: about 40 miles, wide variations in water levels, many obstructions.

Fox River

Oak Point State Park on Route 173 at the Wisconsin border to the dam at Algonquin on Route 62: about 33 miles with many intermediate access points, flows through Grass Lake, Fox Lake, and Pistakee Lake / Algonquin to Yorkville on Route 47: about 45 miles, polluted / Yorkville to Wedron east of Route 23 at junction with Indian Creek: 27 miles, the most scenic "wilderness stretch" of the river / below Wedron backwater of the dam at Dayton, motor boats are found here / For the Fox River in Wisconsin, *see* Wisconsin. Rentals: Aurora, Chicago, DeKalb, Elgin, Evanston, Fox River Grove, Libertyville, Morris, Rockford, and Wheaton.

Green River

Amboy on Route 52 to Deer Grove on Route 88: about 25 miles / Deer Grove to junction with the Rock River near Colona: about 40 miles, shallow with high banks.

Illinois-Michigan Canal

The only canoeable stretch of this once 100-mile-long canal is a 25-mile section from Channahon State Park off Route 66 opposite the mouth of the Kankakee River to 5 miles west of Morris on Route 47. The canal parallels the Illinois River. Some canoeists paddle down the Illinois River and return on the canal, eliminating the need for a car shuttle. Rentals: Chicago.

Illinois-Mississippi Canal

Illinois River opposite Hennepin on Route 29 to junction with the Rock River above Rock Island on Route 92: about 60 miles, the canal parallels Routes 6 and I–80 and is accessible at many points, 21 locks, at mileage 53 from Hennepin is junction of the canal with its feeder from the Rock River at Rock Falls — the feeder is 29 miles long, no locks, slow current, when it reaches the canal it flows in both directions, towards the Illinois River east of the canal and the Rock River west of the canal. Rentals: Chicago and Rockford.

Illinois River

Formed by the junction of the Des Plaines and Kankakee Rivers at Channahon on Route 66 to the Mississippi River at Grafton on Route 100: 272 miles, much commercial traffic, some locks and dams, highly polluted above Havana. Rentals: Chicago and Morris.

Iroquois River

Town of Iroquois on Route 52 to Route 1 at Watseka: about 15 miles, in high water only / Watseka to Aroma Park in Kankakee: 34 miles, pleasant, placid, motor boats near Kankakee. Rentals: Kankakee.

Kankakee River

Indiana border to junction with the Des Plaines River at Channahon on Route 66: 55 miles, pleasant canoeing only from Route 44 in Indiana, just east of the border, to Momence, Illinois, on Route 17, a stretch about 15 miles long; motor boat traffic below Momence. For the Kankakee River in Indiana, see Indiana. Rentals: Kankakee.

Kaskaskia River

Shelbyville Reservoir on Route 16 to Route 128 near Cowden: 20 miles, flows through Hidden Springs State Forest, motor boats on the reservoir / Cowden to Route 40 at Vandalia: 20 miles / Vandalia to Carlyle on Routes 50–127: 25 miles, flows through the Carlyle Reservoir / Carlyle to the Mississippi River at Kellogg: about 40 miles.

Little Wabash River

Considered canoeable only from Carmi on Route 1 to junction with the Wabash River at New Haven on Route 141: 25 miles / Above Carmi in high water only.

Mackinaw River

Kappa on Route 51 to Route 150 near Carlock: 20 miles / Route 150 to Route 9 near Mackinaw: 15 miles / Route 9 to Route 121: 15 miles / Route 121 to Route 29: 20 miles / Route 29 to junction with the Illinois River at Pekin on Route 9: 15 miles / Best stretch is from the point where the Mackinaw River meets Route 9, downstream. Rentals: Bloomington.

Mazon River

A small river, canoeable in spring only, fast with minor rapids. Bridge on Route 113 between Routes 47 and I-55 to a county road bridge off Pine Bluff Road: about 10 miles, downstream. Rentals: Morris.

Pecatonica River

Wisconsin border near Winslow on Route 73 to junction with the Rock River at Rockton on Route 2: about 75 miles, somewhat muddy waters with access points at McConnel at the Route 73 bridge, Freeport off Route 20, and near the town of Pecatonica north of Route 20. For the Pecatonica River in Wisconsin, *see* Wisconsin. Rentals: Chicago and Rockford.

Rock River

Rockton on Route 2 just below the Wisconsin border and the mouth of the Pecatonica River to Rockford on Route 20: about 20 miles / Rockford to Oregon on Route 64: 25 miles / Oregon to Dixon on Route 52: 20 miles, this the most scenic stretch of the river / Dixon to Sterling and Rock Falls (two separate towns, on either side of the river) on Route 30: 15 miles, here the Rock River meets the feeder for the Illinois-Mississippi Canal / Sterling to the Mississippi River near Rock Island on Route 92: about 70 miles, gentle flow, through rural countryside / Some pollution along the entire river / For the Rock River in Wisconsin, *see* Wisconsin. Rentals: Chicago, Fox River Grove, and Rockford.

Saline River

County road at Equality off Route 13 to the Ohio River at Saline Landing: about 25 miles of scenic canoeing through Shawnee National Forest and abandoned salt mining lands / Saline Landing down the Ohio River to Cave-in-Rock State Park on Route 1: about 12 miles.

Salt Creek

Clinton on Routes 10–51–54 to Lincoln on Route 66: about 40 miles, canoeable in high water only, many obstructions / Lincoln to Route 29: about 30 miles / Route 29 to junction with the Sangamon River: about 12 miles.

Sangamon River

Mahomet on Route 150 to Lincoln Trail Homestead State Park on Route 36 west of Decatur: about 35 miles, canoeable only in high water, many obstacles / state park to Carpenter Park in Springfield on Route 66: 23 miles, trips on the Sangamon River usually start at the state park / Springfield to Lincoln's New Salem State Park near Petersburg on Route 97: 22 miles / Petersburg to junction with the Salt Creek: 14 miles / junction to above Beardstown on Route 125 where it meets the Illinois River: 35 miles / Rentals: Champaign and Urbana.

Shoal Creek

Route 40 near Pocahontas to Route 50 near Breese: about 25 miles with some portages / Route 50 to junction with the Kaskaskia River: about 20 miles.

Spoon River

Route 79 east of Elmore to Route 150 near Dahinda: 14 miles / Route 150 to London Mills on Route 116: 22 miles / London Mills to

Route 9 near Blyton: 20 miles / Route 9 to the dam at Bernadotte: 22 miles / Bernadotte to Route 78 at Havana near junction with the Illinois River: 35 miles, shallow in the upper reaches.

Vermilion River (Big Vermilion River)

Primarily a whitewater stream requiring great expertise and not to be confused with the other Vermilion rivers listed below. County road bridge north of Chatsworth on Route 24 to Pontiac on Route 66: 30 miles, canoeable in high water only / Pontiac to Streator on Route 18: about 18 miles / Streator to the bridge at Lowell on Route 178: 17 miles, watch out for turbulence from broken dam / Lowell to the Illinois River at La Salle on Route 51: about 10 miles, particularly dangerous. Rentals: Bloomington and Morris.

Vermilion River (Champaign and Vermilion Counties)

Not to be confused with the other Vermilion rivers listed.

Middle Fork: Potomac on Route 136 to Kickapoo River State Park northwest of Danville on I–74: about 10 miles, canoeable in high water only, a number of interconnected lakes which are canoeable are to be found in the park / park to Danville: 10 miles / Danville to junction with the Wabash River in Indiana: 15 miles.

Salt Fork: Homer on Route 49 to junction with the Middle Fork: about 20 miles. Rentals for the Salt Fork: Champaign and Urbana.

Vermilion River (Little Vermilion River)

Not to be confused with the other Vermilion rivers listed. This river is strictly for whitewater experts, and only in the spring. The recommended stretch consists of 7 miles from north of LaSalle on Route 51 to the Illinois River above LaSalle.

Illinois Rentals

Aurora

Outdoor World, Inc., 629 South Broadway, Aurora, Ill. 60505; telephone: 312–896–1071 / Waters: Fox and Des Plaines Rivers / Trips: 1 or more days / Best canoeing months: spring and early summer / Campsites: yes / Transportation: no / Car-top carriers: yes.

Bloomington

Wildcountry Wilderness Outfitters, 516 North Main, Bloomington, Ill. 61701; telephone: 309–829–3521 / Waters: Mackinaw and Big Vermilion Rivers / Trips: up to 2 days / Best canoeing months: April-June / Campsites: limited availability / Transportation: no / Car-top carriers: yes / Open all year.

Brookfield

T & V Marine, 9436 West 47th Street, Brookfield, Ill. 60513; telephone: 312–485–1031 / Unconfirmed.

Champaign

Mid-West Boating & Camping (Robert L. Hardin), 1804 Bellamy Drive, Champaign, Ill. 61820; telephone: 219–359–3839 / Waters: Salt Fork and Middle Fork of the Vermilion River, the Sangamon and other rivers and lakes / Trips: 1 or more days, guides available / Best canoeing months: no response / Campsites: yes / Transportation: by special arrangement / Car-top carriers: yes, also canoe trailers / Also rents camping equipment and kayaks / Open all year.

Chicago

Chicagoland Canoe Base, Inc. (Ralph C. Frese), 4019 North Narragansett Avenue, Chicago, Ill. 60634; telephone: 312–777–1489 / Waters: Lake Michigan, Des Plaines River, North Branch of the Chicago River, Fox River, and all other Illinois rivers and streams with the exception of the Big Vermilion River / Trips: 1 or more days / Best canoeing months: when the water is open / Campsites: yes / Transportation: no / Car-top carriers: yes / Canoes may be taken out of state / A source of authoritative information on canoeing / Open all year.

Danville

Charles R. Picket, Kickapoo State Park, 2421 Georgetown Road, Danville, Ill. 61832; telephone: 217–446–7111 / Unconfirmed.

DeKalb

H_2O Sports, 716½ West Lincoln, DeKalb, Ill. 60115; telephone: 815–758–1770 / Waters: rivers of northern Illinois and southern Wisconsin / Trips: 1 or more days, guides available / Best canoeing months: April-mid-July / Campsites: yes / Transportation: by special arrangement / Car-top carriers: yes / Also rents camping equipment.

Elgin

Marinetown, 1337 Dundee Avenue, Elgin, Ill. 60120; telephone: 312–695–1133 / Waters: Chain o' Lakes, Fox River, Des Plaines River / Trips: up to 1 day / Best canoeing months: June-September / Campsites: no / Transportation: no / Car-top carriers: yes.

Evanston

Rent-Rite, 1820 Ridge Avenue, Evanston, Ill. 60201; telephone: 312–869–8011 / Waters: Skokie Lagoons, Des Plaines River, Fox River, Chain o' Lakes, and other nearby waterways / Trips: up to 1 day / Best canoeing months: May-September / Campsites: no / Transportation: no / Car-top carriers: yes.

Fox River Grove

Northern Prairie Outfitters, 206 Northwest Highway, Fox River Grove, Ill. 60021; telephone: 312–639–5773 / Waters: Des Plaines and Fox Rivers and other nearby lakes and rivers including some in Wisconsin / Trips: 1 or more days / Best canoeing months: May-October / Campsites: yes / Transportation: yes / Car-top carriers: yes.

204

Greenville
Shoppers Center, 301 East Harris Avenue, Greenville, Ill. 62246; telephone 618–664–2211 / Unconfirmed.

Ingleside
Wooster Lake Camping Resort, 999 East Route 134, Ingleside, Ill. 60041; telephone: 312–546–8700 / Waters: Wooster Lake and Chain o' Lakes / Trips: up to 1 day / Best canoeing months: May-August / Campsites: yes / Transportation: no / Car-top carriers: no / Also rents camping equipment.

Joliet
American Rental Center, 1928 Plainfield Road, Crest Hill, Joliet, Ill. 60435; telephone: 815–729–1466 / Unconfirmed.

Kankakee
A-1 Rental (Glenn H. Mann), 1010 Kennedy Drive, Kankakee, Ill. 60901; telephone: 815–939–3696 / Waters: Kankakee River / Trips: 1–2 days / Best canoeing months: April-October / Campsites: yes / Transportation: no / Car-top carriers: yes / Also rents camping equipment / Open all year.

Reed's Rent All & Sales, Inc., 907 North Indiana Avenue, Kankakee, Ill. 60901; telephone: 815–939–3117 / Waters: Kankakee and Iroquois Rivers / Trips: up to 1 day / Best canoeing months: June-August / Campsites: yes / Transportation: no / Car-top carriers: yes.

Libertyville
Pack and Paddle, Inc., 701 East Park Avenue, Route 176, Libertyville, Ill. 60048; telephone: 312–367–0090 / Waters: Des Plaines River and other area waterways / Trips: 1 or more days / Best canoeing months: May-November /Campsites: yes / Transportation: no / Car-top carriers: yes / Open all year.

Morris
Waupecan Valley Park (Harry D. Gerstung), Route 5, Morris, Ill. 60450; telephone: 815–942–1209 / Waters: Des Plaines, Illinois, Mazon, Big Vermilion, and Fox Rivers / Trips: up to 1 day / Best canoeing months: April-June and October / Campsites: no / Transportation: yes / Car-top carriers: yes.

Mount Carroll
Timber Lake Resort, Timber Lake, Mount Carroll, Ill. 61053; telephone: 815–244–8744 and 244–9300 / Unconfirmed.

Plainfield
Zimmerman Canoes, 503 Lockport, Plainfield, Ill. 60544 / telephone: 815–436–9135 / Unconfirmed.

Plano
Westwood Camping Center, 220 West Main Street, Plano, Ill. 60545; telephone: 312–552–7273 / Unconfirmed.

205

Quincy
Merkel's Marine, 1720 Broadway, Quincy, Ill. 62301; telephone: 217–223–2400 / Unconfirmed.
Rockford
H₂O Sports, 2424 South Alpine, Rockford, Ill. 61108; telephone: 815–226–5658 / *See* DeKalb.
Springfield
West Side Marine, 2936 South MacArthur, Springfield, Ill. 62704; telephone: 217–544–3121 / Waters: nearby waters / Trips: up to 2 days / Best canoeing months: April, May, September, and October / Campsites: yes / Transportation: no / Car-top carriers: yes.
Sterling
Oppold Marina, Stouffer Road south of Woodland Road, Sterling, Ill. 61081; telephone: 815–626–4802 / Unconfirmed.
Urbana
Larimore's Canoe Rental, 5 Florida Court, Urbana, Ill. 61801; telephone: 217–344–5115 / Waters: Salt Fork and Middle Fork of the Vermilion River, Sangamon River, and other Illinois and Indiana waterways / Trips: up to 2 days / Best canoeing months: May-July / Campsites: yes / Transportation: no / Car-top carriers: yes.
Wheaton
Wheaton Rental Center, 908 East Roosevelt Road, Wheaton, Ill. 60187; telephone: 312–668–8200 / Waters: Fox River / Trips: no response / Best canoeing months: April-October / Campsites: no response / Transportation: no / Car-top carriers: yes / Open all year.
Woodstock
Outdoor Recreation, Inc., 1515 South Route 47, Woodstock, Ill. 60098; telephone: 815–338–6088 / Unconfirmed.

Sources of Information

Chicagoland Canoe Trails, Historic Fox Valley Canoe Trails, and *Middle Fork Rendezvous:* three good brochures available from Chicagoland Canoe Base, Inc. (4019 North Narragansett Avenue, Chicago, Ill. 60634).

Illinois Canoeing Guide, Illinois Department of Conservation (State Office Building, Springfield, Ill. 62706), n.d., 64 pp., free. Description of 23 Illinois canoe streams with maps.

Illinois fishing and hunting information is available from Illinois Department of Conservation (State Office Building, Springfield, Ill. 62706).

Illinois Paddling Council (2316 Prospect Avenue, Evanston, Ill.

60201) offers general information, a newsletter, and *Midwest Canoe Livery Guide.*

Illinois tourist information is available from Illinois Division of Tourism (160 North LaSalle Street, Chicago, Ill. 60603 or 222 South College Street, Springfield, Ill. 62706).

Vierling, Philip E. *Illinois Country Canoe Trails,* Illinois Country Outdoor Guides (4400 North Merrimac Avenue, Chicago, Ill. 60630), in two volumes: 1. Fox River, Mazon River, Vermilion River, and Little Vermilion River, n.d., 80 pages, $1.25; 2. Dupage River, Kankakee River, Des Plaines River, and Au Sable River, n.d., $1.25. Available also from Chicagoland Canoe Base, Inc., listed above.

•

MICHIGAN

WHEN MICHIGAN IS MENTIONED, most people are likely to think of Detroit and automobiles. Few, including many canoeists who have never visited the state, would think of Michigan as a leading canoeing state. Yet Michigan has probably the largest number of developed canoe trails of any state, the largest number of canoe liveries, and, although there are no official statistics, the largest number of canoeists. No particular reason is apparent why Michiganians should be so particularly keen on canoeing — residents of other states have at least as many opportunities to canoe — but perhaps they, more than anyone else, feel the need to get away from the automobile. And nowhere else is "remote" nature so close to dense urban settlements.

The Lower Peninsula, a gently rolling countryside, abounds in rivers and has about 11,000 lakes. The eastern and southern portions are heavily industrialized, and many rivers there are polluted. But as you go further north and west you encounter increasingly better waters and sylvan scenery, such as the virgin stands of pines and hemlocks in the Hartwick Pines State Park near Grayling.

Grayling, situated close to the watershed that runs north to south through the center of the Lower Peninsula, is the canoeing capital of the state. Serving both the Au Sable River, running east into Lake Huron, and the Manistee River, running west into Lake Michigan, Grayling is crowded with eager canoeists on fine weekends in the spring. Seasoned canoeists often start their trips some 10 or 20 miles downstream from Grayling to avoid the traffic of the short-trip canoeists.

As you enter the Upper Peninsula you come into rugged country and a second-growth wilderness of maples, birches, and evergreens. The terrain rises towards Lake Superior in the north, forming dramatic cliffs along the shore and providing the few whitewater canoe runs of the state. Because of rich iron and copper ore deposits, some of the nature in the Upper Peninsula is threatened by a renewal of the mining activities which, together with logging, changed the virgin nature of Michigan in the 19th century.

Michigan Waters

Au Sable River
Main Branch: Grayling at old Route 27 to Wakeley Bridge: 25 miles, heavy canoe traffic near Grayling / Wakeley Bridge to Parmalee Bridge: 30 miles / Parmalee Bridge to Mio Dam on Route 33: 25 miles / Mio Dam to McKinley Bridge: 30 miles / McKinley Bridge to Alcona Dam Pond west of Glennie on Route 65: 40 miles / Alcona Dam Pond to Loud Dam on Route 65: 25 miles / Loud Dam to Oscoda on Route 21 at Lake Huron: 70 miles, much slack water in lower reaches of the river.

South Branch: Route 76 bridge southeast of Roscommon on Route 18 to Chase Bridge near Roscommon: 15 miles / Chase Bridge to Smith Bridge on Route 72: 15 miles, most popular "wilderness stretch" / Smith Bridge to McMasters Bridge on Route F 97 on the Main Branch: 10 miles. Rentals: Glennie, Grayling, Luzerne, Mio, Oscoda, and Roscommon.

Au Train River
U.S. Forest Service Campground southeast of Au Train Lake off Route H 03 to Lake Superior: about 10 miles, passes through Au Train Lake.

Belle River
Gratiot Avenue 3½ miles east of Richmond on Route 19 to Marine City on Route 29 near mouth of the St. Clair River: 22 miles.

Betsie River
Green Lake at Interlochen State Park on Route 137 to Route 115 near Thompsonville: 20 miles, canoeable in high water only / Route 115 to Betsie Lake near Elberta on Route 22 on Lake Michigan: 24 miles. Rentals: Honor.

Big Manistee River
See Manistee River.

Black River
Dam at Croswell north of Route 90 to I–94 bridge near Port Huron: about 30 miles, passes through Port Huron State Game Area.

Boardman River
Kalkaska on Route 66 to Grand Traverse Bay at Traverse City on

MICHIGAN
Au Sable River
  Main Branch (1)
  South Branch (2)
Au Train River (3)
Belle River (4)
Betsie River (5)
Black River (6)
Boardman River (7)
Brule River (8)
Carp River (9)
Cass River (10)
Chippewa River (11)
Clam River (12)
Clinton River (13)
Coldwater River (14)
The "Cut" (15)
Escanaba River
  Main Branch (16)
  West Branch (17)
Fence River (18)
Flat River (19)
Flint River (20)
Ford River (21)
Fox River (22)
Grand River (23)
Huron River (24)
Indian River (25)
Kalamazoo River (26)
Little Manistee River (27)
Looking Glass River (28)
Manistee River (29)
Manistique River (30)
Maple River (31)
Menominee River (32)
Millecoquins River (33)
Muskegon River
  Main Branch (34)
  Little Branch (35)
Net River (36)
Ontonagon River (37)
Otter River (38)
Paint River (39)

Paw Paw River (40)
Pere Marquette River
  Main Branch (41)
  South Branch (42)
Pine River (Isabella & Midland) (43)
Pine River (Wexford & Manistee) (44)
Platte River (45)
Portage River (46)
Presque Isle River (47)
Red Cedar River (48)
Rifle River (49)
St. Joseph River (50)
Shiawassee River (51)
Sturgeon River (52)
Sylvania Tract Lakes (53)

Tahquamenon River (54)
Thornapple River (55)
Thunder Bay River
  Main Branch (56)
  South Branch (57)
Tittabawassee River (58)
Two Hearted River (59)
Waiska River (60)
White River (61)

Route 31: about 40 miles with many dams. Rentals: Cadillac, Honor, and Traverse City.

Brule River

Forms the boundary between the Upper Peninsula and Wisconsin; inquire locally about special fishing regulations in effect. Route 73 bridge southwest of town of Iron Bridge to below Route 141 bridge where the Brule River joins the Paint River to form the Menominee River: about 45 miles with some rapids. Rentals: Crystal City.

Carp River

Deer Lake north of Ishpeming off County Road 573 to rapids on old U.S. 41 west of Marquette: about 10 miles.

Cass River

Cass City on Route 81 to Caro Dam on Route 24: 18 miles / Caro Dam to Frankenmuth Dam on Route 83: 20 miles / Frankenmuth Dam to junction with the Saginaw River: 15 miles.

Chippewa River

South Branch: Martiny Lake Wildlife Flooding Project west of Barryton on Route 66 is put-in point. It joins the North Branch at Barryton.

North Branch: Canoeable a few miles upstream of Barryton.

Main Branch: Barryton to Route 20: 15 miles / Route 20 to junctions with the Pine River and Tittabawassee River near Midland on Route 20: 25 miles. Rentals: Mount Pleasant.

Clam River

Dam at Falmouth on county road east of Route 66 to Muskegon River at Church Bridge: 18 miles, few obstructions, few intermediate access points. Rentals: Cadillac.

Clinton River

In Macomb County, part of Huron-Clinton Metroparks. Bloomer State Park No. 2 on 23-Mile Road and Avon Road to Sterling Heights footbridge: 9 miles, through Rochester-Utica State Recreation Area / footbridge to Shadyside City Park in Mount Clemens: 11 miles, closed below Mount Clemens due to Air Force base. Rentals: Pinckney.

In Oakland County, from Drayton Plains Nature Center off Hatchery Road northwest of Pontiac to Dodge Brothers No. 4 State Park: 7 miles, passes through Cass Lake.

North Branch: 31-Mile Road, 2½ miles southeast of Romeo on Route 53 to junction with the Main Branch at Mount Clemens: 25 miles, canoeable in high water only.

Coldwater River

Route 50 to junction with the Thornapple River north of Middleville on Route 37: about 10 miles. Rentals: Middleville.

Crystal River

Route 675 at Crystal Harbor to Lake Michigan: 6 miles. Rentals: Maple City.

The "Cut"

Connects Higgins Lake west of Roscommon and Houghton Lake southwest of Roscommon on Route 21: about 10 miles. Rentals: Roscommon.

Escanaba River

Main Branch: Route 35 at Gwinn to County Road 420 near Gladstone on Lake Michigan: 50 miles, power dams regulate the water.

West Branch: 7 miles north of Ralph on Route G 38 at West Branch Forest Campground to junction with the Main Branch: 12 miles, 2 rapids.

Fence River

About 14 miles west of Witch Lake on Route 95 to Way Dam of Michigamme Reservoir northeast of town of Crystal Falls on Route 2–141: about 16 miles. Rentals: Crystal City.

Flat River

Greenville on Route 57 to Smyrna Dam south of Belding on Route 91: 15 miles, the upper course is shallow in dry weather / dam to dam in Lowell on Route 21: 20 miles.

Flint River

South of Otisville on Route 15 to Bray Road in Flint: 8 miles, passes through Mott Lake, canoeable in high water; a longer run can begin at Columbiaville, 6 miles above Route 15 / Below Flint the river is polluted; it joins the Shiawassee River near Saginaw to form the Saginaw River which flows into Saginaw Bay and is not canoeable.

Ford River

County Road E–1 bridge south of Route G 38 to Lake Michigan, south of Escanaba on Route 2–41: about 20 miles, a few rapids.

Fox River

Seney on Route 28 to Germfask on Route 77: about 30 miles, passes through Seney National Wildlife Refuge. Rentals: Germfask.

Grand River

Control Dam, Michigan Center, east of Jackson to Route 127 bridge north of Jackson: 21 miles, canoeable depending upon water release from dam, when the water is too low there is a 2,500-foot conduit in Jackson which must be portaged / Route 127 to Baldwin Park in Onondaga west of Route 127: 17 miles / Onondaga to town of Eaton Rapids on Routes 50–99: 9 miles / Eaton Rapids to Dimondale dam southwest of Lansing on I–69: 17 miles / dam to Riverside Park in Lansing: 9 miles / portage recommended through Lansing / Tecumseh Park in Lansing to dam in town of Grand Ledge on Route 100: 12 miles / dam to Chief Okemos Burial Ground south of Portland near I–96: 14 miles / Okemos to Portland near I–96: 12 miles, dangerous dam and shallows in Portland / Portland to dam at Lyons near Route 21: 21 miles / Lyons to Ionia on Route 66: 13 miles / Ionia to Saranac south of Route 21: 9 miles / Saranac to Lowell on Route 21 below junction with the Flat River: 8 miles / Lowell to Ada on Route 21: 9 miles / Ada to Comstock Riverside Park in Grand Rapids: 19 miles / 3-mile portage recommended to Plaster Creek / creek to Grand Valley State College: 13 miles / college to marina in Grand Haven on Route 31: 25 miles / channel to Lake Michigan is not recommended for canoeing. Rentals: Dimondale.

Huron River
Proud Lake State Recreation Area near Commerce, via Milford, to Kensington Road: 14 miles, passes through Kent Lake / Kensington Road to H.C.M.A. Canoe Camp near Ore Lake: 10 miles / Ore Lake to Dexter: 17 miles, passes through Hudson Mills Metro Park / Dexter to Ann Arbor on Route 23: 12 miles / Ann Arbor to Ford Dam on Ford Lake: 13 miles / Ford Dam to New Boston: 14 miles, passes through Belleville Lake / New Boston to Pointe Mouille State Game Area on Lake Erie: 22 miles. Rentals: Ann Arbor, Milford, and Pinckney.

Indian River
U.S. Forest Service Widewater Campground west of Steuben off Route 94 to Indian Lake on Route 149: about 50 miles.

Kalamazoo River
Homer on Route 60 to Albion on Route 99: 12 miles / Albion to Battle Creek on Route 66: 20 miles / Battle Creek to Kalamazoo on Route 43: 20 miles / Kalamazoo to Echo Point 2 miles northwest of Allegan on Route 40: 20 miles / Allegan to Lake Michigan at Douglas north of I–196 and Route 31: 20 miles, flows through Allegan Lake and Swan Creek Wildlife Refuge. Rentals: Saugatuck.

Little Manistee River
Route 37 to town of Manistee on Route 31 at Lake Michigan: 40 miles, shallow, obstructed, the only part of the river that is canoeable, mostly used for fishing. Rentals: Wellston.

Looking Glass River
DeWitt City Park north of Lansing to junction with the Grand River near Portland off I–96: about 25 miles. Rentals: Dimondale.

Manistee River
County Road 612 bridge northwest of Grayling to Route 72: 20 miles / Route 72 to CCC road bridge: 20 miles / CCC bridge to Smithville on Route 66: 25 miles / Route 66 to U.S. 131: 37 miles / U.S. 131 to bridge at Sherman on Route 37: 53 miles / Sherman to bridge at Mesick on Route 115: 10 miles / Mesick to Red Bridge: 20 miles, through Hodenpyle Dam backwater / Red Bridge to Tippy Dam: 20 miles, through backwater / Tippy Dam to Manistee Lake: 35 miles. Rentals: Cadillac, Grayling, Hoxeyville, Lake City, and Wellston.

Manistique River
Germfask on Route 77 to town of Manistique on Route 2 at Lake Michigan: about 45 miles. Rentals: Germfask.

Maple River

Route 27 east of Bridgeville to junction with the Grand River at Muir on Route 21: about 25 miles, passes through Maple River State Game Area.

Menominee River

Formed by the junction of the Paint and Brule Rivers, it is the border between the Upper Peninsula and Wisconsin. Route 2 and Route 141 south of Crystal Falls to Route 141 at Niagara: about 30 miles / Niagara to town of Menominee on Route 41: about 80 miles, no major settlements along this stretch, some rapids and dams, feeds into Green Bay.

Millecoquins River

Hiawatha's Sportsmen's Club near Engadine on Route 117 to Lake Michigan: 7 miles. Rentals: Newberry.

Muskegon River

Little Branch: Route 20 bridge east of Big Rapids to Morley on Route 131: 15 miles / Morley to junction with the Main Branch: 15 miles.

Main Branch: Houghton Lake exit at Route 27 to Route 55 bridge east of Merritt: 20 miles, backwater / Route 55 bridge to Canoe Campsite 2 west of Route 27: 35 miles / Canoe Campsite 2 to Route 61 bridge: about 40 miles / Route 61 bridge to Route 66 bridge: 20 miles / Route 66 bridge to Route 10 bridge at Evart: 12 miles / Evart to Hersey south of Route 10: 15 miles / Hersey to the park in Paris on Route 131: 15 miles / Paris to Big Rapids on Route 20: 10 miles / Big Rapids to Rogers Dam on Route 131: 13 miles of backwater / Rogers Dam to Croton Dam north of Route 82: 20 miles of backwater / Croton Dam to Newaygo on Route 37: 15 miles / Newaygo to Muskegon on Route 31 at Lake Michigan: 30 miles.

West Branch: From about 8 miles above Route 55 bridge west of Merritt (bridge on Young Road), scenic, swampland, beaver dams. Rentals for all branches: Big Rapids, Grant, Merritt, Morley, Newaygo, and Roscommon.

Net River

Slightly west of Route 141, 12 miles north of Amasa, to junction with the Paint River below Gibbs City: about 15 miles. Rentals: Crystal City.

Ontonagon River

U.S. 45 bridge southeast of Rockland to Lake Superior at Ontonagon on Route 38: about 30 miles, mostly smooth with some rapids. Whitewater on the South, Middle, and East Branches which form the Main Branch near U.S. 45 bridge. Rentals: Watersmeet.

Otter and Sturgeon Rivers

North of Nisula on Route 38 through Otter Lake to junction with the Sturgeon River slightly below the lake and down the Sturgeon River to Chassel on Route 41: about 50 miles.

Paint River

Gibbs City north of the town of Iron River on Route 2 to Crystal Falls on Routes 141–69: about 20 miles / 2-mile portage from Crystal Falls to Route 69 bridge, from there 9 miles to Little Bull Rapids Power the Sturgeon River slightly below the lake and down the Sturgeon River the Menominee River. Rentals: Crystal City and Watersmeet.

Paw Paw River

County Road CH–681 between Hartford and Lawrence near I–94 to Route 140: 15 miles / Route 140 to junction with the St. Joseph River near Lake Michigan: 15 miles. Rentals: Benton Harbor and St. Joseph.

Pere Marquette River

Main Branch: Bridge south of Baldwin on Route 37 to Bowman Bridge on county road west of Baldwin: 5 miles / Bowman Bridge to Rainbow Rapids: 10 miles, portage rapids if rough / Rainbow Rapids to Lower Branch Bridge south of Branch on Route 10: 10 miles / Branch to the bridge at Custer on Route 10 below junction with the South Branch of the Pere Marquette River: 15 miles / Custer bridge to Scottville bridge on Route 10–31: 7 miles / Scottville to Route 31: 20 miles, into Pere Marquette Lake at Ludington.

South Branch: 13-Mile Road bridge west of Bitely to the bridge at Custer on Route 10 beyond junction with the Main Branch: about 30 miles, with intermediate access points at Huntley Bridge, Campbell Bridge, and Riverview Bridge. Rentals for both branches: Baldwin, Branch, Hoxeyville, Ludington, and Wellston.

Pine River

Isabella and Midland Counties: Route 46 east of Edmore to junction with the Chippewa River near Midland on Route 10: 40 miles, in high water only, obstructions.

Wexford and Manistee Counties: Edgetts Bridge on a county road south of Bristol to Walker Bridge on a state road: about 15 miles / Walker Bridge to Peterson Bridge on Route 37: about 20 miles / Route 37 bridge to Low Bridge south of Route 55: 15 miles into backwater of Tippy Dam of Manistee River, some rough spots. Rentals: Baldwin, Hoxeyville, and Wellston.

Platte River (Lower)

Route 22 bridge northwest of Honor to Lake Michigan: 7 miles, very pleasant. Rentals: Honor.

Portage River

Little Portage Lake northeast of Jackson on I–94 to junction with the Grand River in Jackson: 10 miles. Rentals: Pinckney.

Presque Isle River

U.S. 2 at Marenisco to Lake Superior: about 30 miles, mostly whitewater. Rentals: Watersmeet.

Red Cedar River

Fowlerville on Route 43 east of Lansing to Williamston north of

I–96: 10 miles / Williamston to Potter Park in Lansing: 20 miles. The river is canoeable in spring or high water only. Rentals: Dimondale.

Rifle River

White Ash Bridge east of Rose City on Route 33 to Route 55 east of West Branch: 16 miles / Route 55 to Greenwood Road east of Greenwood: 30 miles / Greenwood Road to Omer on Route 23: 50 miles. Rentals: Omer and West Branch.

Rogue River

12 Mile Road in Rockford on U.S. 131 to junction with the Grand River north of Grand Rapids on I–96: 11 miles.

St. Joseph River

Sturgeon Lake near Colon on Route 86 to dam near Routes 12 and 103 above the Indiana state line: 20 miles / Route 12 through Indiana to the Indiana Turnpike: about 30 miles through Elkhart and South Bend in Indiana, mostly industrial scenery / Indiana Turnpike to the dam at Niles, Michigan, on Route 12: 10 miles / Niles to St. Joseph on Route 33 at Lake Michigan: about 20 miles. Rentals: Benton Harbor, Buchanan, and St. Joseph.

Shiawassee River

Near Holly off I–75 to Shiawassee Dam and Park: 20 miles, in high water only, beware of rattlesnakes / Shiawassee Dam to Corunna on Route 71: 20 miles / Corunna to Route 57 at Chesaning Park: 25 miles / Below Chesaning the Shiawassee River waters are murky and it is not canoeable; the river joins the Flint River southwest of Saginaw to form the Saginaw River which runs into Saginaw Bay and is not canoeable. Rentals: Corunna and Durand.

Sylvania Recreation Area (Sylvania Tract Lakes)

Ottawa National Forest southwest of Watersmeet on Route 535 off U.S. 2: includes a group of lakes interconnected by portages. Rentals: Watersmeet.

Tahquamenon River

County Road 415 north of McMillan on Route 28 to Dollarville Dam near Newberry on Route 123: about 8 hours canoeing, through Dollarville Reservoir / Newberry to Tahquamenon Falls on Route 123: about 30 miles / Tahquamenon Falls to Lake Superior at Whitefish Bay: about 20 miles. Rentals: Newberry.

Thornapple River

Route 50 northeast of Vermontville to Nashville Dam on Route 66: about 15 miles, high water only / Route 66 to Hastings on Route 43: 15 miles, passes through Thornapple Lake / Hastings to Irving dam: 12 miles / Irving to Middleville Dam on Route 37: 6 miles / Middleville Dam to LaBarge Dam, 84th Street: 12 miles / LaBarge Dam to junction with the Grand River at Ada on Route 21: 14 miles. Rentals: Middleville.

Thunder Bay River

South Branch: Fletcher Pond south of Route 32 to junction with the Main Branch midway between Hillman on Route 32 and Long Rapids on Route 65: 17 miles.

Main Branch: Lake 15 southwest of Atlanta on Route 32 to Route 33 bridge: 14 miles / Route 33 bridge to Route 32 bridge: 6 miles / Route 32 bridge to Hillman on Route 32: 10 miles / Hillman to Long Rapids on Route 65: 25 miles / Long Rapids to Alpena Municipal Park on Route 23 at Lake Huron: 23 miles via dams and backwater. Rentals: Atlanta.

Tittabawassee River

Route 30 northeast of Gladwin to junctions with the Chippewa and Pine Rivers at Midland on Route 20: about 30 miles, polluted below Midland, joins the Saginaw River near Saginaw.

Two Hearted River

Whitewaters but canoeable some 15 miles above Route H 37 bridge south of Deer Park. H 37 bridge to Two Heart on Lake Superior: about 20 miles. Rentals: Newberry.

Waiska River

Route 28 south of Brimley to Brimley State Park on Lake Superior: 7 miles.

White River

Hesperia Park on Route 20 to White Lake on Lake Michigan: about 40 miles. Rentals: Montague.

Michigan Rentals

Ann Arbor

Skip's Huron River Canoe Livery, 3780 West Delhi Road, Ann Arbor, Mich. 48103; telephone: 313–769–8686 / Waters: Huron River / Trips: 2 hours and 4 hours / Best canoeing months: May-September / Campsites: yes / Transportation: yes / Car-top carriers: no.

Atlanta

G & L Canoe Livery (Glen and Louise Boger), Box 92, Atlanta, Mich. 49709; telephone: 517–785–4788 / Waters: Thunder Bay River / Trips: 1 hour to 5 days, guides available / Best canoeing months: June-August / Campsites: yes / Transportation: yes / Car-top carriers: yes.

Red Lantern Canoe Livery, Box 285, Route 3, Atlanta, Mich. 49709; telephone: 517–785–3296 / Waters: Thunder Bay River and small lakes / Trips: 1 hour to 5 days / Best canoeing months: July-September / Campsites: yes / Transportation: yes / Car-top carriers: yes.

Baldwin

Baldwin Canoe Rental, Box 265, Baldwin, Mich. 49304; telephone:

616–745–4669 / Waters: Pere Marquette and Pine Rivers / Trips: a few hours to 5 days / Best canoeing months: May-September / Campsites: yes / Transportation: yes / Car-top carriers: yes.

Ivan's Canoe Livery, Box 1013 Route 1, Baldwin, Mich. 49304 (located on Route 1–M37 at Pere Marquette Bridge); telephone: 616–745–3361 / Waters: Pere Marquette River / Trips: 1 or more days, guides available / Best canoeing months: April-October / Campsites: yes / Transportation: yes / Car-top carriers: no / Housekeeping cabins available.

Benton Harbor

Gardner's Favorite Sports & Marine, 741 Riverview Drive, Benton Harbor, Mich. 49022; telephone: 616–925–3247 / Waters: St. Joseph and Paw Paw Rivers / Trips: 1 or more days / Best canoeing months: May-August / Campsites: yes / Transportation: yes / Car-top carriers: yes.

Big Rapids

Sport 'n' Life Canoe Livery (P. Roy Couch), 711 Farnsworth, Big Rapids, Mich. 49307; telephone: 616–796–9284 / Waters: Big and Litte Muskegon Rivers / Trips: 2 hours to 2 weeks / Best canoeing months: September-October / Campsites: yes / Transportation: yes / Car-top carriers: no.

Branch

Branch Canoe Livery, Route 1, Box 191, Branch, Mich. 49402 (located on U.S. 10); telephone: 616–898–2681 / Waters: Pere Marquette River / Trips: ½ hour to 4 days / Best canoeing months: May-October / Campsites: yes / Transportation: no / Car-top carriers: no / Open all year.

Buchanan

Callman-Buchanan Canoe Center (William A. Smoke), East River Road, Buchanan, Mich. 49107; telephone: 616–695–9637 / The Center is operated by the American Canoe Association for training and trips on the St. Joseph River.

Kayak Specialties, 320 North Red Bud Trail, Buchanan, Mich. 49107; telephone: 616–695–9637 / Waters: St. Joseph River / Trips: as long as wanted / Best canoeing months: April-November / Campsites: no / Transportation: yes / Car-top carriers: yes / Open all year.

Cadillac

Chippewa Landing, Box 234, Cadillac, Mich. 49601; telephone: 616–775–3441 or 775–7352 / Waters: Boardman River, Clam River, and Manistee River / Trips: a few hours to two weeks / Best canoeing months: May-October / Campsites: yes / Transportation: yes / Car-top carriers: no / Open weekends only April-May and September-October, daily June-August / Operates its own campsite.

Corunna

Dick's Canoe Livery, 501 East Ferry Street, Corunna, Mich. 48817;

telephone: 517–743–3388 / Waters: Shiawassee River / Trips: up to 1 day / Best canoeing months: June-October / Campsites: yes / Transportation: yes / Car-top carriers: yes.

Crystal Falls

Michi-Aho Resort Motel (Butch Harder), Star Route M–69, Crystal Falls, Mich. 49920; telephone: 906–875–3514 / Waters: Brule, Paint, Net, and Fence Rivers / Trips: 1 or more days, guides available / Best canoeing months: April-June / Campsites: yes / Transportation: yes / Car-top carriers: yes / Also rents camping equipment.

Dimondale

Grand Pointe Marina, Creyts Road "On the River", Dimondale, Mich. 48821; telephone: 517–646–6733 / Waters: Grand, Red Cedar, and Looking Glass Rivers / Trips: 1 or more days / Best canoeing months: April-October / Campsites: yes / Transportation: no / Car-top carriers: yes / Canoe trailer available.

Durand

Borrow's Canoe Rental, 7164 South Geeck Road, Durand, Mich. 48429; telephone: 517–288–4251 from May-October and 517–288–3896 at other times / Waters: Shiawassee River / Trips: up to 2 days / Best canoeing months: May-October / Campsites: yes / Transportation: yes / Car-top carriers: yes.

Falmouth

White Birch Canoe Livery, located on M 55, 4 miles west of U.S. 27, Falmouth, Mich. 49632; telephone: 616–328–4547 / Unconfirmed.

Germfask

Northland Outfitters (Tom and Carma Gronback), Highway M 77, Germfask, Mich. 49836; telephone: 906–586–9801 / Waters: Fox and Manistique Rivers / Trips: 1–8 days, guides available / Best canoeing months: May-September / Campsites: yes / Transportation: yes / Car-top carriers: yes / Complete outfitting for camping.

Glennie

Jane's Canoe Rental, 4217 South State, Glennie, Mich. 48737; telephone: 517–735–2334 / Waters: Au Sable River / Trips: 2 hours to 1 week, guides available / Best canoeing months: June-September / Campsites: yes / Transportation: yes / Car-top carriers: yes.

Grant

Vic's Canoes at Salmon Run Campground, Felch Road, RR 2, Grant, Mich. 49327; telephone: 616–834–5494 or 616–532–7374 / Waters: Muskegon River / Trips: 1 hour to several days / Best canoeing months: May-October / Campsites: yes / Transportation: yes / Car-top carriers: not usually.

Grayling

Borchers Au Sable Canoeing, 101 Maple Street, Grayling, Mich. 49738; telephone: 517–348–4921 / Unconfirmed.

Carlisle Canoe Livery, P.O. Box 150, 110 State Street, Grayling, Mich. 49738; telephone: 517–348–2301 / Waters: Au Sable and Manistee Rivers / Trips: 2 hours to 1 week / Best canoeing months: June-August / Campsites: yes / Transportation: yes / Car-top carriers: no / Also rents camping equipment and manufactures paddles.

Carr's Pioneer Canoe Livery, 217 Alger Street, P.O. Box 252, Grayling, Mich. 49738; telephone: 517–348–5851 / Waters: Au Sable and Manistee Rivers / Trips: 2½ hours to 1 week / Best canoeing months: May-August / Campsites: yes / Transportation: yes / Car-top carriers: yes / Open all year.

Jim's Canoe Livery, RR 3, Box 3119, Grayling, Mich. 49738; telephone: 517–348–9903 / Unconfirmed.

Jolly Redskin Canoe Livery (Bruce and Corrine Smith), P.O. Box 396, Grayling, Mich. 49738; telephone: 517–348–5611 / Waters: Au Sable and Manistee Rivers / Trips: 2½ hours to 1 week / Best canoeing months: June-September / Campsites: yes / Transportation: yes / Car-top carriers: yes.

Penrod's Au Sable Canoe Trips, 100 Maple Street, P.O. Box 432, Grayling, Mich. 49738; telephone: 517–348–3711 / Waters: Au Sable and Manistee Rivers / Trips: 2½ hours to 1 week / Best canoeing months: July-August / Campsites: yes / Transportation: yes / Car-top carriers: yes / Cottages and cabins, some with housekeeping, at rental site.

Ray's Canoe Livery, 200 Ingham Street, P.O. Box 709, Grayling, Mich. 49738; telephone: 517–348–2671 / Waters: Au Sable and Manistee Rivers / Trips: 2½ hours to 1 week / Best canoeing months: May-September / Campsites: yes / Transportation: yes / Car-top carriers: yes.

Shel-Haven Canoe Livery, RR 1, Box 1141 (Diane and Lee Tompkins), Grayling, Mich. 49738; telephone: 517–348–7108 during May-November, and 517–487–3145 at other times / Waters: Manistee River / Trips: 1 to several days, guides available / Best canoeing months: no response / Campsites: yes / Transporation: yes / Car-top carriers: no.

Hastings

Ray Haywood, RR 1 at Airport Bridge, Hastings, Mich. 49058; telephone: 616–945–9968 / Unconfirmed.

Honor

Casey's Corners, Highway M-22 at Platte River, Honor, Mich. 49640; telephone: 616–325–3636 / Waters: Platte River / Trips: up to 1 day / Best canoeing months: May-October / Campsites: no / Transportation: yes / Car-top carriers: yes.

Riverside Canoes (Tom and Kathy Stocklen), RR 1, on Highway M-22 at Platte River, Honor, Mich. 49640; telephone: 616–325–5622 /

Waters: Platte River / Trips: several hours / Best canoeing months: June-August / Campsites: yes / Transportation: yes / Car-top carriers: yes / Also rents motor boats.

Waterwheel Boat and Canoe Livery, Honor, Mich. 49640; telephone: 616–325–3620 / Waters: Platte, Boardman, and Betsie Rivers / Trips: up to 1 day / Best canoeing months: July-October / Campsites: no / Transportation: yes / Car-top carriers: yes.

Hoxeyville

Carl's Canoe Livery (Carl Fortelka), South 15-Mile Road at Walker Bridge, Hoxeyville, Mich. 49641; telephone: 616–862–3251 or 616–797–5156 / Waters: Pine, Manistee, and Pere Marquette Rivers / Trips: 1 or more days / Best canoeing months: May-October / Campsites: yes / Transportation: yes / Car-top carriers: yes.

Lake City

Smithville Landing (F. C. Smith, Jr.), Box 341, Lake City, Mich. 49651; telephone: 616–839–4579 / Waters: Manistee River / Trips: several hours to several days / Best canoeing months: May-October / Campsites: yes / Transportation: yes / Car-top carriers: no.

Ludington

Frontier Canoe & Bait, Rt. 1, Ludington, Mich. 49431; telephone: 616–845–5490 / Waters: Pere Marquette River / Trips: 1–5 days / Best canoeing months: June-August / Campsites: yes / Transportation: yes / Car-top carriers: yes.

Luzerne

Camp Bear Paw Cabins and Canoes, Star Route 4, Box 103, Luzerne, Mich. 48636; telephone: 517–826–3313 / Waters: Au Sable River / Trips: 3 hours to several days / Best canoeing months: May-October / Campsites: yes / Transportation: yes / Car-top carriers: no / Cabins available.

Maple City

Crystal Harbor, Inc., 2 miles northeast of Glen Arbor on Highway 67, Maple City, Mich. 49664; telephone: 616–334–3991 / Waters: Crystal River and nearby lakes / Trips: several hours / Best canoeing months: June-August / Campsites: no / Transportation: yes / Car-top carriers: yes.

Merritt

Happy River Canoe Livery Inc., RR 1, Highway M-55, 6 miles west of Houghton Lake, Merritt, Mich. 49667; telephone: 616–328–4323 / Waters: Muskegon River / Trips: 2 hours to 2 weeks, guides available / Best canoeing months: May-October / Campsites: yes / Transportation: yes / Car-top carriers: yes.

Middleville

Clanland Campground (William D. Campbell), 7690 Irving Road, Middleville, Mich. 49333; telephone: 616–795–3809 / Waters: Thornapple and Coldwater Rivers / Trips: 1 or more days, guides available /

Best canoeing months: May-November / Campsites: yes / Transportation: yes / Car-top carriers: yes / Canoeing instruction offered.

Milford

Heavner Canoe Rental (Alan Heavner), 2775 Garden Road, Milford, Mich. 48042; telephone: 313–685–2379 / Waters: Huron River and other area waterways / Trips: 1 to several days / Best canoeing months: April-mid-October / Campsites: yes / Transportation: yes / Car-top carriers: no.

Mio

Hinchman Acres Au Sable River Canoe Rental (Sam and Natalie Giardina), 702 North Morenci, Box 146, Mio, Mich. 48647; telephone: 517–826–3991/ Waters: Main Branch of the Au Sable River / Trips: 2½ hours to 2 weeks / Best canoeing months: May-October / Campsites: yes / Transportation: yes / Car-top carriers: no / Open all year.

Montague

Happy Mohawk Canoe Livery, 351 Fruitvale Road at County Line Bridge, Montague, Mich. 49437; telephone: 616–894–4209 / Waters: White River / Trips: up to 2 days / Best canoeing months: April-October / Campsites: yes / Transportation: yes / Car-top carriers: yes.

Morley

Tall Pines Campsites and Canoe Rental, Talcott Street, RR 1, Morley, Mich. 49336; telephone: 616–856–4556 or 856–4158 / Waters: Little Muskegon and Big Muskegon Rivers / Trips: up to 2 days / Best canoeing months: April-October / Campsites: no / Transportation: yes / Car-top carriers: yes.

Mount Pleasant

Mountainside Canoes (Donna and John Buckley), Route 2, 4700 West Remus Road, Mount Pleasant, Mich. 48858; telephone: 517–772–5437 / Waters: Chippewa River / Trips: 1 or more days, guides available / Best canoeing months: April-June, September-October / Campsites: yes / Transportation: yes / Car-top carriers: yes.

Newaygo

Derk's Marine Sales and Service, 1672 Croton Drive, Newaygo, Mich. 49337; telephone: 616–652–6738 / Unconfirmed.

Newberry

Dollarville Outdoors (Robert L. Schneider), near Dollarville Dam, Box 209, Newberry, Mich. 49868; telephone: 906–293–8125 or 293–5759 / Waters: Tahquamenon, Two Hearted, and Millecoquins Rivers / Trips: 1 or more days / Best canoeing months: June-August / Campsites: yes / Transportation: yes / Car-top carriers: yes / Also rents camping equipment.

Omer

Russell's Canoes, U.S. 23 north of Omer, Omer, Mich. 48749; telephone: 517–653–2644 / Waters: Rifle River / Trips: 1 hour to 3 days /

Best canoeing months: April-October / Campsites: no / Transportation: yes / Car-top carriers: no.

Oscoda

Lovell's Canoe Rental (Penny and Frank Trudell), 718 West River Road, Oscoda, Mich. 48750; telephone: 517–739–5239 / Waters: Au Sable River / Trips: 1 or more days / Best canoeing months: May-October / Campsites: yes / Transportation: yes / Car-top carriers: no / Housekeeping cottages available.

Pinckney

Hell Creek Ranch, Inc., 10820 Cedar Lake Road, Pinckney, Mich. 48169; telephone: 313–878–3632 / Waters: Clinton, Huron, and Portage Rivers / Trips: up to 1day / Best canoeing months: April-June, September-October / Campsites: yes / Transportation: yes / Car-top carriers: no.

Roscommon

Campbell's Canoe Livery, State Route 144 at bridge, Roscommon, Mich. 48653; telephone: 517–275–5810 / Unconfirmed.

Hiawatha Canoe Livery, 1113 Lake Street, Roscommon, Mich. 48653; telephone: 517–275–5213 / Waters: South Branch of the Au Sable River / Trips: 1½ hours to 6 days / Best canoeing months: May-October / Campsites: yes / Transportation: yes / Car-top carriers: yes.

North Cut Canoe Livery and Sales, Route 2, Box 366, Roscommon, Mich. 48653; telephone: 517–821–9521 / Waters: The "Cut" and Muskegon River / Trips: 1 or more days / Best canoeing months: spring and fall / Campsites: yes / Transportation: yes / Car-top carriers: yes / Also rents camping equipment.

Paddle Brave Canoe Livery-Camp (Chuck and Linda Mires), Box 998, Route 1, Roscommon, Mich. 48653; telephone: 517–275–5273 / Waters: South Branch of the Au Sable River / Trips: 2 hours to 10 days or longer / Best canoeing months: April-October / Campsites: yes / Transportation: yes / Car-top carriers: yes / Also rents camping equipment / Open all year.

Watters Edge Canoe Livery, RR 1, Box 990, Roscommon, Mich. 48653; telephone: 517–275–5568 / Waters: Au Sable River / Trips: 5 hours to 5 days / Best canoeing months: May-October / Campsites: yes / Transportation: yes / Car-top carriers: yes / Open all year.

St. Joseph

Wolf's Enterprises, 1207 Ann Street, St. Joseph, Mich. 49085; telephone: 616–983–1008 / Waters: St. Joseph and Paw Paw Rivers / Trips: 1 or more days / Best canoeing months: May-October / Campsites: yes / Transportation: no / Car-top carriers: yes.

Saugatuck

Gleason's Marina, 650 Water Street, Saugatuck, Mich. 49453; telephone: 616–857–9973 / Waters: Kalamazoo River and other waterways /

222

Trips: half-day to 2 days / Best canoeing months: July-August / Campsites: yes / Transportation: yes / Car-top carriers: no.

Traverse City

Ranch Rudolf, P.O. Box 587, Traverse City, Mich. 49684; telephone: 616–947–9529 / Waters: Boardman River / Trips: up to half a day / Best canoeing months: May-October / Campsites: yes / Transportation: yes / Car-top carriers: no / A resort with lodgings, campground, restaurant, swimming pool, general store, entertainment, cross-country ski rental / Open all year.

Watersmeet

Sylvania Outfitters, West U.S. 2, Watersmeet, Mich. 49969; telephone: 906–358–4766 / Waters: Middle and South Branches of the Ontonagon River, the Sylvania Tract Lakes, and the Paint and Presque Isle Rivers / Trips: 1 or more days / Best canoeing months: May-October for the lakes and May, June, and September for the rivers / Campsites: yes / Transportation: yes / Car-top carriers: yes / Also rents camping equipment.

Wellston

Chippewa Landing-Pine, South of M-55 on M-37, RR 1, Wellston, Mich. 49689; telephone: 616–775–3441 and 775–7352 / Unconfirmed.

Horina Canoe Rental (Emil Horina), RR 1, Highway M-37, Wellston, Mich. 49689; telephone: 616–862–3470 / Waters: Pine River / Trips: 1–3 days / Best canoeing months: no response / Campsites: yes / Transportation: yes / Car-top carriers: yes / Open all year.

Marrik's Pine River Canoe Service, Route 1, Wellston, Mich. 49689; telephone: 616–862–3471 / Waters: Pine, Manistee, and Pere Marquette Rivers / Trips: 1 or more days / Best canoeing months: May-August / Campsites: yes / Transportation: yes / Car-top carriers: yes.

Sportsman's Canoe & Campground Rental (Mary Barber), RR 1, West Caberfae Highway, Wellston, Mich. 49689; telephone: 616–862–3571 / Waters: Pine, Little and Big Manistee Rivers / Trips: several hours to several days / Best canoeing months: May-September / Campsites: yes / Transportation: yes / Car-top carriers: yes.

West Branch

Jacksonville Store & Canoe Rental, 987 East M-55, West Branch, Mich. 48661; telephone: 517–345–0049 / Waters: Rifle River / Trips: 1 or more days / Best canoeing months: June-September / Campsites: yes / Transportation: yes / Car-top carriers: no.

Sources of Information

Canoe Rental Guide, Recreational Canoeing Association (Box 936, Route 1, Roscommon, Mich. 48653), n.d., 24 pp., free. Lists member canoe liveries, restaurants, campgrounds, food stores, and other services.

Carefree Days, West Michigan Tourist Association (136 Fulton East, Grand Rapids, Mich. 49502), free annual publication. Lists campgrounds, trailer parks, sports fishing and canoeing opportunities, and marinas.

Huron-Clinton Metropolitan Authority (600 Woodward Avenue, Detroit, Mich. 48226) publishes canoeing guides and road and park maps in a five-county area.

Michigan Boat Launching Directory, Michigan Department of Natural Resources (Mason Building, Lansing, Mich. 48926), n.d., 52 pp., free.

Michigan fishing and hunting information is available from the Michigan Department of Natural Resources (Mason Building, Lansing, Mich. 48926).

Michigan Grand River Watershed Council (3322 West Michigan Avenue, Lansing, Mich. 48917) supplies free canoe maps of the Grand River and its tributaries.

Michigan Guide to Easy Canoeing, Michigan Department of Natural Resources (Mason Building, Lansing, Mich. 48926), n.d., 32 pp., free. Describes 54 "easy" rivers, most of them with maps.

Michigan tourist information is available from the Michigan Tourist Council (300 South Capitol Avenue, Lansing, Mich. 48926) and the following regional associations: Southeast Michigan Travel and Tourist Association (1200 Sixth Avenue, Detroit, Mich. 48226), East Michigan Tourist Association (1 Wenonah Park, Bay City, Mich. 48706), West Michigan Tourist Association (136 Fulton East, Grand Rapids, Mich. 49502), and Upper Peninsula Travel and Recreation Association (P.O. Box 400, Iron Mountain, Mich. 49801).

Run River Run, Michigan Tourist Council (300 South Capitol Avenue, Lansing, Mich. 48926), a 30-minute film available for screening by groups.

Wilderness Canoe Trail, South Branch Canoe Livery Association (Roscommon, Mich. 48653), n.d., 12 pp., free. Interprets the South Branch of the Au Sable River.

•

WISCONSIN

No STATE HAS THE ATTRACTIONS of its waterways better documented than Wisconsin. And for good reason. Wisconsin has been a leader in designating many of its river systems as official canoe trails, treating them as irreplaceable treasures for its citizens and visitors. Waters run clear and often swiftly, through large forest tracts lined with rock bluffs and sandstone cliffs, toppling over rapids and falls, or they meander their way slowly through marshes, wetlands, hardwood swamps, pastures, and fields. Water birds feel at home, from the ubiquitous ducks to the elusive sandhill cranes. Fish are abundant and beavers keep busy in the company of muskrats, deer, black bears, chipmunks, and raccoons.

Among the longest and most rewarding canoe trails are those originating in the northwestern and north-central parts of the state — the Chippewa, Flambeau, and Namekagon Rivers. In the southwest, the Baraboo River, cutting its way through the Baraboo mountain range, and the Kickapoo River, flowing through the rugged terrain known as the Driftless Area, are popular. The Wisconsin River, rising in the lake region on the Michigan border, flows about 600 miles through the heart of the state to join the Mississippi River at Prairie du Chien. Its most famous tourist attraction is Wisconsin Dells, a 15-mile canyon, 150 feet deep, carved in fantastic shapes out of the sandstone. In the northwest, the Wolf River's middle course is one of the most renowned whitewater runs in the nation — recommended only to star performers or to rubber rafters. The upper and lower courses of the Wolf River are suitable for family canoeing.

Many Wisconsin rivers are too shallow in the dry summer months, and it is always wise to inquire locally about water conditions. In medium and high water, quiet-water canoeists should be alert to the fact that many a smooth Wisconsin river, like a bolting horse, will suddenly jump into wild action with roaring rapids and falls, some of them so rough that even whitewater experts will portage. The reason for this characteristic is that the landscape was shaped by the last ice age, which flattened out much of the countryside while at the same time scraping and carving deep dents and sharp edges into the surface or piling up small but steep hills of rock and gravel, ideal playgrounds for jumping rivers.

The ice age left some 9,000 lakes in the state, most of them in the north. These lakes offer an infinite variety of canoeing trips. It also left the famous Kettle Moraine, near Milwaukee, dotted by miniature lakes, ponds, and waterholes connected by streams or short portages. This area is very popular with canoeing fishermen.

Wisconsin Waters

Bad River
Elm Hoist Trail in Bad River Indian Reservation to Lake Superior downstream from Odanah on Route 2: 26 miles, canoeable in high water only; a trip can be started 12 miles upstream on the Marengo River from the bridge north of Highbridge on Route 13.

Baraboo River

Reedsburg on Route 33 to the dam in the town of Baraboo on Route 113: 28 miles / Route 113 to the Wisconsin River below Portage east of I-90–94: 25 miles. Rentals: Portage and Sauk City.

Bark River

Lake Nemabbin east of Fort Atkinson to junction with the Rock River at Fort Atkinson on Routes 12–26–106: about 30 miles. Rentals: Jefferson.

Bois Brule River

County Highway S in Brule River State Forest southwest of the town of Brule to the Route 2 bridge at Brule: 13 miles / Brule to Lake Superior: 23 miles, several whitewater rapids. Rentals: Brule.

Brule River

Wisconsin Route 55-Michigan Route 73 to junction with the Paint River to form the Menominee River below Routes 2–141: about 45 miles, shallow in dry weather, a few rapids, special fishing regulations, forms a portion of the Wisconsin-Michigan border.

Chippewa River and Lake Chippewa

Lake Chippewa is an artificial lake of 17,000 acres southeast of Hayward on Route 63 with more than 200 miles of shoreline offering a great variety of canoe trips through numerous bays, channels, and island chains.

West Fork: Canoeable from Upper Clam Lake on Route 77 to Lake Chippewa on Highway B bridge: about 24 miles.

East Fork: Glidden on Route 13 to Winter Dam at Lake Chippewa: about 50 miles.

Main Branch: Winter Dam to junction with the Flambeau River and Holcombe Flowage (a lake) on Route 27 southwest of Ladysmith: about 70 miles. The river continues through the cities of Chippewa Falls and Eau Claire to join the Mississippi River near Pepin on Route 35: Rentals: Bruce, Chippewa Falls, and Hayward.

Couderay River

Windigo Lake near Route 27 south of Hayward via portages through Grindstone Lake and Lac Court Oreilles to the beginning of the river at Little Lac Court Oreilles via the town of Couderay on Route 27–70 to junction with the Chippewa River: 28 miles. Rentals: Hayward.

Crawfish River

Route 16 south of Danville on Highway T to Hubbleton on Route 19: 20 miles / Hubbleton to Jefferson on Route 18 and junction with the Rock River: 20 miles.

Crystal River and Chain O' Lakes

Taylor Lake on Route 22 near Waupaca to junction with the Waupaca River below town of Waupaca: 12 miles, through the Chain O' Lakes into the Crystal River, thrilling but safe whitewater. Rentals: Madison and Waupaca.

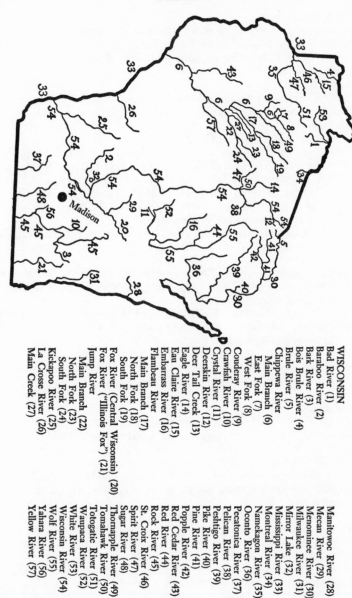

Madison

WISCONSIN

Bad River (1)
Baraboo River (2)
Bark River (3)
Bois Brule River (4)
Brule River (5)
Chippewa River
  Main Branch (6)
  East Fork (7)
  West Fork (8)
Couderay River (9)
Crawfish River (10)
Crystal River (11)
Deerskin River (12)
Deer Tail Creek (13)
Eagle River (14)
Eau Claire River (15)
Embarrass River (16)
Flambeau River
  Main Branch (17)
  North Fork (18)
  South Fork (19)
Fox River (Central Wisconsin) (20)
Fox River ("Illinois Fox") (21)
Jump River
  Main Branch (22)
  North Fork (23)
  South Fork (24)
Kickapoo River (25)
La Crosse River (26)
Main Creek (27)

Manitowoc River (28)
Mecan River (29)
Menominee River (30)
Milwaukee River (31)
Mirror Lake (32)
Mississippi River (33)
Montreal River (34)
Namekagon River (35)
Oconto River (36)
Pecatonica River (37)
Pelican River (38)
Peshtigo River (39)
Pike River (40)
Pine River (41)
Popple River (42)
Red Cedar River (43)
Red River (44)
Rock River (45)
St. Croix River (46)
Spirit River (47)
Sugar River (48)
Thornapple River (49)
Tomahawk River (50)
Totogatic River (51)
Waupaca River (52)
White River (53)
Wisconsin River (54)
Wolf River (55)
Yahara River (56)
Yellow River (57)

227

Deerskin River

Forest Service Road 2178 about 10 miles northeast of town of Eagle River on Routes 17–45–70 to Eagle River: 15 miles, passes through Scattering Rice Lake and a chain of lakes, shallow in dry weather. Rentals: Eagle River.

Deer Tail Creek

Route 27 south of Ladysmith to junction with the Chippewa River at Highway D: 7 miles, canoeable in medium and high water only. Rentals: Bruce.

Eagle River and Eagle Chain O' Lakes

Entry of Eagle River into the chain is between Big Lake and Whitefish Lake on Route 32 east of the town of Three Lakes. The chain consists of 28 interconnected lakes; motor boats are permitted. The Eagle River leaves the chain at the town of Eagle River and joins the Wisconsin River a few miles downstream. Rentals: Eagle River.

Eau Claire River (Northwest Wisconsin)

Eau Claire Reservoir on Route 27 to junction with the St. Croix River at Gordon on Route 53: about 20 miles.

Embarrass River

Middle Branch: Town road off Route 45 about 3 miles north of Wittenberg to Caroline on Highway G north of Marion on Route 45 and junction with the South Branch: 28 miles.

South Branch: Tigerton Dells north of Tigerton on Route 45 to Caroline: about 15 miles / Caroline to junction with the North Branch below Hayman Falls: 5 miles.

North Branch: Tilleda on Highway D north of Route 29 to Hayman Falls: 17 miles / Hayman Falls to town of Embarrass on Route 22: 19 miles / Embarrass to junction with the Wolf River at New London on Route 45: 35 miles.

Flambeau River

Can be started on the Turtle River at Shea Dam 10 miles northeast of Mercer on Route 51 to Highway FF bridge above Turtle Falls, a run of about 15 miles. Continue into Turtle Flambeau Flowage. Or from town of Manitowish Waters on Route 51 down the Manitowish River to Turtle Flambeau Flowage, about 22 miles. Turtle Flambeau Flowage is a 17,000-acre artificial lake with a maze of islands, bays, and channels, and varying water levels.

North Fork: Turtle Flambeau Flowage dam to town of Park Falls on Route 13: about 20 miles, a fast run with several rapids / Park Falls to junction with the South Fork at The Forks, just below Flambeau Falls: 46 miles, whitewater, several rapids, flows through Flambeau River State Forest / The Forks to junction with the Chippewa River at Highway D: 45 miles, whitewater, flows through a group of lakes.

South Fork: Canoeable from Round Lake in Chequamegon National Forest north of Route 70 to junction with the North Fork at The Forks:

228

about 70 miles, several stretches of whitewater. Rentals: Bruce, Chippewa Falls, and Winter.

Fox River (Central Wisconsin)

Portage on Route 33 to Montello on Route 22: 27 miles, passes through Buffalo Lake / Montello to Marquette on Highway H on Lake Puckaway: 11 miles / Marquette to Princeton on Route 73: 16 miles / Princeton to Berlin on Route 49: 19 miles / Berlin to Oshkosh and Lake Winnebago: 27 miles, passes through Lake Butte des Morts / Lake Winnebago is too rough for canoeing. One can also canoe on a canal from Portage to the Wisconsin River. Rentals: Madison, Oshkosh, and Portage.

Fox River ("Illinois Fox")

Mukwonago on County Road ES off Routes 83 and 99 to Waterford on Route 36: 16 miles, flows through Tichigan Wildlife Area / Waterford to Route 50 east of New Munster: 17 miles / Route 50 to Route 173 in Illinois: 10 miles / For continuation, *see* Illinois. Rentals: Madison and Milwaukee.

Jump River

South Fork: Prentice on Route 13 to junction with the North Fork below Big Falls Portage: 33 miles, canoeable only in medium to high water, several whitewater stretches with rapids.

North Fork: U.S. 8 west of Prentice to junction with the South Fork: 19 miles, canoeable in medium and high water only.

Main Branch: Junction of the North and South Forks to Holcombe Flowage and junction with the Chippewa River: 28 miles, upper stretch canoeable in medium to high water only. Rentals: Bruce.

Kettle Moraine State Forest

Not to be confused with an area of the same name southwest of Minneapolis. This area is off Route 45 between Milwaukee and Fond du Lac and has many small lakes and ponds interconnected by streams or short portages. Rentals: Milwaukee.

Kickapoo River

Ontario on Route 33 to La Farge on Route 82: 21 miles / La Farge to Readstown on Route 14: 22 miles / Readstown to Wauzeka on Route 60 and junction with the Wisconsin River: 50 miles, upper section is dammed. Rentals: La Farge, Madison, Ontario, and Wauzeka.

La Crosse River

Sparta on Route 27 to La Crosse and junction with the Mississippi River: 32 miles.

Main Creek

Conrath on Highway G northwest of Sheldon on Route 194 to Holcombe Flowage and junction with the Chippewa River: 8 miles. Rentals: Bruce.

Manitowish River

See Flambeau River.

Manitowoc River

Potter on Route 114 to Clark Mills near Valders on Routes 148–151: 10 miles, smooth except for one rapids before Valders / Valders to Manitowoc: 15 miles, whitewater race course with rocks, canoeable in high water only.

Marengo River

See Bad River.

Mecan River

Route 22 west of Germania to junction with the Fox River slightly below Highway C off Route 23: 14 miles, scenic, flows through Germania Marsh Wildlife Area. Rentals: Wautoma.

Menominee River

Formed by the junction of the Brule and Paint Rivers at the Michigan-Wisconsin border east of Routes 2–141. Generally smooth canoeing through limited access points to town of Menominee on Route 41 in Michigan on Lake Michigan, about 110 miles.

Milwaukee River

Waubedonia Park in Fredonia off Route 84 to Estabrook Park in Milwaukee: 36 miles, mostly scenic, some riffles, some mud, some pollution.

Minocqua Chain of Lakes

Six interconnected lakes on both sides of Route 51 at Minocqua, including Tomahawk Lake, some motor boats. Rentals: Woodruff.

Mirror Lake

Route 23 in Mirror Lake State Park through Lake Delton to the Wisconsin River at Route 12: 6 miles.

Mississippi River

Forms Wisconsin's southwestern border for more than 200 miles, motor boat and commercial traffic, some side channels are used by canoeists. Rentals: Madison, Milwaukee, and Wauzeka.

Montreal River

Route 77 at Hurley to Lake Superior: about 20 miles, the river forms a part of the Wisconsin-Michigan border, several whitewater rapids, the scenic Montreal River Canyon is at the lower end.

Namekagon River

Namekagon Lake north of Highway M between Cable on Route 63 and the town of Clam Lake on Route 77 to bridge on U.S. 63 south of Cable: 14 miles / U.S. 63 to Route 27 bridge at Hayward: 19 miles / Route 27 to Route 53 at Trego: 30 miles / Route 53 to Route 77 between Danbury and Minong: 22 miles / Route 77 to junction with the St. Croix River northeast of Danbury on Route 35: 18 miles. Designated a National Scenic Riverway. Rentals: Grantsburg, Hayward, and Trego in Wisconsin and Taylors Falls in Minnesota.

Oconto River

Tar Dam Road, Forest Service Road 2104, 4 miles north of Mountain on Route 32 to Chute Pond Dam: 13 miles, shallow in dry weather / Chute to Suring on Route 32: 18 miles, rocky riffles / Suring to Pulcifer on Route 22 northeast of Cecil: 22 miles / Pulcifer to town of Oconto Falls on Highway C off Route 22: 12 miles / Oconto Falls to Green Bay below the town of Oconto on Routes 22–41: 21 miles.

Pecatonica River

County Road O near Calamine on Highway G to Darlington on Route 23: 12 miles / Darlington to South Wayne on Route 176: 30 miles. The East Branch joins the Main Branch 4 miles below South Wayne for a 12-mile stretch to the Illinois border. The East Branch is canoeable for about 30 miles from Blanchardville on Route 78 to junction of the East and Main Branches. For continuation, *see* Illinois.

Pelican River

Moen Lake 3 miles east of Rhinelander on Routes 8–47 to Rhinelander: about 20 miles, passes through 2nd, 3rd, 4th, and 5th Lakes and downriver with several easy rapids. Rentals: Rhinelander.

Peshtigo River

Big Joe Landing off Route 139 north of Cavour to Forest Service Road 2134, Burnt Bridge: 13 miles / Burnt Bridge to Caldron Falls Reservoir south of Highway C: 26 miles, many whitewater rapids, for experts only / reservoir to High Falls Reservoir dam: 14 miles / dam to Crivitz on Route 141: 20 miles, several rapids / Crivitz to Green Bay: about 50 miles, smooth waters.

Pike River

Dow Dam Road in Amberg on Route 141 to the Menominee River: 15 miles, whitewater rapids, designated a "wild river."'

Pine River

Pine River Campground on Forest Service Road 2182 west of Route 55 and upstream from the junction with Kimball Creek to Route 55 just below junction with the North Branch of the Pine River: 15 miles, the North Branch is canoeable a few miles upstream / Route 55 south of Alvin to Route 139 north of Long Lake: 15 miles / Route 139 to Route 101 north of Fence: 26 miles, several rapids / Route 101 to Ellwood Landing about half a mile upstream from the Menominee River: 16 miles. Rentals: Madison.

Popple River

Route 55 about 10 miles north of Argonne to the town of Popple River on Route 139: 16 miles, canoeable in high water only / Popple River to Forest Service Road 2159: 14 miles, canoeable in medium or high water / Forest Service Road 2159 to junction with the Pine River northeast of Fence on Route 101: 16 miles.

Red Cedar River

Town of Rice Lake on Routes 48–53 to Route 53 near Chetek: about 30 miles, slow / Route 53 to Sand Creek on Highways U and E north of Route 64: 20 miles / Sand Creek to Colfax on Route 40: 25 miles /

Colfax to Menomonie on Route 29: about 30 miles, passes thrugh Tainter Lake / Menomonie to junction with the Chippewa River below Highway Y east of Route 25: about 25 miles. Rentals: Bruce and Chippewa Falls.

Red River

Gresham on Highway G northwest of Shawano on Route 29 to junction with the Wolf River above Shawano: about 10 miles, canoeable in high water only.

Rock River

Horicon on Routes 28–33 upstream a few miles into Horicon Marsh Wildlife Area, downstream through Sinissippi Lake to Hustisford on Route 60: 10 miles / Hustisford to Watertown on Routes 16–19: 40 miles / Watertown to Jefferson on Route 18: 20 miles / Jefferson to Newville on Route 59 and I-90: 20 miles, passes through Lake Koshkonong / Newville to Beloit on Route 51 on the Illinois border: 25 miles. For continuation, *see* Illinois. Rentals: Horicon, Madison, and Milwaukee.

St. Croix River

St. Croix Flowage dam on Highway Y west of Gordon on Route 53 to junction with the Namekagon River: 20 miles, designated a National Scenic Riverway. For continuation, *see* Minnesota. Rentals: Grantsburg and Trego.

Spirit River

Spirit Falls off Route 86 to junction with the Wisconsin River south of Tomahawk on Route 51: 20 miles, passes through Spirit River Flowage.

Sugar River

Attica on Highway C east of Monticello on Routes 39–69 to the border with Illinois: about 30 miles. About 10 miles below the state line the Sugar River flows into the Pecatonica River; about 10 miles further on, the Pecatonica River joins the Rock River at Rockton, Illionis, on Route 75.

Thornapple River

Route 27 about 8 miles north of Ladysmith to junction with the Chippewa River near Bruce on Route 40: 12 miles, some rapids, long shallow stretches in low water. Rentals: Bruce.

Tomahawk River

Willow Reservoir dam off Highway Y to Prairie Road at entry to Lake Nokomis Flowage on Routes 8–51; about 30 miles, 2 difficult rapids / Prairie Road to Tomahawk on Route 51 and junction with the Wisconsin River: 8 miles of lakes.

Totogatic River

Totogatic Flowage dam on Route 27 north of Hayward to Route 53: 24 miles, canoeable in high water only, some whitewater / Route 53 to

Lake Nancy: 16 miles / Lake Nancy to Namekagon River: 15 miles.
Rentals: Hayward.

Turtle River
See Flambeau River.

Waupaca River
Amherst on Route 10 to junction with the Crystal River near Waupaca on Route 54: about 25 miles / Crystal River junction to junction with the Wolf River: 13 miles, flows through Lake Weyauwega.

White River
Town road bridge at Mason on Highway E off Route 63 to the dam at Routes 112–118: about 15 miles, many minor rapids, the dam is dangerous when open. The White River is unreliable on the stretch from the dam to Lake Superior, dependent as it is upon water release from the dam.

Wisconsin River
Canoeable from Lac Vieux Desert east of Route 45 at the Wisconsin-Michigan border to Highway K near Conover on Route 45: 19 miles / Conover to Route 70 west of the town of Eagle River: 25 miles / Route 70 to dam on Boom Lake near Rhinelander on Route 17: 37 miles, passes through Rainbow Flowage / Rhinelander to Lake Mohawksin at Tomahawk on Route 51: 28 miles, some rapids / Tomahawk to Merrill near Route 51: 27 miles, several rapids / Merrill to Wausau on Route 29: 20 miles / Wausau to Stevens Point: 35 miles, passes through Lake Du Bay, industrialized / Stevens Point to Nekoosa on Route 173: 37 miles, mostly lake canoeing / Nekoosa to Castle Rock Flowage dam on Highway Z north of Route 82: 40 miles, through Petenwell Flowage, all lake canoeing / dam to Lower Dells on Route 23: 33 miles / Lower Dells to Portage on Route 33: 18 miles / Portage to Sauk City on Route 12: 30 miles, passes through Lake Wisconsin / Sauk City to Tower Hill State Park in Spring Green on Route 23: 22 miles / Spring Green to Route 18 at Bridgeport, just before junction with the Mississippi River: 55 miles. Rentals: Eagle River, Madison, Milwaukee, Muscoda, Portage, Rhinelander, Sauk City, and Wauzeka.

Wolf River
Pine Lake off Route 32 at Hiles to Pearson on Highway T east of Route 45 at the town of Summit Lake: 40 miles, relatively quiet and scenic / Pearson to Keshena on Route 47: about 60 miles, very dangerous whitewater, for skilled experts only or rafts / Keshena to near junction of Routes 156 and 187: about 50 miles, smoother than previous stretch / Routes 156–187 to New London on Route 45: about 40 miles / New London to Lake Poygan: about 35 miles. Designated a National Scenic Riverway. Rentals: Madison, Milwaukee, and Oshkosh.

Yahara River
Route 113 at the northern end of Madison to Dyreson Road south of Mud Lake: 14 miles, passes through the four Madison lakes / Dyre-

son Road to junction with the Rock River below Fulton on Route 184: 23 miles, passes through Lake Kegonsa. Rentals: Madison.

Yellow River

Forest Service Road 108 about 10 miles northwest of Perkinstown on Highways M and T to county highway bridge near Gilman on Route 64: about 12 miles, canoeable in medium or high water only, very hazardous and not recommended, flows through Chequamegon Waters Flowage. Below Gilman the Yellow River joins the Chippewa River in Lake Wissota. Rentals: Bruce and Chippewa Falls.

Wisconsin Rentals

Beaver Dam

Spangler Sales, 134 South Spring Street, Beaver Dam, Wisc. 53916; telephone: 414–887–2709 / Waters: local waterways / Trips: up to 1 day / Best canoeing months: June-September / Campsites: no / Transportation: no / Car-top carriers: yes.

Bruce

Voyageur Outfitters of America, Inc. — Chippewa Trails Canoe Rental (Charles E. Hess), U.S. Highway 8, Bruce, Wisc. 54819; telephone: 715–868–9245 or 868–6565 / Waters: Chippewa, Thornapple, Red Cedar, Yellow, Jump, and Flambeau Rivers and Deer Tail and Main Creeks / Trips: 2 hours to 2 weeks, guides available / Best canoeing months: June-September / Campsites: yes / Transportation: yes / Car-top carriers: yes / Bruce is the headquarters of VOA, which operates 7 canoe liveries in Wisconsin, Ohio, and Tennessee and has plans to open others. The chain offers family memberships which grant discounts on rentals, camping, sporting goods, etc.

Brule

Brule River Canoe Rental (Brian and Pam Carlson), Brule, Wisc. 54820; telephone: 715–736–3955 / Waters: Bois Brule River / Trips: 1 to several days, guides available / Best canoeing months: May-mid-October / Campsites: yes / Transportation: yes / Car-top carriers: yes / Also offers kayak and raft trips.

Chippewa Falls

Yellow River Marine, R.R. 5, Chippewa Falls, Wisc. 54729; telephone: 715–723–1289 / Waters: Yellow, Chippewa, Red Cedar, and Flambeau Rivers and other nearby waterways / Trips: 1 or more days / Best canoeing months: May-August / Campsites: yes / Transportation: yes / Car-top carriers: yes.

Danbury

Camp One, Route 1, Box 606, Danbury, Wisc. 54830; telephone: 715–866–7553 / Unconfirmed.

Eagle River

Boat's Port Marina, Eagle River, Wisc. 54521; telephone: 715–479–8000 / Waters: Eagle Chain O' Lakes / Trips: several hours to several days / Best canoeing months: June-September / Campsites: yes / Transportation: no / Car-top carriers: yes.

Cross Roads, Eagle River, Wisc. 54521; telephone: 715–479–9544 / Waters: Eagle Chain O' Lakes / Trips: several hours to several days, guides available / Best canoeing months: May-October / Campsites: yes / Transportation: yes / Car-top carriers: yes / Also rents camping equipment.

Tomlinson Auto & Marine Co., Inc., Box 579, Eagle River, Wisc. 54521; telephone: 715–479–4471 / Waters: Eagle Chain O' Lakes and Wisconsin and Deerskin Rivers / Trips: several hours to several days / Best canoeing months: June-September / Campsites: yes / Transportation: yes / Car-top carriers: yes, may be taken out of state into Michigan and Minnesota / Also rents motor boats and sail boats.

Gordon

Keith's Campground and Canoe Rental, Gordon, Wisc. 54838; telephone: 715–376–2220 / Unconfirmed.

Grantsburg

Wild River Outfitters, Route 1, Box 249, Grantsburg, Wisc. 54840 (located on Highway 70, 4 miles west of Grantsburg); telephone: 715–463–2254 or 463–2602 / Waters: St. Croix and Namekagon Rivers / Trips: 1–4 days / Best canoeing months: May-October / Campsites: yes / Transportation: yes / Car-top carriers: yes.

Hales Corners

Heileman Marine, 10549 West Forest Home Avenue, Hales Corners, Wisc. 53130; telephone: 414–425–1900 / Unconfirmed.

Hayward

Voyageur Canoe Outfitters, Historyland, Hayward, Wisc. 54843; telephone: 715–634–4811 or 634–2601 / Waters: Namekagon, Chippewa, Couderay, and Totogatic Rivers / Trips: 2 hours to more than 2 days / Best canoeing months: April-October / Campsites: yes / Transportation: yes / Car-top carriers: yes / Also rents some camping equipment.

Horicon

Horicon Marsh Canoe Outfitters, Highway 33 at bridge, Horicon, Wisc. 53032; telephone: 414–485–4217 / Waters: Rock River / Trips: up to 1 day / Best canoeing months: April-November / Campsites: yes / Transportation: yes / Car-top carriers: no.

Jefferson

Bark River Camp Grounds, Hanson Road near Rome, Route 1, Box 255, Jefferson, Wisc. 53549; telephone: 414–593–2421 / Waters: Bark River / Trips: up to 2 days / Best canoeing months: May-mid-October / Campsites: yes / Transportation: yes / Car-top carriers: yes.

235

Ladysmith

Flambeau Lodge, Route 1, Ladysmith, Wisc. 54848; telephone: 715–532–5392. / Unconfirmed.

La Farge

Mick's Scenic River Canoe Rentals (David Mick), La Farge, Wisc. 54639; telephone: 608–625–4449 or 625–2490 / Waters: Kickapoo River / Trips: up to 2 days / Best canoeing months: May-mid-Octo-September / Campsites: yes / Transportation: yes / Car-top carriers: yes.

Land O' Lakes

Headwaters Marine, Inc., Box 201, Land O' Lakes, Wisc. 54540; telephone: 715–547–3555 / Unconfirmed.

Madison

Mazinet Sporting Goods and Marina, 55 Bluebill Drive, Madison, Wisc. 53718; telephone: 608–249–9316 / Waters: area waterways / Trips: up to 3 days / Best canoeing months: no response / Campsites: yes / Transportation: no / Car-top carriers: yes.

Outdoor Rentals, Memorial Union, University of Wisconsin, 800 Langdon Street, Madison, Wisc. 53706; telephone: 608–262–7351 / Waters: Wisconsin, Mississippi, Yahara, Kickapoo, Wolf, Pine, Rock, Fox, and Crystal Rivers / Trips: up to several days / Best canoeing months: no response / Campsites: yes / Transportation: no / Car-top carriers: yes / Also rents camping equipment.

Ready Rents Inc., 5621 Odana Road, Madison, Wisc. 53719; telephone: 608–271–0771 / Waters: nearby lakes and the Wisconsin, Mississippi, and Rock Rivers / Trips: as long as you want / Best canoeing months: May-October / Campsites: yes / Transportation: no / Car-top carriers: yes / Also rents camping equipment / Open all year.

Medford

Liske Marine, Route 13, Medford, Wisc. 54451; telephone: 715–748–3242 / Unconfirmed.

Menasha

Waverly Beach Marine, P.O. Box 307, Menasha, Wisc. 54952; telephone: 414–734–6735 / Unconfirmed.

Middleton

N & M True Value Hardware, 6305 University Avenue, Middleton, Wisc. 53562; telephone: 608–836–1771 / Unconfirmed.

Milwaukee

ABC Supply Co., Inc., 3201 West Burnham Street, Milwaukee, Wisc. 53215; telephone: 414–383–1200 / Waters: Rock, Fox, Wolf, Wisconsin, and Mississippi Rivers and Kettle Moraine State Forest / Trips: as long as you want / Best canoeing months: May-September / Campsites: no / Transportation: no / Car-top carriers: yes.

Muscoda

Riverview Hills (Albert Bremmer), R.R. 3, Box 67, Muscoda, Wisc.

53573; telephone: 608–739–3472 / Waters: Wisconsin River / Trips: 1–14 days / Best canoeing months: May-September / Campsites: yes / Transportation: yes / Car-top carriers: yes.

New Lisbon

Wa Du Shuda Canoe, 115 Welch Prairie Road, New Lisbon, Wisc. 53950; telephone: 608–562–3364 / Unconfirmed.

Oconomowoc

Kinn Motors Marine, 650 East Wisconsin Avenue, Oconomowoc, Wisc. 53066; telephone: 414–567–4485 and 567–6070 / Unconfirmed.

Ontario

Beauti-View Resort, on Highway 33 in Ontario, Wisc. (mailing address: Route 1, Box 197, La Farge, Wisc. 54639); telephone: 608–387–4711 or 608–487–2011 / Waters: Kickapoo River and other waterways / Trips: several hours to several days / Best canoeing months: May-November / Campsites: yes / Transportation: yes / Car-top carriers: yes, to local areas only.

Oshkosh

Fox River Marina, Inc. (Russell F. Williams), P.O. Box 2325, Pioneer Harbor, Oshkosh, Wisc. 54901; telephone: 414–235–2340 / Waters: Wolf and Fox Rivers, Lake Winnebago, and Lake Butte des Morts / Trips: 1 or several days / Best canoeing months: May-September / Campsites: yes / Transportation: no / Car-top carriers: yes / Also rents motor boats and sail boats / Resort on premises.

Park Falls

Oxbo Resort (Russell Frey), Route 1, Box 250, Park Falls, Wisc. 54552; telephone: 715–762–4786 / Unconfirmed.

Portage

Baraboo River Canoe Livery, division of VOA Family Canoeing, Cascade Mountain Road, Portage, Wisc. (mailing address: Bruce, Wisc. 54819); telephone: 715–868–6565 or 868–9245 in Bruce or call Portage information for new telephone number / Waters: Fox, Baraboo, and Wisconsin Rivers / Trips: 1 or more days / Best canoeing months: May-October / Campsites: yes / Transportation: yes / Car-top carriers: yes.

Rhinelander

Boom Lake Marine, 1520 Eagle Street, Rhinelander, Wisc. 54501; telephone: 715–362–6519 / Waters: Wisconsin and Pelican Rivers or anywhere else / Trips: 1 or several days / Best canoeing months: June-September / Campsites: yes / Transportation: yes / Car-top carriers: yes / Also rents rafts for the Pelican River.

Richland Center

Richland Canoe Sales and Rentals-Bill's Mobil Service, Highway 14, Richland Center, Wisc. 53581; telephone: 608–647–9990 / Unconfirmed.

Sauk City

Blackhawk Ridge (Isenring Family), Highway 78 South, P.O. Box 92, Sauk City, Wisc. 53583; telephone: 608–643–3775 / Waters: Wisconsin River / Trips: up to 1 day, overnights by arrangement / Best canoeing months: April-November / Campsites: yes / Transportation: yes / Car-top carriers: no response / Also rents camping equipment.

Sauk Prairie Canoe Rental (James and Delores Staff), 106 Polk Street, Sauk City, Wisc. 53583; telephone: 608–643–6589 / Waters: Wisconsin and Baraboo Rivers / Trips: 1 to several days, guides available / Best canoeing months: April-October / Campsites: yes / Transportation: yes / Car-top carriers: yes.

Superior

Northwest Outlet Inc., 1815 Belknap, Superior, Wisc. 54880; telephone: 715–392–8164 / Unconfirmed.

Tomahawk

Tomahawk Trailer and Boat Sales, Highway 51 North, Tomahawk, Wisc. 54487; telephone: 715–453–2824 / Unconfirmed.

Trego

Jack's Canoe Rental (Jack Canfield), Trego, Wisc. 54888; telephone: 715–635–2959 / Waters: Namekagon and St. Croix Rivers / Trips: a few hours to several days / Best canoeing months: June-September / Campsites: yes / Transportation: yes / Car-top carriers: yes / Housekeeping cabins available.

The Wild River Canoe Rental and Sales (John Kaas), Route 1, Box 33, Trego, Wisc. 54888; telephone: 715–635–2966 / Waters: Namekagon and St. Croix Rivers / Trips: a few hours to several days / Best canoeing months: June-September / Campsites: yes / Transportation: yes / Car-top carriers: yes.

Waupaca

Clear Water Harbor, Inc., Route 5, Box 384, Waupaca, Wisc. 54981; telephone: 715–258–2866 / Waters: Crystal River and Chain O' Lakes / Trips: no response / Best canoeing months: April-October / Campsites: no / Transportation: yes / Car-top carriers: no response.

Ding's Dock (Joe Leean), Route 1, Waupaca, Wisc. 54981; telephone: 715–258–2612 / Waters: Crystal River and Chain O' Lakes / Trips: up to 1 day / Best canoeing months: May-September / Campsites: no / Transportation: yes / Car-top carriers: sometimes.

Wautoma

Lake of the Woods Campground, Route 1, Box 207, Wautoma, Wisc. 54982; telephone: 414–787–3601 / Waters: Mecan River / Trips: up to 1 day / Best canoeing months: June-August / Campsites: yes / Transportation: yes / Car-top carriers: no.

Wauwatosa

Marineland, Inc., 5105 West North Avenue, Wauwatosa, Wisc. 53213; telephone: 414–258–5586 / Unconfirmed.

Wauzeka

Kickapoo Canoe Rentals (Paul E. Morel), Box 238, Wauzeka, Wisc. 53826; telephone: 608–875–5065 or 875–5348 / Waters: Kickapoo, Wisconsin, and Mississippi Rivers / Trips: a few hours to several days / Best canoeing months: June-October / Campsites: yes / Transportation: yes / Car-top carriers: no.

Winter

Ballagh's & Biermann's Big Bear Lodge, Inc., Star Route, Winter, Wisc. 54896; telephone: 715–332–5261 / Waters: North and South Forks of the Flambeau River / Trips: 1 or several days / Best canoeing months: May-September / Campsites: yes / Transportation: yes / Car-top carriers: yes (customer must provide his own carrier; they provide canoe only).

Woodruff

Indian Shores Campground, P.O. Box 12, Woodruff, Wisc. 54568; telephone: 715–356–5552 / Waters: Minocqua Chain of Lakes / Trips: 1 or several days / Best canoeing months: May-October / Campsites: yes / Transportation: no / Car-top carriers: yes.

Sources of Information

Canoeing the Wild Rivers of Northwestern Wisconsin, Wisconsin Indianhead Country, Inc. (1316 Fairfax Street, Eau Claire, Wisc. 54701), n.d., $3.50. Description and maps of the Brule, St. Croix, Namekagon, Totogatic, Eau Claire, Yellow, and Clam Rivers.

Canoe Trails of North-Central Wisconsin, Wisconsin Trails (P.O. Box 5650, Madison, Wisc. 53705), 1973, 64 pp., $4.00. Description and maps of the Chippewa, Couderay, Flambeau, Jump, Manitowish, Turtle, Thornapple, and Yellow Rivers and Deer Tail and Main Creeks.

Canoe Trails of Northeastern Wisconsin, Wisconsin Trails (P.O. Box 5650, Madison, Wisc. 53705), 1972, 72 pp., $4.75. Description and maps of the Brule, Deerskin, Embarrass, Manitowish, Menominee, Oconto, Pelican, Peshtigo, Pike, Pine, Popple, Spirit, Tomahawk, Wisconsin, and Wolf Rivers.

Duncanson, Michael E. *Canoe Trails of Southern Wisconsin,* Wisconsin Trails (P.O. Box 5650, Madison, Wisc. 53705), 1974, 62 pp., $4.95. Description and maps of the Baraboo, Crawfish, Crystal, Fox (both), Kickapoo, La Crosse, Lemonweir, Manitowoc, Mecan, Milwaukee, Pecatonica, Pine, Rock, Sugar, Waupaca, Wisconsin, and Yahara Rivers.

Palzer, Robert J. and Joette M. *Whitewater, Quietwater,* Evergreen Paddleways (1415 21st Street, Two Rivers, Wisc. 54241), 1974, 158 pp., $7.95. Description and maps of selected rivers in Wisconsin, upper

239

Michigan, and northeastern Minnesota, plus general information on equipment, techniques, safety, etc.

Vilas County Lake Region, Publicity Department (Box 71, Vilas County Court House, Eagle River, Wisc. 54521), a free map.

Wisconsin fishing and hunting information is available from Wisconsin Department of Natural Resources (Box 450, Madison, Wisc. 53701).

Wisconsin tourist information is available from Wisconsin Department of Natural Resources, Vacation and Travel Services (Box 450, Madison, Wisc. 53701).

Wisconsin Water Trails, Wisconsin Department of Natural Resources (Box 450, Madison, Wisc. 53701), a free brochure.

●

MINNESOTA

"... AND WILDERNESS IS PARADISE ENOW ..." sings Omar Khayyam.

With 15,291 lakes of 10 acres or more in size, 100,000 smaller ponds and wetlands, 25,000 miles of flowing waterways, and a good deal of wilderness, Minnesota, like Maine, is often called a canoeist's paradise. And it is, even though it has a short season lasting barely from May to September, which is further shortened for those sensitive to black flies and mosquitos coming out in force during May and June, when the fishing is best. Thus, there is a canoeing crunch in July and August, leading to some overcrowding of the more accessible waters.

By far the best known and most popular canoeing region is the Boundary Waters Canoe Area, part of the Superior National Forest at the northern end of the state. Together with the Quetico Provincial Park on the Canadian side of the border, they offer practically unlimited canoeing opportunities without serious difficulties through innumerable lakes interconnected by streams and portages. A great portion of the combined area is off limits to motor boats, automobiles, and airplanes. An extension of the park area is under development in the newly created Voyageurs National Park, west of the Boundary Waters Canoe Area.

Excellent family river cruising is found on the Crow Wing River and its tributaries flowing through state forest lands. The mighty Mississippi River rises at the western edge of Minnesota, and 80 miles of its headwaters have been designated as a scenic canoe trail. An enterprising canoeist could paddle about 2,500 miles to the mouth of the Mississippi at New Orleans. The St. Croix River, forming the border between

Minnesota and Wisconsin, is popular with family canoeists in both states.

Because of the vastness of the Minnesota waterways, only a small percentage of them are recorded in published information. Thus, no other state provides more opportunity for adventurous canoeists to explore the less popularized streams and lakes and discover their own pieces of wilderness — virgin stands of pine, alders, and willows reflected in quiet lakes, the muskegs with their black spruce, low shrubs, and sphagnum moss. Canoeists may encounter moose, beaver, timber wolves, and black bears as well as the ever-present mallards and loons. Fish, as can be expected, are abundant, including the official state fish, the walleyed pike.

Minnesota Waters

Big Fork River
Town of Dora Lake on Route 29 to Route 6 bridge: 25 miles / bridge to Big Fork Campground off Route 38 at Big Fork: 9 miles / Route 6 to Route 1 east of Effie: 15 miles / Route 1 to Bowerman Brook at Route 6: 33 miles / Bowerman Brook to Mondo Campground off Route 6: 16 miles / campground to Route 71 at Big Falls: 23 miles / Route 71 to mouth of Sturgeon River off County Road 30: 6 miles / Sturgeon River to County Road 1 at Lindford: 28 miles / Lindford to junction with the Rainy River below Route 11: 20 miles.

Boundary Waters Canoe Area (USA) and Quetico Provincial Park (Canada)
These waters, straddling the Minnesota-Canada border, are in the largest protected wilderness canoeing area in North America with about 1 million acres on the Minnesota side and practically unlimited canoeing on both sides of the border. The area contains thousands of lakes with interconnecting streams or portages allowing for any number of trip variations. Outfitters and the park rangers provide a selection of recommended trips from a few days to several weeks and even longer. Because of the weather, the prime season is from May to early October. Insects are much in evidence in May and June. Many parts of these waters are banned to motor boats. Travel permits are required for all canoeists and they are available free of charge from the offices of the Superior National Forest or from canoe outfitters. Before crossing into Canada, canoeists must check in with the U.S. Customs posts at Ely, Crane Lake, or Grand Marais and canoeists must also check in with any one of several Canadian Customs posts. Camping permits are issued free of charge on the United States side but campsites are limited to one party per site with a maximum of 15 people per party. Canadian permits

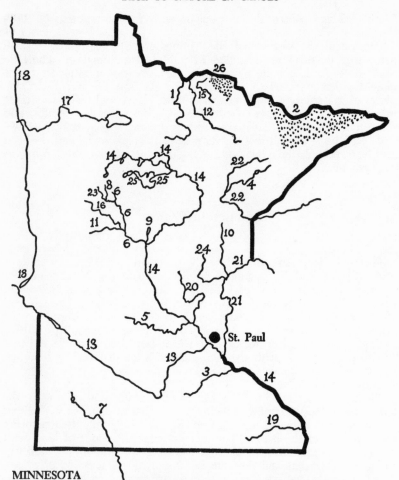

MINNESOTA

Big Fork River (1)
Boundary Waters
  Canoe Area (2)
Cannon River (3)
Cloquet River (4)
Crow River (5)
Crow Wing River (6)
Des Moines River (7)
Fish Hook River (8)
Gull Lakes & River (9)

Kettle River (10)
Leaf River (11)
Little Fork River (12)
Minnesota River (13)
Mississippi River (14)
Rat Root River (15)
Redeye River (16)
Red Lake River (17)
Red River of
  the North (18)

Root River (19)
Rum River (20)
St. Croix River (21)
St. Louis River (22)
Shell River (23)
Snake River (24)
Turtle River (25)
Voyageurs
  National Park (26)

for canoeing and camping cost $2 per canoe per day, or $20 per canoe for up to a stay of 16 days, and these permits can be obtained at any of the Canadian border check points. Rentals: Babbitt, Crane Lake, Duluth, Ely, Grand Marais, and Winton, all in Minnesota.

Cannon River

Route 13 near Waterville to junction with the Straight River below Route 3 north of Faribault: 20 miles, flows through Lake Sakatah and Cannon Lake, canoeable in high water only / junction to the dam at Dundas below Route 3: 15 miles / dam to Lake Byllesby entrance on Route 56: 10 miles, motor boats allowed on lake, water is often low below the exit dam / start again at Cannon Falls off old Route 52 to Route 61 near Harliss: 18 miles / Route 61 to junction with the Mississippi River: 6 miles. Rentals: Minneapolis.

Cloquet River

County Road 44 south of Brimson to St. Louis River near Brookston off Route 2: 60 miles, upper reaches canoeable in high water only, flows through Island Lake Reservoir — watch out for high winds; some whitewater; irregular flow on lower reaches.

Crow River

Middle Fork: Canoeing about 12 miles upstream from New London on Route 23, plus lakes.

North Fork: Route 22 north of Litchfield to Route 15 at Kingston: 17 miles / Kingston to Route 25 south of Buffalo: 40 miles / Route 25 to Mississippi River at Dayton on Route 101: 30 miles, scenic, some pollution. Rentals for both forks: Minneapolis.

Crow Wing River and Lakes

10th Crow Wing Lake north of Akeley on Route 34 through chain of lakes with some portages to Nevis on Route 33 bridge off Route 34: 15 miles / Nevis to junction with the Shell River: 20 miles / junction to Route 18 bridge: 5 miles / bridge to Nimrod on Route 227: 14 miles / Nimrod to Route 30: 25 miles / Route 30 to Motley on Route 210: 12 miles / Motley to the Mississippi River: 15 miles. Rentals: Brainerd, Huntersville, and Nimrod in Minnesota and Grand Forks in North Dakota.

Des Moines River

Lake Shetek State Park north of Route 30 to Talcot Lake Wildlife Management Area: 25 miles / wildlife area to rapids at Windom on Route 60: 23 miles / Windom to Jackson on Route 71: 20 miles and flows through Kilen Woods State Park / Jackson to Iowa state line, near Petersburg east of Route 71: 10 miles / The Des Moines River continues for about 500 miles through Iowa to join the Mississippi south of Keokuk. Rentals: Huntersville.

Fish Hook River

Long Lake on Route 34 east of Park Rapids to Upper Twin Lake and junction with the Shell River: about 20 miles. Rentals: Huntersville.

Gull Lakes and River

Some 30 miles of lake and river canoeing above the junction of the Gull and the Crow Wing Rivers which is 3 miles above Crow Wing State Park on the Mississippi River. Rentals: Brainerd.

Kettle River

Route 73 south of Cromwell to junction with the Moose River at Route 52: 13 miles of whitewater / Moose River junction to Banning State Park on Route 23: 15 miles, easier than the first stretch / Route 23 to junction with the St. Croix River: 25 miles, *very dangerous whitewater*, flows through Sandstone Game Refuge and Chengwatana State Forest.

Leaf River

Route 71 north of Wadena to the Crow Wing River via the lower part of the Redeye River: about 25 miles, in high water only. Rentals: Huntersville and Nimrod.

Little Fork River

Route 53 at Cook to Route 65 at Silverdale bridge: 38 miles, several falls and rapids / Route 65 to Route 217 east of Little Fork: 75 miles, a number of rapids, few access points, flows through Nett Lake Indian Reservation / Route 217 to the Rainy River: 20 miles.

Minnesota River

Ortonville and Big Stone Dam off Route 75 to Route 119 and the entrance to Lac qui Parle: 25 miles, flows through Marsh Lake / Route 119 to the dam at Lac qui Parle State Park on Route 33: 13 miles / park to Route 212 at Montevideo: 13 miles / Montevideo to Granite Falls on Route 212: 16 miles, hydroelectric station at Granite Falls / Granite Falls to Morton on Route 71: 44 miles with rapids / Morton to Route 4 near Fort Ridgely State Park: 20 miles / Route 4 to New Ulm on Route 14: 25 miles / New Ulm to North Mankato on Route 14: 35 miles / North Mankato to St. Peter on Route 99: 15 miles / St. Peter to Henderson on Route 19: 20 miles / Henderson to Route 25 at Belle Plaine: 18 miles / Route 25 to Shakopee on Route 169: 22 miles / Shakopee to the Mississippi River: about 40 miles, urbanized. Rentals: Minneapolis.

Mississippi River

Lake Itasca on Route 200 to Lake Bemidji on Route 2: about 30 miles / Lake Bemidji to Lake Andrusia on Route 8: 15 miles, passes through Wolf Lake / Route 8 to Route 39 at exit of Cass Lake: 10 miles / Route 39 to dam on Lake Winnibigoshish on Route 9: 25 miles / dam to Route 2: 10 miles, flows through Little Winnibigoshish Lake / Route 2 to dam at Grand Rapids on Route 169: 40 miles, passes through several lakes / Grand Rapids to Jacobson on Route 200: 35 miles / Route 200 to junction with Sandy Lake River at Libby on Route 65: 25 miles, rapids / Libby to Route 169: 21 miles, rapids / Route 169 to Aitkin anding off Route 210: 15 miles / Aitkin to dam at Brainerd on Route 25: 45 miles / Brainerd to Little Falls on Route 27: 35 miles / Little Falls to Sauk rapids above St. Cloud on Route 10: 35 miles / St. Cloud to the dam at Anoka on Route 10 northwest of Minneapolis: 55 miles, rapids and obstructions on the entire river course, urbanized and developed below St. Cloud. Rentals: Brainerd and Minneapolis.

Namekagon River
See St. Croix River.

Rat Root River
Route 217 west of Little Fork to Island View on Route 11 and Black Bay of Rainy Lake: about 30 miles of canoeing and one can continue into Voyageurs National Park waters. Rentals: International Falls.

Redeye River
Sebeka on Route 71 to junction with the Crow Wing River: about 25 miles, canoeable in high water only. Rentals: Huntersville and Nimrod.

Red Lake River
Dam at Lower Red Lake on Route 1 to Route 24 at High Landing: 30 miles, flows through Red Lake Indian Reservation / Route 24 to Thief River Falls on Route 59: 30 miles / Thief River Falls to St. Hilaire on Route 32: 10 miles, minor rapids / St. Hilaire to Red Lake Falls on Route 32: 15 miles, many rapids / Red Lake Falls to Crookston on Route 2: 35 miles / Crookston to North Red River at East Grand Forks on Route 220: 45 miles, unattractive. Rentals: Grand Forks, North Dakota.

Red River of the North
Headwaters in Lake Traverse, only a few miles from the headwaters of the Minnesota River, the Red River of the North flows in the opposite direction, forming the border between Minnesota and North Dakota and flowing into Lake Winnepeg. Its waters ultimately reach the Hudson Bay. In Minnesota, it flows through farmlands and it is not popular with canoeists.

Root River
Route 5 bridge south of Chatfield on Route 52 to Route 52 southeast of Chatfield: 5 miles / Route 52 to Route 250 northeast of Lanesboro: 25 miles / Route 250 to Route 43 south of Rushford: 18 miles / Route 43 to Route 76 at Houston: 15 miles / Route 76 to Route 26 at Broken Arrow Slough: 17 miles, 2 miles above junction with the Mississippi River; some whitewater in spring. Rentals: Rushford.

Rum River
Route 95 at Princeton to Route 47: 16 miles / Route 47 to Route 95 at Cambridge: 15 miles / Route 95 to dam at St. Francis on Route 24 off Route 47: 17 miles / St. Francis to the dam at Anoka on Route 10: 20 miles. Rentals: Minneapolis.

St. Croix River

Gordon dam in Wisconsin on Highway Y west of Gordon on Route 53 to Route 35 bridge below the junction with the Namekagon River: 24 miles / Trip may begin on Namekagon River (*see also* Wisconsin) at Namekagon Lake in Wisconsin to Route 35 bridge: 102 miles, with many intermediate access points / Route 35 to mouth of Yellow River at Danbury, Wisconsin, on Route 35: 34 miles / Danbury to Route 70 west of Grantsburg, Wisconsin: 34 miles, some rapids / Route 70 to Nevers dam: 27 miles / dam to Taylors Falls, Minnesota and St. Croix Falls, Wisconsin, on Route 8: 10 miles / Taylors Falls to Stillwater: 28 miles / Stillwater to junction with the Mississippi River at Point Douglas on Route 10: 23 miles. Rentals: Minneapolis, St. Paul, and Taylors Falls in Minnesota and Grantsburg and Trego in Wisconsin.

St. Louis River

Ford Fairlane Taconite Plant off Route 53 south of Virginia to Floodwood City Park off Route 2 and County Road 8: 55 miles, some whitewater rapids / Floodwood to Brookston on County Road 31 off Route 2 and above the mouth of the Cloquet River: 18 miles, whitewater rapids / Brookston to town of Cloquet on Route 33: 17 miles, not canoeable below Cloquet. Rentals: Duluth.

Shell River

Blueberry Lake off Route 41 south of Park Rapids to junction with the Crow Wing River: 25 miles, flows through Twin Lakes. Rentals: Huntersville and Nimrod.

Snake River

Routes 27–65 at McGrath to Mora on Routes 23–65: 37 miles / Mora to junction with the St. Croix River: 40 miles, mostly whitewater.

Turtle River

Route 71 southwest of Tenstrike through Cass Lake to junction with the Mississippi River: about 20 miles.

Voyageurs National Forest

About 220,000 acres, including about 80,000 acres of waterways, is under development by the National Park Service and it is in use. The forest is accessible from International Falls on Route 11 and it offers the same type of wilderness trips that one can find in its immediate neighbor, the Boundary Waters Canoe Area. Rentals: International Falls.

Minnesota Rentals

Babbitt

Duane's Canoe Outfitters (Duane and Elsi Arvola), Highway 21, Babbitt, Minn. 55706; telephone: 218–827–9380 or via Ely, Minn. operator to mobile phone Z-B-8-2438 June-August only for mobile telephone / Waters: Boundary Waters Canoe Area and Quetico Provincial Park and lakes around Babbitt / Trips: a few days to more than a week, guides available / Best canoeing months: May-August / Campsites: yes / Transportation: yes / Car-top carriers: yes / Also rents camping equipment and provides full outfitting, with food, for camping.

Bovey

Cliff Wild's Canoe Trip Outfitting Co., 1731 East Sheridan, Bovey, Minn. 55709; telephone: 218–365–3267 / Unconfirmed.

Brainerd

Sports Craft, Inc., Route 371 North-Route 7, P.O. Box 623, Brainerd, Minn. 56401; telephone: 218–829–1401 / Waters: Mississippi, Crow Wing, and Gull Rivers and many nearby lakes / Trips: 1 or more days / Best canoeing months: June-September / Campsites: yes / Transportation: no / Car-top carriers: yes.

Crane Lake

Campbell's Cabins and Trading Post, Ltd. (Bob Handberg), located on Lac La Croix on the Canadian side of the border (mailing address: Crane Lake, Minn. 55725); telephone: 218–993–2361 / Waters: Quetico Provincial Park / Trips: 1 day to a week or more, guides available / Best canoeing months: July and August / Campsites: yes / Transportation: yes / Car-top carriers: no / Customers arrive by air pick-up service or canoe 35 miles from Crane Lake to Lac La Croix / Also rents camping equipment / Motel rooms and housekeeping cabins available at rental site. Owns and operates Lac La Croix Quetico Air Service, which provides air-lift camping trips with guides into the Quetico area.

Duluth

Taylor Rental Center, 1710 London Road, Duluth, Minn. 55812; telephone: 218–728–4217 / Waters: St. Louis River, Boundary Waters Canoe Area, and other Minnesota waterways / Trips: 2 or more days / Best canoeing months: June-September / Campsites: yes / Transportation: no / Car-top carriers: yes / Also rents camping equipment.

Ely

Beland's Wilderness Canoe Trips (Don Beland), P.O. Box 358–Moose Lake, Ely, Minn. 55731; telephone: 218–365–5837 / Waters: Boundary Waters Canoe Area and Quetico Provincial Park / Trips: 3–30 days, guides available / Campsites: yes / Transportation: yes / Car-top carriers: no / Overnight accomodations / Complete outfitters; does not offer float trips.

Boundary Waters Canoe Outfitters, P.O. Box 569, Ely, Minn. 55731; telephone: 218–365–3201 / Unconfirmed.

Canadian Border Outfitters (Emery and Delores Bulinski), Box 117, Ely, Minn. 55731; telephone: 218–365–5847 / Waters: Superior National Forest and Boundary Waters Canoe Area / Trips: 2 or more days, guides available / Best canoeing months: May-September /

Campsites: yes / Transportation: yes / Car-top carriers: yes / Overnight accomodations / Free canoe instruction / Complete outfitters.

Canadian Waters, Inc. (Jon Marshall Waters), 111 East Sheridan Street, Ely, Minn. 55731; telephone: 218–365–3202 / Waters: Boundary Waters Canoe Area and Quetico Provincial Park / Trips: 2–7 days, including tours with direct air charter flights from Chicago, guides available / Best canoeing months: June-August / Campsites: yes / Transportation: yes / Car-top carriers: yes / Complete outfitters.

Fall Lake Resort and Outfitters, SR 1 Box 3255, Ely, Minn. 55731; telephone: 218–365–4183 / Waters: nearby lakes and rivers / Trips: 1 or more days, guides available / Best canoeing months: May-September / Campsites: yes / Transportation: yes / Car-top carriers: yes / Overnight accomodations / Campsite at base / Cabins available / Complete outfitters.

Fishermen's Headquarters & Canoe Outfitting, 209–223 East Sheridan Street, Ely, Minn. 55731; telephone: 218–365–3324 / Unconfirmed.

Kawishiwi Lodge (Frank Zgonc), P.O. Box 480, Ely, Minn. 55731; telephone: 218–365–5487 or 365–4525 / Waters: Boundary Waters Canoe Area and Quetico Provincial Park / Trips: any length, guides available / Best canoeing months: June-August / Campsites: yes / Transportation: yes / Car-top carriers: yes / Overnight accomodations and cabins with housekeeping / Complete outfitters.

Pipestone Outfitting Co. (Jack and Toni Dulinsky), P.O. Box 780, Ely, Minn. 55731; telephone: 218–365–3788 / Waters: Boundary Waters Canoe Area and Quetico Provincial Park / Trips: any length, guides available / Best canoeing months: May-October / Campsites: yes / Transportation: yes / Car-top carriers: yes / Log cabins with housekeeping / Complete outfitters.

Quetico Superior Canoe Outfitters (Bernie Carlson), Box 89, Ely, Minn. 55731; telephone: 218–365–5480 or in winter 365–5121 / Waters: Boundary Waters Canoe Area and Quetico Provincial Park / Trips: any length / Best canoeing months: June-August / Campsites: yes / Transportation: yes / Car-top carriers: no / Overnight accomodations / Complete outfitters.

Rom's Canoe Country Outfitters (Bill Rom), 629 E. Sheridan Street, P.O. Box 30, Ely, Minn. 55731; telephone: 218–365–4046 or 365–5429 / Waters: Boundary Waters Canoe Area and Quetico Provincial Park / Trips: any length, guides available / Best canoeing months: June-September / Campsites: yes / Transportation: yes / Car-top carriers: yes / Overnight accomodations / Complete outfitters.

Wilderness Outfitters (Jim Pascoe and Bob LaTourell), 1 East Camp Street, Ely, Minn. 55731; telephone: 218–365–3211, 365–4785, or 365–4896 / Waters: Boundary Waters Canoe Area and Quetico Provincial Park / Trips: any period of time, guides available / Best canoeing months: June-August / Campsites: yes / Transportation: yes / Car-top carriers: yes / Overnight accomodations / Complete outfitters / Fly-in service to housekeeping cabins in Canada.

Grand Marais

Blankenburg's Saganaga Outfitter, Grand Marais, Minn. 55604; telephone: 218–388–2217 / Unconfirmed.

Jocko's Canoe Outfitters (Jocko and Lee Nelson), Gunflint Trail, Box 31, Grand Marais, Minn. 55604; telephone: 218–388–2254, in winter 612–831–0755 (winter mailing address: 8624 Kell Avenue South, Bloomington, Minn. 55437) / Waters: Boundary Waters Canoe Area and Quetico Provincial Park / Trips: any length / Best canoeing months: June-August / Campsites: yes / Transportation: yes / Car-top carriers: yes / Overnight accomodations / Complete outfitters.

Northpoint Outfitters, Gunflint Trail, Box 427, Grand Marais, Minn. 55604; telephone: 218–388–2283, in winter 314–343–7199 / Waters: Boundary Waters Canoe Area, Quetico Provincial Park, and other waters in Eastern Canada to Lake Superior / Trips: any length, guides available / Best canoeing months: July-September / Campsites: yes / Transportation: yes / Car-top carriers: no / Fly-in arranged / Overnight accomodations / Complete outfitters.

Seagull Outfitters, Box 119, Grand Marais, Minn. 55604; telephone: 218–388–2271 /Waters: Boundary Waters Canoe Area and Quetico Provincial Park / Trips: any length, guides available / Best canoeing months: May-September / Campsites: yes / Transportation: yes / Car-top carriers: no / Overnight accomodations / Complete outfitters.

Trail Center Outfitters and Canoe Rental, Gunflint Trail, Box 50, Grand Marais, Minn. 55604; telephone: 218–388–2262 / Unconfirmed.

Tuscarora Canoe Outfitters (Jerry and Marie Mark), Gunflint Trail, Grand Marais, Minn. 55604; telephone: 218–388–2221 / Waters: Boundary Waters Canoe Area and Quetico Provincial Park / Trips: 1–21 days, guides available / Best canoeing months: July-September / Campsites: yes / Transportation: yes / Car-top carriers: yes / Overnight accomodations / Complete outfitters.

Hibbing

Adventures Unlimited, Hibbing, Minn. 55746; telephone: 218–263–7578 / Unconfirmed.

Huntersville

Huntersville Outfitters (Dorothy and Turk Kennelly), Highway 18, Huntersville, Minn. (mailing address: Route 4, Menahga, Minn. 56464); telephone: 218–564–4279 / Waters: Crow Wing Lakes and River, Des Moines, Fish Hook, Leaf, Redeye, and Shell Rivers and other nearby waterways / Trips: 1 or more days, guides available / Best canoeing months: April-September / Campsites: yes / Transportation: yes / Car-top carriers: yes / Rents camping equipment and provides partial or complete outfitting.

International Falls

Johnson Canoe Outfitters, Box 90A, Route 9, on Highway 53, 8 miles south of International Falls, Minn. 56649; telephone: 218–377–4411 / Waters: Rat Root River and Voyageurs National Park waters / Trips: any length / Best canoeing months: June-September / Campsites: yes / Transportation: yes / Car-top carriers: no / Complete outfitters.

Point of Pines Marina, Inc., Island View Route, International Falls, Minn. 56649; telephone: 218–224–2227 / Unconfirmed.

Minneapolis

aaRCee Rental Center, 2900 Lyndale Avenue South, Minneapolis, Minn. 55408; telephone 612–827–5746 / Waters: St. Croix and Cannon Rivers and many nearby lakes and rivers / Trips: 1–14 days / Best canoeing months: April-August / Campsites: yes / Transportation: no / Car-top carriers: yes / Complete outfitter.

Ketter Canoeing (Karl L. Ketter), 101 79th Avenue North, Minneapolis, Minn. 55444; telephone: 612–561–2208 / Waters: Mississippi and Minnesota Rivers and other lakes and rivers in the state / Trips: 1 hour to 3 months, guides available / Best canoeing months: May-October / Campsites: yes / Transportation: yes / Car-top carriers: yes: / Also publishes *Canoeing,* a quarterly magazine that is entertaining and informative.

Nimrod

Irv Funk Canoe Outfitters, Highway 12, Nimrod, Minn. (mailing address: Route 2, Box 51, Sebeka, Minn. 56477); telephone: 218–472–3272 / Waters: Crow Wing Lakes and River, Redeye River, Shell River, Leaf River, and other waterways / Trips: 1 or more days, guides available / Best canoeing months: June-September / Campsites: yes / Transportation: yes / Car-top carriers: yes / Also rents camping equipment.

Rushford

Earl's Sales and Service, Inc. (Earl W. Bunke), Box 548, Rushford, Minn. 55971; telephone: 507–864–9781 or 864–9496 / Waters: Root River / Trips: 1 or more days / Best canoeing months: May-September / Campsites: yes / Transportation: yes / Car-top carriers: no response.

St. Paul

Century Camper Center, 1985 Geneva Avenue, St. Paul, Minn. 55119; telephone: 612–777–3141 / Waters: St. Croix River and lakes throughout the state / Trips: any length / Best canoeing months: May-August / Campsites: yes / Transportation: no / Car-top carriers: yes / Also rents camping equipment.

The Voyageurs Concession, 2300 Greenview Drive, St. Paul, Minn. 55112; telephone: 612–633–5582 / Waters: St. Croix and Namekagon Rivers / Trips: 1 hour to 3 days / Best canoeing months: June-August / Campsites: yes / Transportation: yes / Car-top carriers: no.

Taylors Falls

Taylors Falls Canoe Co. (Bob Muller and Dennis Raedeke), Taylors Falls, Minn. 55084; telephone: 612–465–6315 or 465–5051 / Waters: Namekagon and St. Croix Rivers / Trips: 1–4 days / Best canoeing months: May-mid-October / Campsites: yes / Transportation: yes / Car-top carriers: yes.

Wayzata

Voyageur Outpost, 860 East Lake Street, Wayzata, Minn. 55391; telephone: 612–473–5492 / Unconfirmed.

West St. Paul

Marlin Marine Inc., 1034 South Rober Street, West St. Paul, Minn. 55118; telephone: 612–222–7352 / Unconfirmed.

Winton

Border Lakes Outfitters (John E. Farkas and Jack M. Niemi), P.O. Box 158, Winton, Minn. 55796; telephone: 218–365–3783 / Waters: Boundary Waters Canoe Area and Quetico Provincial Park / Trips: any length / Best canoeing months: May-September / Campsites: yes / Transportation: yes / Car-top carriers: no response / Complete outfitters.

Sources of Information

Boundary Waters Canoe Area-Superior National Forest, Forest Service, U.S. Department of Agriculture (P.O. Box 338, Duluth, Minn. 55801), a free brochure with rules, regulations, and suggested canoe routes.

Canoe Trails Through Quetico, Quetico Foundation (20 Victoria Street, Toronto, Ontario, Canada), n.d., 86 pp. An excellent general description of the area including some history, canoe trails in minute detail, portages, and an area map.

The Mighty Mississippi, Aitkin County Park Commission (Court House, Aitkin, Minn. 56431), 75¢. A 95-mile trip map of the river through Aitkin County plus historical data.

Minnesota fishing and hunting information is available from the Minnesota Department of Natural Resources, Division of Fish and Game (St. Paul, Minn. 55101).

Minnesota map sets of all important canoeing trails in the state and Quetico Provincial Park are available, at various prices, from W.A. Fisher Company (123–125 Chestnut Street, Virginia, Minn. 55792).

Minnesota tourist information is available from Minnesota Department of Economic Development, Division of Tourism (51 East 8th Street, St. Paul, Minn. 55101).

Minnesota Voyageur Trips, Minnesota Department of Natural Resources, Division of Parks and Recreation (320 Centennial Building,

St. Paul, Minn. 55155), 1970, 48 pp., $2.00. A detailed description, with maps, of 16 Minnesota canoe trails plus general information on the Boundary Waters Canoe Area.

Olsen, Sigurd F. *The Singing Wilderness,* Alfred A. Knopf (New York N.Y.), 1975, 245 pp., $6.95. A well-known woodsman's loving account of the Boundary Waters and Quetico wilderness area, its flora and fauna.

Quetico Provincial Park, District Manager, Ministry of Natural Resources (Atikokan, Ontario, Canada POT 1CO) or Executive Director, Ministry of Natural Resources, Division of Parks (Toronto, Ontario, Canada M7A 1X5). A free brochure with a map, canoe routes, and other information.

So You're Going to the BWCA, Izaak Walton League of America (Minnesota Division, 106 Times Building, 57 South 4th Street, Minneapolis, Minn. 55401), n.d., 16 pp., free. A pamphlet on the Boundary Waters Canoe Area.

Voyageurs National Park, National Park Service, Voyageurs National Park (P.O. Box 50, International Falls, Minn. 56649). A free brochure.

•

ARKANSAS and MISSOURI

STRADDLING THE ARKANSAS-MISSOURI STATE LINE, the Ozark highlands with their deeply cut valleys have produced some of the finest canoeing streams in the nation. Many of the streams are fed by underground rivers that surface as springs to provide a year-round steady water supply.

On the Missouri side they run swiftly through cuts, between bluffs and wooded slopes, and around hairpin bends, but rarely over such rough terrain that whitewater experience is needed. Nature is at its most versatile with many types of hardwoods and coniferous trees, dogwoods and flowering shrubs, wildflowers and swamp vegetation.

On the Arkansas side, the Ozarks rise to greater heights. Canoeable streams are fewer, with more whitewater, or they are tamed by the dam builders. One of the most beautiful waterways, however, the Buffalo River, has been saved from the heavy hand of the U.S. Army Corps of Engineers and pork barrelling politicians by a last-minute uphill struggle by conservationists. It has remained one of the most beautiful wilderness rivers in the country.

The Missouri Ozark rivers are widely promoted tourist attractions. People come from near and far for float cruises and the most popular streams have become severely overcrowded. On a recent July 4th weekend, 243 canoes passed under a bridge spanning the Current River in a single hour! Unfortunately, the beer-drinking, horseplaying type of canoeist seems to outnumber the nature lover and camper. Even the fish have become upset, and many have buried their heads in the sand. Authorities are so concerned that they are trying to limit the number of canoes that liveries rent. But that doesn't stop people from bringing in their own canoes. Thus, for nature lovers to enjoy the Missouri Ozark rivers they obviously must avoid fine weekends and the peak season and go there on weekdays and in the off-season, or stick to the less popular waterways.

Perhaps because of Missouri's experience, Arkansas canoeing circles are close-mouthed on their rivers, and very little published information is available. After leaving the Ozarks, many of the rivers become placid and wide, but where they are not impounded in reservoirs they reportedly offer much untouched wilderness scenery worth exploring for those who like to paddle rather than float.

By the same token, Missouri canoeing interests, with their entire focus on the Ozarks, seem to have ignored the rivers of the rural plains north of the Missouri River. Yet on superficial inspection, these waters should offer at least as much canoeing potential as the rivers of the other Great Plains states, such as Illinois, Indiana, and Ohio. Practically no information is available on them, however, and the enterprising canoeist is left to his own devices.

The Missouri River, one of the nation's major waterways, is not popular with canoeists because of its heavy commercial traffic and width.

Arkansas Waters

Arkansas River
Rising near Leadville, Colorado, in a pristine state, it arrives in Arkansas at Fort Smith on Route 64 as one of the most harnessed rivers in the country. From Fort Smith it flows for close to 400 miles through the state until it joins the Mississippi River north of Arkansas City on Route 4.

Black River
See Missouri.

Buffalo River
A National Scenic Riverway. Ponca on Route 74 to Pruitt on Route 7: 22 miles / Pruitt to Route 123: 11 miles / Route 123 to Route 65: 30 miles / Route 65 to Route 14 and Buffalo River State Park: 23 miles / Route 14 to town of Buffalo and junction with the White River: 33 miles. Some stretches are too shallow for floating in dry

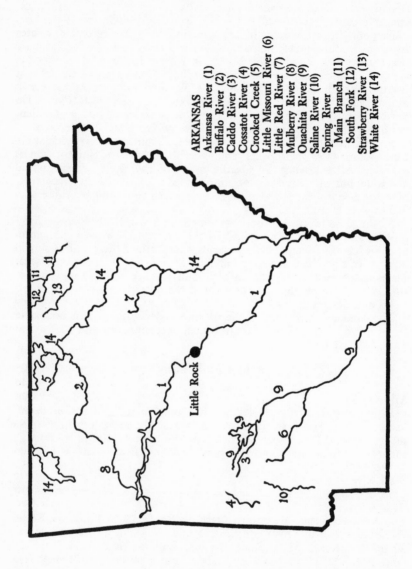

ARKANSAS
Arkansas River (1)
Buffalo River (2)
Caddo River (3)
Cossatot River (4)
Crooked Creek (5)
Little Missouri River (6)
Little Red River (7)
Mulberry River (8)
Ouachita River (9)
Saline River (10)
Spring River
Main Branch (11)
South Fork (12)
Strawberry River (13)
White River (14)

254

weather. In high water the river is canoeable from Boxley, 6 miles above Ponca, a stretch that has some whitewater in the upper reaches. Rentals: Yellville.

Caddo River
Caddo Gap on Route 8 northwest of Glenwood to Amity on Routes 8–84: 25 miles. Rentals: Glenwood.

Cossatot River
Route 246 east of Hatton on Routes 59–71 to Route 380 east of Gillham: about 20 miles, reportedly a beginner's whitewater course / Route 380 to Route 70 east of De Queen: 12 miles, smoother / De Queen to junction with the Little River: about 30 miles. Rentals: Glenwood.

Crooked Creek
Harrison on Routes 62–65 to Yellville on Route 62: about 40 miles / Yellville to junction with the White River below Cotter on Route 62: 20 miles. Rentals: Yellville.

Eleven Point River
See Missouri.

Little Missouri River
Route 84 west of Glenwood to Lake Greeson: 15 miles, some whitewater / Narrows Dam below lake on Route 19 to junction with the Ouachita River: 60 miles, canoeable only when water is released from the lake. Rentals: Glenwood.

Little Red River
Greers Ferry Dam on Route 25 northeast of Heber Springs to Ramsey access off Route 124 west of Pangburn on Route 16: 29 miles, canoeable depending on water release from reservoirs / Ramsey access to junction with the White River: about 50 miles.

Mulberry River
Practically all whitewater, canoeable at high water only. Route 103 bridge north of Clarksville to Cass on Route 23: 23 miles / Cass to Route 215 north of Pleasant Hill: 27 miles / Route 215 to junction with the Arkansas River at the town of Mulberry on Route 64: 10 miles.

Ouachita River
Old Bridge off Route 88 about 6 miles west of ranger station in Ouachita National Forest to U.S. 270 near Pencil Bluff: 20 miles / U.S. 270 to entrance of Lake Ouachita: about 25 miles / lake exit at Blakley Mountain Dam to Camden on Route 79: about 120 miles, passes through Lake Hamilton and gets slower and wider / Camden to Monroe, Louisiana, on I–20: about 170 miles / Monroe to junction with the Red River and from there into the Mississippi River: about 200 miles. Rentals: Glenwood.

Saline River
Route 4 north of Dierks on Route 70 to Millwood Lake, impoundment of the Little River: about 60 miles.

Spring River

South Fork: Canoeable in high water from Salem on Route 9 to Saddle on Route 289: 33 miles / Saddle to junction with the Main Branch: 25 miles.

Main Branch: Thayer, Missouri, on Route 142 to the dam below the town of Mammoth Spring, Arkansas, on Route 63: 8 miles / dam to Hardy on Routes 62–63 and junction with the South Fork: 20 miles / Hardy to Williford on Route 58: 12 miles / Williford to junction with the Black River above Black Rock on Route 63: 30 miles. Rentals: Mammoth Spring.

Strawberry River

Route 56 west of Ash Flat to Route 167 south of Ash Flat: about 20 miles / Route 167 to junction with the Black River southeast of the town of Strawberry on Route 25: about 60 miles.

White River

Town of Crosses on Route 74 southeast of Fayetteville to Beaver Lake: about 40 miles, some whitewater, continues through Table Rock Lake and Bull Shoals Lake, a portion of which is in Missouri; motor boats are permitted but the small coves and inlets are suitable for canoes / Bull Shoals Lake dam on Route 178 to Cotter on Route 62: 18 miles / Cotter to town of Buffalo and junction with the Buffalo River: 15 miles / Buffalo to Norfork and junction with the North Fork of the White River (*see* Missouri for the North Fork): 11 miles / junction to Calico Rock on Route 56: 18 miles / Calico Rock to Guion on Route 58: about 30 miles / Guion to Dam No. 3: 9 miles, because of extreme variations in water level depending on water release from Bull Shoals Lake dam it is important that you camp well above the high water mark. Below Dam No. 3 the river becomes slow and wide and is not popular among canoeists. It continues until it enters the Mississippi River at the mouth of the Arkansas River, a distance of about 200 miles from Dam No. 3. Rentals: Eureka Springs and Yellville.

Arkansas Rentals

Eureka Springs

Starkey Marina, Rural Route 2, Eureka Springs, Ark. 72632; telephone: 501–253–8194 / Waters: Beaver Lake and White River / Trips: 1 or more days / Best canoeing months: all year / Campsites: yes / Transportation: no / Car-top carriers: no response / Open all year.

Glenwood

Caddo River Sporting Goods, Highway 70B East, Glenwood, Ark. 71943; telephone: 501–356–3480 / Waters: Caddo, Cossatot, Little

Missouri, and Ouachita Rivers / Trips: 1–2 days / Campsites: no / Transportation: yes / Car-top carriers: yes / Open all year.

Mammoth Spring

Many Islands Camp, Route 2, Mammoth Spring, Ark. 72554; telephone: 501–856–3451 / Waters: Spring River / Trips: 1 or more days / Best canoeing months: March-November / Campsites: yes / Transportation: yes / Car-top carriers: no.

Yellville

Buffalo River Fishing Resort, Route A, Yellville, Ark. 72687; telephone: 501–449–6235 / Waters: Buffalo and White Rivers and Crooked Creek / Trips: several hours to 7 days, guides available / Best canoeing months: May-June, September, and October / Campsites: yes / Transportation: yes / Car-top carriers: yes / Rents camping equipment with guided trips only.

Robison's Canoe Rental, Route A, Yellville, Ark. 72687; telephone: 501–449–6431 / Waters: Buffalo River and Crooked Creek / Trips: several hours to several days / Best canoeing months: May-June, September, and October / Campsites: yes / Transportation: yes / Car-top carriers: no / Open all year.

Missouri Waters

Beaver Creek

Route 76 southwest of Ava on Route 14 to Route 76 bridge at Brownbranch: 15 miles, canoeable in high water only / Brownbranch to Route 160 at Bull Shoals Lake: 26 miles.

Beaver Lake

See White River in Arkansas.

Big Piney River

Baptist Camp off Route 63 south of Houston to Route 17 west of Houston: 9 miles / Route 17 to old Route 32 bridge: 23 miles / Route 32 to Ross Access off Highway J: 23 miles, this is the last take-out point before entering Fort Leonard Wood Military Reservation, a permit from the post is required to canoe the river through the fort's property / Ross Access through the reservation to I–44 bridge: 28 miles, the most popular take-out point unless one wishes to continue into the Gasconade River, 3 miles downstream. Rentals: Devils Elbow, Duke, Jerome, Licking, Rolla, and Webster Groves.

Big River

Highway E north of Bonne Terre on Route 47 to Route 21 at Washington State Park: 17 miles / park to junction with the Mineral Fork: 4 miles through the park / junction to Route 30 near Cedar Hill: 42 miles / Route 30 to junction with the Meramec River: 15 miles, urban-

Gasconade River (13)
Osage Fork (14)
Huzzah Creek (15)
Jacks Fork River (16)
James River (17)
Lake of the Ozarks (18)
Little Niangua River (19)
Meramec River (20)
Moreau River (21)
Niangua River (22)
Osage River (23)
Pomme de Terre River (24)
Sac River (25)
St. Francis River (26)
Shoal Creek (27)
Spring River (28)
Stockton Lake (29)
Sugar Creek (30)
White River (31)

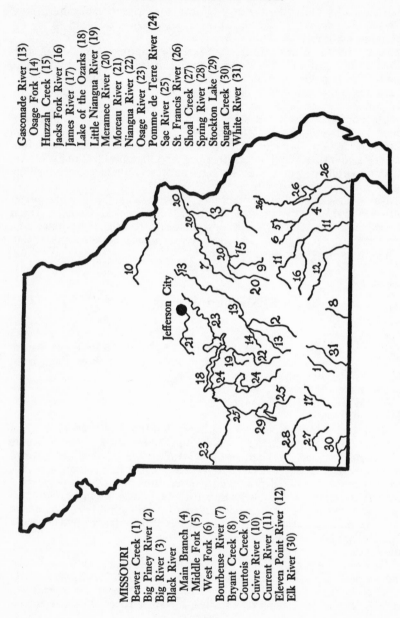

Jefferson City

MISSOURI
Beaver Creek (1)
Big Piney River (2)
Big River (3)
Black River
  Main Branch (4)
  Middle Fork (5)
  West Fork (6)
Bourbeuse River (7)
Bryant Creek (8)
Courtois Creek (9)
Cuivre River (10)
Current River (11)
Eleven Point River (12)
Elk River (30)

258

ized. The Mineral Fork is canoeable for about 14 miles from the bridge on Highway F.

Black River

West Fork: Centerville on Route 21 to the mouth of Mill Creek and junction with the Middle Fork below Iron Bridge: 11 miles, canoeable in high water only.

Middle Fork: Route 21 north of Centerville to Mill Creek and junction with the West Fork: about 6 miles, canoeable in high water only.

Main Branch: Mill Creek to Highway K bridge: 15 miles / Highway K to Highway CC: 8 miles, beginning backwater of Clearwater Lake / Highway CC to Clearwater Lake dam: 10 miles / dam to Leeper on Route 34: 7 miles / Leeper to Williamsville bridge off Route 49: 14 miles / Williamsville to U.S. 67: 7 miles, usual take-out point / U.S. 67 to Poplar Bluff at U.S. 60 bridge: 19 miles. Below Poplar Bluff the river widens and gets slow and muddy; it flows through Arkansas until it joins the White River at Newport on U.S. 67, about 120 miles from Poplar Bluff. Rentals: Annapolis, Jennings, and Piedmont.

Bourbeuse River

Route 19 south of Bem to Highway H bridge south of Gerald on Route 50: 24 miles, canoeable in high water only / bridge to Route 185 at Noser Mill: 22 miles / Route 185 to Route 50 at Union: 48 miles / Route 50 to junction with the Meramec River: 15 miles. The river is winding and slow.

Bryant Creek

Route 14 at Rippee Wildlife Area to Bertha on Highway D: 9 miles, canoeable in high water only / Bertha to Bell bridge on Route 95: 5 miles / Route 95 to Hodgson Mill on Route 181: 9 miles / Route 181 to Tecumseh on Route 160 and junction with the North Fork of the White River and Norfork Lake: 11 miles. Rentals: Tecumseh and West Plains.

Bull Shoals Lake

See White River in Arkansas.

Courtois Creek

Route 8 near Berryman east of Steelville to Meramec River: 11 miles. Rentals: Leasburg and Steelville.

Cuivre River

Route 161 near Middletown to Cuivre River State Park near Route 61 north of Troy: about 30 miles, intermediate access points, the upper stretches are canoeable in high water only / Route 61 to junction with the Mississippi River: about 30 miles. Rentals: Troy.

Current River

An Ozark National Scenic Riverway. Montauk State Park on Route 119 to Akers on Highway K: 17 miles / Akers to Round Spring on Route 19: 19 miles / Round Spring to junction with the Jacks Fork River at Two Rivers Landing: 18 miles / Two Rivers Landing to Owls

Bend on Route 106: 7 miles / Owls Bend to Van Buren on Route 60: 26 miles / Van Buren to Big Spring State Park on Route 103: 5 miles, most canoe trips finish here / park to Arkansas border: 49 miles, motor boats. In Arkansas, the Current River joins the Black River near Pocahontas on Routes 62–67. Rentals: Alley Spring, Eminence, Jadwin, Licking, Rolla, Round Spring, Salem, and Van Buren.

Eleven Point River

Thomasville on Route 99 to Route 19 north of Greer: 17 miles, canoeable in high water only / Route 19 to Riverton on Route 160: 19 miles / Route 160 to Route 142: 10 miles, usual take-out point. It is possible to continue into Arkansas for about 40 miles until the Eleven Point River joins the Black River. In Arkansas, the river is wide and slow. Rentals: Alton and Van Buren.

Gasconade River

Hartville on Route 38 to Highway O bridge near Competition: 32 miles, canoeable in high water only / Competition to Route 32 near Falcon / 13 miles / Route 32 to I–44 below junction with the Osage Fork: 30 miles / I–44 to Route 133: 10 miles / Route 133 to Route 17 near Waynesville: 32 miles / Route 17 to junction with the Big Piney River below Route 28: 26 miles / junction to Routes 28–63 bridge: 32 miles / bridge to Route 89 bridge: 30 miles / Route 89 to Route 50 near Mount Sterling: 17 miles / Route 50 to junction with the Missouri River: 33 miles, the river is very slow on this stretch. Rentals: Devils Elbow, Eldridge, Jerome, Lebanon, Licking, Rolla, Vienna, and Wester Groves.

Osage Fork: Highway ZZ bridge east of Conway on I–44 to Route 5: 17 miles / Route 5 to Route 32: 22 miles / Route 32 to junction with the Gasconade River near I–44: 20 miles. The Osage Fork is shallow in its upper reaches in dry weather. Rentals: Eldridge.

Huzzah Creek

Davisville off Route 49A to Route 8 east of Steelville: 17 miles, canoeable in high water only / Route 8 to junction with the Meramec River: 7 miles. Rentals: Leasburg and Steelville.

Jacks Fork River

An Ozark National Scenic Riverway. Buck Hollow on Route 17 north of Mountain View to Alley Spring on Route 106: 24 miles, canoeable in high water only / Alley Spring to Eminence on Route 19: 6 miles / Eminence to junction with the Current River at Two Rivers Landing near town of Jacks Fork on Highway V: 8 miles. Rentals: Alley Spring, Eminence, Jadwin, Licking, Rolla, Round Spring, Salem, and Van Buren.

James River

Route 125 west of Springfield to Route 65 at Galloway: 10 miles / Route 65 to Route 14 west of Nixa: 18 miles / Route 14 to junction with Finley Creek near Jamesville on Highway U: 10 miles / junction to Galena on Routes 148–13: 24 miles, below Galena backwater of Table Rock Lake. Watch for frequent obstructions on this river. Finley Creek is canoeable only in high water for about 20 miles, starting on Route 125 near Linden.

Lake of the Ozarks

Formed by Bagnell Dam on Route 54, the lake has a shoreline of 1,375 miles with secluded coves and inlets which provide privacy for canoeists from the motor boats, sightseeing boats, water planes, water skiers, etc., who use the lake.

Little Niangua River

Route 54 east of Preston to Highway J bridge at entry to Lake of the Ozarks: 32 miles.

Meramec River

Short Bend on Route 19 northeast of Salem to Woodson K. Woods Wildlife Area off Route 8: 26 miles, canoeable in high water only / Route 8 to Route 19 near Steelville: 20 miles / Route 19 to junction with Huzzah and Courtois Creeks on Highway E: 18 miles / junction to Route 185 at entry to Meramec State Park: 23 miles / Route 185 to Meramec Caverns just below exit from park: 6 miles / caverns to Route 30 near St. Clair: 23 miles / St. Clair to the Mississippi River: 76 miles, urban developments to look at. Rentals: Leasburg, Rolla, Stanton, and Steelville.

Moreau River

North Moreau River: Highway U bridge south of Centertown on Route 50 to junction with the South Moreau River: 20 miles.

South Moreau River: Decatur on Highway AA to junction with the North Moreau River: 14 miles.

Moreau River: Junction of North and South Moreau Rivers to Route 54: 5 miles / Route 54 to the Missouri River at Jefferson City: 30 miles.

Niangua River

Route 32 east of Buffalo to Bennett Spring State Park on Route 64: 30 miles / park to Berry Bluff on Highway E northwest of Eldridge: 27 miles, most popular take-out point / Berry Bluff to Tunnel Dam on Lake Niangua: 10 miles / dam to Lake of the Ozarks: about 6 miles, water may be shut off below the dam. Rentals: Eldridge and Lebanon.

Osage River

I–71 north of town of Nevada to Osceola Dam on Route 82: about 70 miles, slow and muddy, shallow in dry weather / dam to Route 7: about 50 miles, backwater of Lake of the Ozarks / Bagnell Dam of Lake of the Ozarks to the Missouri River below Jefferson City on Route 50: about 80 miles.

Pomme de Terre River

Route 32 at Burns to Pomme de Terre Reservoir at Highway PP east of Route 83: 22 miles.

Sac River

Route 32 below Stockton Lake to Bear Creek inlet: under 2 miles / Bear Creek to junction with Cedar Creek: 21 miles / Cedar Creek to Route 54: 10 miles / Route 54 to Osceola Dam about 4 miles below junction with the Osage River: 24 miles. Bear Creek is canoeable for some 10 miles from Highway P bridge. Cedar Creek is canoeable for 18 miles from Ivy Bridge on Highway K. Rentals: Stockton.

St. Francis River

Highway H bridge south of Farmington on Route 32 to Lake Wappapello on Route 67: about 80 miles, strictly whitewater. The tributaries are canoeable: Little St. Francis River from Route 72 west of Fredericktown and Big Creek from Highway E east of Millcreek.

Shoal Creek

Dam at Ritchey on Highway W north of Route 60 to Route 71 south of Joplin: 28 miles, much whitewater / Route 71 to Scherhorn Park south of Galena, Kansas, on Route 26: 14 miles / park to junction with the Spring River: 3 miles. Rentals: Quapaw, Oklahoma.

Spring River

Highway V 3 miles west of Mount Vernon on Route 39 to Route 97 bridge: 7 miles / Route 97 to dam at Route 66 near Carthage: 23 miles, obstructions, especially in low water / Route 66 to Route 71: 1 mile, low water / Route 71 to Route 43: 15 miles / Route 43 to Route 171: 7 miles / Route 171 to Highway P west of Joplin: 11 miles / Highway P to Baxter Springs, Kansas, on Route 166: 20 miles / For continuation, *see* Kansas. Rentals: Quapaw, Oklahoma.

Stockton Lake

A 25,000-acre reservoir with 250 miles of shoreline of which 45 miles are set aside for camping and wildlife conservation. Motor boats are permitted but there are quiet inlets for canoeing. The lake empties into the lower part of the Sac River. Rentals: Stockton.

Sugar Creek and Elk River

Big Sugar Creek: Route 90 east of Huckleberry State Forest to junction with the Little Sugar Creek just above Route 71 bridge: 25 miles, the upper reaches are canoeable in high water only.

Little Sugar Creek: Route 90 northeast of Jane on Route 71 to junction with the Big Sugar Creek just above the Route 71 bridge: 8 miles, canoeable only in high water.

Elk River: Junction of the Big and Little Sugar Creeks to Route 43 near the Oklahoma border: 23 miles, below this point the river enters Lake of the Cherokees in Oklahoma.

Table Rock Lake

See White River in Arkansas.

White River

North Fork: Route 76 in Mark Twain National Forest to Hebron on Highway AA off Route 181: 19 miles, canoeable in high water only /

Hebron to Twin Bridges on Route 14: 3 miles / Route 14 to Tecumseh on Route 160 and Norfork Lake: 26 miles, motor boats on the lake / lake exit at Salesville in Arkansas to junction with the Main Branch at Norfork, Arkansas: 5 miles. *See* Arkansas for the Main Branch. Rentals: Caulfield, Tecumseh, and West Plains.

Missouri Rentals

Alley Spring
Alley Spring Canoe Rental (Staples Family), Alley Spring, Mo. 65466; telephone: 314–226–3386 / Waters: Jacks Fork and Current Rivers / Trips: 1 or more days / Best canoeing months: March-October / Campsites: yes / Transportation: yes / Car-top carriers: no / Open all year.

Alton
Hufstedler's Canoe Rental, Riverton Rural Branch, Alton, Mo. 65606; telephone: 417–778–6116 / Waters: Eleven Point River / Trips: 1 or more days / Best canoeing months: May-September / Campsites: yes / Transportation: yes / Car-top carriers: no / Open all year.

Woods" Canoe Rental (Don Woods), R.R. 2, Box 216, Alton, Mo. 65606; telephone: 417–778–6497 / Waters: Eleven Point River / Trips: 1 or more days, guides available / Best canoeing months: April-November / Campsites: yes / Transportation: yes / Car-top carriers: yes / Open all year.

Annapolis
Midwest Floats and Campgrounds (Jim and Mary Henson, mgrs.), Route 1, Box 138, Annapolis, Mo. 63620; telephone: 314–637–2278, or contact owners, Jim and Doris O'Brien at 14565 Ladue Road, Chesterfield, Mo. 63017, telephone: 314–469–1791 / Waters: Black River / Trips: 1–3 days / Best canoeing months: May-October / Campsites: yes / Transportation: yes / Car-top carriers: no response / Open all year.

Caulfield
Sunburst Ranch (Belle and Leroy Webb), Star Route, Caulfield, Mo. 65626; telephone: 417–284–3443 / Waters: North Fork of the White River / Trips: 1 or more days, guides available / Best canoeing months: no response / Campsites: yes / Transportation: yes / Car-top carriers: no.

Chesterfield
See Annapolis, Mo.

Devils Elbow
Hiawatha Camp Grounds, Box 345, Devils Elbow, Mo. 65457; telephone: 314–336–4068 / Waters: Big Piney and Gasconade Rivers /

Trips: 1 or more days, guides available / Best canoeing months: March-November / Campsites: yes / Transportation: yes / Car-top carriers: yes / Affiliated with GO-E-Z Float Trips in Webster Groves, Mo. / Open all year.

Duke

The Last Resort (Richard Sphar), formerly Herb & Lea's Resort, Route 1, Duke, Mo. 65461; telephone: 314–435–6669 / Waters: Big Piney River / Trips: 1–4 days, guides available / Best canoeing months: May-September / Campsites: yes / Transportation: yes / Car-top carriers: no / Housekeeping cabins available at base.

Eldridge

Blue Springs Resort (Don Reagan), Eldridge, Mo. 65463; telephone: 417–286–3507 / Waters: Niangua and Gasconade Rivers / Trips: 1 or more days / Best canoeing months: April-October / Campsites: yes / Transportation: yes / Car-top carriers: yes / Housekeeping cabins available / Open all year.

Eminence

Bales Canoe Rental, Eminence, Mo. 65466; telephone: 314–226–3434 / Unconfirmed.

Eminence Canoe Rental (Stanley Smith), Eminence, Mo. 65466; telephone: 314–226–3642 / Waters: Jacks Fork and Current Rivers / Trips: 1–7 days / Best canoeing months: March-October / Campsites: yes / Transportation: yes / Car-top carriers: no / Open all year.

Two Rivers Canoe Rental (Joe and Darlene Devall), Eminence, Mo. 65466; telephone: 314–226–9478 / Waters: Jacks Fork and Current Rivers / Trips: 1–7 days, guides available / Best canoeing months: April-November / Campsites: yes / Transportation: yes / Car-top carriers: yes, only for Current and Jacks Fork Rivers / Also rents camping equipment / Open all year.

Windy's Canoe Rental, Box 151, Eminence, Mo. 65466; telephone: 314–226–3404 / Waters: Jacks Fork and Current Rivers / Trips: no response / Best canoeing months: April-October / Campsites: yes / Transportation: yes / Car-top carriers: no response.

Jadwin

Jadwin Canoe Rental (Darrel Blackwell), Jadwin, Mo. 65501; telephone: 314–729–5229 / Waters: Jacks Fork and Current Rivers / Trips: 2 hours-5 days, guides available / Best canoeing months: April-November / Campsites: yes / Transportation: yes / Car-top carriers: yes / Open all year.

Jennings

Gunwhale Canoe Rentals, 2527 OEPTS, Jennings, Mo. 63136; telephone: 314–388–0125 or 314–862–2543 / Waters: Black River / Trips: 1 or more days / Best canoeing months: May-October / Campsites: yes / Transportation: yes / Car-top carriers: yes.

Jerome

Gasconade Valley Canoe Rental, General Delivery, Jerome, Mo. 65529; telephone: 314–762–2526 / Waters: Gasconade and Big Piney Rivers / Trips: 1–3 days / Best canoeing months: May-September / Campsites: yes / Transportation: yes / Car-top carriers.

Leasburg

Al Keyes Canoe Rental, Leasburg, Mo. 65535; telephone: 314–245–6437 / Waters: Meramec River and Courtois and Huzzah Creeks / Trips: 4 hours-5 days / Best canoeing months: April-October / Campsites: yes / Transportation: yes / Car-top carriers: no / Open all year.

Lebanon

Niangua & Osage Fork Canoe Rentals (Dwight Maggard), Route 3, Lebanon, Mo. 65536; telephone: 417–532–7616 / Waters: Niangua River and Osage Fork of the Gasconade River / Trips: a few hours to several days / Best canoeing months: April-October / Campsites: yes / Transportation: yes / Car-top carriers: no / Open all year.

Sand Spring Resort (Paul and Mayme Burtin), Highway 64, Bennett Spring State Park, Lebanon, Mo. 65536; telephone: 417–532–5857 / Waters: Niangua River / Trips: 1–3 days, guides available / Best canoeing months: May-October / Campsites: yes / Transportation: yes / Car-top carriers: no / Motel and housekeeping units at base.

Vogels Resort, Brice Route, Lebanon, Mo. 65536; telephone: 417–532–4097 / Waters: Niangua River / Trips: 2 hours-2 days / Best canoeing months: May-September / Campsites: yes / Transportation: yes / Car-top carriers: yes, for Niangua River only.

Licking

Big M Resort, Star Route 7, Box 124, Licking, Mo. 65542; telephone: 314–674–3488 / Waters: Big Piney, Gasconade, Current, and Jacks Fork Rivers / Trips: 1 or more days, guides available only if booked in advance / Best canoeing months: April-November / Campsites: yes / Transportation: yes / Car-top carriers: yes / Housekeeping cabins available / Open all year.

Big Piney River Resort (Ken Everett), Rural Ozark Route 7, Box 419, Licking, Mo. 65542; telephone: 314–674–2779 / Waters: Big Piney River / Trips: 1–6 days, guides available / Best canoeing months: March-October / Campsites: yes / Transportation: yes / Car-top carriers: yes.

OK Cottage Resort (Mrs. O.K. Rennick), Licking, Mo. 65542; telephone: 314–674–3140 / Waters: Big Piney River / Trips: 1 or more days, guides available / Best canoeing months: May-November / Campsites: yes / Transportation: yes / Car-top carriers: no / Housekeeping cabins available.

Ray's Riverside Resort, Route 7, Box 417, Licking, Mo. 65542; telephone: 314–674–2430 or 674–3931 / Unconfirmed.

Morrison

Roland Meyer, Fredericksburg Ferry on Highway J, Morrison, Mo. 65061; telephone: 314–294–5621 / Unconfirmed.

Piedmont

Clearwater Store's, Inc., Route 3, Piedmont, Mo. 63957; telephone: 314–223–4813 / Waters: Black River / Trips: 1 or more days / Best canoeing months: May-September / Campsites: yes / Transportation: yes / Car-top carriers: no response.

Rolla

Aaron's Boats & Motors, Business Loop 44 West, Rolla, Mo. 65401; telephone: 417–364–2431 / Waters: Gasconade, Big Piney, Meramec, Jacks Fork, and Current Rivers / Trips: 1 or more days / Best canoeing months: spring to fall / Campsites: yes / Transportation: no / Car-top carriers: yes / Open all year.

Ozark Equipment Co., Highway 63 and Black Street, Rolla, Mo. 65401; telephone: 314–364–2180 / Unconfirmed.

Round Spring

Carr's Canoe Rental, Round Spring, Mo. 65467; telephone: 314–858–3240 / Waters: Current and Jacks Fork Rivers / Trips: 1–10 days / Best canoeing months: May-October / Campsites: yes / Transportation: yes / Car-top carriers: yes / Open all year.

Sullivan's Canoe Rental, Point Rivers, Round Spring, Mo. 65467; telephone: 314–858–3237 or 314–689–2536 / Unconfirmed.

St. Louis

Marlin's Sports Shop, 5408 Hampton Avenue, St. Louis, Mo. 63109; telephone: 314–481–4681 / Waters: anywhere in Missouri / Trips: any length, guides available / Best canoeing months: June-October / Campsites: yes / Transportation: no / Car-top carriers: yes / Also rents camping equipment / Open all year.

Salem

Akers Ferry Canoe Rental (G.E. Maggard), Cedar Grove Route, Box 90, Salem, Mo. 65560; telephone: 314–858–3224 / Waters: Current and Jacks Fork Rivers / Trips: a few hours to several days, guides available / Best canoeing months: April-November / Campsites: yes / Transportation: yes / Car-top carriers: yes / Open all year.

Current River Canoe Rental (Russell Sandlin), Gladden Star Route, Salem, Mo. 65560; telephone: 314–858–3250 or during the winter in Eminence, Mo. at 314–226–5517 / Waters: Current River / Trips: 1–6 days / Best canoeing months: May-October / Campsites: yes / Transportation: yes / Car-top carriers: no / May 1-October 1 rentals at Pulltite Campground; November 1-April 30 rentals from Eminence.

Silver Arrow Canoe Rental (George and Dennis Purcell), Gladden Star Route, Salem, Mo. 65560; telephone: 314–729–5770 / Waters: Current and Jacks Fork Rivers / Trips: a few hours to several days, guides available / Best canoeing months: April-November / Campsites: yes / Transportation: yes / Car-top carriers: yes, for Current and Jacks Fork Rivers only / Also rents camping equipment / Open all year.

Wild Rivers Canoe Rental, Cedar Grove Route, Salem, Mo. 65560; telephone: 314–858–3230 or 858–3317 / Unconfirmed.

Stanton

Stanton Fina Service, P.O. Box 8, Stanton, Mo. 63079; telephone: 314–927–5224 / Waters: Meramec River / Trips: 1 or more days / Best canoeing months; March-October / Campsites: yes / Transportation: yes / Car-top carriers: yes / Open all year.

Steelville

B & H Canoe Rental (Karen Wood), Route 1, Box 104A, Steelville, Mo. 65565; telephone: 314–775–5505 or 314–781–1492 and 314–647–5216 in St. Louis / Waters: Meramec River and Courtois and Huzzah Creeks / Trips: 1 or more days / Best canoeing months: June-September / Campsites: yes / Transportation: yes / Car-top carriers: yes.

Bass Canoe and Boat Sales and Rental, Box 61, Steelville, Mo. 65565; telephone: 314–786–8517 / Unconfirmed.

Payne's Boat Company (Ken Payne), R.R. 1, Box 10, Steelville, Mo. 65565; telephone: 314–775–2575 / Waters: Meramec River and Huzzah Creek / Trips: up to 4 days / Best canoeing months: May-October / Campsites: yes / Transportation: yes / Car-top carriers: no / Open all year.

J.W. Ray Canoe & Boat Rental, Route 1, Box 277, Steelville, Mo. 65565; telephone: 314–775–5697 / Waters: Meramec River / Trips: 1 or more days / Best canoeing months: March-October / Campsites: yes / Transportation: yes / Car-top carriers: no response / Open all year.

Thornton's Canoe Rental, Route 1, Box 285, Steelville, Mo. 65565; telephone: 314–775–5523 / Waters: Meramec River / Trips: 1 or more days / Best canoeing months: May-August / Campsites: yes / Transportation: yes / Car-top carriers: no response.

Stockton

Orleans Trail Boat Dock and Marina, Route 3, Stockton, Mo. 65785; telephone: 417–276–3940 / Waters: Sac River and Stockton Lake / Trips: as long as you want / Best canoeing months: June-September / Campsites: yes / Transportation: yes / Car-top carriers: yes / Also rents houseboats.

Sullivan

The Service Center, Camp Rest-A-While, Route 1, Box 1, Sullivan, Mo. 63080; telephone: 314–927–5224 / Unconfirmed.

Tecumseh

Nelson's Canoe Rentals (Betty Nelson), Tecumseh, Mo. 65760; telephone: 417–284–3488 / Waters: North Fork of the White River and

Bryant Creek / Trips: a few hours to 2 days, guides available / Camp-sites: yes / Transportation: yes / Car-top carriers: no.

Troy

Castle's Canoe Rental & Float Trips, Highway 61, Troy, Mo. 63379; telephone: 314–528–7525 / Waters: Cuivre River / Trips: 1 or more days / Best canoeing months: May-September / Campsites: yes / Transportation: yes / Car-top carriers: yes.

Van Buren

Big Spring Canoe Rental (Roy L. Gossett), formerly Neil Canoe and Jon Boat Rental, P.O. Box 396, Van Buren, Mo. 63965; telephone: 314–323–4447 and 323–8330 during the day or 323–4356 in the evening / Waters: Current and Jacks Fork Rivers; also Eleven Point River by advance appointment only / Trips: 2 hours-5 days / Best canoeing months: April-October / Campsites: yes / Transportation: yes / Car-top carriers: yes / Main office in Van Buren is open all year, canoeing office adjacent to KOA Campground is open from April 1-October 31.

Vienna

Indian Ford Resort, Vienna, Mo. 65582; telephone: 314–422–3484 / Waters: Gasconade River / Trips: 1 or more days / Best canoeing months: May-July and October / Campsites: yes / Transportation: yes / Car-top carriers: no response.

Webster Groves

GO-E-Z Float Trips, subsidiary of Hiawatha Camp Grounds, 8394 Big Bend, Webster Groves, Mo. 63119; telephone: 314–962–8434 / Waters: Big Piney and Gasconade Rivers / Trips: 1 or more days, guides available / Best canoeing months: March-November / Camp-sites: yes / Transportation: yes / Car-top carriers: yes / Open all year / *See also* Devils Elbow.

West Plains

Twin Bridges Canoe Rental, S.S. Route, Box 230, West Plains, Mo. 65775; telephone: 417–256–7507 / Waters: North Fork of the White River, Bryant Creek, and other waterways / Trips: 1 or more days, guides available / Best canoeing months: April-October / Campsites: yes / Transportation: yes / Car-top carriers: yes / Also rents camping equipment / Open all year.

Sources of Information

Arkansas fishing and hunting information is available from Arkansas Game and Fish Commission (State Capitol Grounds, Little Rock, Ark. 72201).

Arkansas tourist information is available from Arkansas Department of Parks and Tourism (Capitol Building, Room 149, Little Rock, Ark. 72201).

Hawksley, Oz. *Missouri Ozark Waterways*, Missouri Conservation

Commission (Jefferson City, Mo. 64101), 1974, 114 pp., $1.00. Detailed guide to 37 major float streams of the area plus useful general observations on canoeing practices and equipment; one of the best books of its kind.

Mid-South River Guide, Bluff City Canoe Club (P.O. Box 4523, Memphis, Tenn. 38104), n.d., 24 pp., $1.00. Describes 6 rivers in Missouri, Arkansas, and Tennessee.

Missouri Fishing, Missouri Tourist Commission (308 East High Street, Box 1055, Jefferson City, Mo. 65101), n.d., 19 pp., free. Describes fishing opportunities and regulations.

Missouri Vacation Guide, Missouri Division of Tourism (P.O. Box 1055, Dept. M075, Jefferson City, Mo. 65101), n.d., 43 pp., free.

Nolen, Ben and R. E. Narramore. *Texas Rivers and Rapids*, available from Ben Nolan (P.O. Box 673, Humble, Texas 77338), includes the Buffalo and Cossatot Rivers in Arkansas. *See* Texas for more information on this publication.

The Ozark Society (Box 2914, Little Rock, Ark. 72203) has publications on the Buffalo and Mulberry Rivers and other information on Arkansas waterways.

•

THE DAKOTAS, NEBRASKA, and IOWA

" . . . FROM THE TOP OF THIS MOUND we beheld a most butifull landscape: Numerous herds of buffalow were Seen feeding in various directions; the Plain to North N.W. & N.E. extends without interruption as far as Can be seen." Thus the entry of William Clark in his diary on August 25, 1804, when he stood on a mount along the Missouri River, a few miles above what is today Vermillion, South Dakota, on the most memorable canoe trip ever made — the Lewis and Clark expedition commissioned by President Thomas Jefferson "to explore the Missouri river and such principal streams of it, as, by its course & communication with the waters of the Pacific Ocean, may offer the most direct & practicable water communication across the continent . . . "

Lewis and Clark, encountering the peaks of the Rockies, failed to locate a "practicable" river route from the Atlantic to the Pacific Oceans, but their trip remains the outstanding example of advance planning and circumspection in execution of any canoe expedition, and any novice keen on proving his ability as a wilderness canoeist would be well advised to study its record.

Meriwether Lewis and William Clark would hardly recognize the Missouri River today as it flows through the Dakotas and along the boundaries of Nebraska and Iowa. So much of it is lake rather than river, among the lakes the huge 364,000-acre Lake Sakakawea in North Dakota. And many other stretches are channeled. But there are at least three sections that may give a modern canoeist an inkling of what Lewis and Clark encountered in a virgin state: the 60-mile stretch from Garrison Dam on Lake Sakakawea to Bismarck, North Dakota; the 40 miles from Fort Randall Dam at the exit of Lake Francis Case in South Dakota to Niobrara, Nebraska; and the 60 miles from Gavins Point Dam at the exit of Lewis and Clark Lake on the South Dakota-Nebraska border to Ponca, Nebraska, also on the state line.

Apart from the Missouri River, the Little Missouri River, and the Red River, which flows north into Canada, there is practically no published information on the waterways of the Dakotas. It was not clear as this book went to press whether there is a lack of canoeable waters or a lack of communication between canoeists.

In Nebraska and Iowa the story is different. Nebraska (meaning "flat river" in Indian) is largely drained from west to east by the Platte River (meaning "flat" in French). Together with the North Platte River, the wide and shallow Platte is canoeable across the entire width of the state, except perhaps for some spots during the summer when too much water is diverted for irrigation purposes. This diversion of water is a problem for canoeists with several Nebraska rivers, but otherwise a number of rivers offer very attractive canoeing through rolling plateaus and past limestone bluffs, most popular among them the Niobrara River and the Calamus River.

Iowa, even flatter than the Dakotas and Nebraska, and almost 95 percent cultivated, offers great scenic surprises in its river courses. Most of the state's woods are ribbon developments along the river banks. Limestone canyons alternate with lush meadows. The Upper Iowa River — a separate river and not to be confused with the Iowa River — is the most widely favored by canoeists and fishermen, but the Yellow, Red Cedar, Shellrock, and Wapsipinicon Rivers, among others, are no less attractive.

North Dakota Waters

Little Missouri River

Medora on I–94 to Route 85 south of Watford City: a 4-day trip if the waters are slow, a 2-day trip in fast water. The Little Missouri is usually canoeable until the end of June. This stretch passes through the Petrified Forest and 3 separate sections of the Theodore Roosevelt Na-

NORTH DAKOTA
Little Missouri River (1)
Missouri River (2)
Red River (3)

SOUTH DAKOTA
Big Sioux River (1)
Missouri River (2)

271

tional Memorial Park. Route 85 bridge to backwater of Lake Sakakawea on Route 22: about 35 miles. Rentals: Watford City.

Missouri River

Enters North Dakota from Montana at Buford southwest of Williston on Route 85, the river is soon backed up for about 150 miles as a result of Garrison Dam on Lake Sakakawea near Riverdale on Route 200. There is good canoeing from Riverdale to Bismarck on I–94 for about 80 miles. Below Bismarck is backwater of Oahe Reservoir, which runs from North Dakota into South Dakota ending at Oahe Dam at Pierre, South Dakota, on Routes 14–34, a 200-mile stretch. *See* South Dakota and Nebraska. Rentals: Watford City.

Red River

The Red River forms the boundary between North Dakota and Minnesota and flows into Canada. White Rock, South Dakota, on Route 81, where South Dakota, North Dakota, and Minnesota meet at the exit from Lake Traverse, to Pembina, North Dakota, on Route 81 and the Canadian border: about 200 miles. The most popular stretch is from Grand Forks, North Dakota, on Route 2 to Winnepeg, Canada, on Route 75, a stretch of about 100 miles. Rentals: Grand Forks.

North Dakota Rentals

Bottineau

Larson Marine, Inc., Lake Metigoshe, Bottineau, N.D. 58318; telephone: 701–263–4888 / Unconfirmed.

Grand Forks

4 Season Outfitters (Bob Wood), 512 North Washington, Grand Forks, N.D. 58201; telephone: 701–7750–657 / Waters: Red River and, in Minnesota, the Red Lake River and Crow Wing Chain / Trips: 1 or more days / Best canoeing months: June-September / Campsites: yes / Transportation: no / Car-top carriers: yes / Also rents camping equipment.

Watford City

Dixon Canoe Outfitters, Route 85, Watford City, N.D. 58854; telephone: 701–842–3448 / Waters: Little Missouri, Missouri River, and, in Montana, the Yellowstone River / Trips: up to 4 days / Best canoeing months: April-June / Campsites: yes / Transportation: yes / Cartop carriers: yes, they will rent the canoe but canoeist must have his own carrier.

South Dakota Waters

Big Sioux River

Route 14 west of Brookings to Route 77 south of Brookings: 15 miles / Route 77 to local road near Ward: 10 miles / Ward Road to

Route 13 north of Flandreau: 15 miles / Route 13 to Route 34 at Egan: 15 miles / Route 34 to Route 77 at town of Dell Rapids: 20 miles / Dell Rapids to city of Sioux Falls on I-90: 30 miles / southeast of Sioux Falls the river forms the state line between South Dakota and Iowa to junction with the Missouri River at Sioux City on I-29, about 160 miles.

Missouri River

Lake Oahe Dam at Pierre on Routes 14–34 to Fort Randall Dam at Pickstown on Route 18: about 150 miles. *See* North Dakota and Nebraska.

South Dakota Rentals

None.

Nebraska Waters

Big Blue River

Rarely canoeable above Crete on Route 82 southwest of Lincoln. Crete to Route 41 at Wilber: about 12 miles, canoeable primarily in spring and high water / Route 41 to DeWitt on Route 103: 10 miles / DeWitt to Riverside Park in Beatrice on Route 77: 15 miles / Beatrice to Barneston on Route 8 above the Kansas border: about 25 miles / Barneston to Marysville, Kansas, on Route 36: about 20 miles / below Marysville is backwater of Tuttle Creek Lake.

Calamus River

Route 7 about 19 miles north of Brewster to Route 183 about 12 miles north of Taylor: about 35 miles / Route 183 to junction with the North Loup River at Burwell on Routes 11–91: about 20 miles. Rentals: Lincoln.

Dismal River

Route 97 about 14 miles south of Mullen to Route 83 about 14 miles south of Thedford: about 30 miles / Route 83 to Dunning on Route 2 and junction with the Middle Loup River: 25 miles. Rentals: Lincoln.

Elkhorn River

West Point on Routes 32–275 to Dead Timber Recreation Grounds on Routes 91–275: 18 miles / recreation grounds to Winslow on Route 77–275 and junction with the Logan River: about 20 miles / Winslow to Route 91 east of Nickerson: 10 miles / Route 91 to Route 30 at Arlington: 12 miles / Arlington to Two Rivers Recreation Grounds and junction with the Platte River west of Gretna on Route 6: about 30 miles. Rentals: Lincoln.

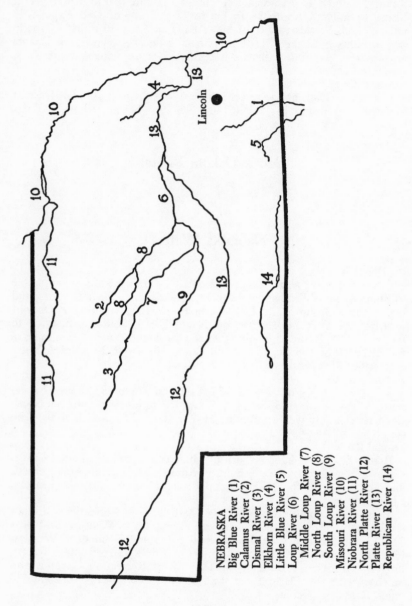

NEBRASKA
Big Blue River (1)
Calamus River (2)
Dismal River (3)
Elkhorn River (4)
Little Blue River (5)
Loup River (6)
Middle Loup River (7)
North Loup River (8)
South Loup River (9)
Missouri River (10)
Niobrara River (11)
North Platte River (12)
Platte River (13)
Republican River (14)

Little Blue River

Hebron on Route 81 to Route 136 west of Fairbury: about 30 miles /
Route 136 to Steele City on Route 8 near the Kansas border: 15 miles /
Steele City to Tuttle Creek Lake on Route 77 in Kansas: about 30 miles.

Loup River

Middle Loup River: Route 83 at Thedford to Dunning on Route 2
and junction with the Dismal River: 30 miles / Dunning to Milburn
Dam on Route S-21A: 25 miles / Milburn Dam to Route 183 south of
Sargent: 25 miles / Sargent to Route 70 at Arcadia: 20 miles / Arcadia
to Loup City on Route 92: 15 miles / Loup City to junction with the
South Loup River below Boelus on Route 58: 25 miles / junction with
South Loup River to junction with North Loup River below St. Paul on
Route 92: 25 miles.

North Loup River: Route 183 at Taylor to Burwell on Routes 11–91
and junction with the Calamus River: 20 miles / Burwell to Route 70
at Ord: 20 miles / Ord to Scotia on Route 22: 20 miles / Scotia to
junction with the Middle Loup River below Route 281: 25 miles.

South Loup River: Pressy Recreation Grounds on Route 21 to Route
183 about 8 miles north of Miller: 25 miles / Route 183 to Pleasanton
on Route 10: 20 miles / Pleasanton to Ravenna on Route 2: 10 miles /
Route 2 to junction with the Middle Loup River below Boelus on Route
58: 12 miles, unreliable water conditions due to diversion of water for
irrigation purposes.

Loup River: Formed by confluence of Middle and North Loup Rivers
below Route 281. Route 281 to Route 14 at Fullerton: 30 miles / Fullerton to junction with the Platte River at Columbus on Routes 30–81:
about 40 miles.

Missouri River

The river forms part of the border with South Dakota. Fort Randall
Dam in South Dakota on Routes 18–281 to Niobrara, Nebraska, on
Route 12: 50 miles, scenic, good for canoeing / Niobrara through Lewis
and Clark Lake to Gavins Point Dam on Route 81: about 40 miles /
dam to Ponca State Park at Ponca off Route 12: 60 miles, scenic, good
canoeing / Ponca to Sioux City, Iowa, on Route 73–77: 20 miles. *See*
South Dakota and Iowa. Rentals: Lincoln.

Niobrara River

Route 97 south of Nenzel and north of Nebraska National Forest to
power dam east of Valentine on Route 83: about 40 miles / Valentine
to Meadville on local road north of Ainsworth on Route 20: about 50
miles / Meadville to Route 183 south of Springview: 7 miles / Route
183 to Route 7: 12 miles / river continues for about 75 miles to junction with the Missouri River at town of Niobrara on Routes 10–12.
Rentals: Lincoln.

Platte River

Main Branch: Formed by confluence of North and South Platte Rivers at town of North Platte on Routes 70–83, canoeable all the way to junction with the Missouri River below Omaha, about 350 miles, except for dry periods in the summer months when the waters are diverted for irrigation. Many access points from Route 30 between town of North Platte and Columbus, the waters are usually adequate for canoeing year round below Columbus. Columbus on Routes 30–81 to Route 15 at Schuyler: 25 miles / Schuyler to Route 77 at Fremont: about 35 miles / Fremont to Route 92 at Venice: 20 miles / Venice to Two Rivers Recreation Grounds and confluence with the Elkhorn River: 5 miles / recreation grounds to Louisville on Route 50: 15 miles / Louisville to Plattsmouth on Route 34: 15 miles, junction with the Missouri River is about 4 miles above Plattsmouth. Rentals: Lincoln.

North Platte: Henry on Route 26 on the Wyoming border to Scottsbluff on Route 71: about 25 miles / Scottsbluff to Route 26 at Bayard: about 20 miles / Bayard to Bridgeport on Route 385: 15 miles / Bridgeport to Broadwater on Route 92: 15 miles / Broadwater to Oshkosh on Route 27: about 35 miles / below Oshkosh is backwater of Lake McConaughy / Kingsley Dam below Lake McConaughy on Route 61 to Hershey bridge north of Route 30: about 40 miles /Hershey to Cody Park in town of North Platte on Route 83 and junction with the South Platte River: 18 miles. *See* Wyoming.

Republican River

Route 83 at McCook to Route 47 at Cambridge: about 30 miles / Cambridge to Route 283 at Arapahoe: about 20 miles / Route 283 to Oxford on Route 136: about 20 miles / Oxford to Route 183 at Harlan Reservoir: about 25 miles, canoeable in spring and high water only, below the reservoir the water level depends on release from the dam / Harlan Reservoir dam to Route 10 south of Franklin: 15 miles / Route 10 to Route 281 south of Red Cloud: about 25 miles / Route 281 to Superior on Route 14 at the Kansas state line: about 30 miles, some stretches tend to run dry in summer with water being diverted for irrigation.

Nebraska Rentals

Lincoln

Holmes Lake Marina, 3150 South 58, Lincoln, Nebr. 68506; telephone: 402–488–6173 and 402–489–7225 / Waters: Platte, Elkhorn, Missouri, Niobrara, Dismal, and Calamus Rivers / Trips: 1 or more days / Best canoeing months: April-September / Campsites: yes / Transportation: yes / Car-top carriers: yes / Also rents some camping equipment.

Iowa Waters

Boone River

Route 60 south of Webster City to junction with Des Moines River north of Stratford on Route 175: 23 miles, scenic, minor rapids. Rentals: Boone.

Cedar River

Otranto north of St. Ansgar to dam on Route 105 northwest of St. Ansgar: 7 miles, a second dam 1½ miles downstream / St. Ansgar to dam at Mitchell on Route 177: 5 miles / Mitchell to Route 9 and Osage Spring Park: 5 miles / Osage to Floyd on Route 218: 12 miles / Floyd to Charles City on Route 18 and Main Street dam: 10 miles / Charles City to lake at Nashua off Route 218: 15 miles / Nashua to junction with the Shellrock River about 8 miles north of Cedar Falls on Route 218: about 35 miles / Cedar Falls to Cedar Rapids on Routes 30–218: about 70 miles, major rapids / below Cedar Rapids the river is smoother and wider to junction with the Iowa River at town of Columbus Junction on Route 92: about 70 miles. Rentals: Cedar Falls.

Des Moines River

East Fork and West Fork join 20 miles above Fort Dodge. Kalo 7 miles southeast of Fort Dodge on Route 20 to Lehigh on Route 50: 11 miles, scenic / Lehigh to junction with the Boone River north of Stratford on Route 175: 12 miles / from this point the river gets wider and is impounded on its roughly 250-mile course to junction with the Mississippi River at Keokuk on Route 61. Rentals: Boone.

Iowa River

Bigelow Park north of Alden on Route 20 to town of Iowa Falls on Route 65: 15 miles / Iowa Falls to Eagle City southeast of Iowa Falls: 12 miles / Eagle City to town of Steamboat Rock on Route 118: 12 miles / Steamboat Rock to Eldora on Route 57: 6 miles / Eldora to Union: 20 miles / Union to Albion northwest of Marshalltown on Route 14: 20 miles / Albion to Route 30 southeast of Marshalltown: 30 miles / Route 30 to Route 63 at Tama: 15 miles / Route 63 to Route 212 south of Belle Plaine: about 30 miles / Route 212 to Route 411 at Marengo: 20 miles / Marengo to Route 149 at Amana: 15 miles / Amana to Route 218 on Coralville Reservoir: about 20 miles / Route 218 through reservoir to Coralville Dam: 15 miles / the Iowa River is free-flowing below the reservoir dam to junction with the Cedar River at Columbus Junction on Route 92: about 40 miles / Columbus Junction to confluence with the Mississippi River about 3 miles from Toolesboro on Route 99: about 30 miles. Rentals: Cedar Falls and North Liberty.

Little Sioux River

Route 71 at town of Sioux Rapids to Linn Grove on Route 264: 7

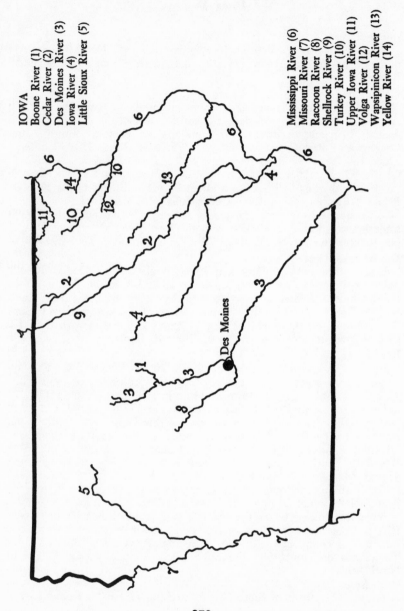

IOWA
Boone River (1)
Cedar River (2)
Des Moines River (3)
Iowa River (4)
Little Sioux River (5)

Mississippi River (6)
Missouri River (7)
Raccoon River (8)
Shellrock River (9)
Turkey River (10)
Upper Iowa River (11)
Volga River (12)
Wapsipinicon River (13)
Yellow River (14)

Des Moines

miles / Linn Grove to Route 10 at Peterson: 8 miles / Peterson to Route 10 between Peterson and Sutherland: 5 miles / Route 10 to Brasch Bridge east of Larrabee on Route 59: 12 miles / bridge to Cherokee on Routes 3–59: 12 miles / Cherokee to Washta on Route 31: 25 miles / Washta to town of Little Sioux off Route 75 near junction with the Missouri River: about 60 miles, river is slow and wide.

Mississippi River
Forms entire eastern boundary of Iowa for more than 300 miles from New Albin on Route 26 to Keokuk to Route 61, backwater sloughs too shallow for power boats offer pleasant canoeing. Rentals: Decorah.

Missouri River
Enters Iowa at Sioux City on Route 73–77. From Sioux City the Missouri River forms the Iowa border with Nebraska for more than 250 miles, mostly channelized. *See* Nebraska and Missouri.

Raccoon River
Henderson Park in Jefferson on Route 4 to bridge north of Dawson on Route 335 off Route 141: 20 miles / Dawson to Route 141 west of Perry: 6 miles / Route 141 to Route 64 about 4 miles west of Dallas Center: 15 miles / Route 64 to Riverside Park in Adel on Routes 6–169: 7 miles / Adel to Des Moines on Route I–235 and junction with the Des Moines River: about 35 miles.

Shellrock River
Albert Lea Lake in Minnesota about 18 miles west of Austin, Minnesota, to Route 65 south of Northwood, Iowa: about 25 miles / Northwood to Plymouth on Route 288: 18 miles / Plymouth to town of Rock Falls northeast of Mason City on Route 65: 4 miles / Rock Falls to town of Nora Springs on Route 18: 7 miles / Nora Springs to Rockford on Route 147: 10 miles / Rockford to Clarkville on Route 188: 25 miles / Clarkville to junction with the Cedar River about 8 miles above Cedar Falls on Route 218: 20 miles. The most scenic stretch is between Northwood and Rockford. Rentals: Cedar Falls.

Turkey River
Spillville on Route 325 to Route 24 at Fort Atkinson: 10 miles / Route 24 to Route 150 at Eldorado: 20 miles / Route 150 to Route 18 at Clermont: 13 miles / Route 18 to Elgin on Route 172: 10 miles / Elgin to dam at Elkader on Route 13: 18 miles / Elkader to Garber: 17 miles / Garber to junction with the Mississippi River east of Millville on Route 52: 15 miles. The most popular stretch is between Elgin and Garber.

Upper Iowa River
1 mile north of town of Lime Springs, Iowa, on Routes 63–157 to Florenceville Dam on the Minnesota state line south of Granger, Minnesota: 12 miles, canoeable in high water only / dam to Kendallville, Iowa, on Route 139: 12 miles / Kendallville to Bluffton: 15 miles /

Bluffton to Decorah on Route 52: 15 miles, very scenic from Kendallville to Decorah / Decorah to Lower Dam south of Sattre: 17 miles / Lower Dam to Route 13: 20 miles, scenic, some rapids / Route 13 to junction with the Mississippi River near New Albin on Route 182: about 20 miles, dredged in lower section. Rentals: Cedar Falls and Decorah.

Volga River

Town of Volga on Route 112 southwest of Elkader on Route 56 to Route 13 at Osborne south of Elkader: 8 miles / Osborne to Littleport: 10 miles / Littleport to junction with the Turkey River at Garber: 10 miles.

Wapsipinicon River

Independence on Route 20 to Quasqueton on Route 282: 12 miles / Quasqueton to Troy Mills: 10 miles / Troy Mills to Central City on Route 13: 14 miles / Central City to Stone City west of Anamosa on Route 151: 15 miles / Stone City to Anamosa on Route 151: 6 miles, scenic all the way but especially good near Stone City and Anamosa / Anamosa to junction with the Mississippi River about 4 miles north of Princeton on Route 67: about 60 miles. Rentals: Cedar Falls.

Yellow River

Route X26 at Volney south of Rossville on Route 13 to junction with the Mississippi River north of Marquette on Route 13: 18 miles, scenic.

Iowa Rentals

Boone

Reynoldson Marine, Inc., 104 West Third Street, Boone, Iowa 50036; telephone: 515–432–4984 / Waters: Des Moines and Boone Rivers and other nearby waters / Trips: 1–2 days / Best canoeing months: April-July / Campsites: yes / Transportation: no / Car-top carriers: yes / Also rents camping trailers.

Cedar Falls

Olsen Boat House, Inc., P.O. Box 397, Cedar Falls, Iowa 50613; telephone: 319–277–4444 / Waters: Cedar, Shellrock, Iowa, Upper Iowa, and Wapsipinicon Rivers and other nearby waterways / Trips: 1 or more days / Best canoeing months: June-September / Campsites: yes / Transportation: yes / Car-top carriers: yes.

Decorah

Erickson Sport Center & Texaco Service, State Street South, Decorah, Iowa 52101; telephone: 319–382–4748 / Waters: Upper Iowa River / Trips: 1 or more days / Campsites: yes / Transportation: yes / Car-top carriers: yes.

Oneota Canoe Sales and Rentals, 616 Center Street, Decorah, Iowa

52101; telephone: 319–382–2332 / Waters: Upper Iowa and Mississippi Rivers / Trips: 1 or more days, guides available / Best canoeing
months: May-July / Campsites: yes / Transportation: yes, by special
arrangement only / Car-top carriers: yes / Also rents some camping
equipment.

Des Moines

Ahrens & Johnson, Inc., 621–25 Des Moines Street, Des Moines, Iowa
50316; telephone: 515–244–3533 / Unconfirmed.

North Liberty

Marina 218 Inc., U.S. Highway 218 North, North Liberty, Iowa
52317; telephone: 319–626–2411 / Waters: Iowa River and other
nearby waters / Trips: 1 or more days / Best canoeing months: spring
to fall / Campsites: yes / Transportation: yes / Car-top carriers: yes /
Open all year.

Sources of Information

Black Hills, Badlands, and Lakes Association (P.O. Box 539, Sturgis,
S.D. 57785) offers general tourist information.

Canoeing Nebraska, Nebraska Game and Parks Commission (2200
North 33rd Street, Lincoln, Nebr. 68503), a free, 8-page pamphlet.

Iowa Canoe Trips, Iowa Conservation Commission (300 Fourth
Street, Des Moines, Iowa 50319), a free, 14-page pamphlet describing
12 rivers with maps.

Iowa fishing and hunting information is available from Iowa Conservation Commission (300 Fourth Street, Des Moines, Iowa 50319).

Iowa tourist information is available from Iowa Development Commission (250 Jewett Building, Des Moines, Iowa 50309).

Knudson, George E. *The Upper Iowa River,* Luther College Press
(Decorah, Iowa 52101), 1971, 69 pp., $1.25. A very detailed description
including geology, archeology, plants and wildlife, and history.

Nebraska fishing and hunting information is available from Nebraska
Game and Parks Commission (2200 North 33rd Street, Lincoln, Nebr.
68503).

Nebraska tourist information is available from Nebraska Department
of Economic Development (P.O. Box 94666, Lincoln, Nebr. 68509).

North Dakota fishing and hunting information is available from North
Dakota Game and Fish Department (Bismarck, N.D. 58501).

North Dakota tourist information is available from North Dakota
Highway Department, Travel Division (Bismarck, N.D. 58501).

South Dakota fishing and hunting information is available from South
Dakota Game, Fish, and Parks Department (State Office Building,
Pierre, S.D. 57501).

KANSAS and OKLAHOMA

To ANYONE NOT FAMILIAR WITH KANSAS AND OKLAHOMA, "in the middle of nowhere" and "flat as a pancake" are the descriptions that come to mind most often. In the middle of these states, of course, they are. But the flatness, as Mark Twain said about the report of his death, "is greatly exaggerated."

Both states tilt from an elevation of well above 4,000 feet above sea level in the west to a few hundred feet in the east. Both offer attractive mountain ranges. Kansas has the Smoky Hills in the northwest, marked by rugged sandstone formations, and the Flint Hills in the southeast, with their lush hillsides and valley pastures. Oklahoma has the pine-and-oak-covered Ouachitas in the southeast, the extensions of the Ozarks in the northeast, and the Wichitas in the southwest.

In both states, rivers run from west to east, with most of those in southern Kansas tilting south into Oklahoma.

Most Kansas rivers are more free flowing than those in Oklahoma. The Arkansas River in Kansas, for instance, arriving from Colorado, is canoeable most of the year from about Dodge City, but in Oklahoma it begins to be subjected to its numerous impoundments.

Oklahoma, as the dust bowl of the 1930s, has been more conscious than almost any other state about preserving the precious waters of its rivers and has built many reservoirs. Thus, most of its water sports take place on artificial lakes. Many of these reservoirs have fjord-like tributaries that offer attractive flat water canoeing, and it is worthwhile to write for the brochure *Oklahoma Lakes* listed at the end of this chapter.

In addition, Oklahoma has an officially designated canoe trail in the Illinois River and shares with Missouri and Kansas the Spring River, about to be preserved as a canoe trail.

Kansas has a problem inasmuch as most of its rivers have not been declared navigable. Permission must be obtained in order to float many of them or to use access points. The Kansas Canoe Association, which provided all of the information on Kansas canoeing used in this chapter, is actively at work to have the best canoeing streams declared official canoe trails.

Kansas Waters

Arkansas River
Canoeable from Dodge City on Route 56 to the Oklahoma state line near Arkansas City, Kansas, on Route 77 for more than 300 miles with

282

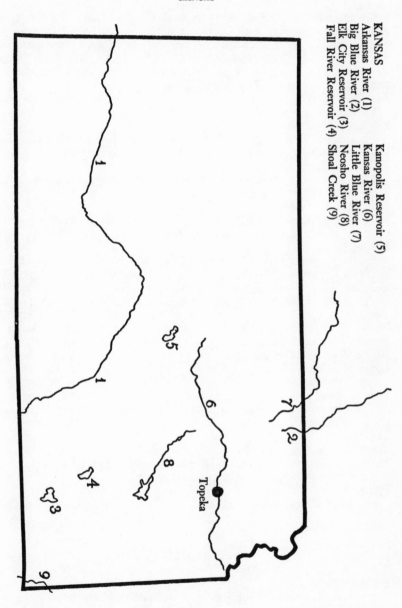

KANSAS
Arkansas River (1)
Big Blue River (2)
Elk City Reservoir (3)
Fall River Reservoir (4)

Kanopolis Reservoir (5)
Kansas River (6)
Little Blue River (7)
Neosho River (8)
Shoal Creek (9)

many intermediate access points at road bridges. There are developed canoe trails from Raymond southeast of Great Bend on Route 56 to Sterling on Route 14, a 25-mile stretch, and the popular 60-mile stretch from Mulvane on Route 53 bridge south of Wichita to Arkansas City on Route 77. The upper course of the Arkansas River is canoeable only in spring and high water. Rentals: Wichita.

Big Blue River
See Nebraska.

Elk City Reservoir
Located north of Route 96 at the town of Fall River, the reservoir has has good canoeing and one can also canoe the feeder streams.

Fall River Reservoir
Located north of Route 96 at the town of Fall River, the reservoir has good canoeing and one can also canoe the feeder streams.

Kanopolis Reservoir
Located southeast of Ellsworth on Route 156, the reservoir has good canoeing and one can also canoe the feeder streams.

Kansas River
Route 77 below Milford Reservoir Dam near Junction City to Ogden south of Route 18: 15 miles / Ogden to Route 18 at Manhattan: 15 miles / Manhattan to Route 99 at Wamego: 20 miles / Wamego to bridge south of Route 24 at Rossville: 30 miles / Rossville to Topeka south of Route 24: 20 miles / Topeka to Lawrence on Route 40: 30 miles / Lawrence to Route 7 at town of Bonner Springs: 30 miles / Bonner Springs to junction with the Missouri River at Kansas City on Route 69–169: 20 miles.

Little Blue River
See Nebraska.

Neosho River
Town of Neosho Rapids on Route 130 to John Redmond Reservoir: about 10 miles, 1 rapid.

Shoal Creek
Route 43 at Joplin, Missouri, to Scherhorn Park at Galena, Kansas, on Route 66: 6 miles / Galena to junction with the Spring River: 3 miles. *See also* Missouri. Rentals: Quapaw, Oklahoma.

Spring River
See Missouri and Oklahoma.

Kansas Rentals

Prairie Village
Canoeing Outfitters Rental & Sales, 6209 West 76th Terrace, Prairie Village, Kans. 66208; telephone: 913–381–9823 / Waters: all Ozarks

waterways / Trips: 1 or more days / Best canoeing months: April-October / Campsites: yes / Transportation: no / Car-top carriers: yes.
Wichita
  Kansas Sailing Center, 3216 Turnpike Drive, Wichita, Kans. 67210; telephone: 316–684–2268 / Waters: Arkansas River and all Kansas, Missouri, and Arkansas rivers and lakes / Trips: 1 or more days / Best canoeing months: April-September / Campsites: no response / Transportation: no / Car-top carriers: yes.

Oklahoma Waters

Broken Bow Reservoir
  Main access is via Route 259A off Route 259 north of town of Broken Bow on Route 7–70. Rentals: Broken Bow.
Illinois River
  Twin Falls on Route 59 north of Watts to Chewey bridge east of Route 10: 22 miles / Chewey to Comb's Bridge off Route 10 south of Scraper: 15 miles / Comb's Bridge to Routes 51–62 east of Tahlequah: 21 miles / Tahlequah to Carter's Landing and backwater of Tenkiller Reservoir: 14 miles. Rentals: all along the river, see rentals section.
Kiamichi River
  Canoeable in season from various points along Route 2 between Clayton and Antlers to Hugo Reservoir northeast of Hugo on Route 271, a stretch of about 100 miles. Below the reservoir one can canoe for about 20 miles to junction with the Red River which forms the Oklahoma-Texas border.
Mountain Fork River
  East of Smithville on Route 4 to backwater of Broken Bow Reservoir: about 25 miles, some minor rapids, no boats allowed below the reservoir. Rentals: Broken Bow.
Pine Creek Reservoir
  Located on Route 3 northwest of Wright City on Route 98, many secluded sidearms, drained by the Little River.
Spring River
  Baxter Springs, Kansas, on Route 166 to Promenade Bridge in Oklahoma south of Baxter Springs: 8 miles / bridge to Twin Bridges Recreation Area on Route 10: 12 miles / from the recreation area the Spring River flows into Lake O' the Cherokees where there is little canoeing. Rentals: Quapaw.

Oklahoma Rentals

Broken Bow
  Beavers Bend Marina, Broken Bow, Okla. 74728; telephone: 405–494–6455 / Waters: Broken Bow Reservoir and Mountain Fork River /

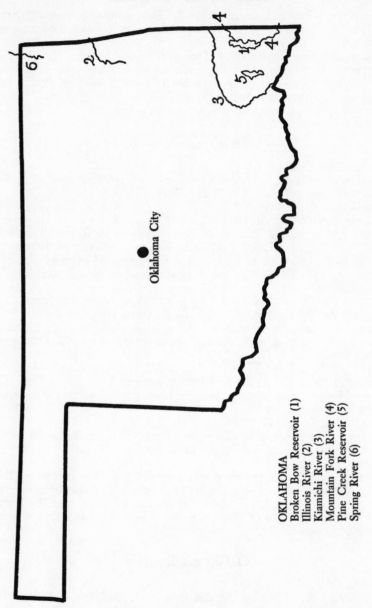

OKLAHOMA
Broken Bow Reservoir (1)
Illinois River (2)
Kiamichi River (3)
Mountain Fork River (4)
Pine Creek Reservoir (5)
Spring River (6)

Trips: 1 or more days, guides available / Best canoeing months: March-October / Campsites: yes / Transportation: no / Car-top carriers: yes.
Illinois River Canoe Rentals
A number of rental services along the river, all of them on the 70-mile stretch between Tenkiller Reservoir and Watts. All of them, with one exception, offer shuttle service: Twin Falls: 918–254–6238 / Riverside Park: 918–868–2269 / Riverside Camp: 918–456–4787 / Rock-A-Way Camp: 918–456–9788 or 456–3031 [no transportation] / Hanging Rock Camp: 918–456–3088 / Arrowhead Camp: 918–456–4974 / Eagle Bluff Camp: 918–456–3031 / Peyton's Place: 918–456–3847 / Green River: 918–456–4867 / Sparrow Hawk Camp: 918–456–8371 / Cherokee Floats: 918–456–8511 / Tahlequah Floats: 918–456–6949 / Whitehouse River Ranch: 918–456–9329 / Float Inn: 918–456–5681.
Quapaw
Quapaw Float Trips (Terry Fitzgibbon), Box 701, Quapaw, Okla. 74363; telephone: 918–674–2557 / Waters: Spring River and Shoal Creek / Trips: 1–2 days / Best canoeing months: May-August / Campsites: yes / Transportation: yes / Car-top carriers: yes.

Sources of Information

Floating the Illinois, Oklahoma Department of Wildlife Conservation (1601 North Lincoln, Oklahoma City, Okla. 73105), a free brochure with a river map, mileages, and canoe rental services.

Kansas Canoe Association (Jim Nighswonger, President; Box 2885, Wichita, Kans. 67201) furnished all of the information on Kansas waterways in this chapter.

Kansas fishing and hunting information is available from Kansas Forestry, Fish, and Game Commission (P.O. Box 1028, Pratt, Kans. 67124).

Kansas tourist information is available from Kansas Economic Development Commission (State Office Building, Topeka, Kans. 66612). *Kansas Travel Guide*, a 24-page free brochure which is one of their publications, is recommended.

Oklahoma fishing and hunting information is available from Oklahoma Department of Wildlife Conservation (1601 North Lincoln Boulevard, Oklahoma City, Okla. 73105).

Oklahoma tourist information is available from Oklahoma Department of Tourism and Recreation (504 Will Rogers Building, Oklahoma City, Okla. 73105), ask especially for *Oklahoma Lakes*.

TEXAS

LIKE EVERYTHING ELSE IN TEXAS, canoeing opportunities are on a grand scale, with some 80,000 miles of waterways, many of them canoeable. The scenic variety is also exceptionally wide, from arid desert to tropical bayou jungle.

In the western sections, semi-desert prevails, covered with cacti, yucca, and mesquite. The rivers often run dry or go underground, and after rains flash floods may surprise canoeists.

The most dramatic canyons line the Rio Grande at Great Bend National Park and further downstream. Some of them are suitable for family canoeing while others are strictly for the whitewater experts, or canoeable with a guide.

The Guadalupe, San Marcos, and Colorado Rivers, in the Austin-San Antonio region, are among the most popular canoeing streams. The vegetation is lusher here than farther west. Cottonwoods, palmettos, giant bald cypresses, pecans, oaks, and shrubbery thickets line the banks, interspersed with dramatic bluffs and cliffs.

The Big Thicket National Preserve north of Beaumont is one of the few virgin wilderness and wildlife areas left in the country, with an infinite variety of subtropical plants and rare animals. Almost impenetrable on land, it can be canoed on the Village Creek, Pine Island Bayou, and Neches River.

Relatively unspoiled bayous can be found right within the limits of the Houston metropolitan area on the Armand and Dickinson Bayous.

Many Texas waterways are exceptionally well recorded by the Texas Parks and Wildlife Department. Visitors from other states can easily chart their own ways, but they should be prepared for long distances between access points on some of the rivers.

Few canoe shuttle services are available in Texas. Most rental services rent only for car-top carrying, but usually allow customers to take the canoes just about anywhere within the state.

Texas Waters

Angelina River
Route 84 east of Reklaw to Route 204: 5 miles / Route 204 to Route 21 east of Alto: 23 miles, canoeable only in high water / Route 21 to

TEXAS

Angelina River (1)
Armand Bayou (2)
Attoyac Bayou (3)
Bastrop Bayou (4)
Big Cypress Bayou (5)
Blanco River (6)
Bosque River (7)
Brazos River (8)
Clear Creek (9)
Colorado River (10)
Concho River (11)
Devils River (12)
Dickinson Bayou (13)
Frio River (14)
Guadalupe River (15)
Lampasas River (16)
Lavaca River (17)
Leon River (18)
Little River (19)
Little Wichita River (20)
Llano River
Main Branch (21)
North Llano River (22)
South Llano River (23)
Medina River (24)
Navidad River (25)
Neches River (26)
Nueces River (27)
Paluxy River (28)
Pecos River (29)
Pedernales River (30)

Pine Island Bayou (31)
Red River (32)
Rio Grande (33)
Sabine River (34)
San Antonio River (35)
San Bernard River (36)
San Gabriel River (37)
San Jacinto River (38)
San Marcos River (39)
San Saba River (40)
Trinity River
Main Branch (41)
Elm Fork (42)
Village Creek (43)
Wichita River (44)

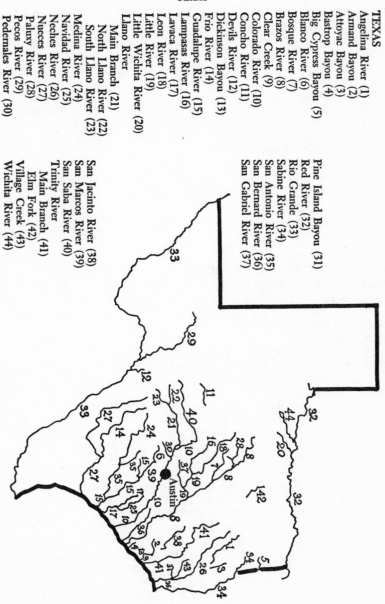

289

Route 7 southwest of Nacogdoches: 34 miles / Route 7 to Route 59: 12 miles / Route 59 to Sam Rayburn Reservoir: 20 miles / reservoir exit at Route 255 along Angelina National Forest to Bevelport on Highway 2799: 18 scenic miles / Bevelport to B.A. Steinhagen Lake: 7 miles, the Angelina River joins the Neches River in the lake. Rentals: Dickinson and Houston.

Armand Bayou

Unspoiled bayou scenery at the edge of Houston, upstream or downstream from Bay Area Park at Bay Area Boulevard, off I-45, southeast of Houston, or upstream from Clear Lake Park on Clear Lake. Rentals: Dickinson and Houston.

Attoyac Bayou

Route 138 southeast of Garrison on Route 59 to Route 7 at Martinsville: 10 miles / Martinsville to Route 21 just above Sam Rayburn Reservoir: 18 miles.

Bastrop Bayou

Route 288 north of Freeport and Clute to Highway 2004 off Route 523: about 15 miles, power boats below this point.

Big Cypress Bayou

Lake O' The Pines outlet at Route 726 to Route 59 at Jefferson: 14 miles / Route 59 to Caddo Lake State Park on Route 43 just above Caddo Lake: 20 miles / Canoeable only intermittently above Lake O' The Pines; the bayou joins the Red River below Caddo Lake at Shreveport, Louisiana.

Blanco River

Town of Blanco on Route 281 to junction with the San Marcos River below town of San Marcos on I-35: 64 miles, some whitewater, canoeable only after heavy rains.

Bosque River

Canoeable after heavy rains from about 40 miles above the Route 6 bridge west of Iredell. Route 6 to Clifton on Route 219: 35 miles, may get too shallow during dry spells / Clifton to Lake Waco north of Route 6 and Waco Dam: about 30 miles / The Bosque River joins the Brazos River in Waco. Rentals: Waco.

Brazos River

Generally speaking, it is not canoeable above Possum Kingdom Reservoir west of Fort Worth. Route 16 below the dam at Possum Kingdom Reservoir to Route 180 west of Mineral Wells: 42 scenic miles, however the water level is dependent upon the release of water from the reservoir / Route 180 to Route 281 south of Mineral Wells: 35 miles, also scenic and dependent upon water release / Route 281 to Lake Granbury: 41 miles, slower than the first stretches / Lake Granbury dam to Route 67 east of Glen Rose: 30 miles / Route 67 to Lake Whitney (recreational area): 36 miles / Lake Whitney dam on Route 22 to Waco on Route 84: 40 scenic miles / Waco to Route 7 west of

Marlin: 39 miles / Route 7 to Route 79 just below the mouth of the Little River: about 40 miles / Route 79 to the Gulf of Mexico: about 300 miles, the river is canoeable and is reported to be scenic. Rentals: Arlington, College Station, Dallas, Dickinson, Euless, Fort Worth, Richardson, Waco, and Wichita Falls.

Clear Creek

Edge of Houston from Route 528 off I-45 to Galveston County Park on Route 3: about 15 miles. Rentals: Dickinson and Houston.

Colorado River

Some 300 miles of this river above the junction with the San Saba River just above Route 190 are intermittently canoeable after rains. San Saba River junction to Bend on Route 580: 25 miles / Bend to Lake Buchanan: 25 miles, scenic / Lake Buchanan to Austin: a series of lakes and reservoirs / Austin on Route 183 to Bastrop on Route 71: 50 miles, with fairly reliable flow controlled by reservoirs / Bastrop to Smithville on Routes 71–77: 24 miles / Smithville to La Grange on Route 77: 32 miles, scenic / La Grange to Columbus on Route 71: 43 miles / Columbus to East Matagorda Bay: about 140 miles, slow coastal stream. Rentals: Austin, College Station, Euless, Houston, San Antonio, and San Marcos.

Concho River

The river is formed at San Angelo at the confluence of the North Concho River and the South Concho River; the branches are canoeable from time to time. The Concho River from South Concho Park in San Angelo to junction with the Colorado River above the bridge on Highway 2134: 55 miles.

Devils River

Routes 163–189 northeast of Juno to Baker's Crossing on Route 163: intermittently canoeable, the river goes underground at points / Route 163 through Rough Canyon Recreation Area to Amistad Reservoir: 44 miles, mostly whitewater.

Dickinson Bayou

Route 3 bridge near Dickinson southeast of Houston upstream to I-45: about 3 miles / Route 3 downstream to Route 146: about 7 miles. Rentals: Dickinson.

Frio River

Kent Creek on Route 336 north of Leakey to Concan on Route 127 via Garner State Park: 31 miles, some whitewater / Concan to Nueces River junction near Three Rivers on Routes 72–281: a long stretch of about 125 miles, usually too dry to canoe. Rentals: San Antonio.

Guadalupe River

Waring east of Comfort on I-10 to Route 281 north of San Antonio: 59 miles, some rapids / Route 281 to Canyon Reservoir: 10 miles / reservoir dam to New Braunfels on I-35: 24 miles, whitewaters dependent upon water release from the reservoir / New Braunfels to Gonzales on

Route 183: about 40 miles, slow, winding / Gonzales to Hochheim on Route 183: about 20 miles, scenic / Hochheim to Cuero on Routes 77A–183: 25 miles / Cuero to Victoria on Route 59: about 50 miles / Victoria to San Antonio Bay: about 35 miles. Rentals: Austin, Canyon Lake, Dickinson, Euless, Houston, San Antonio, San Marcos, and Spring Branch.

Lampasas River

Canoeable in high water only. Highway 1047 southwest of Hamilton to Rumely on Route 580: 47 miles / Rumely to Kempner on Route 190: 4 miles / Route 190 to Route 440 at Ding Dong: 30 miles / Ding Dong to Stillhouse Reservoir: 10 miles / Stillhouse Reservoir to junction with the Leon River: 18 miles. Rentals: Waco.

Lavaca River

Route 111 near Navidad Community northwest of Edna to Route 616 west of Lolita: about 30 miles, the river then merges with the Navidad River and flows for 15 miles to Lavaca Bay. Rentals: San Antonio.

Leon River

Proctor Lake dam on U.S. 67 to Gatesville on U.S. 84: about 100 miles with many intermediate access points, canoeable only when water is released at the dam or after heavy rains / Gatesville to Mother Neff State Park just above Belton Reservoir on Route 236: 46 miles / reservoir dam to junction with the Lampasas River to form the Little River, a mile below Route 436: 18 miles. Rentals: Waco.

Little River

Route 436 southeast of Belton just above junction of the Leon and Lampasas Rivers which form the Little River to Route 439 south of Rogers: 25 miles / Route 439 to Route 36 at Cameron: 46 miles / Route 36 to junction with the Brazos River just above Route 79: 28 miles, the Little River meets the San Gabriel River 10 miles southwest of Cameron on this stretch. Rentals: Austin, College Station, and Waco.

Little Wichita River

Canoeable a few miles upstream from Route 281 at Scotland. Lake Arrowhead to junction with the Red River: 30 miles, waters depend on how much is released from the dam of the lake; the Red River forms the Texas-Oklahoma border in this area. Rentals: Wichita Falls.

Llano River

South Llano River: Canoeable in high water from U.S. 377 southwest of Telegraph to the confluence with the North Llano River at town of Junction on I–10.

North Llano River: Canoeable only after very heavy rains for some 10 miles up Route 290 from Junction.

Main Branch: Junction to Routes 87–29 south of Mason: 54 miles / Route 87 to town of Llano on Routes 16–29: 30 miles, scenic /

Llano to Lyndon B. Johnson Lake: 20 miles. Rentals: Austin and San Antonio.

Medina River

Town of Medina on Route 16 to Bandera on Route 16: 20 miles, some whitewater / Bandera to Bandera Falls: 13 miles, backwater of Lake Medina / Lake Medina to confluence with the San Antonio River south of San Antonio: 64 miles, placid, not very attractive. Rentals: Canyon Lake, Euless, San Antonio, San Marcos, and Spring Branch.

Navidad River

Morales Crosses 2 miles east of Morales on Route 111 to Route 59 southwest of Ganado: 22 miles / Route 59 to slightly west of Lolita on Route 616: 21 miles, the Navidad River joins the Lavaca River near Lolita. Rentals: San Antonio.

Neches River

U.S. 175 below Lake Palestine northwest of Jacksonville to U.S. 84 west of Rusk: 30 miles / U.S. 84 to Route 21 at edge of Davy Crockett National Forest: 30 miles / Route 21 to Route 7 along forest: 32 miles / Route 7 to Route 94: 18 miles / Route 94 to Route 59: 24 miles / Route 59 to Route 69: 44 miles / Route 69 to B.A. Steinhagen Lake: 30 miles, one waterfall / lake exit to Evadale on Route 96: 54 miles / Route 96 to Beaumont on the Gulf of Mexico: 40 miles, tidal waters below Beaumont used by ocean-going vessels. Rentals: Dickinson and Houston.

Nueces River

Route 335 bridge 11 miles north of Barksdale to Route 55 at Barksdale: 12 miles / Barksdale to Route 55 bridge below Camp Wood: 10 miles / Camp Wood bridge to Route 55 near junction of Route 334: 15 miles, tricky in high water / From this point to Nueces Bay: about 300 miles, usually too dry for good canoeing except after very heavy rains. Rentals: San Antonio.

Paluxy River

Bluff Dale on Route 377 via Dinosaur Valley State Park to junction with the Brazos River at Glen Rose below Route 144: about 30 miles, some rapids, after heavy rains only. Rentals: Arlington, Euless, and Fort Worth.

Pecos River

Route 11 southeast of Grandfalls to U.S. 67–385 southwest of McCamey: about 40 miles, after heavy rains only / U.S. 67–385 to Route 290 east of Sheffield: 63 miles, canoeable after rains but beware of flash floods / U.S. 290 to Highway 2083 near Pandale: 64 miles, rugged, many rapids / Pandale to junction with the Rio Grande: 55 miles, canyons, some rapids.

Pedernales River

Above Johnson City on Route 281, after heavy rains only, dangerous whitewater. Route 281 to Route 71: 39 miles, backwater of Lake Travis, scenic, may be too shallow in dry spells. Rentals: Austin, Canyon Lake, San Antonio, San Marcos, and Spring Branch.

Pine Island Bayou

Route 770 near Saratoga to Route 326 south of the town of Sour Lake: 21 miles, flows through Big Thicket National Preserve / Route 326 to U.S. 69–96–287 at Beaumont: 28 miles. Rentals: Dickinson and Houston.

Red River

Canoeable intermittently after good rains from north of Quanah on Route 283 to I–35 above the backwaters of Lake Texoma. Below the lake the river is dependent upon the release of water from the power dam. The most popular stretch begins at Denison Dam on Route 75A and runs for 30 miles to Route 78. Below this point there are few access points, the waters are wild and the country rugged. The Red River flows from Texas into Arkansas and from there into Louisiana. Rentals: Arlington, Dallas, Euless, Fort Worth, Richardson, and Wichita Falls.

Rio Grande

Not canoeable above Presidio. Presidio on Route 67 through Colorado Canyon to Lajitas on Route 170: about 50 miles / Lajitas through Santa Elena Canyon to Castolon in Big Bend National Park: 26 miles, permits required to canoe in the park, difficult whitewaters at all times other than dry spells / Castolon to Talley: about 40 miles, an easier stretch / Talley to Solis: 12 miles, through Mariscal Canyon, difficult, with "tight squeeze" shoot / Solis to Boquillas del Carmen: 20 miles, easier, through Vincente and Hot Springs Canyons to the ranger station at Boquillas / Boquillas del Carmen to Stillwell on Highway 2627: 26 miles, easier, goes through Boquillas Canyon / Stillwell to Langtry on Route 90: 135 miles, remote, inaccessible, goes through a number of canyons, for whitewater and wilderness canoeists only / Langtry to the Gulf of Mexico: about 500 miles of fairly easy canoeing from any access point, passes through Amistad Reservoir. Rentals: San Antonio and Terlingua.

Sabine River

Rarely canoeable above Route 42 west of Longview. Route 42 to Route 149 south of Longview: 22 miles / Route 149 to Route 43 north of Tatum: 22 miles / Route 43 to Routes 59–1749 north of Carthage: 18 miles / Route 1749 to Route 79 northeast of Carthage: 12 miles / Route 79 to Toledo Bend Reservoir: 16 miles / reservoir exit at Route 692 to Route 190 near Bon Wier: 56 miles, wide, slow / Route 190 to Route 12 at Deweyville: 60 miles / Route 12 to Sabine Lake: 30 miles, the lake feeds into the Gulf of Mexico. Rentals: Dallas, Dickinson, Euless, Houston, and Richardson.

San Antonio River

Downtown San Antonio to Floresville on Route 97: 48 miles /

Floresville to Route 123 north of Karnes City: 40 miles, scenic / Route 123 to junction with the Guadalupe River near San Antonio Bay: about 150 miles, slow, murky waters. Rentals: San Antonio.

San Bernard River

Cat Spring on Highway 1088 to Highway 1093 west of Wallis: 24 miles, canoeable in high water, many obstructions / Route 1093 to Route 59 northeast of Hungerford: 27 miles / Route 59 to the Gulf of Mexico: 70 miles. Rentals: Houston.

San Gabriel River

North Fork: Canoeable after heavy rainfalls only, from Route 243 northeast of Burnet to I–35 at Georgetown: 43 miles.

South Fork: Canoeable after heavy rainfalls only, from Route 243 southwest of Bertram to I–35 at Georgetown: 34 miles.

Main Branch: I–35 to junction with the Little River near Route 487: 55 miles. Rentals: Austin, College Station, and Waco.

San Jacinto River

West Fork is rarely canoeable above Lake Conroe in Sam Houston National Forest. From exit of Lake Conroe at Route 105 to Route 59 at Humble: about 45 miles, dependent upon release of water from the lake. Lake Houston and the Houston Ship Canal are below Route 59. The West Fork joins the San Jacinto River at Lake Houston, northeast of the city. Rentals: Houston.

San Marcos River

Town of San Marcos on I–35 to Luling City Park on Route 80: 43 miles, with intermediate access points at Martindale and Fentress, scenic, some rapids, log jams / Luling to Gonzales on Route 183: 39 miles, joins the Guadalupe River at Gonzales. Rentals: Canyon Lake, College Station, Dickinson, Euless, Houston, San Marcos, and Spring Branch.

San Saba River

Fort McKavett on Route 864 and Highway 1674 to Menard on Route 83: 23 miles, canoeable in high water only / Menard to U.S. 87–377 south of Brady: 47 miles / U.S. 87–377 to junction with the Colorado River near town of San Saba on Route 16: 64 miles. Rentals: Austin and Waco.

Trinity River

Elm Fork: Lewisville Dam at exit of Garza-Little Elm Lake (Corps of Engineers Park) to California Crossing Park in Dallas: 22 miles. Rentals: Arlington, Dallas, Euless, Fort Worth, and Richardson.

Main Branch: Formed by the confluence of the Elm Fork and West Fork near Dallas, polluted and murky for about 200 miles but canoeable. Route 7 west of Crockett to Route 21 northeast of Midway: 33 miles, not as bad as some stretches / Route 21 to Lake Livingston: 44 miles / lake exit east of Camilla to Route 59 south of Goodrich: 10 miles, dependent upon release of water from the lake's dam / Route 59 to Route 105: 22 miles / Route 105 to Route 162: 19 miles / Route 162 to U.S. 90 at Liberty: 29 miles with suburban developments / U.S. 90 to I–10: 28 miles, swamp wilderness, passes through Wallisville Lake / I–10 to Trinity Bay: 8 miles, bayou scenery. Rentals: Dickinson and Houston.

Village Creek
Big Thicket National Preserve from Village Mills on U.S. 69–287 to northeast of Kountze: 15 miles / northeast of Kountze to Route 327: 9 miles / Route 327 to U.S. 96: 19 miles / U.S. 96 to junction with the Neches River: 6 miles / In good water, canoeable an additional 25 miles upstream from the Alabama and Coushatta Indian Reservation via Big Sandy Creek, which flows into Village Creek. Rentals: Dickinson and Houston.

Wichita River
Canoeable in the backwaters of Lake Kemp about 10 miles upstream from Highway 1919 / Lake Kemp to Diversion Reservoir: 14 miles / reservoir dam to downtown Wichita Falls on Route 287: about 50 miles, water level depends on release from reservoir / Wichita Falls to junction with the Red River: 55 miles, in high water only. Rentals: Wichita Falls.

Texas Rentals

Arlington
Southwest Canoe 'n' Kayak Outfitters, 2002 West Pioneer Parkway, Arlington, Texas 76013; telephone: 817-461-4503 /Waters: Brazos and Trinity Rivers and other waterways / Trips: 1 or more days / Best canoeing months: spring and fall / Campsites: yes / Transportation: no / Car-top carriers: yes / Also rents camping equipment / Open all year.

Austin
Armadillo Canoe Rentals (J. Howard Barnett), Zilker Park, Austin, Texas; telephone: 512-441-2534 / Unconfirmed.

Down River Sports (David Bowen), 5213 Avenue G, Austin, Texas 78751; telephone: 512-451-8349 / Waters: many waterways in Texas / Trips: 1 or more days / Best canoeing months: March-June, August-October / Campsites: yes / Transportation: no / Car-top carriers: yes.

Wilderness/Whitewater Supply, 5400 Burnet Road, Austin, Texas 76756; telephone: 512-476-3712 / Unconfirmed.

Canyon Lake
Whitewater Sports, Star Route 2, Box 22, Canyon Lake, Texas 78130; telephone: 512-964-3800 / Waters: Guadalupe and San Marcos Rivers, Canyon Lake, and other nearby waters / Trips: several hours to 2 days, guides available / Best canoeing months: March-November / Campsites: yes / Transportation: yes / Car-top carriers: yes / Rents some

camping equipment / Also rents 12-man rafts, offers rafting trips, and operates a kayak instruction school / Open all year.

College Station

Canoes Ltd. (Dr. Mickey Little), 1212 Berkeley, College Station, Texas 77840; telephone 713-846-7307 / Waters: Brazos, Colorado, and San Marcos Rivers and other waterways / Trips: 1 or more days / Best canoeing months: March-November / Campsites: no / Transportation: no / Car-top carriers: yes / Offers canoeing instruction and is booking agent for canoe camping trips / Open all year.

Dallas

"Doc" Baker's Canoe Rentals (John T. Baker), 115 East Woodin Boulevard, Dallas, Texas 75216; telephone 214-946-3100 or 214-371-0434 / Waters: many large and small waterways / Trips: 1 or more days, guides available, Baker has guide permits for Rio Grande and Big Bend National Park canoeing / Best canoeing months: all year / Campsites: yes / Transportation: yes / Car-top carriers: yes.

Dickinson

Creek Canoe Co., 605 Pine Drive, Dickinson, Texas 77539; telephone: 713-337-2612 / Waters: many waterways including Armand and Dickinson Bayous, Clear Creek, and Angelina, San Marcos, Brazos, and Guadalupe Rivers / Trips: several hours to several days, guides available / Best canoeing months: spring and fall / Campsites: yes / Transportation: yes / Car-top carriers: yes / Also rents kayaks / Open all year.

Euless

Woodbine Canoe Rental (Joe Butler), 706 Janann Street, Euless, Texas 76039; telephone: 817-267-4008 / Waters: Brazos, Trinity, Red, Colorado, and Sabine Rivers with whitewater canoeing on the San Marcos, Guadalupe, Medina Rivers, and other waterways / Trips: 1 day to several weeks, guides available / Best canoeing months: April-June, September and October / Campsites: yes / Transportation: no / Car-top carriers: yes / Trailers offered free for 4 or more canoes / Arranges about 10 guided and catered trips a year / Rents some camping equipment and offers free canoeing instruction to small groups by appointment.

Fort Worth

Wilderness Outfitters, Inc., 1704 South University, Fort Worth, Texas 76107; telephone: 817-332-2423 / Waters: anywhere / Trips: short or longer trips; including organized, guided trips of a weekend to 7 days in Texas, Oklahoma, and Arkansas waters primarily for beginners and family canoeists with camping equipment and car-top carriers / Best canoeing months: all year / Campsites: yes / Transportation: yes / Car-top carriers: yes / Also rents camping equipment / Open all year.

Houston

Texas Canoe Trails Inc., Houston Canoe Sales Inc., 8566 Katy Freeway #127, Houston, Texas 77024; telephone: 713-467-8764 / Waters:

many Texas waterways including the Angelina, Guadalupe, San Marcos, Colorado, and Neches Rivers / Trips: 1 or more days, guides available / Best canoeing months: January-June, September-November / Campsites: yes / Transportation: yes / Car-top carriers: yes / Rents some camping equipment / Also rents kayaks and rafts from several other locations and operates campsites.

Wilderness Equipment Inc., 638 Westbury Square, Houston, Texas 77035; telephone: 713-721-1530 / Waters: many Texas waterways / Trips: 1 or more days / Best canoeing months: spring, summer, and fall / Campsites: no / Transportation: no / Car-top carriers: yes / Rents camping equipment / Open all year.

New Braunfels

White Water Sports, 1311 River Crest, New Braunfels, Texas 78130; telephone: 512-625-2800 / Unconfirmed.

Richardson

High Trails Canoe Co. (Bob Narramore), 530 East Main, Richardson, Texas 75080; telephone: 214-234-0202 / Waters: many Texas waterways, two locations on the Brazos River with car shuttles while Richardson location provides canoes for trailers and car-top carriers to other rivers / Trips: 1 or more days, guides available / Best canoeing months: April, May, September, and October / Campsites: yes / Transportation: no, except as noted / Car-top carriers: yes.

San Antonio

Whole Earth Canoe Sales and Rentals, 2539 Bitters Road, San Antonio, Texas 78217; telephone: 512–656–3436 / Waters: Rio Grande, Medina, Colorado, Guadalupe, and Nueces Rivers, and many other waterways / Trips: 1 or more days, guides available / Best canoeing months: March-mid-July and October / Campsites: yes / Transportation: no / Car-top carriers: yes / Closed during deer season (November 15-January 1) and low water (July 15-September).

San Marcos

Goynes Canoe Livery, Route 2, Box 43 G (Pecan Park), San Marcos, Texas 78666; telephone. 512–392–6171 / Waters: San Marcos, Guadalupe, and Colorado Rivers, and other waterways / Trips: several hours to several days, guides available / Best canoeing months: February-December / Campsites: yes / Transportation: yes, only to San Marcos River / Car-top carriers: yes / Also rents camping equipment and operates a campground at the renting site / Offers guided and fully outfitted wilderness river trips in Texas and Mexico arranged by Texas Canoe Outfitters at the same address / Open all year.

Spring Branch

Guadalupe Canoe Rental (Linda and Mike Clark), Route 281 N on the Guadalupe River (mailing address: P.O. Box 8, Spring Branch, Texas 78070); telephone: 512–885–4671 / Waters: Guadalupe, Medina, San Marcos Rivers, and other waterways / Trips: 1 or more days, guides available / Best canoeing months: February-November / Campsites: yes / Transportation: yes / Car-top carriers: yes / Also rents camping equipment / Open all year.

Terlingua

Villa de la Mina, P.O. Box 47, Terlingua, Texas 79852; telephone: 915–364–2446 / Waters: Rio Grande and Santa Elena, Mariscal, Boquillas, and Colorado Canyons / Trips: 4 hours to 2 days, with guides only / Best canoeing months: late summer and fall / Campsites: yes / Transportation: yes / Car-top carriers: no / Also rents 6-man rafts / Operates a lodge with accomodations and meals / Open all year.

Waco

Burleson Outfitters, Inc., 1028 South Valley Mills Drive, Waco, Texas 76711; telephone: 817–752–8965 / Waters: throughout Texas / Trips: up to several days / Best canoeing months: all year / Campsites: yes / Transportation: no / Car-top carriers: yes / Also rents camping equipment / Open all year.

Wichita Falls

Wichita Falls Canoes & Kayaks, 4034 Kemp, Wichita Falls, Texas 76308; telephone: 817–692–9645 / Waters: Wichita and Little Wichita Rivers, Red and Brazos Rivers / Trips: 1 day or more / Best canoeing months: April-October / Campsites: along river banks / Transportation: sometimes / Car-top carriers: yes / Open all year.

Sources of Information

Belisle, Harold J. and Josselet, Ron. *An Analysis of Texas Waterways,* Texas Parks and Wildlife Department (John H. Reagan Building, Austin, Texas 78701), n.d., 240 pp., free. Belisle is Head, Trail and Waterway Section, and Josselet is Trail and Waterway Planner for the department. The book is an excellent, detailed description with maps of "all the rivers, streams, and bayous in the State of Texas that are capable of supporting ... canoeing, kayaking, and rafting."

Nolen, Ben M. and R.E. Narramore. *Texas Rivers and Rapids,* published by Ben M. Nolen (P.O. Box 673, Humble, Texas 77338), 1974, 128 pp., $6.55. This is a commercial venture, with advertising, and is also available from many of the rental services and canoe sales companies in the state. It is a good guide and has maps of Texas rivers plus a few in Mexico, Arkansas, Colorado, and Oklahoma.

Texas fishing and hunting information is available from Texas Parks and Wildlife Department (John H. Reagan Building, Austin, Texas 78701).

Texas tourist information is available from Texas Tourist Development Agency (Box 12008, Austin, Texas 78711).

PART FOUR

THE WEST

•

MONTANA

MONTANA HAS ONE OF THE BRIGHTEST canoeing gems in the country — the longest free-flowing wilderness section left on the entire 2,400-mile length of the Missouri River. It starts at Fort Benton and runs for 160 miles through remote country, unbridged, unpopulated, and untrammeled, and ends at the backwater of Fort Peck Lake. Green banks with stands of cottonwood and poplar soon give way to dramatic rock formations and barren badlands. Wildlife abounds. The river flow poses no serious problem to canoeists. Campsites are easy to find. Few intermediate access points exist. Most canoeists make the entire 6-day trip, stocking up with provisions and drinking water at Fort Benton. A shuttle service to a take-out point at Kipp State Park on Route 191 is available in Fort Benton.

Montana offers an even longer float trip than the Missouri — the almost 600 miles of the Yellowstone River from the boundary of Yellowstone National Park to the confluence with the Missouri River at the North Dakota state line. The upper course, just below the park, has dangerous whitewater. The most popular section is between Livingston west of Billings and Pompeys Pillar below Billings. But there is nothing to stop a canoeist doing the entire length. Main highways parallel the entire course. Thus, access to the river and shuttling is no problem, but to the wildlife purist the proximity to automobile traffic may be a slight flaw.

As a canoeist ventures more and more into the mountains he will find that most sizeable rivers share their valleys with roads — an inevitable necessity of topography. This is true of many of Montana's mountain streams, especially on the west side of the Continental Divide, which crosses Montana on a line running roughly north to south, west of Great Falls, skirts Butte, then turns west to the Idaho border to form the Idaho state line, then turns south to Wyoming.

Among the most popular of these west-side streams are the Clark Fork, Big Blackfoot, and Bitterroot Rivers, the latter used by Lewis and Clark during their descent to the Pacific Ocean.

Historical reminders of Lewis and Clark abound in Montana. At Loma on the Missouri River they made the momentous decision to ignore the Marias River and continue on the Missouri. (The Marias River, today, is good for a wilderness float of about 4 days starting at Tiber Reservoir.) About Great Falls, Lewis wrote in his diary: ". . . the grandest sight I ever beheld." At Three Forks the expedition picked the Jefferson River and continued up the Beaverhead River until all water travel became imposssible.

Thus, Montana streams can be enjoyed both for their scenery and their history (and there is much of it following Lewis and Clark). A word of caution: check the mountain streams carefully for whitewater stretches, and the rivers in the lower regions for lack of water in late summer.

Montana Waters

Beaverhead River

Clark Canyon Dam on I–15 to Dillon on Route 91: about 30 miles / Dillon to junction with the Jefferson River below town of Twin Bridges on Routes 41–287: about 35 miles.

Big Blackfoot River

Lincoln on Route 200 to junction with the Clearwater River near Greenough on Route 200: about 50 miles / Greenough to Bonner on Route I–90 and junction with the Clark Fork River: about 40 miles, some difficult stretches, rafts are safer on this stretch than canoes.

Big Hole River

Dam at town of Divide on Routes 91 and I–15 to Glen on Route 91: 25 miles / Glen to junction with the Beaverhead River near town of Twin Bridges on Routes 41–287: 25 miles.

Bitterroot River

Darby on Route 93 to junction with Clark Fork River near Missoula on Routes 10–12: about 80 miles, many intermediate access points off Route 93 which parallels the river.

Clark Fork River

Town of Deer Lodge on I–90 to Garrison on I–90 and Route 12: 15 miles / Garrison to Drummond on I–90: 25 miles / Drummond to Clinton on I–90: about 30 miles / Clinton to Missoula on I–90 and Route 200: 25 miles / Missoula to St. Regis on I–90 and Route 10: about 70 miles / St. Regis to junction with the Flathead River near Paradise on Route 200: about 20 miles / Paradise to backwater of Noxon Rapids Reservoir: about 40 miles.

Dearborn River

Route 287 north of town of Wolf Creek to junction with the Missouri River below Craig on I–15: about 12 miles, too shallow in dry spells.

Flathead River

Main Branch: Columbia Falls on Route 40 to Flathead Lake: about 30 miles / Flathead Lake: about 30 miles long / Flathead Lake exit to Dixon on Route 200: about 50 miles / Dixon to junction with Clark Fork River above Paradise on Route 200: about 35 miles.

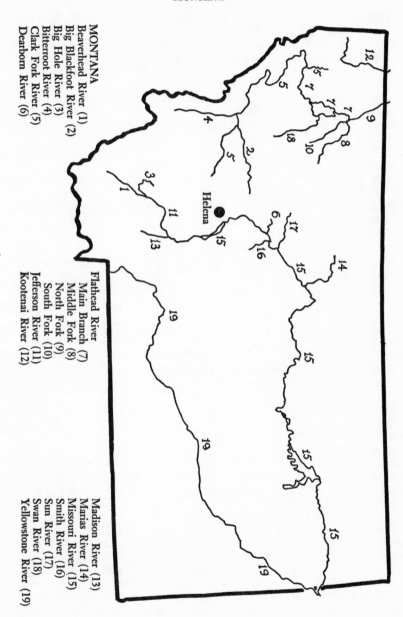

MONTANA
Beaverhead River (1)
Big Blackfoot River (2)
Big Hole River (3)
Bitterroot River (4)
Clark Fork River (5)
Dearborn River (6)

Flathead River
Main Branch (7)
Middle Fork (8)
North Fork (9)
South Fork (10)
Jefferson River (11)
Kootenai River (12)

Madison River (13)
Marias River (14)
Missouri River (15)
Smith River (16)
Sun River (17)
Swan River (18)
Yellowstone River (19)

Middle Fork: Essex on Route 2 to junction with the North Fork above Coram on Route 2: about 40 miles, mostly difficult whitewater in the upper stretches getting easier as the lower stretches are reached.

North Fork: On the Canadian border below town of Flathead in British Columbia on Route 486 to junction with the Middle Fork above Coram on Route 2: about 50 miles.

South Fork: Flows through almost inaccessible wilderness country with difficult whitewater spots from about 50 miles above Hungry Horse Reservoir. The reservoir is itself about 30 miles long. Reservoir dam to Coram on Route 2 and junction with the Middle and North Forks: about 5 miles.

Jefferson River

Junction with the Beaverhead River below town of Twin Bridges on Routes 41–287 to junction with the Madison and Gallatin Rivers and the headwaters of the Missouri River at town of Three Forks on Route 10: about 40 miles.

Kootenai River

Dam at Libby at exit from Lake Koocanusa to Libby on Route 2: about 20 miles / Libby to Troy on Route 2: about 18 miles, impassable, Kootenai Falls, stay away! / Troy to Bonners Ferry, Idaho, on Route 2: about 35 miles, the river continues through Idaho into Kootenai Lake in British Columbia.

Madison River

Bridge at Varney 13 miles above Ennis on Route 287 to Ennis Lake below Ennis: 16 miles / Ennis Lake to bridge east of Norris on Route 287: 15 miles, dangerous whitewater / Norris to town of Three Forks on Route 10 and junction with the Jefferson and Gallatin Rivers at the headwaters of the Missouri River: about 25 miles.

Marias River

Dam at Tiber Reservoir on Route 366 to junction with the Missouri River at Loma on Route 87: about 80 miles, intermediate access points from private property, permissions necessary.

Missouri River

Headwaters at town of Three Forks on Route 10 to dam at Toston on Route 287: about 30 miles / Toston to Townsend on Routes 12–287: about 15 miles, backwater of Canyon Ferry Lake / Townsend to Hauser Lake dam: about 40 miles of lake canoeing through Canyon Ferry Lake / dam to Holler Lake: about 20 miles / Holler Lake dam to Ulm on I–15: about 50 miles, near Great Falls which has been much changed by a power plant since Lewis and Clark visited it in 1805 / Stretch from Great Falls to Fort Benton on Route 230 off Route 87 offers only a few short canoeing courses; the 160-mile stretch of unspoiled canoeing begins at Fort Benton / Fort Benton to ferry at Loma on Route 87: 20 miles / Loma to ferry at Virgelle on local road: 20 miles / Virgelle to Citadel Rock: 23 miles / Citadel Rock to Route

236 ferry: 27 miles / Route 236 ferry to Winifred Road ferry: 14 miles / Winifred Road ferry to Cow Island Landing: 23 miles / landing to Route 191 and James Kipp State Park: 27 miles / Route 191 to backwater of Fort Peck Reservoir: 10 miles, the reservoir is about 180 miles long / Fort Peck Reservoir dam on Route 24 to South Dakota state line at Nohly, Montana, on Route 58: about 180 miles. Rentals: Fort Benton.

Smith River
Fort Logan on Route 360 to Route 330 west of Eden on local road: about 70 miles / Route 330 to junction with the Missouri River at Ulm on Route I–15: about 20 miles.

Sun River
Route 287 north of Augusta to Vaughn on I–15 and Route 89: about 50 miles, gets dry in late July.

Swan River
Access points off Route 209 for about 30 miles into Swan Lake at town of Swan Lake on Route 209. Swan Lake and the Swan River are east of Flathead Lake.

Yellowstone River
Boundary of Yellowstone National Park at Gardiner on Route 89 to Livingston on I–90: about 80 miles, mostly whitewater / Livingston to Big Timber on Route 191: about 35 miles / Big Timber to Columbus on Routes 306–307: about 50 miles / Columbus to Billings on I–90: about 40 miles / Billings to Bighorn on I–94 and Route 47 and junction with the Big Horn River: about 60 miles / Bighorn to Forsyth on I–94 and Route 12: about 45 miles / Forsyth to Miles City on I–94 and Route 12: about 60 miles / Miles City to Terry on I–94 and Route 253: about 50 miles / Terry to Glendive on I–94 and Route 254: about 45 miles / Glendive to Sidney on Routes 16–23: about 60 miles / Sidney to North Dakota Route 200 between Fairview, Montana, and Cartwright, North Dakota: about 20 miles / Route 200 to junction with the Missouri River near Nohly, Montana, on Route 58: about 12 miles. Rentals: Watford City, North Dakota.

Montana Rentals

Fort Benton
Missouri River Cruises (Bob Singer), P.O. Box 1212, Fort Benton, Mont. 59442; telephone 406–622–3295 / Waters: Missouri River / Trips: up to 7 days / Best canoeing months: late June-August / Campsites: yes / Transportation: yes, for canoe renters and for canoeists with their own canoes / Car-top carriers: no / Pick-up service from Great Falls Airport.

Somers
   Westlake Marina, Box 278, Somers, Mont. 59932; telephone: 406–857–3301 / Unconfirmed.

Sources of Information

   Historic Upper Missouri River, Missouri River Cruises (P.O. Box 1212, Fort Benton, Mont. 59442), $5.00, a contour map of sections of the upper Missouri River.
   Montana fishing and hunting information is available from Montana Department of Fish and Game (Helena, Mont. 59601).
   Montana tourist information is available from Montana Highway Commission, Advertising Department (1315 8th Avenue, Helena, Mont. 59601).
   Montana's Popular Float Streams, Montana Department of Fish and Game (Helena, Mont. 59601), a free brochure.
   "The Wild Missouri," Montana Department of Fish and Game (Helena, Mont. 59601), a free reprint of the article which appeared in the May-June 1973 issue of *Montana Outdoors* magazine.

•

WYOMING and IDAHO

YELLOWSTONE NATIONAL PARK, GRAND TETONS, JACKSON HOLE, Flaming Gorge, Bighorn Canyon, Hell Canyon, River of No Return, Snake River, Craters of the Moon National Monument, Lost River Range — these are some of the names that spur the imagination of vacationers seeking the most spectacular in outdoor recreation and make Wyoming and Idaho two of the most popular tourist states. Unfortunately, these attractions include only limited flat water canoeing.
   As with most whitewater mountain streams, Wyoming and Idaho rivers have flat water sections, and there are also many quiet mountain lakes. The famous Snake River, for instance, has relatively flat water for about 60 miles below Jackson Lake in Wyoming, and there are also a few flat water stretches in Idaho, but it is always a very fast river, particularly in the spring, and an upset can be dangerous in the cold water. Somewhat safer canoeing can be found on the mountain lakes of Grand Teton National Park and Yellowstone National Park, with a breath-taking background of snow-covered mountain ranges. But canoeists must be alert to sudden mountain winds gathering speed in narrow valleys.

The flattest canoeing in Wyoming is on the North Platte River going east into Nebraska; and Idaho has a fairly smooth river in the St. Joe, in the northern section of the state.

A great many visitors enjoy the Wyoming and Idaho rivers on safely conducted raft trips. *Family Water Sports in Big Wyoming*, a free brochure, and publications of the Idaho Outfitters and Guide Association, listed at the end of the chapter, offer the names and addresses of outfitters and guides.

Most canoe liveries in these states have given up renting because of the high mortality rate of canoes when used by inexperienced paddlers.

Wyoming Waters

Big Horn National Forest
Between Big Horn Lake and Sheridan on Route 14 are a group of canoeable lakes — Meadowlark, Sibley, and West Ten Sleep Lakes.

Buffalo River
Turpin Meadow bridge off Routes 26–287 to junction with the Snake River at Moran on Routes 26–89–187–287: 25 miles, canoeable in high water only.

Grand Teton National Park
In addition to the Snake River and Jackson Lake, the smaller Jenny Lake, Leigh Lake, Phelps Lake, and String Lake offer good canoeing. Canoeists, kayakers, and rafters must register with the Chief Ranger's Office, Grand Teton National Park, Moose, Wyo. 83012. Rentals: Jackson Hole.

Green River
Whiskey Grove Campground near Kendall on Route 352 to Route 187–189 north of Daniel: about 35 miles, some rapids in the upper course / Route 187–189 to Daniel on Route 189: 20 miles / Daniel to backwater of Fontenelle Reservoir near town of Big Piney on Route 189: about 40 miles / Fontenelle Dam to town of Green River on Route I–80: about 90 miles / below town of Green River is backwater of Flaming Gorge Reservoir and one can canoe from Green River to the Flaming Gorge Dam in Utah, about 90 miles.

Gros Ventre River
Kelly on Route 115 to junction with the Snake River near Jackson on Routes 26–89–187: about 20 miles, some rapids to be portaged below Slide Lake; the lower course is smooth.

Hoback River
Various access points in parkland from Routes 187–189 above Bondurant to junction with the Snake River at Hoback Junction on Routes 28–89–187–189: up to 40 miles, depending on put-in point, canoeable in good water conditions only.

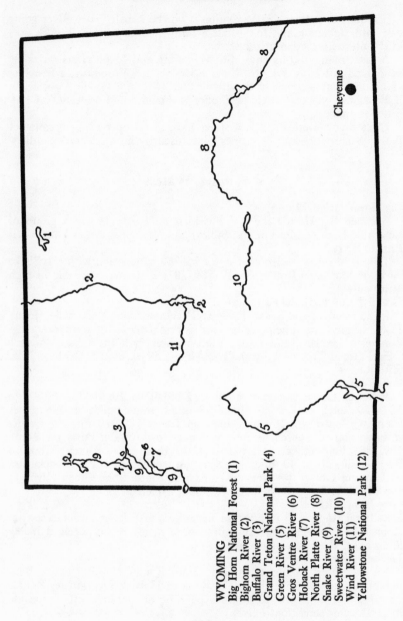

WYOMING
Big Horn National Forest (1)
Bighorn River (2)
Buffalo River (3)
Grand Teton National Park (4)
Green River (5)
Gros Ventre River (6)
Hoback River (7)
North Platte River (8)
Snake River (9)
Sweetwater River (10)
Wind River (11)
Yellowstone National Park (12)

North Platte River

Canoeable from below Alcova Dam on Route 220 to Route 220 bridge between Alcova and Casper: 15 miles / Route 220 bridge to Bessemer Landing off Route 220: about 20 miles, the river's most popular stretch / Bessemer Landing to Casper on Route 25: 15 miles / Casper to Glenrock on Route 95: 30 miles / Glenrock to Douglas on Route I–25: about 50 miles / Douglas to Glendo Reservoir on Routes 26–87: 15 miles / Glendo Dam to Guernsey on Route 26: 20 miles / Guernsey to Torrington on Routes 26–85: about 50 miles. For continuation, see Nebraska. Rentals: Casper.

Snake River

Rises in Yellowstone National Park. Park boundary to Flagg Ranch on Routes 89–287: 3 miles, whitewater, passes through Flagg Canyon / Flagg Ranch to Jackson Lake entrance: 6 miles, quiet water / Jackson Lake Dam to Moose on Routes 26–89: 25 miles, flat but with fast water / Moose to Wilson bridge on Route 22: 14 miles / Wilson to Hoback Junction on Routes 26–89–187–189: 19 miles, river picks up speed on the last 5 miles of this stretch / Hoback Junction through Snake River Canyon to Palisades Reservoir at Alpine on Route 26–89: 23 miles, dangerous, whitewater, for rafts only. For continuation, see Idaho. Most of the stretch described is in Grand Teton National Park. Canoeists, kayakers, and rafters using the Snake River in Grand Teton National Park must register with the Chief Ranger's Office, Grand Teton National Park, Moose, Wyo. 83012. Rentals: Jackson Hole.

Sweetwater River

Local road east of Jeffrey City on Route 287 to Pathfinder Reservoir: about 120 miles, some whitewater.

Wind River and Bighorn River

Above Boysen Reservoir, a good deal of whitewater with few access points; below Boysen Dam the river becomes increasingly flat, it changes its name to Bighorn River and parallels Route 20 to Greybull for about 100 miles. Greybull on Route 20 to Bighorn Reservoir near Route Alternate 14: about 40 miles.

Yellowstone National Park

Good canoeing on Lewis Lake, Shoshone Lake, and the 7-mile Lewis River connecting the two lakes as well as on the South and Southeast Arms of Yellowstone Lake. Permits are required from the Park Superintendent, Yellowstone National Park, Wyo. 82190.

Wyoming Rentals

Casper

Grizzly Fly Shop, 1000 North Center Street, Casper, Wyo. 82601; telephone: 307–234–9774 / Waters: North Platte River and nearby reservoirs / Trips: up to 2 days, guides available / Best canoeing months: May-September / Campsites: yes / Transportation: no / Car-top carriers: yes.

Jackson Hole

Teton Trailsports, Box 468, Jackson Hole, Wyo. 83001; telephone: 307–733–4924 / Waters: Jackson Lake and Snake River / Trips: up to 2 days / Best canoeing months: June-September / Campsites: yes / Transportation: no / Car-top carriers: no response / Also rents camping equipment.

Idaho Waters

Priest River

Priest Lake to mouth of Priest River at town of Priest River on Route 2–195: about 35 miles of fairly flat and safe water.

St. Joe River

Avery to St. Joe east of St. Maries on Route Alternate 95: about 35 miles of fairly flat and safe water.

Salmon River

Above Riggins on Route 95 the Salmon River is the "River of No Return," running for more than 150 miles through an almost shoreless, winding canyon. Riggins to junction with the Snake River about 60 miles above Lewiston on Route 95: about 80 miles, a few easy whitewater and flat water stretches interspersed with many dangerous rapids and chutes, this section of the river is described in detail in *Lower Salmon River Guide* listed at the end of the chapter.

Snake River

Enters Idaho from Wyoming via Palisades Reservoir on Route 26. It is canoeable from the reservoir dam for about 35 miles through fairly flat water. It then crosses the entire state and has a series of spectacular falls — Idaho Falls, American Falls, and Twin Falls. The waters are dammed and calmer near Nampa and Caldwell, both on Route I–80N. Then the river turns north, forming the Idaho-Oregon border and shoots for about 75 miles through Hell Canyon, the deepest gorge in the country. Flatter and safer waters are to be found for the last 80 miles above Lewiston on Route 95 where the Snake River enters Washington. It runs for about 750 miles in Idaho.

Idaho Rentals

None.

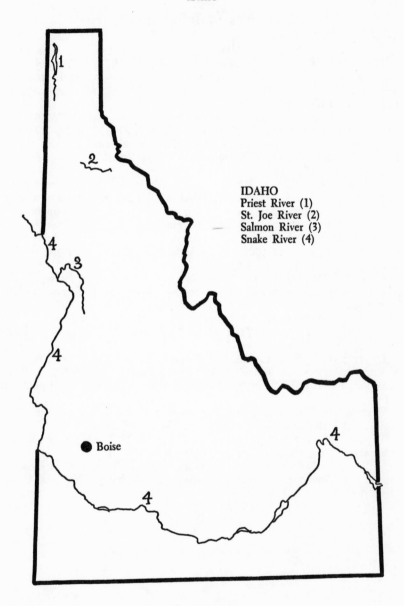

IDAHO
Priest River (1)
St. Joe River (2)
Salmon River (3)
Snake River (4)

● Boise

Sources of Information

Evans, Laura and Buzz Belknap. *Dinosaur River Guide*, Westwater Books (P.O. Box 365, Boulder City, Nev. 89005), 1973, 64 pp., price unknown. Detailed description of the Green River with sectional maps for Wyoming, Utah, and Colorado, and description and maps of the Yampa River in Colorado.

Huser, Verne and Buzz Belknap. *Snake River Guide*, Westwater Books (P.O. Box 365, Boulder City, Nev 89005), 1972, 72 pp., price unknown. Detailed description and sectional maps of the Snake River and Jackson Lake in Wyoming, including list of concessioners and guides.

Family Water Sports in Big Wyoming, Wyoming Travel Commission (2320 Capitol Avenue, Cheyenne, Wyo. 82002), a free brochure which lists boating waters, float and fishing waters, plus concessioners and commercial operators of float trips and guided tours.

Idaho fishing and hunting information is available from Idaho Fish and Game Department (600 South Walnut, P.O. Box 25, Boise, Idaho 83707).

Idaho Outfitters and Guides Association (P.O. Box 95, Boise, Idaho 83701) offers a free annual brochure on wilderness outfitters, guides, boat trips, and ranches.

Idaho tourist information is available from Idaho Department of Commerce and Development (108 State Capitol Building, Boise, Idaho 83707).

Lower Salmon River Guide, U.S. Department of the Interior, Bureau of Land Management, Resource Area Headquarters (Route No. 3, Cottonwood, Idaho 83522), a free, 19-page booklet with maps and description.

Wyoming fishing and hunting information is available from Wyoming Game and Fish Department (Cheyenne, Wyo. 82002).

Wyoming tourist information is available from Wyoming Travel Commission (2320 Capitol Avenue, Cheyenne, Wyo. 82002).

Yellowstone National Park information is available from U.S. Department of the Interior, National Park Service, Yellowstone National Park, Wyo. 82190.

COLORADO, NEW MEXICO, UTAH, and ARIZONA

WHEN YOU DRIVE SOUTH FROM LEADVILLE, COLORADO, the highest town in the United States at an altitude of 10,200 feet, you see a sparkling little stream alongside the road. It rushes heedlessly through a wide, treeless valley, carpeted with alpine grass and flowers and flanked by a chain of snow-capped 14,000-footers. It is the Arkansas River. About 1,500 miles later, much impounded and polluted, it ends its life in the Mississippi River in Arkansas.

In addition to the Arkansas River, the Rockies in Colorado give birth to three other mighty rivers — the Colorado River, the Rio Grande, and the North and South Platte Rivers which come together in Nebraska to form the Main Branch.

The Colorado River is joined in Utah by another great river, the Green River. It originates in Wyoming, runs through the famous Flaming Gorge Reservoir into Utah, and with a loop into Colorado becomes one of the attractions of the Dinosaur National Monument, which contains the greatest assembly of dinosaur fossils found anywhere in the world. After traversing the uncanoeable Desolation Canyon, the Green River offers one of the greatest flat water attractions in the country — about 120 miles of peaceful float through completely unpopulated canyon scenery. This is the place for whoever wants to get away from it all. The Colorado River offers a similar picturesque float trip from about 70 miles above the junction with the Green River.

Otherwise, the pickings for the flat water canoeist are slim in the four states, and they get slimmer the further one goes southwest into the desert. In Arizona, with the exception of the Colorado River below Lake Mead, there seems to be no canoeing whatsoever. But rafting through the Grand Canyon is a tourist thrill. The Rio Grande in New Mexico has a few flat stretches, and so has the Yampa River in Colorado.

Colorado Waters

Arkansas River
Whitewater above Canon City. Canon City on Route 50 to Florence on Route 67: 10 miles, easy and scenic / Florence to Pueblo on Route I–25: about 40 miles / Pueblo to Holly on Route 89: about 180 miles,

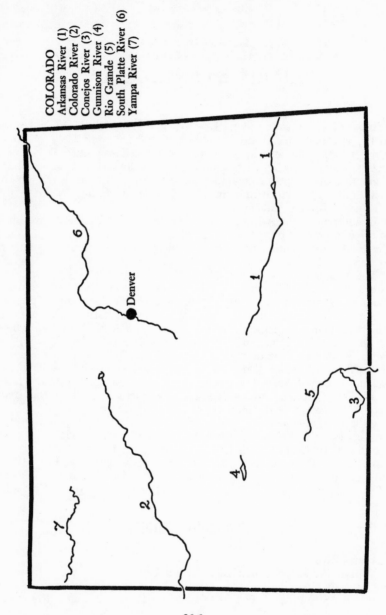

COLORADO
Arkansas River (1)
Colorado River (2)
Conejos River (3)
Gunnison River (4)
Rio Grande (5)
South Platte River (6)
Yampa River (7)

passes through John Martin Reservoir, Holly is about 4 miles from the Kansas border, the Arkansas River is flat and runs through rural country. Rentals: Denver.

Colorado River

Granby on Route 40 to town of Hot Sulpher Springs on Route 40: 10 miles, minor rapids / Hot Sulpher Springs to Parshall on Route 40: 6 miles, through Byers Canyon, not canoeable / Parshall to Kremmling on Route 9–40: 15 miles, easier stretch / Kremmling to town of State Bridge on Route 131: about 25 miles, dangerous whitewater, passes through Gore Canyon / State Bridge to Glenwood Canyon Reservoir: about 60 miles, several rapids but mostly flat / Shoshone dam on Routes 6–24 to New Castle on Routes 6–24: 25 miles, some impassable stretches, other sections range between intermediate to difficult whitewater / New Castle to Utah state line: about 120 miles, waters range from intermediate difficulty to flat water, many intermediate access points along Routes 6, 24, and I–70. Rentals: Denver and Fort Collins.

Conejos River

Canoeable from about 30 miles west of Antonito off Route 17 to Aspen Glade near Antonito, a stretch that is scenic, fast, and has few obstacles. The section between Antonito and junction of the Conejos River with the Rio Grande northeast of Lasauses is about 25 miles long and flows through open farmland with barbed wire fences.

Green River

See New Mexico and Utah.

Gunnison River

Town of Gunnison on Route 50 to Blue Mesa Reservoir: about 10 miles.

Rio Grande

Town of Wagon Wheel Gap on Route 149 to Baxterville on Routes 149–160: about 20 miles / Baxterville to Del Norte on Routes 112–160: about 20 miles, reportedly easy / Del Norte to Alamosa on Route 160–281: about 50 miles, whitewater below Del Norte / Alamosa to Route 142 east of Manassa: 25 miles / Route 142 to Route 248 east of Lobatos: 10 miles, easy / Route 248 begins a difficult whitewater stretch into New Mexico. For continuation, *see* New Mexico. Rentals: Fort Collins.

South Platte River

Deckers on Route 67 to town of South Platte: 13 miles, intermediate whitewater with many rapids / South Platte to Kassler: 7 miles, dangerous whitewater / Kassler to Englewood, a suburb of Denver: 7 miles, minor rapids, obstructed and unattractive through city of Denver / north of Denver the South Platte River becomes a flat river running through farmland with many diversion dams used for irrigation until it reaches the Nebraska state line. *See also* Nebraska. Rentals: Denver and Fort Collins.

Yampa River

Craig on Route 13–789–40 to Juniper Springs south of Route 40: about 50 miles, canoeable in favorable medium water conditions / Juniper Springs to Route 40 east of Maybell: 15 miles / Route 40 to Sunbeam on Route 318: 20 miles / Sunbeam to Lily: 30 miles / Lily to boundary of Dinosaur National Monument: 18 miles / park entrance to junction with the Green River at Echo Park in Dinosaur National Monument: 45 miles, permit required, write to Superintendent, Dinosaur National Monument, Dinosaur, Colo. 81610 / the lower course of the river has dangerous whitewater and is suitable only for rafts. Rentals: Fort Collins.

Colorado Rentals

Boulder

Colorado Whitewater Specialists Inc., 2047 Broadway, Boulder, Colo. 80302; telephone: 303–449–4620 / Waters: anywhere in the region / Trips: conducts guided canoe trips / Rents for car-top carriers / Also rents camping equipment.

Denver

Grayling Paddlecraft Ltd., 1200 South Bannock Street, Denver, Colo. 80223; telephone: 303–744–9133 / Waters: South Platte, Arkansas, and Colorado Rivers and many other waterways / Trips: 1 or more days / Best canoeing months: April-October, low water after July / Campsites: yes / Transportation: no / Car-top carriers: yes / Manufactures canoes and kayaks / Open all year.

Fort Collins

Colorado Whitewater Specialists Inc., 1127 West Elizabeth, P.O. Box 1416, Fort Collins, Colo. 80522; telephone: 303–493–3369 / Waters: South Platte, Colorado, and Yampa Rivers, Rio Grande, and other waters / Trips: 1 or more days, guides available / Best canoeing months: May-October / Campsites: yes / Transportation: no / Car-top carriers: yes / Also rents camping equipment, sailboats, and rafts.

New Mexico Waters

Gila River

Canoeable in spring run-off only. Route 15 south of Gila Cliff Dwellings National Monument to Cliff on Route 180: about 50 miles, whitewater in upper course / below Cliff the river is mostly uncanoeable due to diversion of waters for irrigation purposes.

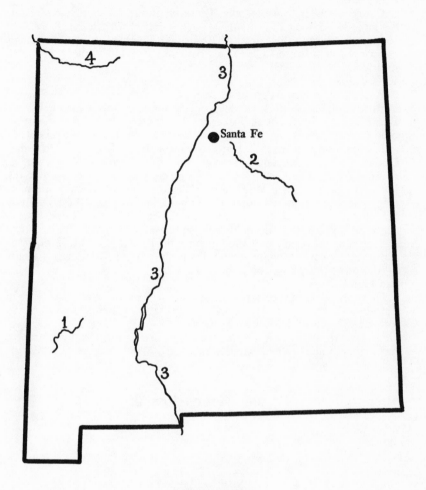

NEW MEXICO
Gila River (1)
Pecos River (2)
Rio Grande (3)
San Juan River (4)

Pecos River

Canoeable in high water only. Pecos on Route 63 southeast of Santa Fe to I–84–85 west of Soham: about 30 miles, whitewater / I–84–85 to town of Anton Chico west of Route 84: about 30 miles, increasingly calmer waters / Anton Chico to Santa Rosa on I–40: about 50 miles, mostly flat.

Rio Grande

Route 248 in Colorado east of Antonito to Route 111 in New Mexico northwest of Taos on Route 64: about 50 miles, dangerous whitewater / Route 111 to Route 96 at Taos Junction southwest of Taos: about 15 miles, whitewater / Route 96 to Rinconado on Route 64: about 12 miles, some smooth water but mostly whitewater / Rinconado to Otowi Bridge on Route 4: about 35 miles, mostly flat with several irrigation dams / Route 4 to Cochiti: about 30 miles, spectacular whitewater run for rafts, passes through White Rock Canyon / below Cochiti are many irrigation dams, channelization and impoundments make the river uninteresting and often impossible to canoe for lack of water / the river is canoeable again due to adequate release of water from Caballo Reservoir east of town of Truth or Consequences on Routes 85 and 52 and one can canoe the Rio Grande to the Texas state line at El Paso on Route I–10. For continuation, *see* Texas.

San Juan River

Depends on release of water from Navajo Dam on Route 511 east of Farmington. Dam to Blanco on Route 64: about 25 miles, some whitewater / Blanco to Shiprock on Route 550–666: about 75 miles, generally smooth, many irrigation dams / the river is not usually canoeable to Bluff in Utah. For continuation, *see* Utah.

New Mexico Rentals

None.

Utah Waters

Colorado River

Town of Westwater in Utah near the Colorado state line to Moab on Route 163: about 70 miles, dangerous whitewater / Moab to junction with the Green River: about 70 miles, popular flat water float trip / junction to Glen Canyon Reservoir: about 50 miles / Glen Canyon Reservoir dam in Arizona through the Grand Canyon to Mead Lake: not canoeable. Rentals: Moab.

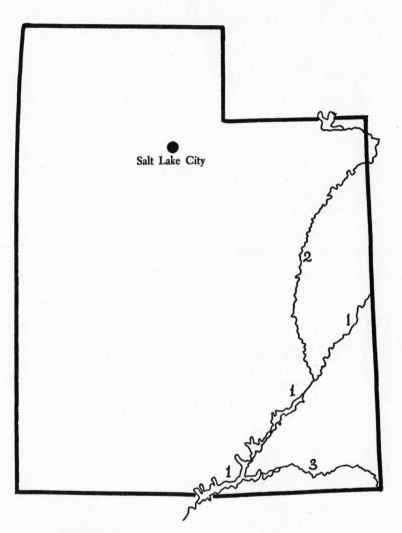

UTAH
Colorado River (1)
Green River (2)
San Juan River (3)

Green River

Enters Utah for the first time from Wyoming through Flaming Gorge Reservoir, a 100-mile twisting and often narrow lake ending at Flaming Gorge Dam on Route 260 / below dam is a popular float trip, mostly for rafters, to Little Hole Campground, a 7-mile stretch, or one can go on for an additional 20 miles or so to Indian Crossing boat ramp in Browns Park in Dinosaur National Monument in Colorado, water level dependent on release from dam, several minor rapids / Browns Park through Dinosaur National Monument to Lodore Ranger Station in Colorado: 30 miles / Lodore Ranger Station to Echo Park and junction with the Yampa River, still in Dinosaur National Monument: 20 miles, difficult whitewater / Echo Park in Colorado to Split Mountain Campground in Utah: 25 miles, difficult whitewater, passes through Whirlpool Canyon in Colorado / boating permit required for the stretch from Lodore Ranger Station to Split Mountain Campground, write to Superintendent, Dinosaur National Monument, Dinosaur, Colo. 81610 / Split Mountain Campground to Jensen on Route 40: 20 miles / Jensen to Ouray on Route 88: about 50 miles / Ouray to town of Green River on Route 6–50: about 120 miles, passes through Desolation Canyon and Gray Canyon, an uncanoeable string of rapids, suitable for rubber rafts only / Green River to junction with the Colorado River in Canyonlands National Park: about 120 miles, popular flat water float trip with wilderness camping, intermediate access point at town of Mineral. Rentals: Moab.

San Juan River

Bluff on Route 163 to town of Mexican Hat on Route 163: 25 miles, some whitewater / Mexican Hat to Clay Hill Crossing above backwater of Glen Canyon Reservoir: 57 miles, some intermediate whitewater about 20 miles above Clay Hill Crossing, canoeable in late May and June only, after which the river dries up. For continuation, *see* New Mexico. Rentals: Moab.

Utah Rentals

Moab

Tex's River Expeditions, P.O. Box 67, Moab, Utah 84532; telephone: 801–259–5101 / Waters: Green, Colorado, and San Juan Rivers / Trips: 1–7 days / Best canoeing months: March-October / Campsites: yes / Transportation: yes / Car-top carriers: no response / offers a wide range of activities other than canoeing and has many facilities nearby.

Orem

Sports Specialties, 170 South State, Orem, Utah 84057; telephone: 801–225–2457 / Unconfirmed.

Sources of Information

Arizona fishing and hunting information is available from Arizona Game and Fish Commission (2222 West Greenway Road, Phoenix, Ariz. 85023).

Arizona tourist information is available from Arizona Department of Economic Planning and Development, Travel Information Section (1645 West Jefferson, Phoenix, Ariz. 85007).

Colorado fishing and hunting information is available from Colorado Department of Natural Resources, Division of Wildlife (6060 Broadway, Denver, Colo. 80216).

Colorado tourist information is available from Colorado Visitors Bureau (225 West Colfax Avenue, Denver, Colo. 80202) and information on outdoor recreation is available from Colorado Division of Parks and Outdoor Recreation (1845 Sherman, Room 101, Denver, Colo. 80203).

Evans, Laura and Buzz Belknap. *Dinosaur River Guide*, Westwater Books (Box 365, Boulder City, Nev. 89005), 1973, 64 pp., price unknown. Detailed description of the Green River and Yampa River with sectional maps.

New Mexico fishing and hunting information is available from New Mexico Department of Game and Fish (State Capitol, Santa Fe, N. Mex. 87501).

New Mexico tourist information is available from New Mexico Department of Development, Tourist Division (113 Washington Avenue, Santa Fe, N. Mex. 87503).

Ungnade, Herbert E. *Guide to the New Mexico Mountains*, University of New Mexico Press (Albuquerque, N. Mex. 87106), 1972, 235 pp., $7.50. Includes a chapter on river boating in the state.

Utah fishing and hunting information is available from Utah Division of Wildlife Resources (1596 West North Temple, Salt Lake City, Utah 84116).

Utah tourist information is available from Utah Travel Council (Council Hall, Capitol Hill, Salt Lake City, Utah 84114).

•

OREGON and WASHINGTON

WATER, WATER EVERYWHERE; innumerable streams cascading down steep mountain slopes; a galaxy of riffles, rapids, haystacks, and chutes to satisfy even the most fastidious whitewater fan, but rather spotty pickings for the leisurely flat water paddler who wants to drift and dream. That, in a nutshell, is the canoeing appeal of the western parts of the two states which also offer some of the most spectacular scenery in the nation and share a very similar topography and climate.

Both Oregon and Washington are neatly divided into two uneven halves by the Cascade Mountains which run from north to south parallel to the Pacific Ocean. Closer to the shore is the lower Coast Range, which catches the lion's share of the rainfall — up to 200 inches annually at Mount Olympus west of Seattle, by far the most precipitation in the country. Enough rain remains for the western slopes of the Cascades to allow a myriad of streams and rivers to carry water to the Pacific Ocean, usually in a tearing hurry, through dramatic forested mountain gorges or lush farmed valleys. The peak rainy season is from November to March, but many rivers feed on melting snow until late in the summer. Some impounded rivers, regulated by water released from reservoirs, such as the Yakima and Skagit Rivers in Washington, generally have a good water supply all year.

The larger, eastern portions of the two states, in the rain shadow of the Cascades, are semi-arid. In the volcanic areas of Oregon, some rivers disappear completely into the porous lava or sand. Others, however, richly endowed with water from the peaks of the Cascades, stay on course. One of the most attractive is the Deschutes River, originating in the dramatic volcanic section of the Cascades north of the famous Crater Lake. A part of its course offers relatively safe flat water canoeing.

At the Oregon-Washington state line, the great Columbia River has cut a gorge through the Cascade Range. With waterfalls plunging hundreds of feet over cliffs into the river, and with its many parks and overlooks, the gorge has become one of the greatest tourist attractions of the two states. The Columbia River itself is rarely canoed because of its width and frequent impoundments.

Another great scenic river is the Rogue River in the southwest coastal region of Oregon. The upper course is primarily whitewater used by organized raft parties, and on the lower course tourists are carried upriver by jet powered boats. This leaves only a relatively short stretch in the middle for safe and quiet paddling.

By far the longest flat water run in the two states is the 180 miles of the Willamette River between Eugene and Portland, Oregon — a river saved in the nick of time from death by pollution. It flows primarily through lush farmland with dramatic mountain views. Many other rivers that start as whitewater get calmer in their lower courses, but careful local research is needed to discover the safe sections.

Both Washington and Oregon have many attractive lakes, but again local research will help discover those that offer some seclusion from power boats and high winds.

Oregon Waters

Deschutes National Forest

Excellent lake canoeing on Wickiup Reservoir, Crane Prairie Reservoir, Cultus Lake, Davis Lake, Summit Lake, Odell Lake, and some connecting streams. Accessible from forest roads off Routes 58 and 97 south of Bend, which is on Route 97, and east of Eugene, which is on Route I–5.

Deschutes River

Wickiup Reservoir Dam on forest road west of Route 97 at LaPine and south of Bend to Benham Falls: about 45 miles, a relatively easy run with minor whitewater, dangerous whitewater from Benham Falls to Lake Chinook / Lake Chinook to the Columbia River above town of The Dalles on Route I–80N: abut 150 miles, no published information.

Detroit Lake

Lake is located at Detroit on Route 22. Power boats are on the lake but there is good flat water canoeing several miles upstream on the tributaries — the Breitenbush River, French Creek, Blowout Creek, Kinney Creek, and North Santiam River. The North Santiam River, which drains the lake below the dam, is mostly whitewater to its junction with the South Santiam River northeast of Albany on Route 99. Rentals: Detroit.

John Day River

Junction of North and South Forks at Kimberly on Route 19 to town of Service Creek on Routes 19–207: about 30 miles / Service Creek to Route 218 west of Fossil: about 70 miles, some whitewater / the river continues until it joins the Columbia River at John Day Lock and Dam on Route I–80N.

Owyhee River

Route 95 at Rome to Lake Owyhee: about 75 miles, mostly whitewater, but the lake is narrow and offers fairly good canoeing / Lake Owyhee dam to junction with the Snake River: about 50 miles.

Rogue River

Designated a "wild" and "scenic" river. Whitewater float trips usually start at Grave Creek near town of Grants Pass on Route I–5 and end at Agness, about 55 miles. Smoother canoeing is to be found below Agness. Agness to the Pacific Ocean at town of Gold Beach on Route 101: about 40 miles, jet powered boats carrying tourists are to be found on the lower reaches.

Willamette River

Formed by junction of the Middle and Coast Forks above Springfield on Route I–5, both forks have much whitewater and hazards. Junction to Eugene on Route I–5: about 2 miles, rapids / Eugene Greenway riverside park in Eugene to Harrisburg on Route 99: 21 miles / Harris-

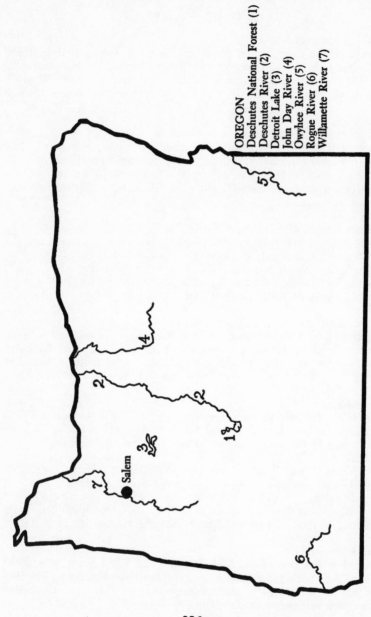

OREGON
Deschutes National Forest (1)
Deschutes River (2)
Detroit Lake (3)
John Day River (4)
Owyhee River (5)
Rogue River (6)
Willamette River (7)

Salem

burg to Peoria on county road west of Shedd on Route 99E: 19 miles / Peoria to Albany on Routes 20–99: 23 miles / Albany to Independence on Route 51: 25 miles / Independence to Salem on Route 22: 12 miles / Salem to Newberg on Route 219: 35 miles / Newberg to Oregon City on Routes 43–99E: 25 miles / Oregon City to Willamette Park in Portland: 10 miles / Portland to junction with the Columbia River: 16 miles. Rentals: Oregon City.

Oregon Rentals

Corvallis
Riverview Marina, 781 N.E. 2nd Street, Corvallis, Ore. 97330; telephone: 216–788–8709 / Unconfirmed.

Detroit
Detroit Lake Resort (Arthur and Barbara Whiteley), 115 Breitenbush Road, P.O. Box 466, Detroit, Ore. 97342; telephone: 503–854–3423 / Waters: Detroit Lake and connecting creeks and rivers / Trips: up to 1 day / Best canoeing months: May-September / Campsites: yes / Transportation: no / Car-top carriers: no response.

Oregon City
Sportcraft Landing, Inc. (Ken, Wayne, and Winnie Dye), 1701 Clackamette Drive, P.O. Box 111, Oregon City, Ore. 97045; telephone: 503–656–6484 / Waters: Willamette River / Trips: 1 or more days / Best canoeing months: June-October / Campsites: yes / Transportation: yes / Car-top carriers: yes / Open all year.

Portland
The Canoe Rack, 3003 N.E. Alberta, Portland, Ore. 97211; telephone: 503–288–5395 / Unconfirmed.

Washington Waters

Chelan Lake
Access from Chelan on Route 97 to this 50-mile-long, narrow lake with dramatic scenery.

Columbia River
Traverses the state for about 1,000 miles from the Canadian border to the Pacific Ocean, forming the border between Washington and Oregon for the last 300 of these miles. It is impounded and populated along its course, offering only limited stretches of quiet canoeing.

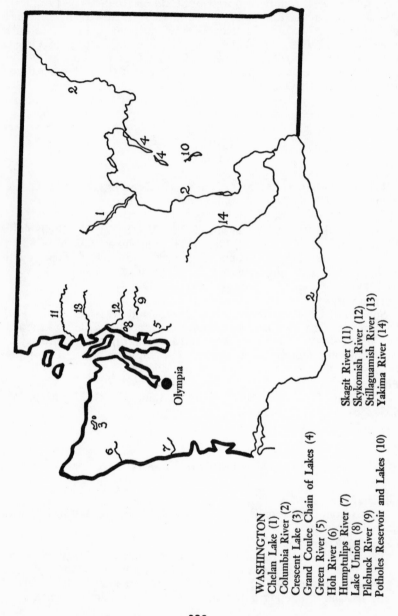

WASHINGTON
Chelan Lake (1)
Columbia River (2)
Crescent Lake (3)
Grand Coulee Chain of Lakes (4)
Green River (5)
Hoh River (6)
Humptulips River (7)
Lake Union (8)
Pilchuck River (9)
Potholes Reservoir and Lakes (10)

Skagit River (11)
Skykomish River (12)
Stillaguamish River (13)
Yakima River (14)

Crescent Lake

A very scenic lake on Route 101 in Olympic National Park.

Grand Coulee Chain of Lakes

In the old river bed of the Columbia River along Route 17 north of town of Soap Lake, 3 portages.

Green River

Hanson Dam east of Palmer to Route 169 north of Enumclaw: about 20 miles, the river continues through populated areas into Puget Sound.

Hoh River

Route 101 south of town of Forks to the Pacific Ocean: about 15 miles, some whitewater; more difficult whitewater is found from about 20 miles above Route 101.

Humptulips River

Wynoochee Lake Road east of Route 101 and north of town of Humptulips to Humptulips on Route 101: about 15 miles, scenic, some intermediate whitewater / Humptulips to North Bay on the Pacific Ocean: about 30 miles.

Lake Union and Union Bay

Good canoeing along secluded shore spots near Seattle's Museum of History and Industry on Route I-5.

Pilchuck River

Route 92 southwest of town of Granite Falls to Snohomish on Route 2: about 20 miles, some intermediate whitewater.

Potholes Reservoir and Potholes Lakes

North of Othello on Route 26 is interesting canoeing on the sidearms of the reservoir and among the sand dunes. Also pleasant canoeing on the chain of lakes, below the reservoir dam, connected by portages.

Skagit River

Above Rockport on Route 20 is mostly difficult whitewater with water level varying dangerously dependent upon release of water from the power dam. Below Rockport is mostly smooth water with minor rapids. Rockport to Concrete on Route 20: about 15 miles / Concrete to town of Sedro Woolley on Route 9: about 30 miles / Sedro Woolley to town of Skagit on Skagit Bay: about 30 miles.

Skykomish River

Above town of Gold Bar on Route 2 is difficult whitewater. Gold Bar to Monroe on Routes 2–203: about 15 miles, light to intermediate whitewater. About 8 miles below Monroe, the Skykomish River joins the Snoqualmie River to form the Snohomish River which continues for about 40 miles to Puget Sound, the water is mostly flat.

Stillaguamish River

South Fork: Town of Granite Falls north of Route 92 to Arlington on Route 530: about 15 miles, fast but without serious hazards; joins the North Fork at Arlington / Arlington to mouth of river: about 20 miles, mostly flat.

Yakima River

Town of Cle Elum on Route 10 to Ellensburg off Route I–90: about 30 miles / Ellensburg to Yakima on Route I–82: about 40 miles, some minor rapids on the upper portion / Yakima to junction with the Columbia River: about 120 miles, many intermediate access points off Routes 12 and 22.

Washington Rentals

Ashford

The Lodge, Inc., Box 86, Ashford, Wash. 98304; telephone: 206–569–2312 / Waters: United States and Canadian Rocky Mountain waterways / Trips: 1 or more days, guided trips only for groups and individuals may join regularly scheduled trips / Best canoeing months: July-September / Campsites: yes / Transportation: yes / Car-top carriers: no / Also offers canoeing instruction.

Ocean Shores

Merle's Boat Rentals, Ocean Shores Marina, Ocean Shores, Wash. 98551; telephone: 206–289–3391 / Unconfirmed.

Seattle

The Boathouse, 9808 17th Avenue S.W., Seattle, Wash. 98106; telephone: 206–763–0688 / Waters: many lakes and rivers within driving distance of Seattle / Trips: 1 or more days / Best canoeing months: March-September / Campsites: yes / Transportation: no / Car-top carriers: yes / Also rents canoe trailers / Open all year.

Sources of Information

Furrer, Werner. *Water Trails of Washington*, Signpost (16812 36th Street West, Lynnwood, Wash. 98036), 1973, 31 pp., $2.50. Brief descriptions of 19 canoeing waters with maps.

Garren, John. *Oregon River Tours*, Binford & Mort, Publishers (2536 S.E. 11th, Portland, Ore. 97202), 1974, 128 pp., $4.00 Detailed description and maps of Oregon rivers.

Oregon fishing and hunting information is available from Oregon State Game Commission (P.O. Box 3503, Portland, Ore. 97208).

Oregon tourist information is available from Oregon State Highway Division, Travel Information (Salem, Ore. 97310).

Washington fishing and hunting information is available from Washington Department of Game (600 North Capital Way, Olympia, Wash. 98504).

Washington tourist information is available from Washington Department of Commerce and Economic Development, Travel Development Division (General Administration Building, Olympia, Wash. 98504).

Willamette River Recreation Guide, Oregon State Highway Division, State Parks and Recreation Section (Salem, Ore. 97310), a free map with mileages and detailed description.

•

CALIFORNIA and NEVADA

As WITH MANY OTHER FEATURES of California life, its canoeing is different from the rest of the country. Its topography is unique, its climate is unique, and most of its rivers are different in scenic character and water supply from those found in other states.

Topographically, the state is bound in the east by the solid and soaring Sierra Nevada mountain range and in the west by the lower but more complex Coastal Range with its rugged, rocky coastline. In between lies a vast central plain, drained by two large rivers — the Sacramento flowing south and the San Joaquin flowing north, and both finding their exit to the sea through the gap in the Coastal Range at San Francisco Bay.

Except for the heights of the Sierra Nevada, California knows no real winter, but it has extreme summer heat in its Central Valley and in the arid lands in the south. It has only one relatively short rainy season, usually starting in November and ending in March, with the heaviest fall occurring in the north and in the High Sierra where it turns to snow. The state relies heavily on reservoirs and irrigation for its agriculture.

These conditions create three distinct types of rivers in terms of water supply: rain fed, spring run-off fed, and reservoir fed. Each has its own flow characteristics and canoeing season, often very short.

The rivers hugging the coast of the northwest in the redwood forests rely largely on rain. Those coming down from the Sierra slopes with their majestic sequoias, pines, and firs are best in the spring run-off unless impounded. Among the waterways supplied year-round by reservoirs are the Sacramento River, American River, and the popular Russian River. They run through rich farmland or the hilly grassland with its emerald green carpet in the rainy season turning to a golden straw color in the summer. The heavily scented eucalyptus trees shed a delicate pattern of shade and light on the invitingly smooth picnic grounds beneath them. In its most popular stretches, the Russian River on busy weekends often gets so crowded that it looks more like a Disneyland attraction than a piece of nature. The Colorado River, arriving from Nevada and forming the California-Arizona border on its last leg to the sea, is also a popular year-round float trip through desert scenery spotted with cacti, sagebush, and Joshua-trees, or through productive irrigated farmland.

I would caution against venturing too far out into San Francisco Bay and other tidal waters. Winds, waves, and currents can be fierce. But somewhat inland between Sacramento and Stockton are canoeable canals that have turned a marsh into rich farmland. And many smaller mountain lakes, listed in Ann Dwyer's book (see the end of the chapter) are lovely spots for enjoying nature in a canoe.

On the Nevada side, the Sierras drop abruptly. There are a few reservoirs and rivers at their edge in Nevada, such as the Truckee River — which also runs into California — and Pyramid Lake, in an Indian reservation. A few of them, as well as some irrigation channels, look canoeable, but canoeing, in contrast to other recreation activities, does not seem to be a publicized sport in Nevada. There are no canoe rentals in the state and no specific information on Nevada's waters could be found for this book.

California Waters

American River
Nimbus Dam in Fair Oaks off Route 50 to Watt Avenue off Route 50 east of Sacramento: 13 miles, minor rapids / Watt Avenue to Discovery Park in Sacramento and junction with the Sacramento River: 12 miles. Rentals: Columbia, Fair Oaks, and Stockton.

Bear River
Camp Far West Reservoir dam northeast of Wheatland to Route 65 southeast of Wheatland: 5 miles / Route 65 to confluence with the Feather River: 12 miles.

Big River
Tidal round trip canoeing about 8 miles upstream from Mendocino on Route 1. The upper stream is difficult to reach, either from a dirt road off Little Lake Road from Mendocino, about 11 miles back to Mendocino, or from Orr Springs Road off Route 101 north of Ukiah to Mendocino: about 40 miles, some whitewater. Rentals: Mendocino.

Cache Creek
Rumsey on Route 16 to Guinda on Route 16: 6 miles / Guinda to dam at Capay on Route 16: about 15 miles.

Russian River (21)
Sacramento River (22)
Salmon River
  Main Branch (23)
  North Fork (24)
  South Fork (25)
San Joaquin River (26)
Scott River (27)
Smith River (28)
Stanislaus River (29)
Trinity River
  Main Branch (30)
  South Fork (31)
Truckee River (32)
Tuolomne River (33)
Van Duzen River (34)
Yuba River (35)

CALIFORNIA
American River (1)
Bear River (2)
Big River (3)
Cache Creek (4)
Calaveras River (5)
Carmel River (6)
Colorado River (7)
Eel River
  Main Branch (8)
  South Fork (9)
Feather River (10)
Garcia River (11)
Gualala River (12)
Klamath River (13)
Mad River (14)
Mattole River (15)
Merced River (16)
Mokelumne River (17)
Navarro River (18)
Noyo River (19)
Redwood Creek (20)

Calaveras River

Canoeable during run-off season only. Route 26 at Bellota to Route J3 at Stockton: about 15 miles. Rentals: Stockton.

Carmel River

Flow depends on reservoir release in rainy season. Town of Carmel Valley on Route G16, Esquiline Road east of the town of Carmel, to Route 1 at Carmel: about 15 miles.

Colorado River

The river runs through Nevada, Arizona, and California on the stretch described here. Hoover Dam on Route 93 southeast of Las Vegas, Nevada, to Willow Beach Park off Route 93 in Arizona: 15 miles, dangerous variations of water levels depending on water release from dam / park to Eldorado Canyon east of Nelson on Nevada Route 60: about 15 miles, below canyon is backwater of Lake Mohave / Davis Dam on Lake Mohave at Nevada Route 77 and Arizona Route 68 to Needles, Arizona, on I-40: about 30 miles, dependent upon water release from dam, great variations of water levels / Needles to Lake Havasu City, Arizona, on Lake Havasu at Route 95: about 35 miles, the river forms the California-Arizona border / below Parker Dam of Lake Havasu at Earp, California, on Route 62 to Lost Lake Resort: about 15 miles / Lost Lake Resort to Agua Quin Park above Palo Verde dam off California Route 95 north of Blythe: about 30 miles / Blythe on Route 60 to Walters Camp: 18 miles / Walters Camp via Picacho State Recreation Area to Imperial Dam northeast of Yuma, Arizona, on I-8: about 50 miles. Rentals: Lake Havasu City and Topock in Arizona and Azusa, Blythe, and Lynwood in California.

Eel River

Main Branch: Dos Rios on Route 162 to Alderpoint east of Route 101 at Garberville: about 50 miles, popular scenic camping trip but for canoeists with advanced whitewater skills only / Alderpoint to town of Eel Rock east of Myers Flat on Route 101: 18 miles / Eel Rock to junction with the South Fork at the town of South Fork on Route 101: 14 miles / junction to Rio Dell on Route 101: about 24 miles, minor rapids, heavy winds. Rentals: Greenbrae and Klamath.

South Fork: Follows Route 101 more or less from just northwest of Cummings to the town of South Fork and junction with the Main Branch, a total of about 75 miles. The first 25 miles, from near Cummings to near Piercy, is intermediate whitewater; the stretch from Piercy to junction with the Main Branch is generally easy with a few portages around the different spots. The Middle Fork above Dos Rios is mainly whitewater.

Feather River

Dam at Oroville on Route 70 to east of Gridley on Route 99: about 20 miles / Gridley to Yuba City on Routes 99–70–20 junction with the Yuba River: 18 miles / Yuba City to junction with the Sacramento River near Sacramento: about 30 miles. Rentals: Fair Oaks and Stockton.

Garcia River

Dirt road off Iverson Road off Route 1 south of Point Arena to Eureka Hill Road east of Point Arena: 5 miles / Eureka Hill Road to Route 1 south of Manchester: 7 miles.

Gualala River

South Fork: Stewarts Point-Skaggs Spring Road east of town of Stewarts Point on Route 1 to Annapolis Road and junction with the Wheatfield Fork of the Gualala River: 6 miles.

Main Branch: Formed by junction of the South Fork and Wheatfield Fork at Annapolis Road to Route 1 at town of Gualala: 9 miles.

Wheatfield Fork: Stewarts Point-Skaggs Spring Road to junction with the South Fork: 18 miles.

Klamath River

Iron Gate Reservoir off I–5 east of Hornbrook to I–5: 11 miles / I–5 to town of Klamath River on Route 96: 22 miles, whitewater / Klamath River to town of Horse Creek on Route 96: 9 miles, flat water / Horse Creek to Hamburg on Route 96: 8 miles, one minor rapid / Hamburg to town of Seiad Valley on Route 96: 9 miles, whitewater / Seiad Valley to town of Happy Camp on Route 96: 26 miles, easy except for a 3-mile stretch of difficult whitewater between Fort Goff and Thompson Creek / From Happy Valley the river flows southwest but at Weitchpec, about 70 miles downstream, the river meets the Trinity River and makes an abrupt turn to the northwest. On this northwestern section, about 10 miles from Weitchpee at Cappell Creek on Route 169, the Klamath River is wild whitewater, suitable only for rafts; however, the stretch from Cappell Creek to Klamath Glen near Route 101 is relatively easy, 27 miles long, wide and windy, and motor boats in the lower reaches. Rentals: Greenbrae and Klamath.

Mad River

Ruth Lake off Route 36 to Route 36: about 8 miles, minor rapids / Route 36 to Butler Valley Road, about 15 miles east of Eureka on Route 101: 35 miles, heavy whitewater, most of it is not canoeable / Butler Valley Road to Blue Lake on Route 299: 16 miles, one rapids to be portaged.

Mattole River

Ettersburg west of Redway on Route 101 to Honeydew on Mattole Road: 18 miles, 2 difficult rapids which can be portaged / Honeydew to Petrolia on Mattole Road: about 20 miles.

Merced River

McConnell State Recreation Area east of Route 99 at Delhi to Hageman County State Park west of Delhi: about 10 miles / Hageman

County State Park to George J. Hatfield State Park Recreation Area and junction with the San Joaquin River on Route J18: about 10 miles. Rentals: Stockton.

Mokelumne River

Comanche Reservoir dam on Buena Vista Road east of Route 88 to Mackville Road north of Routes 12–88 at Clements: 6 miles / Mackville Road to Route J5 north of Routes 12–88 at Lockeford: 7 miles / Route J5 to I-5 in Lodi: 12 miles / I-5 to Route J12: 6 miles, passes through Lodi Lake / Route J12 to junction with the Sacramento River at Thornton near Route J8: 10 miles. Rentals: Stockton.

Navarro River

Philo on Route 128 to Paul M. Dimmick State Park: 16 miles, twisting waterway, minor rapids / park to town of Navarro-by-the-Sea on Route 1: 10 miles, tidal and windy in lower parts.

Noyo River

Tidal canoeing a few miles upstream of Fort Bragg on Route 1. The upper section is hard to reach, from a dirt road north of Route 20 and west of Willits for a 20-mile scenic stretch of intermediate whitewater to Fort Bragg.

Redwood Creek

Route 299 about 20 miles east of Arcata to Lacks Creek: about 16 miles, minor rapids; rafts only below Lacks Creek.

Russian River

Ukiah on Route 101 to Hopland on Route 101: 16 miles / Hopland to Pieta Creek: 5 miles / Pieta Creek to Cloverdale on Route 101: 8 miles, popular advanced whitewater run / Cloverdale to Geyserville on Route 101: 10 miles / Geyserville to Alexander Valley Road bridge: 5 miles / bridge to Healdsburg on Route 101: 15 miles / Healdsburg to Mirabel Park: 10 miles / Mirabel Park to Guerneville on Route 116: 9 miles / Guerneville to Reins Beach: 8 miles, below Reins Beach wide, windy, and tidal. Rentals: Greenbrae and Healdsburg.

Sacramento River

Dam at Lake Siskiyou off I–5 south of town of Mount Shasta to Lake Shasta north of Redding on Route 299: about 35 miles of very difficult whitewater / Lake Shasta dam to Red Bluff on I–5: about 50 miles, intermediate whitewater / Red Bluff to Colusa on Route 20: about 100 miles, mostly flat / Colusa to Knights Landing on Route 113: 45 miles, below Knights Landing is the Sacramento metropolitan area and tidal waters. Rentals: Los Molinas and Stockton.

Salmon River

South Fork: Cecilville to town of Forks of Salmon on local road: about 20 miles, heavy whitewater.

North Fork: Town of Sawyers Bar to Forks of Salmon on local road: about 12 miles, heavy whitewater.

336

Main Branch: Forks of Salmon to town of Somes Bar on Route 96 and junction with the Klamath River: about 15 miles, heavy whitewater.

San Joaquin River

Route J16 bridge northeast of Westley on Route 33 to Airport Way in San Joaquin City on Route J4 below confluence with the Stanislaus River: 15 miles / Airport Way to junction of Route 120 and I–5: 18 miles / I–5 to Stockton Water Channel in Stockton west of I–5: 20 miles / many sloughs and channels which are canoeable between Stockton and San Francisco Bay. Rentals: Stockton.

Scott River

Callahan on Route 3 to Etna on Route 3: 12 miles / Etna to Fort Jones on Route 3: 10 miles / Fort Jones to Scott River Canyon: about 10 miles, below Fort Jones and through the canyon to the junction with the Klamath River is a stretch usable only by rafts.

Smith River

Jedediah Smith Redwoods State Park on Route 199 east of Crescent City to tidewater: about 10 miles, above the park both forks of the Smith River are whitewater.

Stanislaus River

Knights Ferry off Route 108 to Oakdale on Route 120: 14 miles, minor rapids in the upper section / Oakdale to Riverbank on Route J7 off Route 108: 8 miles / Riverbank to Route 99 southeast of Ripon: 15 miles / Route 99 to Airport Way in San Joaquin City on Route J4 below confluence with the San Joaquin River: 25 miles. Rentals: Columbia, Greenbrae, and Stockton.

Trinity River

Main Branch: Lewiston below Lewiston Lake to Douglas City on Route 299: 16 miles / Douglas City to Junction City on Route 299: 14 miles / Junction City to junction with the North Fork: 7 miles / junction to Big Bar on Route 299: 9 miles, dangerous whitewater / Big Bar to Cedar Flat above Burnt Bridge Gorge: 15 miles, intermediate whitewater, the 9-mile gorge is not canoeable / Hawkins Bar below gorge to junction with the South Fork: 9 miles, intermediate whitewater / junction to Hoopa on Route 96: 24 miles, minor rapids / Hoopa to junction with the Klamath River at Weitchpec on Route 96: 9 miles, difficult whitewater.

South Fork: Canoeable from about 8 miles above the junction with the Main Branch, one minor rapids on this stretch. The South Fork is generally not canoed above this stretch.

Truckee River

Tahoe City on Routes 28–29 to River Ranch on Route 89: 4 miles / River Ranch to town of Truckee on Route 89 and I–80: 12 miles, some intermediate whitewater / Truckee to Boca on I–80: 8 miles, some intermediate whitewater / Boca to Floriston on I–80: 6 miles, easy whitewater / Below Floriston is dangerous whitewater. The river continues to Pyramid Lake Indian Reservation in Nevada; much diversion of water for irrigation.

Tuolumne River
La Grange on Route 132 to Turlock Lake State Park: about 6 miles. Rentals: Stockton.

Van Duzen River
Route 36 below Bridgeville to Carlotta on Route 36: about 24 miles, one major rapids below Grizzly Creek Redwoods State Park.

Yuba River
Parks Bar bridge on Route 20 northeast of Marysville on Route 20 to Yuba City on Route 20 and junction with the Feather River: 15 miles, some rapids in the upper portion. Rentals: Stockton.

California Rentals

Azusa
Pack "n" Paddle (Ernie Doiron), 18320 East Alosta, Azusa, Cal. 91702; telephone: 213–339–8410 / Waters: Colorado River and coastal waters / Trips: 1 or more days, guides available / Best canoeing months: all year / Campsites: yes / Transportation: yes / Car-top carriers: yes / Other locations in Blythe, California, and Topock, Arizona / All reservations through Azusa office / Also rents kayaks, rafts, camping equipment, and canoe trailers / Offers instruction on canoeing and kayaking / Offers packaged group tours from Los Angeles to the Colorado River and surf trips / Open all year.

Blythe
See Azusa.

Columbia
Zephyr River Expeditions, P.O. Box 529, Columbia, Cal. 95310; telephone: 209–532–6249 / Waters: Stanislaus and American Rivers and other waterways / Trips: 1–2 days, guided raft trips only / Best months: April-October / Campsites: yes / Transportation: yes / Car-top carriers: no / Complete outfitters / Also operates a whitewater school.

Fair Oaks
W. C. "Bob" Trowbridge, 8877 Winding Way, Fair Oaks, Cal. 95628; telephone: 916–967–2526 / Waters: American and Feather Rivers / Trips: 1–5 days / Best canoeing months: March-October / Campsites: yes / Transportation: yes / Car-top carriers: yes / Also rents rafts.

Greenbrae
Canoe Trips West, Inc. (Ann Dwyer), 2170 Redwood Highway, Greenbrae, Cal. 94904; telephone: 415–461–1750 / Waters: Corte Madera Creek as well as guided trips on the Eel, Klamath, Russian, and

Stanislaus Rivers / Trips: several hours to 8 days, guides available / Best canoeing months: all year / Campsites: yes / Transportation: only for guided trips / Car-top carriers: yes / Canoe and kayak instruction / Open all year.

Healdsburg

W. C. "Bob" Trowbridge, Box 942, Healdsburg, Cal. 95448; telephone: 707–542–0598 or 707–433–4116 or 433–4103 / Waters: Russian River / Trips: 1–2 days / Best canoeing months: March-October / Campsites: yes / Transportation: yes / Car-top carriers: yes

Klamath

Klamath Kruises, P.O. Box 5, Klamath, Cal. 95548; telephone: 707–482–4191 / Waters: Eel and Klamath Rivers / Trips: 3–7 days / Best canoeing months: May-September / Campsites: yes / Transportation: yes / Car-top carriers: yes / For more information or reservations contact W. C. "Bob" Trowbridge, 625 B Street, Santa Rosa, Cal. 95401; telephone: 707–542–0598.

Lake Havasu City (Arizona)

Jon and Ruth Finley, Box 144, Lake Havasu City, Ariz. 86403; telephone: 602–855–2186 / Located on the Colorado River, border between California and Arizona / Waters: Colorado River / Trips: 2-, 4-, or 6-day trips / Best canoeing months: all year / Campsites: yes / Transportation: no / Car-top carriers: yes / Open all year.

Los Molinas

Nelson Howe, 24630 Tehama-Vina Road, Los Molinas, Cal. 96055; telephone: 916–384–2851 / Waters: Sacramento River / Trips: 2–6 days / Best canoeing months: May-September / Campsites: yes / Transportation: yes / Car-top carriers: yes / For more information or reservations contact W. C. "Bob" Trowbridge, Box 942, Healdsburg, Cal. 95448; telephone: 707–542–0598.

Lynwood

Lane's Marine Sales & Service, Inc., 11120 Atlantic, Lynwood, Cal. 90262; telephone: 213–631–3506 or 213–638–8717 / Waters: Colorado River, coastal rivers and bays, and local lakes / Trips: 1 or more days / Best canoeing months: April-November / Campsites: yes / Transportation: no / Car-top carriers: yes / Open all year.

Mendocino

Catch A Canoe (Bob and Kathy McMillen), Highway 1 and Comptche Road, Mendocino, Cal. 95460; telephone: 707–937–0273 / Waters: Big River / Trips: several hours to several days / Best canoeing months: June-November / Campsites: yes / Transportation: no / Car-top carriers: no response.

Santa Rosa

W. C. "Bob" Trowbridge, 625 B Street, Santa Rosa, Cal. 95401; telephone: 707–542–0598. *See also* Fair Oaks, Healdsburg, Klamath, Lake Havasu City, and Los Molinas.

Stockton

Gray's Rent-A-Canoe and West Coast Canoe and Kayak Training School, 437 East Fremont #3, Stockton, Cal. 95202; telephone: 209–463–3234 / Waters: American, Mokelumne, Stanislaus, Tuolumne, Sacramento, Feather, Yuba, Merced, Jan Joaquin, Calaveras Rivers and also foothill lakes / Trips: 1 or more days, guides available / Best canoeing months: March-July / Campsites: yes / Transportation: yes, by special arrangement only / Car-top carriers: yes / Also rents kayaks / Open all year.

Sources of Information

California fishing and hunting information is available from California Department of Fish and Game (1416 9th Street, Sacramento, Cal. 95814).

California tourist information is available from California Division of Tourism and Visitor Services (1400 10th Street, Sacramento, Cal. 95812) and Southern California Visitors Council (705 West 7th Street, Los Angeles, Cal. 90017).

Dwyer, Ann. *Canoeing Waters of California*, G.B.H. Press (125 Upland Road, Kentfield, Cal. 94904), 1973, 95 pp., $4.00. Detailed descriptions of many waterways plus maps.

Lakes of California, Pacific Gas and Electric Company (San Francisco, Cal.), is a 48-page free brochure available from the utility.

Martin, Charles. *Sierra Whitewater: A Paddler's Guide to the Rivers of California's Sierra Nevada*, Fiddleneck Press (P.O. Box 114, Sunnyvale, Cal. 94088), 1974, 192 pp., $5.95. As the title indicates, this book is devoted almost exclusively to whitewater; maps.

Nevada tourist information is available from Nevada Department of Economic Development (Carson City, Nev. 89701).

Schwind, Dick. *West Coast River Touring: Rogue River Canyon and South*, The Touchstone Press (P.O. Box 81, Beaverton, Ore. 97005), 1974, 221 pp., $5.95. Detailed description of 170 "river runs" from the Rogue River in Oregon to the Salinas River in California plus a scientist's approach to water conditions, canoeing techniques, etc.

•

ALASKA

ALASKA, LIKE NO OTHER STATE OF THE UNION, offers true wilderness canoeing away from the crowds in a variety of scenic settings that include coastal fjords, alpine mountain ranges, glaciers, dense forests, lakes, swamps, muskegs, Arctic tundra, and above all, clean fast streams and mighty rivers. The season is short and summer temperatures are comparable to those of the Boundary Waters in Minnesota and the Allagash in Maine — and so are the insects. Alaskan waters are strictly for the wilderness camper and whitewater expert. No one should venture there without a great deal of experience or a guide.

The U.S. Department of the Interior has designated 12 canoe trails accessible from highways. Information on these and detailed maps are available from the Bureau of Land Management, Alaska State Office (555 Cordova Street, Anchorage, Alaska 99501).

In addition, there are two official canoe routes in the Kenai National Moose Range on Kenai Peninsula southwest of Anchorage. Information and route maps are available from U.S. Department of the Interior, Fish and Wildlife Service, Kenai National Moose Range (P.O. Box 500, Kenai, Alaska 99611).

Innumerable other waterways, inaccessible by road, may challenge the imagination of wilderness canoeists. Some can be reached by plane.

The only canoe rental service that provided information for this book is Wilderness Canoe Trails, 6.9 Mile Chena Hot Springs Road, Fairbanks, Alaska 99701 (telephone: 907–488–2601), operated by Harold Dinkins. Mr. Dinkins offers guided canoe trips anywhere in Alaska and he furnishes automobile transportation and all necessary equipment, including tents and food. Canoeists should bring their own sleeping bags, personal items, and fishing tackle.

A trip especially recommended by Mr. Dinkins and not listed in the Alaska Canoe Trails publication of the U.S. Department of the Interior starts at the headwaters of Beaver Creek, 30 miles northeast of Fairbanks, and ends at the new North Slope road across the Yukon River, a mere 21 days in the wilderness.

Mr. Dinkins also rents a limited number of canoes to those who want to go it alone, and he provides shuttle service to put-in and take-out points. However, do-it-yourselfers must bring their own food and camping equipment. Food, including the dehydrated variety, and other supplies can be purchased in Fairbanks.

Travel information is available from Alaska Department of Economic Development, Division of Tourism (Pouch E, Juneau, Alaska 99811). Hunting and fishing information is available from Alaska Department of Fish and Game (Subport Building, Juneau, Alaska 99811). Information on ferry service is available from Alaska Marine Highway (Pouch R, Juneau, Alaska 99811), and information on U.S. Forest Service cabins is available from the U.S. Forest Service, Tongass National Forest, Juneau, Alaska 99811 or Chugach National Forest, 121 Fireweed Lane, Anchorage, Alaska 99501.

BIBLIOGRAPHY

WITH THE INCREASING POPULARITY OF CANOEING has come a great many books about canoes, canoeing techniques, and equipment — at least 60 books are listed in the *Grumman Book Rack*. The classics among them are *Malo's Complete Guide to Canoeing and Canoe Camping* and Bill Riviere's *Pole Paddle & Portage*. But for anyone carried away by the art of canoeing, it is always interesting to learn many different viewpoints, new insights, and technical facts. This bibliography offers a selection of general books on various subjects. Books devoted to specific areas are listed at the end of the individual chapters.

When looking at available maps, it becomes obvious that U.S. geography is governed by the automobile. Most maps are dominated by a heavy multi-colored grid of highways. Rivers are practically faded out or omitted completely. Thus, it is not always easy to pin down the courses of individual rivers and their access points.

In states where canoeing is supported by state authorities or canoeing interests, maps for individual rivers have been published, and these are listed at the end of the chapters. For all other areas the reader will be best served by U.S. Geological Survey maps and nautical charts for coastal waterways published by the Coast and Geodetic Survey of the U.S. Department of Commerce.

With all maps, it must be remembered that river courses and coastal waters can change rapidly. A canoeist venturing out on new water for the first time should always get up-to-date information from local sources, like rental operations.

American Red Cross. *Basic Canoeing*, n.d., 67 pp., 75¢. Promotes canoeing safety; describes boats, paddling techniques, safety precautions, rescue procedures; many diagrams.

————*Canoeing*. Doubleday & Co. (Garden City, N.Y.) and the American Red Cross (Washington, D.C.), 1974, 6th edition. Very detailed discussion of canoeing techniques and safety with many photographs.

Angier, Bradford and Zack Taylor. *Introduction to Canoeing*, Stackpole Books (Harrisburg, Pa.), 1973, 191 pp., $3.95. A good over-all review for the beginner, covers canoes, equipment, camping, cruising, etc.

Bearse, Ray. *The Canoe Camper's Handbook*, Winchester Press (New

York, N.Y.), 1974, 366 pp., $7.95. Heavy stress on camping, equipment, outdoor cooking, map reading, reviews some wilderness waters, very readable.

Canoe Magazine (1999 Shepard Road, St. Paul, Minn. 55166) is the official publication of the American Canoe Association. It is published bi-monthly.

Colwell, Robert. *Introduction to Water Trails in America*, Stackpole Books (Harrisburg, Pa.), 1973, 220 pp., $3.95. A selective review of some canoeing trails within easy reach of larger cities.

Davidson, James West and John Rugge. *The Complete Wilderness Paddler*, Alfred A. Knopf, Inc. (New York, N.Y.), 1976, 259 pp., $10.00. A breezily written "how to" book on wilderness canoeing built around a trip taken by the authors down a river in remote Labrador.

DeVoto, Bernard, ed. *The Journals of Lewis and Clark*, Houghton Mifflin Company (Boston, Mass.), 1952, 502 pp., $3.95.

Fillingham, Paul. *The Complete Book of Canoeing & Kayaking*, Drake Publishers, Inc. (New York, N.Y.), 1974, 138 pp., $12.95. The focus here is on techniques, cruising, camping, racing, with diagrams and photographs.

The Grumman Book Rack, Grumman Allied Industries (Marathon, N.Y.), is a free listing of 60 books on canoeing.

Kemmer, Rick. *A Guide to Paddle Adventure: How to Buy Canoes and Kayaks and Where to Travel*, Vanguard Press, Inc. (New York, N.Y.), 1975, 295 pp., $10.00. This book stresses detailed descriptions and specifications of canoes, kayaks, paddles, camping equipment, etc. and includes a selective description of key canoeing waters.

Malo, John W. *Malo's Complete Guide to Canoe Camping*, Quadrangle/The New York Times Book Co. (New York, N.Y.), 1975, 221 pp., $8.95. All-encompassing general primer on equipment, techniques, camping, canoe associations, sources of information, with photographs and diagrams.

————*Wilderness Canoeing*. The Macmillan Company (New York, N.Y.), 1971, 167 pp., $3.95. An excellent guide to finding wilderness waters and surviving there in relative comfort and safety.

McPhee, John. *The Survival of the Bark Canoe*, Farrar, Straus & Giroux (New York, N.Y.), 1975, 144 pp., $7.95. A beautifully written book about a man who makes birch-bark canoes by hand.

Michelson, Mike and Keith Ray. *Canoeing*, Henry Regnery Company (Chicago, Ill.), 1975, 154 pp., $10.00. An easy primer on canoeing techniques and equipment.

Morris, Dan and Inez. *Camping by Boat*, The Bobbs-Merrill Company (New York, N.Y.), 1975, 238 pp., $5.95. Includes a 30-page chapter on canoe camping plus some general hints on handling a canoe safely.

Nautical charts for coastal waterways are available from the U.S. Department of Commerce, Coast and Geodetic Survey (Washington, D.C.)

and also from many marine dealers on coastal waters who tend to stock these maps of their areas.

Perry, Ronald H. *Canoeing for Beginners,* Association Press (New York, N.Y.), 1974, 126 pp., $2.50. A condensed primer, in large print, for the very beginning beginner.

Riviere, Bill. *Pole Paddle & Portage,* Litton Educational Publishing (Cincinnati, Ohio), 1969, 259 pp., $6.95. Excellent over-all review of canoeing techniques and equipment plus a summary of canoeing waters in many states of the Union, with a glossary, maps, and list of information sources.

U.S. Geological Survey (Reston, Va. 22092) provides indexes for geological survey maps for each state and lists of local Federal map distribution centers and map dealers. This information is also available from the Federal Center, Denver, Colo. 80225.

Wilderness Camping Magazine (1597 Union Street, Schenectady, N.Y. 12309) is the official publication of the United States Canoe Association. It is published bi-monthly.

Wilderness Sports Catalogue is available from Wilderness Sports Corporation (Eagle Valley, N.Y. 10974). It lists kits of U.S. Geological Survey maps for many canoeing and fishing waters throughout the United States at a charge over and above the cost of the maps if purchased from the U.S.G.S. Maps of Canadian waters are also available.

NOTES

NOTES

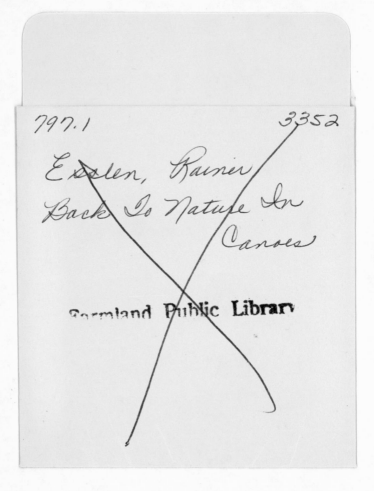